The Silent Guns of Two Octobers

The Silent Guns of Two Octobers uses new as well as previously under-appreciated documentary evidence to link the Cuban missile crisis to the Checkpoint Charlie tank standoff to achieve the impossible—craft a new, thoughtful, original analysis of a political showdown everyone thought they knew everything about. Ultimately the book concludes that much of the Cold War rhetoric the leaders employed was posturing and that neither had any intention of starting a nuclear war. Theodore Voorhees reexamines Khrushchev's and Kennedy's leadership, decisions, and rhetoric in light of the new documentary evidence available to solve five mysteries. Voorhees examines the impact of John F. Kennedy's domestic political concerns about his upcoming first midterm elections on his handling of the Cuban missile crisis through his use of back-channel dealings with Khrushchev during the lead-up to the crisis and in the closing days, when the two leaders managed to reach a settlement.

Theodore Voorhees Jr. is Senior Counsel at Covington & Burling LLP.

The Silent Guns of Two Octobers

Kennedy and Khrushchev Play the Double Game

Theodore Voorhees Jr.

Second Edition

University of Michigan Press
Ann Arbor

New and updated edition published 2021

Published in the United States of America by the
University of Michigan Press
Manufactured in the United States of America
Printed on acid-free paper

A CIP catalog record for this book is available from the British Library.

Library of Congress Cataloging-in-Publication data has been applied for.

First published September 2021

Library of Congress Cataloging-in-Publication Data

Names: Voorhees, Theodore, Jr., 1949– author.
Title: The silent guns of two Octobers : Kennedy and Khrushchev play the double game / Theodore Voorhees, Jr.
Description: Ann Arbor : University of Michigan Press, 2020. | Includes bibliographical references and index.
Identifiers: LCCN 2019044530 (print) | LCCN 2019044531 (ebook) | ISBN 9780472131921 (hardcover) | ISBN 9780472126712 (ebook)
Subjects: LCSH: Cuban Missile Crisis, 1962. | Checkpoint Charlie, Berlin, Germany, 1961–1989. | Cold War—Diplomatic history. | Kennedy, John F. (John Fitzgerald), 1917–1963. | Khrushchev, Nikita Sergeevich, 1894–1971. | United States—Foreign relations—Soviet Union. | Soviet Union—Foreign relations—United States.
Classification: LCC E841 .V66 2020 (print) | LCC E841 (ebook) | DDC 909.82/5—dc23
LC record available at https://lccn.loc.gov/2019044530
LC ebook record available at https://lccn.loc.gov/2019044531

ISBN 978-0-472-03871-8 (paper: alk. paper)
ISBN 978-0-472-12960-7 (e-book)

Contents

Digital materials related to this title can be found on the Fulcrum platform via the following citable URL: https://doi.org/10.3998/mpub.12110650

Acknowledgments

I am grateful for the encouragement I received from scholars, friends, colleagues, and a few mentors with whom I shared my evolving ideas that set this book project in motion. I am indebted to Cold War and missile crisis scholars Philip Nash, David Barrett, Gregg Herken, Jim Hershberg, and Edward Luttwak, who read early versions of my work in progress and offered helpful comments. I received assistance from the library staffs at the John F. Kennedy Presidential Library; Yale University Library Special Collections; Georgetown University, Booth Center for Special Collections; National Defense University Special Collections; the National Archives and Records Administration; and the Institute of World Politics. I am indebted to my law firm, Covington & Burling LLP and its librarian, Larry Guthrie, for their support of my research efforts at every stage, and to my assistant, Karen Lee Banks. IWP professor Dave Thomas graciously provided leads and insights and shared useful materials retrieved from his eclectic personal collection of declassified Cold War military and intelligence artifacts. Many friends and colleagues offered encouraging feedback along the way, including Mary Ann Bell, Walter Earle, Tom Geoghegan, Richard Nash Gould, Charles Miller, Brad Snyder, and Col. H. Wayne Whitten USMC. I am grateful for the help of Elizabeth Demers, my editor at University of Michigan Press, who corrected most of my bad writing habits. Finally, this project would not have reached fruition without the tremendous boost I received late in the process from two outstanding Cold War historians: Sheldon Stern and Marty Sherwin. Neither Sheldon nor Marty had any reason to respond to the persistent inquiries of a complete stranger apart from their natural kindness and irrepressible fascination with the iconic Cold War events covered in this book, and their dedication to the chief and endless task of all historians: to set the record more straight than it was when they found it.

Introduction

AT ABOUT 5:00 P.M. Berlin time on the evening of October 27, 1961, two and a half months after the Soviet bloc's sudden erection of the Berlin Wall blocking the flight of refugees to the West, ten Soviet T-54 tanks came into position on the eastern side of the wall at the Friedrichstrasse Plaza border crossing, their cannons aimed at the American zone. A short time later, ten US Army M-48 Patton tanks stood directly opposite, approximately one hundred yards away on the American side of the crossing known as "Checkpoint Charlie." Within hours the confrontation had sharply escalated as the number of battle tanks working their way toward the plaza had grown to thirty for each side. By this time US president John F. Kennedy and Soviet premier Nikita S. Khrushchev had become personally engaged and were directing events. The dispute had begun over a seemingly minor matter of bureaucratic protocol on the rules for determining whether US civilian officials crossing over to East Berlin in government vehicles could be stopped by East German border guards for an inspection of their credentials. But the spectacle of heavy tanks menacing one another across a tense Cold War border seemed to threaten a "hot" war that could escalate to nuclear Armageddon.

Exactly one year later, on Saturday evening October 27, 1962, the world witnessed an even more alarming confrontation that once again set off nuclear alarm bells. This time the Soviets had been secretly ferrying nuclear-armed medium- and intermediate-range ballistic missiles (MRBMs and IRBMs)[1] to Cuba, about one hundred miles off the coast of the United States. Just the month before, Kennedy had twice formally declared that he would not countenance a Soviet military installation in the Western Hemisphere, and so it seemed that an American armed attack or even full-scale invasion would soon make good on the president's "red line" warning. Tensions mounted sharply earlier in the day when a Soviet surface-to-air (SAM-2 or

SA-2) missile stationed in Cuba brought down an American U-2 surveillance plane, killing the pilot. At the same time, unbeknownst to the Americans, Cuba's defiant leader, Fidel Castro, had sent Khrushchev an urgent message imploring his patron to launch an immediate nuclear missile attack on the United States to prevent what he feared was an imminent invasion of his country.

The Checkpoint Charlie tank standoff on the evening of October 27, 1961, and the climactic moments of the Cuban missile drama on the evening of October 27, 1962, were among the most perilous episodes of the Cold War. The news media at the time and later historians looking back used apocalyptic hyperbole to describe each scene: Checkpoint Charlie was "the most dangerous place on earth"; the Cuban missile crisis placed the world "on the brink"; the superpowers were "eyeball to eyeball"; humanity's clock had reached "one minute to midnight."[2] These dire images reflected how many people felt on those two momentous October days one year apart. Yet each time people who had gone to bed wondering whether they would live to see the light of day woke up to discover that the storm had suddenly—even miraculously—disappeared. A solution had somehow been found and the drawn guns were safely back in their holsters. How was it possible that two seemingly earthshaking crises could have been defused so abruptly?

The simple answer initially disseminated in the West was that a resolute American president had stood up against Soviet aggression each time and that his courage and good sense prevailed. In both instances it seemed that Khrushchev had been compelled to "back down." On the morning of October 28, 1961, the Soviet tanks began to leave Friedrichstrasse Plaza first, followed by reciprocal withdrawals of US armor. Exactly one year later, it was Khrushchev again who appeared to be in retreat when Soviet radio broadcast on the morning of October 28, 1962, that Moscow had accepted the American president's demand for removal of Soviet missiles from Cuba in exchange for an American pledge not to invade.[3]

Later revelations would ultimately confound this early, simplistic, US-centric narrative. Although key deal terms that helped resolve each crisis would remain shrouded in secrecy for decades and, in the case of the tank crisis resolution, even up to this day, the gradual opening of previously classified Soviet and American archives has given rise to a new stream of revelations and reappraisals.

The one-day tank staredown across a Berlin plaza certainly did not match the later Cuban drama either in scale or in the magnitude and duration of the public anxiety that arose as each crisis unfolded. Nevertheless, the brief, nerve-racking episode at Checkpoint Charlie provided a first critical test for whether the American and Soviet leaders could find a way to draw back from an imminent hot-war precipice. The steps each side took to defuse the ticking time bomb in Berlin would foreshadow some of the most consequential aspects of the more complex and far-ranging missile crisis that unfolded in Cuba a year later.

Most Western commentators initially adopted the Kennedy administration's somewhat triumphalist narrative of the two Cold War military showdowns,[4] in which each crisis began with an audacious Soviet military provocation and ended after the Americans countered by calling up their own forces, demonstrating a readiness to stand their ground.[5] The Soviet leader seemed like a reckless adventurer, the American president a strong but coolheaded keeper of the peace, and above all the victor.[6] This appealing US self-assessment fit well with popular conceptions of the rival leaders at the time. On one side stood the young, attractive, and eloquent US president, John F. Kennedy: a modern, Harvard-educated, lofty-minded man of wealth and sophistication.[7] On the other side was the aging, rotund, rumpled, crude, minimally educated veteran of the Stalin era, Nikita S. Khrushchev, who had famously taken off his shoe at a United Nations General Assembly meeting and pounded the desk in a boisterous gesture of defiance against the West.[8]

In the years that have followed these popular and polarizing images, however, many previously classified government documents from US and Soviet archives have come to light, revealing a fuller and more complex picture, both of the two national leaders and of the key driving forces that shaped the arc of the Kennedy-Khrushchev crisis years, especially the Cold War showdown over the Soviet ballistic missiles in Cuba. Most important, it turned out that almost all of the deliberations of the Kennedy administration's top advisers during the Cuban drama—a group that became known as the "ExComm," short for Executive Committee of the National Security Council—had been secretly tape-recorded by the president. Thus, the exact words of the ExComm participants, including the president himself, became an anchor part of the primary source missile crisis record when they were transcribed and published in the 1990s.[9] Moreover, the growing historical literature assessing the missile crisis from Khrushchev's standpoint was notably strengthened by the contributions of Soviet scholars Timothy Naftali, Aleksandr Fursenko,[10] and Jonathan Haslam;[11] by excellent biographies of Khrushchev by William Taubman[12] and the Soviet leader's son and confidante, Sergei Khrushchev;[13] by Soviet ambassador Anatoly Dobrynin's memoirs, published in 1995;[14] by Philip Nash's detailed analysis of the US concessions, long kept secret, that facilitated the quick resolution of the Cuban missile crisis;[15] by Michael Beschloss's comprehensive 1991 examination of the Kennedy-Khrushchev Cold War rivalry;[16] and by the more recent contributions of Michael Dobbs and Sheldon Stern.[17] It is fair to say that the world now knows better than to blindly revere Kennedy or blithely disdain Khrushchev for the methods the two leaders used to manage the sharpest East-West confrontation of their time.

Early hints of the eventual need for this more sober appraisal are captured in a photograph taken of the two leaders sitting together at the Vienna summit in early June 1961—the only time the two would meet face-to-face. The premier looked more seasoned, solemn, even serene than the prevailing public view of him; the president less poised, more uncertain.

It has also become apparent that there were a surprising number of parallels in the ways the two crises were resolved. Both superpower leaders made major concessions to restore tranquility, though Khrushchev's "quids" were exhibited largely in the open, while Kennedy's "quos" were exchanged under condition of secrecy. Although the Checkpoint Charlie standoff was a frightening moment and the Cuban missile crisis seemed to ExComm participants to pose some of the most complex and intractable challenges to world peace that arose during the Cold War, the rival leaders managed in both crises to cut the knot with lightning speed.[18] How was that possible?

The simple answer is that the sudden, seemingly miraculous, restoration of peaceful coexistence was possible because both the underlying point of dispute and the ultimate deal terms that ended each crisis were matters under the personal control of each leader. When Kennedy and Khrushchev chose to settle, each man had the authority and the power to do so almost instantaneously. The two leaders personally directed all key decisions down to precise details, most dramatically as the Cuban confrontation unfolded.[19] While both leaders were surrounded by expert counselors and under pressure from allies advancing their own agendas, it has become increasingly clear that Khrushchev and Kennedy felt free to reject the views of their closest advisers and brush aside the consternation they caused their alliance partners.

Although the main focus of this book will be the Cuban missile crisis, I will briefly address the Checkpoint Charlie tank standoff because the process used to settle that confrontation served as a template that yields clues to unraveling some of the mysteries that arose a year later, in particular by helping to decode obscure but revealing statements made by the missile crisis principals. The more complete record that is now available places a considerable degree of personal responsibility on both Kennedy and Khrushchev for dangerous missteps that precipitated the missile crisis no less than for their more sober acts of forbearance that produced a peaceful outcome. It now seems fair to classify each man's leadership style as a combination of vision and blindness, of deep thinking and shallow cunning, of reckless hubris and fearful prudence.

Taking a step further, it is time to examine whether the Soviet provocation in Cuba warranted the state of alarm that was raised across the world and has been colorfully dramatized in many retellings thereafter. It is now reasonably clear that neither Kennedy nor Khrushchev, whatever his publicly stated position, actually believed that his adversary's actions presented a problem whose *substantive importance* warranted even a conventional military engagement, far less a nuclear showdown. Further, neither leader had any intention whatsoever of being the first to order the use of a nuclear weapon. Both men recognized, albeit for distinctly different reasons, that any battlefield use of a nuclear weapon would have horrific consequences, even aside from the vast destruction it would unleash on others.[20] Further, because both men were convinced that it might be difficult to prevent an outbreak of conventional fighting from escalating to a nuclear exchange, they were intent on avoiding any armed conflict even at the lowest ground-level of engagement.[21] However frequently their public statements invited confrontation, when it became evident that a military clash might be imminent, both leaders were quick to seek a settlement, even if that meant offering extraordinarily generous, even potentially humiliating concessions they believed might be needed to achieve a quick deal.

This explains the striking fact that at no point during the approximately one thousand days the two leaders waged their personal Cold War rivalry did either Kennedy or Khrushchev affirmatively seek, far less countenance, open fighting between their two militaries at even the lowest level of bullets and shells, let alone nuclear-armed bombers or missiles.[22] In fact, it appears that the two leaders displayed many of the same basic instincts as they waged their global "cold" rivalry, and tried to keep their respective forces under tight control in circumstances where thousands of armed men held their fingers on the triggers of conventional and nuclear weapons on numerous potential battlefields. And they did so all while obeying the same rule: that the two nuclear-armed superpowers must never allow their troops to actually start shooting at one another.

To be sure, both leaders had to deal with subordinates who seemed to relish the prospect of a fight. During the Berlin crisis Kennedy had to muzzle his handpicked special representative on the scene, General Lucius Clay, who wanted to conduct a quixotic, tank-led "raid in force" into East Berlin that would knock down portions of the Berlin Wall on the way back to West Berlin.[23] Khrushchev, too, had to deal with his own loose cannon in East Germany, or German Democratic Republic (GDR). GDR president Walter Ulbricht ordered his East Berlin border guards to conduct provocative identity checks in spite of adamant American objections backed by US battle tanks, and he urged Khrushchev to allow him to erect a steel barrier that would block the full width of the Friedrichstrasse, a move that might have triggered the kind of provocative raid-in-force maneuver that General Clay had dreamed up and that the more cautious US secretary of state had provisionally approved.[24]

During the Cuban missile crisis a year later, war hawks on both sides eagerly raised the temperature by urging ever more extreme measures. From the beginning, US civilian and military leaders, most notably the president's brother, Attorney General Robert F. Kennedy, and US Air Force chief of staff General Curtis LeMay, advocated air strikes against Soviet positions in Cuba, followed by an invasion. On October 19, 1962, the fourth day of the crisis, LeMay even tried to shame the president into the path of war by comparing Kennedy's restrained naval quarantine plan to British prime minister Neville Chamberlain's infamous "appeasement at Munich," and by insinuating that the Soviets had the president "on the run."[25] Khrushchev, for his part, once again faced the considerable challenge of restraining a belligerent ally. As noted, on the critical night of October 27–28, 1962, Khrushchev learned of Castro's doomsday appeal for a preventive Soviet nuclear first-strike attack against the United States, and this convinced the Soviet premier that it was time to strike a quick deal, even one calling for a Soviet retreat from his risky Cuban adventure. Khrushchev also had to abide criticism from China, his country's primary Cold War ally, whose leaders accused him initially of weakness and later of "adventurism" and "capitulationism."[26]

Of course both Kennedy and Khrushchev faced high uncertainty, especially during the Cuba incident, because there was always the danger that men lower down the chains of command might pull the trigger, whether by mistake, through personal belligerence, through fear, or all three.[27] Nor were these hypothetical risks. During the Cuban crisis an American destroyer dropped relatively harmless practice depth charges on a submerged Soviet submarine as a signal to come to the surface, not knowing that the Soviet vessel carried a torpedo with a nuclear warhead. Unexpectedly, that seemingly restrained act led the submarine's captain to fear an attack might be underway and may actually have damaged the Soviet vessel. While that scenario would have justified a nuclear response under standard Soviet naval protocol, none was launched, but only (according to some reports) after a close vote of the submarine's senior officers. Similarly, the Russian officer in charge of the SAM-2 missile installation that shot down the American U-2 aircraft on October 27, 1962, was not acting under orders of his Soviet chain of command, but rather had decided that the overflight signaled an imminent US invasion.

Kennedy and Khrushchev also utilized essentially the same personal, back-channel diplomacy tool kit of formal and informal signaling, negotiation, and compromise as they endeavored to walk each confrontation back from tit-for-tat provocations to a restoration of the status quo ante. In doing so each leader often found himself disregarding or flatly rejecting the recommendations of his top advisers, substituting instead his own preferred solution communicated to his adversary across secret channels. On Kennedy's side these back channels most often started with his brother, but senior White House adviser Theodore Sorensen and press secretary Pierre Salinger were occasionally deputized to send or receive these private, high-level communications. The president also used friendly journalists like Charles Bartlett and Frank Holeman for these purposes. Bartlett played a key role as a deputized personal representative of the president at critical junctures of the negotiations between Kennedy and Khrushchev leading to the final resolution of the crisis. Khrushchev sometimes launched these secret exchanges using his ambassador to the United States, Anatoly Dobrynin, or Dobrynin's assistant at the Soviet embassy in Washington, Alexander Zinchuk. But in most instances the intermediary preferred by both leaders was GRU colonel Georgi Bolshakov, an officer in the Soviet military intelligence service[28] who had served in Washington, DC, for many years under cover as an information counselor at the Soviet embassy and a journalist or editor of the magazine *USSR*.[29] Khrushchev's son Sergei described Bolshakov's crucial role as that of "a private and unofficial channel of communications" and a "trusted person" who by combining the functions of "journalist, superb interpreter, and Soviet military intelligence" possessed the "versatility" needed to "cope with his complex and extremely responsible new duties."[30]

Bolshakov first met Robert Kennedy on May 9, 1961 after an introduction by their mutual friend, Frank Holeman. Within a matter of days the GRU agent began serving as a trusted go-between helping the White House and the Kremlin lay plans for the Vienna summit. The president's brother would subsequently meet or speak by telephone with Bolshakov on dozens of occasions over the ensuing eighteen months, including one and possibly two private sessions with the president in the White House that will be discussed at length in chapter 5. Bolshakov was well known in Washington circles as a lively and affable Russian figure, and many stories describe his close friendship with the youthful attorney general. Bolshakov attended parties at Bobby Kennedy's Hickory Hill residence, arm-wrestled with the president's brother, and roughhoused with his large and boisterous brood of children. And, as would be revealed many years later in Bolshakov's documentation of his experiences during the Cuba crisis, there was a final, personal parting of the two friends in Kennedy's car on the night of October 27, 1962, shortly after the attorney general left his momentous session with Soviet ambassador Dobrynin at which the specific details of the president's Turkey-for-Cuba missile-trade proposal to end the crisis were conveyed. See chapter 8.

Khrushchev's son-in-law, Alexei Adzhubei, who attended several meetings with President Kennedy at which Bolshakov was also present, reported that, during one such meeting on January 30, 1962, "Kennedy sent Salinger and [US interpreter Alexander A.] Akalovsky away, and asked Bolshakov to be the interpreter." At a second private meeting at the White House on the evening of the next day, where Bolshakov most likely would again have been the sole interpreter, the president told Adzhubei "that he personally welcomes the contact which existed between Bolshakov and Robert Kennedy, insofar as it gives him the possibility to manage without the services of a translator from the State Department." Adzhubei then added his own view that "these observations show that surely in the presence of Akolovsky [*sic*] and even [White House press secretary] Salinger . . . the president speaks with a completely different tongue and is visibly more tense."[31]

As a more complete record of the White House and Kremlin back-channel contacts and secret deliberations during the summer and fall of 1962 has gradually emerged from previously classified archives of both governments, historians have encountered surprising mysteries that challenge previous narratives. Some of the unearthed facts have been so singular and jarring that many historians have been content to leave them largely unexplored. The aim of this book is to closely examine five of these mysteries and pursue the evidence in greater depth.

WHY DID KHRUSHCHEV BACK DOWN FROM THE CUBAN CONFRONTATION SO QUICKLY?

> The enemy is strong, not weaker than we are. . . . That is why he could play the same trump card against us that we were trying to use against him—the position of strength card.
>
> —NIKITA S. KHRUSHCHEV, JANUARY 8, 1962

> We must retreat.
>
> —KHRUSHCHEV, SPEAKING TO THE PRESIDIUM ON OCTOBER 28, 1962

Khrushchev almost immediately recognized that he would have to back down as soon as he learned from President Kennedy's October 22 speech that the United States had discovered his missiles in Cuba and was determined to have them removed. From that moment the Soviet chairman knew he needed to find a face-saving exit from his Cuban gamble. He had anticipated that the missile secret might be prematurely exposed, and he had already reconciled himself to negotiating for a settlement, fully expecting the American president not to escalate to war. He was correct in his assumptions. Why?

The United States held an overwhelming strategic nuclear advantage over the Soviet Union during 1961 and 1962—perhaps as much as seventeen to one—and diverging trends in the two sides' strategic arms procurement policies meant that the US advantage would likely grow larger before the Soviets could begin to catch up. Recognition of this stark power asymmetry is indispensable to understanding why the two leaders—especially Khrushchev as the chief instigator—were able to settle literally overnight. Because Khrushchev knew he stood in a position of extreme strategic weakness, he made no effort to develop a war plan, he held his strategic weapons back from war readiness, and he did not want to precipitate conventional fighting (far less a nuclear exchange), all because he knew his side would lose.

HOW DID KHRUSHCHEV'S TRANSFER OF BALLISTIC MISSILES ACROSS THE ATLANTIC OCEAN ELUDE DETECTION?

> N.S. Khrushchev is satisfied with the president's order to curtail the U.S. planes' inspections of Soviet ships in open waters. . . . [Khrushchev] would like to understand what John F. Kennedy means by "placing the Berlin question on ice."
>
> —GEORGI BOLSHAKOV, QUOTING KHRUSHCHEV, AUGUST 2, 1962

> Nothing will be undertaken before the American Congressional elections that could complicate the international situation or aggravate the tension in the relations between our two countries. We shall follow this course, provided there are no actions taken on the other side which would change the situation.
>
> —KHRUSHCHEV TO KENNEDY VIA DOBRYNIN TO SORENSEN, SEPTEMBER 6, 1962

President Kennedy made an imprudent decision on July 31, 1962, when he sent word to Khrushchev that he was prepared to trade favors if Moscow would be willing to temporarily forbear from exacerbating tensions over Berlin so that the president and his party could avoid domestic political damage from foreign troubles during the run-up to the US midterm elections, set for November 6, 1962. Kennedy privately shared his personal political vulnerability with Khrushchev and offered as a quid pro quo an accommodation affecting America's national security at a meeting in the White House on July 31, 1962, with Georgi Bolshakov. This unwise bargain, motivated by the president's preoccupation with his weakening domestic political standing, would yield a bitter harvest of presidential missteps, lax surveillance, and leader-to-leader misunderstandings over the ensuing two and a half months that might have produced disastrous consequences for the United States in October 1962.

Kennedy erupted in anger when he received irrefutable evidence on October 16 that Khrushchev had been surreptitiously transporting ballistic missiles to Cuba under cover of personal assurances to the president that only defensive weapons were involved and that the Kremlin was granting the White House a kind of armistice in international tensions so that Kennedy could attend to his party's midterm elections free of foreign distractions. The president's enraged response was spontaneous and personal: "He can't do this to me!" He felt that he had been tricked and at least temporarily outmaneuvered in what he would tell British prime minister Harold Macmillan a few days later had been Khrushchev's "double game." Yet Kennedy, too, was engaged in a double game of his own, one in which the president would ultimately hold the winning hand.

ONCE DISCOVERY OF THE SOVIET MISSILES HAD PROVED THE PRESIDENT'S REPUBLICAN CRITICS RIGHT, HOW DID HE AVOID THE POTENTIAL POLITICAL FALLOUT?

He neither contradicted nor confirmed my reference to . . . missile preparations.

—THEODORE C. SORENSEN, SEPTEMBER 6, 1962, REFERRING TO COMMENTS BY DOBRYNIN ABOUT THE NATURE OF THE SOVIET ARMS SHIPMENTS TO CUBA

It seems to me, Mr. President, in your public presentation simultaneous or subsequent to an action, your hand is strengthened somewhat if the Soviets have lied to you, either privately or in public.

—ROSWELL GILPATRIC TO KENNEDY, OCTOBER 16, 1962

One of the enduring tropes of the Cuban missile crisis narrative is that the Kennedy administration, in particular the president and his brother, consistently demonstrated competence and good faith, whereas Khrushchev took advantage of the Americans by disseminating "barefaced lies" about the Soviet arms buildup. The Soviets had indeed been misleading, especially in Khrushchev's double olive branch assurances to Kennedy, first, that the Kremlin would observe a pause in international tensions through the US midterm elections and, second, that the Soviet military assistance to Cuba was not a problem for the United States because it was entirely "defensive" in substance and purpose.

The president's response to Khrushchev's artifice was yet another reciprocating version of the double game the two were playing. Kennedy was infuriated by the chairman's devious offer of a pause in tensions through the midterm elections—crudely calling it "Khrushchev's horseshit" in a private conversation with his brother—yet he never mentioned this embarrassing setback to his expectations in any public discussion. Rather, the president and his brother focused their response to the chairman's perfidy on the Kremlin's misleading characterization of the Cuba arms shipments as "defensive." Yet here the Kennedy brothers faced a problem: Was the word "defensive" obviously or necessarily false? After all, the United States had justified its recent deployment of ballistic missiles in Europe as a defensive move designed to provide deterrence. So a stronger case was needed to show that the Soviet claims about defensive arms were not ambiguous, self-serving rhetoric but rather outright lies.

Robert Kennedy took on this challenge. In particular, the attorney general would later insist that in his separate discussions with Dobrynin and Bolshakov, he had received not simply the Soviet "defensive" weapons and purposes party line but had been assured with greater specificity that the military equipment Khrushchev was sending to Cuba did not include "ground-to-ground" missiles, or "surface-to-surface" missiles, or missiles "capable of reaching the United States." President Kennedy would add that Soviet foreign minister Andrei Gromyko had similarly told him "barefaced lies" about the nature of the Soviet weapons being shipped to Cuba when the two met for a White House discussion on October 18, 1962, two days after the president had learned the true facts. The official notes of the Kennedy-Gromyko meeting would soon refute the president's claim, however.

As to Robert Kennedy's assertion that Dobrynin and Bolshakov made the specific, untrue statements noted above, this claim turns out to have been based entirely on the undocumented word of the attorney general alone. Moreover, a close examination of the younger Kennedy's accounts shows them to have been internally inconsistent and contradicted by contemporaneous documented accounts of others.

Indeed, the evidence strongly suggests that Robert Kennedy's belated articulation of his "flat lies" narrative was almost certainly his after-the-fact effort to give himself an excuse for having carelessly assumed that ambiguous statements in the Soviet Union's public disinformation campaign—which consistently used a repetitive formulation that the arms sent to Cuba were solely "defensive" weapons being installed for "defensive" purposes—must necessarily have meant no ground-to-ground or long-range missiles. The Kremlin's defensive-only messaging had turned out to be a conventional example of Soviet doublespeak, whose ambiguity was transparently obvious and self-serving to many observers, but not, apparently, to the president or to his brother. In other words, the problem was the president's and attorney general's credulity, not Dobrynin's or Bolshakov's factual dishonesty.

HOW WAS IT POSSIBLE FOR KENNEDY AND KHRUSHCHEV TO SETTLE SUCH A COMPLEX CRISIS IN SIX DAYS?

The only offer we would make, it seems to me, that would make any sense, the point being to give him some out, would be giving him some of our Turkey missiles.

—PRESIDENT KENNEDY, OCTOBER 18, 1962

The greatest difficulty for the president is the public discussion of the issue of Turkey . . . the president can't say anything public in this regard about Turkey.

—ROBERT KENNEDY TO DOBRYNIN, OCTOBER, 27, 1962

Khrushchev first learned that Cuba had become a crisis at the same time as the rest of the world—when he received the text of President Kennedy's October 22 televised speech announcing discovery of Soviet missiles and US imposition of a naval quarantine around Cuba. The speech demonstrated to the chairman that the American president did not want a fight. The announcement that the Americans were initiating a comparatively modest naval maneuver rather than an abrupt armed attack on the missile sites came as an enormous relief to the Kremlin since the Soviet leaders had worried that discovery of the missiles before they became operational could have precipitated immediate US air strikes or even a massive invasion.

Indeed, the need for restraint was exactly the message the president had wished to convey to his adversary. Whereas the president's preference would have been to do nothing provocative, he had felt hemmed in by his own redline warning to the Soviets coupled with intense domestic political pressures to take strong action against the Russians as his party faced the run-up to the crucial US midterm elections. This was dramatically demonstrated by a private conversation the Kennedy brothers had on October 23, 1962, which was inadvertently captured on the secret White House taping system. They agreed that the president "would have been impeached" if he had done "anything less" in response to the Soviet missiles in Cuba than the minimal quarantine he had imposed. This decision to act with extreme restraint, whatever may have been the political motive, nonetheless was a critical step needed to keep the crisis on a path toward peaceful resolution.

At the same time, however, the president needed to project strength and even threat. If the Kremlin could play a double game of defense-offense, so could the president. Accordingly on the same day that the quarantine came into effect, the president simultaneously ordered a superelevated military alert that set the world's nerves on edge and caused a state of near-panic in the Kremlin. US strategic nuclear forces had been upgraded to so-called DEFCON-3 alert status on October 22, 1962, the day of the president's address to the nation, and two days later this alert level was further elevated to DEFCON-2, just one alert step short of all-out war. Curiously, messages of this kind changing the DEFCON rating were "routinely transmitted" by the Pentagon "*en clair*, in an unclassified form," making them open to Soviet interception. The momentous DEFCON-2 order was immediately picked up by GRU agents in Washington, and the Kremlin was promptly informed by the Soviet ambassador.[32] This hyperelevated alert level meant that the US Strategic Air Command's (SAC) fleet of long-range bombers carrying nuclear warheads and target instructions was set on around-the-clock rotating launch cycles, sending one-eighth of these enormous aircraft aloft toward their predetermined bombing destinations in the Soviet Union. While each attacking aircraft squadron was in due course called back at a prearranged check point en route to its targets, its place was immediately taken by the next designated set of attack aircraft in rotation so that the Kremlin was under unrelieved threat of imminent attack from a continuously replenishing cycle of oncoming strategic bombers. Notably, the Kremlin took no comparably extreme attack-readiness or countering steps.

Kennedy had thus determined to send Khrushchev double signals that simultaneously pointed in opposite directions. On the one hand he refrained from mounting any actual attack on Soviet missile bases in Cuba, opting instead to announce a relatively passive naval quarantine that would take several days to put in place, let alone engage approaching ships. This was clearly meant to be a sign of the president's sober restraint, and that is how Khrushchev and his colleagues at the Kremlin immediately interpreted it—with great relief. On the other hand, the president's DEFCON-2 alert unmistakably signaled to the Soviets the dire peril into which their gamble in Cuba had placed them. This message, too, was immediately understood by its intended recipients—with great anxiety.

Then, in the days that immediately followed, both Khrushchev and Kennedy were literally tripping over one another to be first to make a settlement proposal that would be so generous that his adversary would be unable to turn it down. As a result, each leader quickly signaled his willingness to make opening concessions that were actually *even more generous than the initial proposal he would see first from his adversary*.

Kennedy led off the bidding on October 23, the day after his speech to the nation, by launching his Turkey-for-Cuba missile swap-out proposal through the Bolshakov back channel using two separate journalist emissaries. The offer to remove an established US ballistic missile installation close to the Russian border would have been an excellent outcome at the end of prolonged negotiations, but to see it as the American president's opening offer must have been truly startling to the Kremlin audience. Equally startling to the Americans was Khrushchev's opening offer, that he would remove the missiles in exchange for a simple pledge by the president not to invade Cuba. After hearing Khrushchev's message, a relieved President Kennedy promptly sent his ExComm advisers to their homes for a good night's rest. Both "opening" proposals were more generous than the other side had expected. This made it possible to close a quick deal.

It was crucial to Kennedy that his Turkey-for-Cuba missile concession be kept secret, however, and Robert Kennedy left no doubt that secrecy was critical due to the president's domestic political concerns. Back-channel negotiations and concealment of deal terms were needed to avert the political embarrassment feared by both leaders, but especially by Kennedy, not only over the way the crisis had arisen, but also at the prospect of the domestic political damage he would likely sustain if his willingness to make major concessions became known. Ironically, the president's missile-trade offer, which he connived to keep secret, was not a sign of weakness but was instead a demonstration of sensible leadership.

DID THE WORLD REALLY COME CLOSE TO A NUCLEAR APOCALYPSE DURING THE CUBAN MISSILE CRISIS?

And we call ourselves the human race.

—JOHN F. KENNEDY, REACTING TO A BRIEFING ON US PLANNING FOR SCENARIOS IN WHICH IT MIGHT BECOME NECESSARY TO USE NUCLEAR WEAPONS, JULY 20, 1961

It is necessary to conduct an aggressive policy, but we need to advance rationally, not to resemble a gambler, in this game, who bets whatever is left in his pocket and then grabs a pistol and shoots himself.

KHRUSHCHEV'S "MENISCUS" SPEECH, NOTING THE NEED TO EXERCISE CAUTION IN THE FACE OF US STRATEGIC MILITARY SUPERIORITY, JANUARY 8, 1962

The persistent use of apocalyptic language in reevaluations of the Cuban missile crisis over the last half century largely ignores the accumulating evidence that both leaders were desperate to find a quick exit. Certainly Kennedy, after his initial shock upon learning that Khrushchev had double-crossed him, was determined not to launch any American missiles or even to allow his military to discharge any conventional weapons. Previously secret records from Soviet archives and memoirs have by now made it clear that Khrushchev likewise had no interest in going to war over his Cuban gambit. And because he held unquestioned control over Kremlin decision-making throughout the crisis, Khrushchev's recognition of the Soviet Union's extreme nuclear vulnerability meant that there was no chance the Russians would intentionally start a fight that might escalate, far less initiate use of nuclear weapons themselves. For the same reason, there was no chance that Khrushchev would risk provoking an American first strike by authorizing even a conventional attack on Berlin, from Cuba, or in any other area that the United States had designated as a sphere of its vital national interest. Thus, there was no meaningful Soviet strategic alert, far less any actual war plan during the Cuban crisis, and for good reason: had the Americans learned of such steps, they would likely have accelerated their own military preparations toward an eventual showdown the Soviets would have had no chance of winning.

Kennedy, too, shrank from allowing any outbreak of fighting between the superpowers out of fear of a nuclear escalation, but his thinking was markedly different from Khrushchev's. Whereas Khrushchev rightly feared his country would lose a nuclear war and face virtual extinction in the process, Kennedy recoiled from the prospect of even a single nuclear detonation on American soil, regardless of who might come out the technical "winner" in an ensuing war. He concluded that any nuclear use that would lead to mass casualties on home soil or even for allies in Europe was unacceptable regardless of the outcome. Add to that Kennedy's abhorrence of using nuclear weapons and his view that the threat posed by the missiles in Cuba was more of a problem for him in terms of domestic politics and the midterm elections than any serious national security concern, and it becomes clear that neither leader wanted a fight, and so neither would unleash a nuclear blow or retaliation.

That leaves the question whether nuclear escalation might have occurred anyway either by accident or by unauthorized action down the chain of command. Here, too, the historical record now available demonstrates that the chance of the victim of such an accidental nuclear strike retaliating in kind would be minuscule for the same reasons. Short of a massive breakdown in communications, approval from the top of either aggrieved side would have been needed, and both Khrushchev and Kennedy would have readily appreciated the folly of tit-for-tat nuclear escalation in the accident scenario that could have materialized. In these circumstances both leaders had sufficient authority to make the needed stand-down decision—even in the face of mass casualties from a limited nuclear strike against their country—and see to it that their orders would be obeyed in the face of inflamed opposition within their respective governments. Even in the scenario of a nuclear strike launched by mistake or a rogue actor, a decision to hold fire rather than to unleash nuclear retaliation would reap reputational benefits for the self-restraining superpower in the eyes of the world. And these benefits would have been far more weighty in terms of the pausing side's long-term interests than would the domestic political problems that the prudent leader would face from vengeful elements within his government and populace.

The literature covering the Cuban missile crisis of October 1962 is vast, and this latest contribution will not attempt to recapitulate the full sequence of well-documented events. Rather, the objective is to focus on several important dimensions of the iconic confrontation that have received comparatively scant attention in the literature, principally the overarching influence of America's global dominance in strategic nuclear strength in 1962, which prevented Khrushchev from backing up his Cuba gamble with any real display of military force (chapter 1); the revealing precedent offered by the 1961 Checkpoint Charlie tank standoff in Berlin, which displayed the president's signature method of resolving an incipient military conflict with the Soviets by use of back-channel diplomacy and generous deal terms wrapped in secrecy (chapter 2); Kennedy's misguided attempt to counter Khrushchev's boasting and restore his own credibility as a superpower leader by dropping multiple hints that the United States might be thinking about exploiting its nuclear dominance, which overreached, leading his impulsive Soviet counterpart to launch Operation Anadyr and bring on the crisis in Cuba (chapter 3); the matching rhetoric of both sides to justify their overseas nuclear missile deployments as defensive rather than offensive measures (chapter 4); the extraordinary lengths to which President Kennedy was willing to go in order to obtain Khrushchev's back-channel-brokered agreement to a pause in superpower tensions over Berlin and Cuba through the US midterm elections (chapters 5 and 6); the trap the president unwittingly set for himself by his belated red-line pronouncement, unquestionably made to shore up his domestic political position as the US midterm elections approached, that Soviet offensive missiles in Cuba would not be tolerated (chapter 7): the cover story of Soviet lying that the two Kennedy brothers devised in order to construct a more appealing narrative of events that preceded their belated discovery in Cuba of the very kinds of ballistic missiles that the president's Republican critics had long been warning about (chapter 8); and the president's role as the author and finisher of the secret missile trade deal that eventually settled the Cuban missile crisis (chapter 9).

The book then closes in chapters 10 and 11 with a critique of the orthodox view, offered by many crisis commentators, that the Cuban drama brought the world close to nuclear Armageddon. Chapter 10 traces the multiple negotiating strategies President Kennedy was lining up alternately to entice and to impose pressure on Khrushchev to remove the missiles while yet averting a nuclear showdown. In addition to the much-discussed Turkey-for-Cuba missile swap and Cordier ploy, Kennedy was formulating a further, even higher-stakes, fallback plan that would have allowed Khrushchev to "grab" West Berlin without determined resistance from the United States, which in turn would provide cover for a US military invasion of Cuba—in effect a Berlin-for-Cuba exchange. Chapter 11 reviews the meticulous steps that both Kennedy and Khrushchev took to muzzle their respective militaries so that the risk of an accidental escalation to nuclear warfare would be minimized. This final chapter also considers the risks that arise in any foreign policy conflict as a consequence of unpreventable mistakes, accidents, and other misadventure. Hopefully readers will gain a better appreciation for how the military and political dynamics that were at work in 1962 prompted both superpower leaders to defuse the crisis quickly, even if that meant each man would need to resist responding with force when right and clear justification were on his side, and to offer exceedingly generous and potentially humiliating terms in order to preserve the peace. The lesson—perhaps counterintuitive to generations who have long accepted that the world came close to a nuclear holocaust in October 1962—is that the fearsome prospect of nuclear war-fighting of any kind virtually guaranteed that the crisis would be settled with remarkable speed and certainly well before the parties came anywhere near a point of no return.

CHAPTER 1

Kennedy Holds All the Cards

The enemy is strong, not weaker than we are.

—NIKITA S. KHRUSHCHEV, JANUARY 8, 1962

ANY DISCUSSION OF the Cuban missile crisis must begin with an appreciation of the substantial military advantage the United States enjoyed over its Soviet adversary in 1962 both in strategic striking power at the global level and in theater forces in any contest over Cuba. One of the most-cited comments attributed to Joseph Stalin was his cynical response to Winston Churchill's assertion that he should heed the Vatican's insistence on Polish autonomy. The Soviet dictator's response was, "How many divisions did you say the Pope had?"[1]

Seventy-one years later, Lieutenant General Frederick Hodges, commander of US Army forces in Europe, made a less cynical observation about the West's ability to counter increasing Russian military pressures in Eastern Europe. Noting that the Kremlin had spent heavily to strengthen its military capabilities and narrow the gap that favored NATO forces, Hodges cautioned: "We're not interested in a fair fight against anyone. We want to have overmatch in all areas."[2]

What do these two comments made decades apart by leaders from such different backgrounds have in common? To the soldier's way of thinking, the correlation of forces vitally matters when one considers how to respond in a looming conflict. In considering whether the impending missile crisis during the late summer and fall of 1962 would bring the world close to war, a military mind would appraise the military forces on each side. Khrushchev certainly paid close attention to this. And he did not like what he saw.

The decisive factor in 1962 was the overwhelming American superiority both in strategic nuclear firepower and in conventional forces marshaled in the Caribbean conflict zone. This meant that Khrushchev would always take the greatest care to avoid initiating hostilities, not only in Cuba but in any location, about any matter that the United States had declared a vital security interest. Khrushchev might complain, boast, or issue threats in respect of declared American interests, but he had to refrain from precipitating military conflict because to do so would expose the Soviet Union to an ultimate test he knew his country could not win or survive.

Kennedy, too, was constrained by the nuclear imbalance, but in a different way. For the American president, use of nuclear weapons was anathema. In the midst of the ExComm's deliberations during the Cuban missile crisis, Kennedy famously referred to the possibility of an American resort to nuclear weapons as "a hell of an alternative"[3] and "obviously the final failure."[4] Like Khrushchev, Kennedy indulged in public boasting about his country's nuclear forces, and during the lead-up to the crisis he and his brother on several occasions recklessly insinuated that the United States might be actively considering the conditions under which a nuclear first strike might be launched against the Soviet Union. Yet while Khrushchev's false boasting concealed his private recognition that his country's inferiority in nuclear weapons meant the Soviet Union would never actually use these weapons against its main adversary, Kennedy's reciprocal but accurate boasting about America's nuclear prowess, and his imprudent hints about launching a nuclear first strike, concealed his adamant moral aversion to using these weapons under any circumstances.

Contrary to the spurious fears of a "missile gap" in favor of the Soviets that had emerged during the late 1950s, by 1962 it had become clear that America held the strategic nuclear advantage by a significant margin.[5] Both the United States and Soviet Union possessed a triad of strategic nuclear forces consisting of land-based ballistic missiles, long- and medium-range bombers, and submarine-launched ballistic missiles (SLBMs). The United States held a numbers advantage in the critical categories of intercontinental ballistic missiles (ICBMs) and SLBMs that were capable of hitting the Soviet homeland. But the critical difference between the strategic forces of the two superpowers in 1961 and 1962 was air power rather than missile power, and the tremendous American advantage there was due mainly to the differential geographies of the two rival Cold War alliances. The United States had alliances with numerous countries located along the Soviet bloc periphery, and this allowed the forward basing of many American strategic bombers that could quickly reach major military and urban targets within the USSR on repeatable two-way missions. In addition, some of the air forces of US NATO allies located near the Soviet bloc were equipped with US nuclear ordnance, thereby adding to the weight of a US strategic attack on the Russian homeland. Equally important, these overseas air bases in friendly countries provided the US Air Force with recovery touch-down locations for attacking bombers returning from their long-distance missions low on fuel.

The Soviet Union enjoyed no similarly advantageous geographic proximity to its main adversary. As a result, many Soviet bombers could not realistically reach the US homeland unless they took off from hard-to-use Arctic airfields whose extreme weather conditions made permanent basing impractical. And even if such raids from Arctic airstrips could be managed, for many Russian air crews those flights would be one-way suicide missions with little or no prospect of returning home or making a safe landing at a welcoming airfield. And that meant there would be no effective repeat strike capability using those aircraft.

Even putting aside the trouble this posed for combat morale, it also meant that the aggregate weight of Soviet airborne nuclear power fell short of the comparable bombing capability of the SAC and America's NATO allies, because the Soviet air force could manage, for all practical purposes, only a single, significant striking wave of attack, whereas SAC would be able to launch repeat air attacks followed by return to base, reloading, and multiple follow-on missions.

The United States had many allies located along or near the Soviet Union's borders, and this allowed the basing of American and allied military aircraft carrying nuclear bombs within striking distance of Russia's largest cities and key military installations. In 1961 and 1962 SAC medium- and long-range aircraft were based in Great Britain, France, Germany, Italy, Greece, Turkey and the Netherlands, among other locations within striking distance of the USSR.[6] These bombers could therefore drop their payloads on target, return to their bases, reload, and repeat the procedure, an advantage that would be critically important to the outcome of any prolonged military struggle.

The United States also had comparatively advanced, in-flight refueling capabilities that expanded the reach of its US-based long-range bomber force, allowing two-way missions launched from the continental United States. By contrast, the Soviet Union had no air force bases along the periphery of the United States, and had to depend on its remote and inhospitable

Arctic bases for attacks on targets inside the US homeland.[7] Russia's longest-range bombers had only limited in-air refueling capability.[8] For many of the Russian bombers, a flight plan with the United States as the target would run a high risk of futility due to American air defenses, and in any event would amount to a one-way suicide mission because fuel limitations would rule out a return home or to other friendly soil.[9]

With regard to ballistic missiles, the United States in 1961 and 1962 could reach Soviet targets both with its ICBMs based in the continental United States and with IRBMs located along the periphery of the Soviet Union at installations in three NATO countries: Great Britain, Italy, and Turkey. The Soviets, by contrast, had a smaller number of ICBM missiles and only four launching pads, and before October 1962 they had no land-based MRBMs or IRBMs within striking distance of the United States. This meant that the main threat of the Soviet rocket forces was to US allies and American forces based in Europe rather than the continental United States. NATO vulnerability posed many complications for collaboration between the United States and its European allies, but it nonetheless amounted to an "enormous advantage in killing power" for the US military in the superpower rivalry.[10]

The US intelligence community regularly produced estimates of Soviet nuclear striking capabilities and advised the president of the findings in national intelligence estimates (NIEs). By 1961, the availability of satellite photographic imagery through the secret US Corona program greatly enhanced intelligence gathering. As a result, estimates of Soviet nuclear striking power sharply declined during 1960–1961.[11]

With ICBMs, for example, the US intelligence community estimated in NIE 11-8-59, issued on February 9, 1960, entitled "Soviet Capabilities for Strategic Attack through Mid-1964," that "the probable Soviet ICBM program would provide on the order of 140–200 ICBMs on launcher in mid-1961."[12] By June 7, 1961, however, the intelligence estimators found themselves "still unable to confirm the location of any ICBM launcher facilities other than those at the test range."[13] On September 21, 1961, a new NIE (11-8/1-61) provided a "sharp downward revision" of the prior figures and estimated "that the present Soviet ICBM strength" was "in the range of 10–25 launchers from which missiles can be fired against the US."[14] The new NIE further concluded that "this force level will not increase markedly during the months immediately ahead."

By January 10, 1962, the "Memorandum to Holders of Annexes A and B, NIE 11-4-61"[15] had once again raised the estimate of Soviet ICBM strength, calculating that "in mid-1962 the USSR will probably have a total of 35–50 launchers from which ICBMs can be fired against the US, including those at first and second generation operational launching complexes in the field as well as R&D launchers at Tyuratam."[16] As of July 6, 1962, the estimated number of operational Soviet ICBM launchers remained at 50.[17]

In point of fact, these NIE estimates significantly overstated the actual "operational" Soviet ICBM capability. The true number of Soviet ICBMs may have been as low as four. The Kennedy administration knew this by September 1961: "How many ICBMs were the Soviets now thought to have? Not 500 or 200 or 100 or even 50, but *four*—just four SS-6 missiles."[18] As noted by William Taubman, citing research by Sergei Khrushchev: "It wasn't until the 1960s that the first Soviet ICBMs, a grand total of four of them, actually became operational."[19] Taubman probably meant to say a grand total of four ICBM *launching pads* rather than ICBM missiles. As Russian rocket engineer Boris Chertok later revealed, the Soviets had manufactured "many" ICBM rockets by late 1962, but they possessed only four ICBM launch pads.[20]

By way of contrast, the United States was able to bring the following numbers of Atlas, Titan and Minuteman ICBMs to essentially fire-on-command alert status during the key days of the Cuban missile crisis: 132 on October 22, 147 on October 24, 152 on October 26, 171 on October 28, and 181 on October 30.[21]

Further, unlike many of the US missiles, all of the Soviet ICBMs were vulnerable to sudden destruction by both distant and nearby US strategic attack forces owing to their known locations in a small number of above-ground installations,[22] the vulnerability of Soviet defenses against a bombing attack,[23] the unstable fuel design of Soviet ICBMs requiring time-consuming fuel loading,[24] and their highly limited state of launch readiness.[25] As Roger Hilsman, the US State Department's director of the Bureau of Intelligence and Research at the time, observed a few years later, just as the United States was moving rapidly toward introduction of its more modern Minuteman ICBM, the Soviets discovered that their giant first-generation rocket was "too big, too bulky to serve as a practical weapon." The need for a "more streamlined missile" meant that the Soviet ICBM program "must have been set back many months."[26]

Moreover, the level of targeting accuracy that Russian ICBMs were capable of achieving at the time was weak at best.[27] The United States had gained an additional layer of reassurance about these Soviet shortcomings from an informant, GRU colonel Oleg Penkovsky, who "insisted that Kennedy should be 'firm,' assured his American handlers that Khrushchev was 'not ready for any war,' and revealed what he had been told in confidence by the head of the Soviet State Committee on Coordination of Scientific Research: 'You know . . . with respect to ICBMs, up to now we don't have a damn thing. Everything is only on paper, and there is nothing in actual existence.'"[28]

As noted above, the United States also had overseas missile installations on the territory of allies around the periphery of the Soviet bloc that were capable of launching Thor and Jupiter IRBMs against targets in Russia. By the time of the Cuban missile crisis these would include fifteen Jupiters in Turkey, thirty Jupiters in Italy, and sixty Thors in Great Britain.[29] Prior to Operation Anadyr, Khrushchev had no similar IRBM or MRBM missiles capable of reaching the continental United States.

Thus, while there is an argument that for a short period after the 1957 launch of *Sputnik* the Soviets may have benefited from a kind of "missile-*technology* gap" owing to their brief lead in the capability to launch long-range ballistic missiles able to lift nuclear warheads,[30] that lead did not translate into any meaningful superiority in strategic ICBM military might.

The US estimates of Soviet long-range air power capable of reaching the continental United States remained steady, and the numbers were small in relation to figures for comparable US air power. As of June 7, 1961, NIE 11-8-61 concluded that the Soviets could field at most only about four hundred bombers and tankers on two-way missions against the United States if staged from Arctic bases and able to be refueled in-flight, but that only two hundred of these aircraft, including eighty heavy bombers, had the capability of arriving over North America given realistic operational limits and not counting combat attrition as they faced formidable US air defenses.[31] As to the requirement of Arctic staging, the NIE estimators observed that "the facilities available at these airfields, together with the adverse operational conditions in the Arctic, impose limitations on the number of aircraft which can be launched for simultaneous attack."[32]

In the NIE dated August 24, 1961, it was similarly estimated that the Soviet Union possessed two hundred medium and heavy bombers that would be capable of reaching the continental United States and returning to their bases (two-way missions).[33] The NIE also noted that the Soviets possessed "a considerably larger gross capability" to conduct one-way (i.e., suicide) bombing missions employing "medium bombers" and "crews who had not had Arctic training."[34]

These figures did not take account of battle attrition, however, that is, the losses those attacks would suffer from interception by US aircraft and other antiaircraft defenses. An analysis conducted in 2012 found that attrition would most likely have been almost total: "Air defense interceptor aircraft, many (or perhaps all) armed with nuclear Genie or Falcon air-to-air missiles would likely have prevented any Soviet bomber from reaching its target."[35]

By contrast, SAC was able to deploy the following numbers of strategic bombers based in the United States and supporting in-air tankers on "emergency war order" (EWO) ready status, at a twenty-four-hour force generation level during the Cuban missile crisis: 912 bombers and 402 tankers on October 24, 1962, and 1,436 bombers and 916 tankers on October 25, 1962. Each of the bombers carried nuclear weapons and targeting orders, referred to as combat mission folders, which gave them the precise coordinates of the Soviet target they were being ordered to hit and destroy.[36] When SAC reached peak strength during DEFCON-2, approximately sixty-five airborne B-52s were "'target effective' at any given time."[37]

The United States was also able to deploy strategic bombers from overseas forward bases in allied countries closer to the Soviet Union in Morocco, Spain, and the United Kingdom. These bases also provided an important "recovery" option for aircraft returning from bombing runs over the Soviet Union, including planes that were either damaged or low on fuel.[38] Aware of the fact that the proximity of overseas bases to Soviet targets also meant these forward deployments were vulnerable to Soviet attack, SAC planners developed a measured strategy that involved rotating B-47 "Stratojet" long-range bombers to ten forward bases—four in Britain, three in Spain, and three in Morocco—for periods limited to "just 21 days, in contrast with the normal 90-day rotation that had been instituted in 1948."[39] Under a program called "Operation Reflex Action," SAC began rotations of B-47 aircraft carrying "the all-new eleven-foot-long, six thousand pound four megaton MK-39 thermonuclear bombs." These aircraft were deployed first to the Sidi Slimane airbase in Morocco in 1957 on an experimental basis, and thereafter the program expanded to include bases in Spain (Zaragosa) and England (Greenham Common, Fairford, Brize Norton, Lakenheath, and Upper Heyford).[40] During the Cuban missile crisis these Reflex aircraft were "EWO configured and available to support any aborted sortie" from the continental United States.[41] In England, Upper Heyford hosted twenty-three B-47s from the USAF 98th and 398th bomb wings. At all times after 1957, one-third of these Reflex aircraft were able to be launched "within 15 minutes of a warning to maximize the chances of a strike being successfully mounted."[42]

As noted previously, the Soviets had no bombers permanently based in the Western Hemisphere that were capable of delivering a nuclear attack on the United States. The US Air Force, by contrast, maintained a permanent overseas fleet of approximately 450 medium bombers and fighter bombers stationed in allied countries along the periphery of the Soviet bloc and capable of carrying nuclear bombs. These included American Martin B-57 Canberra medium bombers and their British counterparts based in Germany, which used the "toss bombing" technique "whereby the attacking aircraft approached the target at low level, released the weapon in a climb and turned away to escape the blast."[43]

In addition, the British Royal Air Force's strategic bombing capability, referred to as its V-Force with combat ranges from 2,607 to 6,000 miles, consisted of Valiant, Vulcan, and Victor bombers equipped with US nuclear bombs. In 1962 the Soviet targets assigned to the RAF's V-Force "covered 48 cities, 6 air defense targets and 3 long-range air force bases." During the Cuban missile crisis there were "three Valiant squadrons at RAF Marham equipped with US nuclear weapons and assigned to the operational control of SACEUR [Supreme Allied Commander Europe]."[44]

Overseas-based American tactical fighter bombers armed with nuclear bombs included F-100 Super Sabres and F-84F Thunderstreaks.[45] During the Cuban missile crisis, some "37 USAF tactical aircraft were prepared" at air bases in Europe and Turkey, "with nuclear weapons loaded in readiness."[46] As will be seen, Khrushchev attempted to match the imbalance he faced by transporting to Cuba a number of IL-28 Beagle light bombers, which had a combat radius of six hundred miles and were capable of carrying atomic bombs. Yet, as Dobbs has reported, the American F-100s "were designed to carry much more powerful bombs than the IL-28s and were much faster." The "two-stage thermonuclear bomb" carried by the F-100 "had several hundred times the destructive power" of the IL-28's "relatively crude atomic bombs."[47]

Similarly, the CIA estimators in 1962 concluded the United States held a heavy advantage over the Soviet Union in numbers of submarine-launched missiles with nuclear warheads that could reach the enemy's home territory. The United States estimated that the Soviets possessed eight missile-carrying submarines as of early 1962. Importantly, however, the Soviet SLBMs could only be launched from the surface, and were only capable of reaching targets at a range of 350 nautical miles or less.[48] This left such attack vessels highly vulnerable to interdiction by US naval and air defense forces. The net result was that submarine-launched missiles "added nothing to the Soviet strategic deterrent in the early 1960s," due to a combination of "noisy" diesel-powered submarines constituting two-thirds of the fleet, which "could be easily detected," and serious limitations on the remainder due to "the long transit time from their home bases, the short range of their missiles, and their inability to launch without surfacing and going through a time-consuming procedure."[49]

By contrast, the United States had a formidable combination of nuclear weapons that could be delivered to the Russian homeland by SLBMs: "At the end of 1961, the United States had a strategic triad of more than 1,650 long-range bombers, 30 Atlas D ICBMs, 32 Atlas E ICBMs, 1 Titan ICBM, and 80 Polaris missiles at its disposal, and these capabilities were rapidly growing."[50] During the Cuban crisis, three Polaris-armed US submarines stationed at the naval base in Holy Loch in Scotland "slipped quietly out to sea accompanied by their tender ship."[51]

Thus, when Kennedy and Khrushchev compared the raw numbers of nuclear weapons that could actually be launched to hit targets on their respective homelands in an all-out initial exchange, the figures overwhelmingly favored the United States. According to one estimate, deliverable bomb/missile/warhead numbers favored the United States by 3,559 to 538, not counting reload capacity.[52] Beschloss found that the differential was even greater, with the United States having "roughly six thousand nuclear warheads against roughly three hundred for the Soviets—a twenty-to-one advantage."[53] Secretary of Defense Robert McNamara later stated that the imbalance was 5,000 US strategic nuclear warheads to 300 for the Soviets.[54] McMahon has computed the size of the US advantage at seventeen to one.[55] Soviet general Anatoly I. Gribkov later agreed with the seventeen-to-one figure, which "everybody understood . . . very clearly," though the magnitude of Soviet strategic nuclear inferiority was "never said in public."[56] Boris Chertok, the Soviet rocket engineer, also put the US advantage in nuclear weapons able to strike the adversary's home territory at 5,000 units to 300 units (roughly seventeen to one).[57]

Whichever of these figures was the most accurate, all pointed to a daunting asymmetry indicating that, while the United States had to anticipate sustaining at least some serious damage and loss of life in the event of a wide-scale nuclear exchange, the Soviet Union would most likely suffer near-absolute national extinction. But this state of affairs was not solely the result of a US strategic military buildup. Khrushchev himself had consciously launched a policy in the late 1950s that slowed Soviet missile procurement pending further progress on their new generation solid-fuel missile system, thereby allowing the United States to widen its lead.

In the wake of the drama produced by the Soviet Union's successful launch of its *Sputnik* satellite on October 4, 1957, Washington and Moscow were both determined to develop ICBMs that could take advantage of the heavy lift and intercontinental range capabilities that the Russian space rocket had demonstrated. However, the two superpowers set out to do so on two different timetables. The United States moved quickly out of fear that the Russians held a dangerous lead in this military competency. The Soviets, by contrast, would soon experience technological difficulties in their development efforts, and they also faced more severe budgetary constraints than their rival. Feeling pressure to devote greater resources to his domestic economy, Khrushchev chose to forgo the drastic steps that would narrow the American advantage.

The first public US response to the *Sputnik* challenge was an embarrassing failure. The highly anticipated and heavily publicized launch of a navy Vanguard missile intended to place the first US satellite in orbit exploded a few feet from takeoff on December 6, 1957.[58] But the Eisenhower administration's commitment to enhanced strategic capability was growing steadily at deeper levels of what the president would later call the "military industrial complex." And while Eisenhower used that term as a warning against uncontrolled military spending, the gains produced by the country's commitment to ICBM development would soon reward the effort in the form of enhanced deterrence.

The elements of the US strategic missile buildup that were most important for an understanding of the balance of nuclear power during 1961 and 1962 were the advances in ICBM and SLBM weapons. The Gaither Committee, established by Eisenhower in May 1957 to review the nation's strategic military posture, delivered its report to the National Security Council on November 7, 1957, only a month after the Soviet Union's surprise launch of *Sputnik*, the world's first artificial earth satellite. The title of the committee's report, "Deterrence and Survival in the Nuclear Age," reflected the committee's worry about an impending window of "increasing threat" of Soviet attack, "which may become critical in 1959 or 1960." The committee recommended a number of responses of which "the highest priority was to reduce SAC vulnerability and to increase the strategic retaliatory capability of U.S. nuclear forces."[59] The committee urged increased production of ICBMs from 80 to

600, with rapid phase-in of hardened launch sites, accelerated development of six Polaris submarines carrying 16 SLBMs each, and deployment of 240 Thor and Jupiter IRBMs, eventually to be stationed overseas.[60]

A month after the Gaither report's release, the air force successfully flight-tested its first Atlas ICBM, and these missiles became operational in above-ground launch sites by June 1959.[61] By the end of the Eisenhower presidency the country had surpassed the Gaither Committee's recommended missile system force levels.[62] The first Minuteman-1 missile, designed to be launched from hardened underground sites and powered by more manageable solid fuel, was successfully flight-tested on February 1, 1961, and the first units were brought into service at Malmstrom Air Force Base in Montana at the height of the Cuban crisis. On October 27, 1962, the first two Minuteman missiles became operational at Malmstrom, followed by seven more the next week.[63]

After four years of development, the United States launched its first nuclear-powered ballistic missile submarine (SSBN), the *George Washington*, at the end of 1959. The vessel went to sea on its first patrol in November 1960. Between 1960 and 1966 the United States launched forty-one SSBNs, nicknamed "boomers," each carrying sixteen Polaris nuclear-armed missiles. By October 1962, the United States had "almost total underwater superiority"; Polaris submarines "based in Scotland were able to patrol the borders of the Soviet Union at will," whereas the Soviet submarine fleet "was largely confined to the Arctic Ocean, posing no significant threat to the United States."[64]

During the same period and in direct contrast to the rapid US strategic arms buildup during the late 1950s, the Soviets chose to slow down. Khrushchev wrote to the Presidium on December 8, 1959, seeking "far-reaching cuts in armaments . . . even without conditions for reciprocity from other states, and for a significant reduction in numbers of men under arms."[65] Fursenko and Naftali have described the critical decision that Khrushchev advocated before his Presidium colleagues at a fateful meeting on December 14, 1959. The basic issue was one familiar to American policymakers: with limited available resources, what should take priority in USSR planning, guns or butter? After painting a concerning picture about the pressing need for measures to strengthen a weak Soviet economy and greatly improve the lives of the people, Khrushchev made the point that for this to happen it would be necessary to "reduce[] the cost of the Cold War so that more money could flow into the civilian economy," even though this meant taking a "huge risk."[66]

The Soviets had a first-generation ICBM missile, the R-7A (also referred to by US analysts as the SS-6), but their Strategic Rocket Forces were limited in numbers of launch pads, and their ICBMs operated from unprotected aboveground launch facilities. Further, the Soviet ICBMs could not be brought quickly to launch-ready status, for several reasons. First, they "were not loaded with warheads, and it would take at least six hours to get them loaded."[67] Moreover, these missiles were powered by hard-to-manage liquid fuel. Soviet rocket forces Marshal Moskalenko gave Khrushchev a sobering message about the qualitative disparity in the two superpowers' respective ICBM force readiness at a February 1962 meeting of the Defense Council at Pitsunda. Whereas the American solid-fuel Minuteman could be held at launch readiness almost indefinitely, the Soviet R-7A's "unstable liquid fuel" had to be drained after thirty days "to avoid an explosion."[68] The volatility of the fuel used in Soviet ballistic missiles was dramatically demonstrated on October 24, 1960, when the fuel of an R-7 rocket (possibly an R-16 prototype) exploded on its launch pad at the Baikonur test range, killing at least seventy-four Soviet engineers, including Marshal Mitrofan Nedelin, the head of the country's Strategic Rocket Forces.[69]

The USSR had two more modern ICBM missiles in development—the R-9 and the R-16—but these systems most likely would not be ready for deployment before 1965. According to Fursenko and Naftali, Khrushchev faced a stark choice: his adversary was able "to deliver a crippling strike on the USSR with one order," whereas the Kremlin had no comparable capability. Nor was the situation likely to change soon given the pace of US investment in next-generation nuclear weapons, which was faster than what the Kremlin was able to manage.[70]

In these gloomy circumstances, Khrushchev surprisingly did not propose a "crash rearmament program" or even an "acceleration of the development of the next generation of missiles." He did just the opposite, recommending to the Presidium a "diplomatic strategy" consisting of "a dramatic unilateral cut in the Soviet armed forces." Perhaps even more surprisingly, the Presidium "adopted Khrushchev's strategy of unilateral disarmament after hearing nothing but praise from his hand-picked military chiefs," and in doing so it took "a huge strategic risk" by creating "a Soviet window of vulnerability," leaving the Kremlin "far weaker" than its adversary.[71]

In the years leading up to the Cuban missile crisis, the Soviet Union was taking no significant steps to bolster its "strategic air and ballistic missile defenses." Facing the "successive crises of 1961 and 1962 over Berlin and Cuban missiles . . . which could well have stimulated the Soviets to take drastic steps to improve their strategic defense capabilities," the Kremlin demurred. To the contrary, "Even as the Cuban crisis was brewing the Soviets were reducing their commitment to strategic defense from what it was in 1961. By 1963 the commitment of resources to strategic defense had fallen to its lowest level for the entire 1955–1972 period."[72]

It was against this backdrop of steadily growing US advantage in strategic military power that a tense superpower confrontation would flare up in Berlin, culminating in the famous, literally cinematic, tank standoff at the Berlin Wall's Checkpoint Charlie in late October 1961. And the resolution of that military face-off would provide a kind of blueprint and preview in miniature of the momentous missile crisis that would unfold in the Caribbean exactly one year later.

CHAPTER 2

Cat-and-Mouse Games at the Berlin Wall

A wall is a hell of a lot better than a war.
—PRESIDENT KENNEDY, AUGUST 1961

LIKE THE CUBAN CRISIS, the Checkpoint Charlie tank stand-off involved rival leaders who claimed to be pursuing defensive policies but whose actions led to soldiers on both sides looking nervously down their adversaries' gun barrels. Both incidents featured frantic efforts at the highest levels to defuse the confrontation, crisis diplomacy over back channels, the appearance on both occasions of a shadowy GRU colonel serving as trusted emissary, and an abrupt end to each crisis achieved by deals wrapped in secrecy. The Berlin tank incident was always low level, inadvertent, and lacking in military necessity, and was thus readily contained. Yet the sequence of events leading from confrontation to peaceful denouement in Berlin turned out to foreshadow in remarkable detail the Cuban drama a year later.

The Berlin incident that began with the erection of the infamous Berlin Wall on August 13, 1961, and culminated with the tank stand-off at Checkpoint Charlie two and a half months later on October 27–28, featured major provocations that might have escalated to military conflict. The wall was begun under cover of night and without notice, and the construction continued under the watchful eyes of armed Soviet and GDR soldiers. Nervous observers in West Berlin and throughout the world can be forgiven for having feared that this dramatic Soviet provocation might lead to fighting. As it turned out, the drama was more political than military, and each side's steps were carefully calibrated to avoid a conflict.[1]

In the aftermath of the Vienna summit, Berlin had become the most significant zone of tensions, and President Kennedy rightly anticipated that

Khrushchev would increase pressure on the foothold the Western powers maintained in that city. The Soviet chairman had long been pursuing a goal of entering into a separate peace treaty with the GDR, one that would confer on East Germany sovereign rights over its territory and therefore a legal basis for seeking to block US access rights to West Berlin. Former secretary of state Dean Acheson was asked to develop recommendations for how the president should respond. Acheson's report, delivered to the president on June 28, 1961, called for a muscular policy in the face of what he called "an issue of resolution between the U.S.A. and the U.S.S.R." on which "the whole position of the United States is in the balance." Acheson called the path of negotiation in these circumstances "worse than a waste of time and energy." What was needed was a policy based on military responses to predefined contingencies that would show the Soviets that, in the words of a former British ambassador to Moscow, "what they want to do is not possible."[2]

The problem for the president was that US strategic policy at the time was based upon the concept of massive retaliation for any Soviet military thrust threatening Berlin. Recognizing that the Western allies were severely outmanned and outgunned by the Red Army in the German theater, the US military's only recourse in the event of a major Soviet attack on Berlin or West Germany was thought to be the prompt, almost automatic unleashing of a nuclear counterattack, potentially escalating to the apocalypse of uncontrolled strikes and counterstrikes, leading to mutually assured destruction (MAD). Both the nuclear retaliation tactic and the strategic MAD doctrine were embodied in a so-called Single Integrated Operational Plan referred to in shorthand at the time as SIOP-62.

Kennedy's court historian, Arthur Schlesinger Jr., was deeply troubled by the tone of the Acheson report and feared the president might be bullied into adopting too martial a policy on Berlin in particular as the president was trying to vindicate his reputation for leadership following the Bay of Pigs disaster. The Pulitzer Prize–winning professor composed a quick response to Acheson's recommended approach, which advised the president "that the Cuban fiasco was a result of 'excessive concentration on military and operational problems' in the preparatory stage while underestimating the political issues."[3]

After receiving a warm reaction from Kennedy, Schlesinger enlisted the help of part-time Kennedy adviser and future secretary of state Henry Kissinger, who drafted an alternative, more nuanced approach to the looming Berlin confrontation that appealed to the president.[4] The president also received a memorandum from Thomas Schelling, a Harvard professor and expert on nuclear strategy. According to McGeorge Bundy, who served as President Kennedy's national security advisor, Schelling's "very intelligent" July 5, 1961, memorandum, entitled "Nuclear Strategy in the Berlin Crisis," made a "deep impression" on the president when he read it during a brief vacation retreat at his home in Hyannis, Massachusetts.[5] The memorandum urged the president to consider that, if it became necessary to actually use a nuclear weapon in battle, the chief value of such use would be the signal of intention it sent to the Soviets, not the military value of the target it destroyed: "The purpose of nuclears is to convince the Soviets that the risk of general war is great enough to outweigh their original tactical objectives, but not so great as to make it prudent to initiate it pre-emptively." This counseled in favor of planning "for a war of nerve, of demonstration, and of bargaining, not of tactical target destruction." Destruction of targets would be "incidental to the message the detonation conveys to the Soviet leadership." The limited number of targets selected for destruction should be treated as "a 'proposal' that must be responded to. And they are an added catalyst to general war. This is an argument for a selective and threatening use of nuclears rather than large-scale tactical use."[6]

The Schelling memorandum thus introduced the notions of signaling, selectivity, demonstration, and bargaining into the president's thinking on US nuclear strategy. If it were to become necessary for the president to use a nuclear weapon, it would be best to do so in a selective and restrained way designed to signal to the Soviets a willingness to engage in first use but also a desire to limit use and an intention to bargain back to a mutual stand-down. This same thinking would inform the president's approach to the new set of military response guidelines being prepared for hypothetical Soviet aggression against Western forces in West Berlin, as described below, and it would appear again one year later as President Kennedy faced the more concrete challenge posed by his Soviet rival's missile installations in Cuba.

At a meeting of his top advisers on July 8, 1961, the president instructed the Pentagon to come up with a plan "for non-nuclear resistance in the case of a Berlin confrontation" and told his assembled advisers that he wanted "new options beyond the current choice between 'holocaust or humiliation.'"[7] The plan was officially issued on October 23, 1961, as National Security Action Memorandum 109, "U.S. Policy on Military Actions in a Berlin Conflict."[8] The policy gave the president multiple intermediate steps he could take in the face of a Soviet challenge to allied positions in West Berlin and around its access routes. These began with "tripartitely agreed probes of Soviet intentions by a platoon or smaller force on the ground and by fighter escort in the air," and included a range of further nonnuclear and even nonmilitary options scaling up from "economic embargo, maritime harassment, and UN action," "expanding non-nuclear air action . . . to gain local air superiority," and "expanding non-nuclear ground operations into GDR territory in division and greater strength, with strong air support."

If these nonnuclear steps proved unavailing, then NSAM 109 approved graduated use of nuclear weapons consistent with Schelling's principles of signaling, selectivity, demonstration, and bargaining. Thus, resort to nuclear force was to begin with selective attacks "for the primary purpose of demonstrating the will to use nuclear weapons." If this failed, then there would be "limited tactical employment of nuclear weapons to achieve in addition significant tactical advantage." Only if this step failed to end the fighting, then NSAM 109 contemplated escalation to "General Nuclear War."

The president sent NSAM 109 to the supreme allied commander Europe (SACEUR), General Lauris Norstad, with a covering letter that emphasized his intention to take as many intermediate measures as possible before resorting to a nuclear strike so as to avoid "going off half-cocked." The president placed "as much importance on developing our capacity and readiness to fight with significant non-nuclear forces as on measures designed primarily to make our nuclear deterrent more credible." He believed the US "nuclear deterrent will not be credible to the Soviets unless they are convinced of NATO's readiness to become engaged on a lesser level of violence and are thereby made to realize the great risks of escalation to nuclear war."[9]

Eventually, there would be parallel major revisions to SIOP-62 that would culminate in a fundamentally transformed "flexible response" policy that came into effect on August 1, 1962, under the new designation SIOP-63.[10] The revised policy distinguished among three categories of target: nuclear-threat, other military, and urban-industrial.[11] A wide range of flexible responses were made available to the president, numbering four thousand or more;[12] however, SIOP-63 still "required the use of massive numbers of nuclear weapons," and conceivably could have inflicted enormous civilian damage and casualties "even without direct attacks on urban-industrial targets."[13]

It was in the midst of the transition from massive retaliation and MAD to flexible response that the president was called upon to react to the erection of the Berlin Wall on August 13, 1961, and then to the Checkpoint Charlie tank stand-off in Friedrichstrasse Plaza on October 27. On both occasions, political solutions won out over military approaches that presented too high a risk of conflict. Khrushchev wanted a wall to stop the embarrassing outflow of political refugees seeking a new and better life in the West, and he also wanted Western recognition of self-governance rights for the nascent GDR border authorities in East Berlin. Kennedy mainly wanted to preserve the status quo for Western power occupation rights in West Berlin and to do so peacefully. But he also wanted to be seen as a strong leader, a desire that existed in tension with his more cautious basic objective. Both leaders would end up getting exactly what they wanted on Saturday morning October 28, 1961, and in the process a signature form of Kennedy crisis resolution diplomacy was revealed.

John F. Kennedy had arrived at the White House after having accused his predecessor of weakness in the face of the Soviet threat. The new president wished to present an entirely new image of toughness and nerve. Nevertheless, and to his great dismay, Kennedy's first two foreign policy challenges turned out to be near-disasters, as the Bay of Pigs invasion became a humiliating fiasco, followed by the Vienna summit in which public opinion held that Khrushchev had "bullied" the younger and less experienced president. A June 30, 1961, *Time* magazine story stated that by the "crucial test of reality," the new president's "system is not working. In the field of foreign policy, the record is sorry. When trouble has struck, the Kennedy solution has seemed to be activity instead of action."[14]

In the aftermath of the Bay of Pigs and Vienna setbacks, Kennedy felt an acute need to demonstrate to the American public and the broader world community his "toughness" and resolution in the face of seemingly relentless Soviet expansion. Nevertheless, the president's next foreign policy challenge proved that circumspection and discretion were the better part of valor. Over many months the GDR had been experiencing a steady flow of its population crossing the border to the Federal Republic of Germany (FRG) in the hope of a better life beyond the Iron Curtain. Especially problematic was the exodus of the most highly trained segments of the GDR's workforce.

The solution was simple. Khrushchev set the stage on August 7 by public assurances designed to make clear that the Soviet Union would take no hostile steps to infringe interests of the Western powers in Berlin: "Any barring of access to West Berlin, any blockade of West Berlin, is entirely out of the question."[15] As one leading Cold War scholar has noted, Khrushchev's "threatening tone at least temporarily disappeared."[16] Then, on the morning of August 13, 1961, residents of the western sector of Berlin awoke to the spectacle of a barbed-wire barrier going up across the center of their city and the sounds of construction as a concrete wall was rapidly erected. Their shock gave way to anger as the citizens of West Germany and especially the people of West Berlin looked to the Western occupying powers to push back. Kennedy's response was silence.[17] He felt that the Berlin Wall was the least dangerous resolution to a critical problem the Soviets were facing. However painful the wall might seem to West Germans and all Berliners, it was far preferable in the president's estimation to the only other alternative—active Western defiance against a core Kremlin initiative vital to Soviet interests. As Kennedy privately and pithily summed up the situation: "A wall is a hell of a lot better than a war."[18]

Notably, the president did not undertake any major military actions in response to the Berlin Wall. Rather, he opted to take two largely symbolic steps. First, he quickly dispatched Vice President Lyndon Johnson and General Lucius D. Clay, the hero of the 1948 Berlin airlift, to go to West Berlin in order to boost its people's flagging morale by underscoring America's determination to support the city in the aftermath of its traumatic bisection. Simultaneously, Kennedy sent a modest reinforcement of US troops into Berlin in order to strike a balance between his intent to show support and his desire not to provoke the Soviets, calling the army detachment "our hostage to that intent."[19] He ordered that a small battle group of fifteen hundred US Army troops be deployed from West Germany to West Berlin in time to be greeted by the two high-level US emissaries. Khrushchev saw no real threat because he considered the reinforcements to be "of no military significance," except to put more men "in West Berlin's mousetrap."[20]

There soon followed a second chapter to the Berlin Wall drama. Although the wall effectively stopped the flow of refugees from the GDR, it soon brought to the fore a long-standing dispute over the occupying powers' rights under conventions that had been set in place at the end of World War II to move at will through the entire occupied city of Berlin. The problem was that GDR guards—referred to derogatively in the West as "VOPOs" (short for *Volkspolizei*)—manned the few routes of access and egress through the wall dividing the city that were left open, but heavily guarded. Because the United States did not officially recognize the GDR as a sovereign entity, US officials—most notably General Clay—did not believe VOPOs had authority to stop US military or civilian officials from exercising their rights to transit the city freely. Clay was adamant on the subject; as he would later tell his biographer, allowing GDR guards to control the border crossing "would have undermined our whole legal position to be in Berlin—which was based on the quadripartite status of the city."[21]

By selecting Lucius Clay as his personal representative, with ambassadorial rank, for the Berlin assignment, Kennedy had chosen a highly popular local hero owing to the prominent role the general had played in marshaling food supplies and other relief for Berlin's beleaguered population in 1949 when the Soviets had blocked all ground transportation routes transiting Soviet-occupied East Germany. But Clay was also an aggressive and independent-minded military man who was used to giving orders and having them obeyed. With his own distinguished military record and now bearing unusual and ill-defined status as the president's personal representative in Berlin, Clay quickly introduced tension in the overlapping authorities of the US military leaders who were already in place, including SACEUR Lauris Norstad and the commander of US Army forces in Europe, General Bruce C. Clarke.

Just over a month after Clay assumed his new role in West Berlin on September 19, 1961, he had an opportunity to test the resistance of the VOPOs and their Soviet patrons. On Sunday evening October 22, 1961, E. Allan Lightner Jr., the senior US diplomat in West Berlin, was traveling by private car with his wife on an evening excursion to the theater in East Berlin. Lightner refused to show his identification papers to the VOPO guards on the GDR-patrolled Friedrichstrasse Plaza side of Checkpoint Charlie. A Soviet official summoned to the scene apologized, but the next day the East German News Agency "announced that civilians crossing the Berlin sector border had to show identification cards."[22]

Clay had written a private letter to President Kennedy just a few days before on October 18 calling attention to tensions at that particular border crossing and recommending that US forces be authorized to act aggressively to protect their crossing rights: "I feel strongly that prompt reaction is essential when an incident occurs which threatens a right, and that even a delay of a few hours makes it impossible to take action without increasing the risk of war." In the same letter he cited resistance he was experiencing from "the Military Command," and he included a nonsubtle and borderline insubordinate reference to Norstad in this regard: "I have respect for our military leadership in Europe and I know the limits of its authority. I am concerned that even as able a Commander as Norstad can report as the American Commander without being influenced by his NATO hat. Perhaps independent viewpoints would be more valuable." Clay added that he could "not accept the recommendations I do make to be tossed lightly aside at higher headquarters in Europe."[23]

This was not General Clay's first tangle with authorities who disagreed with his view that only a display of American military force could stop a determined Soviet challenge to Western rights in Berlin. The 1948 Soviet blockade of West Berlin had ultimately been defeated by a sustained airlift of supplies to the city's beleaguered population, but Clay, an "able soldier with a huge ego, inflated further by his position as Military Governor of Germany," had advocated a more dramatic military response: "to ram through an armored column, like the cavalry rescuing a wagon train." The general argued that "a determined movement of convoys with troop protection would reach Berlin"; Undersecretary of State Robert Lovett called Clay's idea "silly." The airlift plan ultimately saved West Berlin. But Clay had strong opinions and a long memory; on his flight to Berlin thirteen years later, Clay would tell Vice President Johnson that "if only he had been allowed to smash through that armored column" into West Berlin, "there would have been no Korean War," and that "if he were the President right now, he'd tear down that wall." These comments failed to impress Charles "Chip" Bohlen, the State Department representative whom the president had added to the mission as "a diplomatic hedge on Clay's warlike instincts," but they presaged a curious and dangerous episode that soon followed.[24]

For five days after the initial October 22, 1961, incident involving Lightner, the controversy surrounding US civilian governmental officials attempting to cross the border yet refusing to present their credentials to the VOPOs escalated from verbal exchanges and civil disobedience to the more provocative pressures that arose as transiting US officials received armed escorts, initially consisting of jeeps carrying soldiers. By October 27, however, a more ominous situation emerged as the US military response escalated to deployment of M-48 Patton battle tanks to the checkpoint, with their cannons trained on the opposite side of the plaza. Soviet tanks soon appeared on the eastern side of the checkpoint and for twenty-four hours the prospect of increasing numbers of tanks coming forward to face off muzzle to muzzle seemed to presage a pitched battle.

From General Clay's standpoint, this seemingly minor point of border crossing protocol was a matter of international significance to the post–World War II status of US rights as one of the four occupying powers. To the general's way of thinking, which he expressed forcefully to Dean Rusk and most likely to the president directly,[25] it was critically important for the

United States to stand on its rights and deny to the GDR any putative authority as a self-proclaimed sovereign to exercise border control in any area of Germany. VOPOs and other upstart GDR officials were mere pretenders to state authority; in Clay's eyes only Soviet officials were legitimate participants in the postwar Four Power accords with recognized jurisdiction over these territories. The United States would win this confrontation, Clay believed, if it could be demonstrated that the Soviets exercised actual control over the Berlin Wall checkpoints and that the VOPOs were acting as mere puppets. That theory prompted Clay to "crow" to the press after Allan Lightner's first contested border crossing eventually drew an apology from a local Soviet military official that the "'fiction is now destroyed' that it was the East Germans who were responsible for preventing Allied access to East Berlin."[26]

That initial Soviet apology did not end the war of nerves, however, and border crossings over the next few days continued to draw VOPO resistance requiring US military escorts, eventually escalating to American battle tanks. Clay believed he had a mandate from the president "to prevent the loss of any additional authority in Berlin to the Communists, whatever the risks this might entail." And indeed, in response to Clay's request "the White House did authorize a series of daily probes by civilian officials accompanied by an armed escort to defend the right of Western allied diplomats to cross the sector boundary."[27]

Clay had long sensed, however, that a tougher Soviet stance might be imminent, and so, drawing on his 1948 experience challenging the Soviet blockade, he had a month earlier devised a more belligerent contingency plan to demonstrate US resolve. He had directed a covert military exercise to be conducted "in a secluded forest on the outskirts of Berlin" where American tanks equipped with bulldozer blades practiced knocking down portions of a mock Berlin Wall that had been built to simulate the real wall. When General Clarke, the US Army commander in Europe, learned of this secret exercise, he shut it down. But Clay was not deterred; when he learned that the Soviets might close the Checkpoint Charlie access route entirely, he believed that, if this should happen, a squadron of US blade-equipped tanks would venture through the closed border crossing and then forcibly knock (or "nose") down portions of the Berlin Wall on their way back to the US side of the border.[28] Clay would later refer to his plan as a "raid in force."

On October 26, 1961, Clay received qualified approval for his "raid in force" idea from NATO supreme commander Lauris Norstad, who "authorized the commander of U.S. forces in Berlin, General Albert Watson to use 'the present [Clay] plan for 'nosing' down the Friedrichstrasse barrier" if the

VOPOs attempted to close down the border crossing. Norstad also instructed Watson "to prepare an alternative plan in which the tanks would 'nose down' different portions of the Wall simultaneously, 'if practicable from a military standpoint,'" although he emphasized that the alternate plan for damaging the wall "will not under any circumstances be placed in action without specific approval from me."[29]

Unfortunately for Clay, Soviet intelligence had photographed his clandestine "raid in force" drills back in September and reported them to Moscow.[30] Khrushchev was concerned and possibly alarmed; he later recorded in his memoirs that "they were preparing bulldozers to break down our border installations. The bulldozers would be followed by tanks and wave after wave of jeeps with infantry men."[31] When Clay asked for Rusk's reaction to his "raid in force" idea in a telegram that reached Washington at 1:00 p.m. on October 26, the secretary of state consulted the White House, and Clay's audacious plan was rejected. Rusk's telegram to Clay at 8:11 p.m. made it clear that the administration had "decided that entry into East Berlin is not a vital interest" warranting use of force, and was therefore willing to accept "that the Soviets could, in the case of East Berlin, as they have done previously in other areas under their effective physical control, isolate their unwilling subjects."[32] Rusk's telegram was accompanied by a note from Foy Kohler, the State Department official who was overseeing Berlin events, who confirmed that the president had personally approved the instruction.[33]

Nevertheless, the evening of October 27 found ten American tanks, some equipped with bulldozer blades, facing an equal number of Soviet tanks across the Checkpoint Charlie divide, with each side preparing to order further armored reinforcements, potentially numbering thirty tanks per side. The Soviets, forewarned about Clay's tank-bulldozer drills, and seeing bulldozer blades attached to some of the tanks lining up at Checkpoint Charlie, presumably feared that a raid on the wall was at hand. General Clay quixotically claimed that the Russian side's readiness to commit up to thirty tanks represented a victory of sorts for the United States. He explained his reasoning in a telephone conversation with President Kennedy, placed by the president at approximately 5:00 p.m. Washington time over an unsecured line. Clay expressed his opinion that the Soviets had intentionally set the number at exactly thirty tanks as a signal of *restraint* and *moderation* because they surely knew that this figure matched the total number of American tanks stationed in West Berlin.[34] Clay was further emboldened by the thought that the show of Soviet tank strength was an additional sign that the US side had won the confrontation. His roundabout thinking was that the call-up of tanks as a show of Soviet military muscle, like the arrival of Soviet monitors overseeing the VOPOs several days earlier, offered further proof that the Kremlin was in charge of border affairs in East Berlin, and that the VOPOs were mere underlings without autonomous authority.[35]

The president initially offered jaunty support for his special representative over the open telephone line,[36] but in truth the general had demonstrated that his bellicose approach to dealing with tensions at the Berlin border crossing was in direct opposition to the president's desire to tacitly accept Soviet bloc control over East Berlin and its borders and terminate the confrontation as peacefully and as quickly as possible. With so many opposing tanks arrayed muzzle to muzzle in a tight urban plaza, and with General Clay dreaming up ever more aggressive displays of US military might, it was time for the White House and the Kremlin to get directly involved.

The president had earlier opened his back-channel route to Khrushchev by directing his brother to contact Georgi Bolshakov. Two discussions ensued between the GRU colonel and the US attorney general: a preliminary conversation at 5:30 p.m. on October 26 while Berlin tensions were still at an early stage, and then a second, more urgent telephone call late in the evening (Washington, DC, time) on October 27. The first conversation set the stage for a resolution; the second sealed the deal. Within a matter of hours after the second call, the tank escalation had ended and a sequence of graduated tank pullbacks began, resulting in the disappearance of all armored vehicles from Checkpoint Charlie by late Saturday morning, October 28. When the sun rose, television, radio, and newspaper audiences around the world learned that the Soviet tanks had begun leaving the checkpoint first, followed by seriatim withdrawals of equal numbers of tanks from each side, until no armor remained visible at either end of the plaza. It appeared to the public that the Soviets had retreated, and that the Kennedy administration had finally won a serious East-West confrontation. This impression of a victorious outcome proved to be long-lasting.

Of course appearances can be deceiving. It was not until 1978 that the public first learned from Arthur Schlesinger that President Kennedy had used a secret channel to resolve the crisis, and even then the former Kennedy administration insider revealed only the *existence* of the Bolshakov connection, and not any of the *specific terms* of the brokered arrangement. Schlesinger's account left the impression that President Kennedy's direct involvement alone was enough to persuade Khrushchev to remove his tanks first. Garthoff's 1991 *Foreign Policy* article, which endeavored to correct the record promoted by Schlesinger based on Garthoff's access to official Soviet sources that had become available after the collapse of the Soviet Union, revealed a further important feature of the actual back-channel bargain: Kennedy had asked Khrushchev to move his tanks back first, but he "promised that if Khrushchev did so, the American tanks would withdraw in turn."[37]

Yet even that was not the full story. Unfortunately, Garthoff, writing in the early 1990s, may not have had access to a further critical element of the Kennedy-Khrushchev discussion that proved to determine the outcome. Based on their further review of emerging Soviet archives, Fursenko and Naftali uncovered additional details of the Robert Kennedy / Georgi Bolshakov discussions, as revealed in their 2006 book, *Khrushchev's Cold War*. Additionally, subsequent declassification of cable traffic between Washington and Berlin filled in important details of decisions made by President Kennedy that would enable Khrushchev to withdraw his forces from the Friedrichstrasse Plaza with confidence that Moscow's main objectives in the confrontation had been achieved.

The first conversation between Robert Kennedy and Georgi Bolshakov took place at 5:30 p.m. (Washington time) on October 26. No notes or memoranda have been found recording the attorney general's version of what transpired. Bolshakov, however, prepared notes that he promptly cabled back to Moscow. According to a summary of the cable prepared by Fursenko and Naftali, "Kennedy hoped Khrushchev would realize that it was in his interest to help his American counterpart during this difficult period." Bolshakov conveyed Kennedy's appeal that "the Soviet and Western sides should avoid any actions in Germany or Berlin that could lead to sad incidents," and that "if Khrushchev would give similar instructions to his forces, [President] Kennedy would do the same."[38]

The White House thus established an expectation of reciprocity and set the stage for developing a bilateral agreement to defuse the Berlin crisis under which both sides would refrain from their recent, respective provocative actions. But what were the "sad incidents" that had "happened recently," and what actions, specifically, would each side be expected to avoid? That additional detail was not specified in Bolshakov's cable, but the Rusk telegram aborting General Clay's "raid in force" idea only a matter of hours after Robert Kennedy's conversation with Bolshakov almost certainly supplies part of the answer.

The Soviet tanks facing American tanks, still fitted out with bulldozer blades during the evening of October 27 (Berlin time), got President Kennedy's immediate attention once again, and a meeting was held in the Oval Office at 5:00 p.m. (Washington time) on October 27. In attendance were the president, National Security Adviser Bundy, the attorney general, the secretaries of state and defense, advisers Kohler and Assistant Secretary of Defense Paul Nitze, and General Lyman Lemnitzer, the chairman of the Joint Chiefs of Staff. No official memorandum was prepared recording discussions at that meeting. However, General Lemnitzer's handwritten notes, maintained in the library of the National Defense University, confirm that the United States would make several concessions to the Soviets to end the crisis.[39] Along with official cables immediately ensuing, they show that the president made three decisions, two of which were important concessions to the Soviets: (1) Rusk's order rejecting General Clay's plan to conduct a raid to knock down portions of the Berlin Wall or initiate other border crossings with armed military escort (referred to by Lemnitzer as "probes with military force") was confirmed, (2) an effort would be made to get the Soviets to allow military personnel in uniform entering East Berlin to pass without further checks ("Mil[itary] pers[onnel] will be in uniform," "State will try to get uniform OK & Fr[iedrichstrasse] agreement re: mil[itary] personnel"), and (3) the United States would discontinue border crossings by civilian government officials who would be subject to VOPO checks of their passes ("Will not send in US civilians who show passes to VOPOS").

Early in the October 27 Oval Office meeting, at approximately 5:00 p.m. Washington time, President Kennedy telephoned General Clay in Berlin. Mysteriously, the president placed his call on an open line—sometimes referred to in French vernacular as *en clair*. This had the ironic consequence that the sole documented version of the Kennedy-Clay conversation came from Soviet intelligence intercepts. According to the KGB's records, Kennedy told Clay that "it would be best to send over only people in uniform until we hear from Thompson [US ambassador to Soviet Union located in Moscow]."[40]

The president's directive to stop provocative border crossings by civilian US officials—which had precipitated the protocol controversy—was therefore shared with the Soviets at precisely the same time that it was communicated to US officials in Berlin.[41] The directive was then formalized in a telegram from Rusk to the US mission in Berlin dispatched at 10:03 p.m. in the evening of October 27, Washington time,[42] which ordered a stand-down of aggressive US "probes," which had "accomplished their purpose." Further probes by "U.S. personnel wearing civilian clothes and riding in official U.S. vehicles or privately owned vehicles bearing plates of

U.S. Armed Forces and using armed guards or military escort" were to be "deferred," and civilian officials were ordered to "refrain from going into East Berlin," with the exception of one civilian official who was authorized to "attempt daily to enter East Berlin in a privately owned vehicle without armed escort." US military personnel would continue to enter East Berlin so long as they did so in uniform. The State Department's public position would be that the armed probes had successfully demonstrated "direct Soviet responsibility for unilateral action taken by Communists" as well as US official "unwillingness [to] recognize East German authorities with respect to US official civilian personnel."

At the conclusion of the 5:00 p.m. Oval Office meeting, the president asked his brother to contact Bolshakov immediately. The two met at 11:30 p.m. Once again, Robert Kennedy made no known notes of the meeting or of the message he asked the GRU officer to convey to Khrushchev. In an oral history he provided several years later, Kennedy revealed only that he had sent an ultimatum to the Soviet chairman demanding that his tanks be removed from Friedrichstrasse Plaza "[with]in twenty-four hours."[43] As before, Bolshakov's cable (maintained in official Kremlin files) tells a more complete story: Robert Kennedy "asked the Kremlin for a period of four to six weeks without headlines about Berlin," warning that "a period of relative moderation and calm" was needed to avoid "a negative effect on future developments."[44]

Robert Kennedy's pleas for a four- to six-week period during which both sides would "take the necessary measures" to establish "moderation and calm" embraced not only removal of both side's tanks from the Friedrichstrasse Plaza but also the two steps that the president had communicated to Soviet intelligence via his telephone conversation with Clay and officially put in place as memorialized in the official orders from the White House quoted above. Given Khrushchev's willingness to publicly withdraw his armor first, it stands to reason that he knew from the intercepted phone call and Robert Kennedy's remarks to Bolshakov that the president was taking reciprocal steps to stand down, and that he had been informed through Bolshakov that those steps would be the quid pro quo. It therefore follows that Robert Kennedy must have communicated to Khrushchev through Bolshakov—as the president had already partly revealed over the *en clair* phone line—the president's decision to discontinue the two US practices that the Soviets had taken to be serious provocations: the forward deployment of bulldozer-bladed tanks and the defiance by border-crossing US civilian officials of VOPOs conducting identity checks. Fursenko and Naftali neatly summarized the mutual concessions that framed the deal: "From that point forward, the U.S. stopped its military escorts of civilians, and Clay no longer challenged East German authority at the border points." In exchange for the US "retreat[] on the principle," the Soviet tanks "would withdraw first at 10:30 a.m. on Saturday morning, October 28."[45]

Finally, it is noteworthy that the foregoing arrangements were effectuated with almost no documentation created by either side that might reveal the actual terms of the deal. No formal record has been found of the White House discussions on the evening of October 27, 1961. On the Soviet side, Bolshakov promptly cabled his message to GRU headquarters in Moscow, "where it was already approximately 7:00 A.M., October 28," but "no trace of the cable has been found in Kremlin archives." Thus there is no firm, surviving documentation of the US message prompting Khrushchev's decision to withdraw his forces first at Checkpoint Charlie. Secrecy was useful to both sides. Nevertheless, at the conclusion of a "tough, bitter encounter" between Khrushchev and GDR leader Ulbricht on November 2, 1961, in the immediate aftermath of the Friedrichstrasse showdown, where Khrushchev had to deliver the hard message that "he could not force the Berlin issue" and would have to further delay the process toward a peace treaty with East Germany, the "only concessions [Khrushchev] threw to the East German were some suggestions for tightening civil controls at the border."[46] Border-crossing protocol had evidently been the heart of the deal.

Kennedy had thus opted for acquiescence and stability over confrontation and assertion of occupation prerogatives. The result was abandonment of Clay's proposed raid and a return to the status quo ante, which required abiding by VOPO interventions at the border crossing. The US Berlin Command would make "no further attempt to have American officials in civilian clothes escorted into the Soviet sector by armed GIs," with the result that "the Ulbricht regime's right to oblige all foreign civilians to show their identity papers in order to gain admission to East Berlin was thus tacitly accepted."[47] As Campbell Craig later noted, the Kennedy administration had determined to "back down, but perform a little ritual defiance to show that it was not beaten."[48]

Nor was the American concession a narrow, short-term gesture. The core principle of the Checkpoint Charlie border accommodation—granting the GDR the control rights of a sovereign over its side of the East-West border in Berlin—was an enduring change in US policy. A secret CIA handbook distributed at the end of 1961 confirmed that the United States had acquiesced in a change to the border-crossing protocol at the behest of the VOPOs, at least for US officials seeking to cross the border while traveling out of uniform in US-registered vehicles: "In October, the East Germans began demanding identification from such individuals and at present, Allied officials not in uniform are not permitted to enter the Soviet sector except on official business."[49]

President Kennedy himself then underscored the change in policy when he held a White House meeting at the end of January 1962 with Khrushchev's son-in-law, Alexei Adzhubei, who was also the editor of the official Soviet newspaper, *Izvestia*. In a private meeting held after more official events with only Adzhubei present and with Bolshakov most likely acting as interpreter for both men, the president made the following statement, according to Adzhubei's subsequent top-secret report on his visit submitted to the Kremlin: "Kennedy continued. 'I see things realistically. Insofar as you object to international control of the highway [between West Berlin and West Germany], it is senseless for us to insist on it. After all the officers of the GDR are already (I thanked the president for pronouncing the full name, the German Democratic Republic, before me for the first time) putting their stamps [in documents]. The important thing is not who is affixing the stamps.'"[50]

What General Clay had initially resisted as a fundamental challenge to US rights had been acceded to in a change of policy toward GDR sovereignty that was still resonating almost a year later among top administration officials. In August 1962 Khrushchev was still pressing his intention to sign a separate peace treaty with the GDR that would turn over to the East Germans even broader sovereign rights over their country. The Kennedy administration was steadfastly opposed, knowing that such a treaty would threaten continuation of Western rights to keep military forces in West Germany and West Berlin. Against this backdrop, and with little sign of diplomatic progress, Kennedy administration officials considered it an advantage that the US side had shown at least some accommodation to the exercise of GDR rights over border matters. Thus, Rusk wrote to President Kennedy on July 28, 1962, that "the Western powers were now prepared to accept East German personnel substituting for Soviets in implementing existing ground access procedures."[51] A few days later, Llewelyn Thompson, returning to Washington after the end of his term as US ambassador to the Soviet Union, made it clear that this was a change in broad policy and not merely a minuscule alteration of an arcane matter of border-crossing protocol. The secret White House taping system that the president had recently installed recorded Thompson telling the president on August 6, 1962, that Rusk had done "a good job" in Geneva "laying out the [US] case to Gromyko." The secretary of state had "made quite clear we weren't going to take any action which would show that [East Germany] weren't a sovereign state in effect."[52]

And as the presidential recording system would confirm three weeks later, this policy change represented the president's thinking and not simply the viewpoint of the secretary of state. In a discussion between the president and his national security adviser, McGeorge Bundy, at a White House meeting to discuss Berlin issues on the afternoon of August 29, 1962, Bundy noted that VOPO demands for the display of passes by US officials crossing the border had been a matter on which "we did engage our prestige very strongly . . . at the end of last year. And we did regard it as a serious matter, and we refused to circulate people who were asked for their passes in what we regarded as inappropriate circumstances." The president's response made clear that US policy should remain as it had been in October 1961—that American officials would refrain from mounting those border challenges and simply stop going "over there":

> PRESIDENT KENNEDY: Well then we just say, "All right, we won't go over."

It was one thing if a confrontation occurred over US access to occupied *West* Berlin "along the autobahn," which would continue to require a vigorous US response. But regarding US acceptance of the VOPOs' assertion of control over US access to *East* Berlin—a matter that Bundy observed "we settled a year ago," the president reconfirmed that the US policy of mute acquiescence would remain in place: "So we just won't go over there. There's no value in going over there anyway."[53]

The Berlin tank standoff was settled within a matter of hours. Had it not been for the fact that the incident took place in a heavily populated urban area easily accessible to national and international media, the incident would not have taken on such iconic proportions. Nevertheless, the denouement in Berlin foreshadowed almost precisely what would occur exactly one year later on the larger world stage set by the missile crisis. Four key elements in particular were decisive in both episodes: a dramatic show of US force to demonstrate resolve, use of back channels rather than conventional diplomatic means to engage in negotiations, the willingness of each leader to concede what his adversary wanted most on substance, and the determination by both parties, but the United States in particular, to ensure that no written record of the precise agreement would be left to cause political problems.

The first element was a dramatic show of force, arguably disproportionate to the dispute at hand. In this instance, it was the arrival of US battle tanks shouldering aside normal commuter traffic in the heart of a modern European city and transforming a historic urban plaza into a Cold War battle station. As a response to a border crossing guard's insistence on seeing a driver's paperwork, this display of armored force was arguably disproportionate to the perceived threat and a dangerously destabilizing escalation. Nevertheless, it was the considered decision of the US chain of command.

The second element was use of a back channel rather than conventional diplomacy, and in both crises the chosen off-the-books intermediary was the same shadowy figure, GRU officer Georgi Bolshakov. Bolshakov's more complex involvement in the Cuban crisis will be described in greater detail subsequently, but in the Berlin incident it came down to a single late-evening conversation with Robert Kennedy on October 27, 1961. The content of the verbal message that Robert Kennedy conveyed from the president to the Soviet chairman via the GRU officer in that critical discussion was memorialized only by Bolshakov, and it proved to determine the outcome: the tanks of both sides rolled back within a matter of hours and the dispute over border-crossing protocol magically evaporated. The choice of back-channel diplomacy was unquestionably validated by these simple, immediate, definitive, positive, and effectual results.

The third element—both sides' eagerness to be generous in order to escape a looming fight—was also key. The Americans abruptly ended their border provocations and thereby granted tacit acceptance of what the Soviets wanted most: recognition of the GDR border guards' authority to check and verify identities of all nonmilitary persons, including US officials, seeking to enter East Berlin. The matter of principle that General Clay had thought to be vital to US interests was traded away in the twinkling of an eye.[51] As Campbell Craig correctly concluded, when faced with "a vivid possibility of war with the Soviet Union," the American leaders "found themselves backing away from flexible response" and "began to worry much more about finding ways to avoid war." The tank showdown of October 27, 1961, proved to be the last meaningful military confrontation in that tight spot: "Other than some desultory skirmishes over air access in February [1962], that was the end of direct Cold War conflict in Berlin."[55]

Khrushchev, for his part, was equally willing to give Kennedy what the American president wanted most: postponement of the premier's campaign to sign a peace treaty with the GDR, and a peaceful resolution presentable as a successful demonstration of American resolve. Khrushchev had no interest in pressing the peace treaty measure to the point of armed confrontation. As he made clear to Polish Communist leader Wladyslaw Gomulka, he was concerned that "signing a peace treaty with the GDR might exacerbate the situation." He was adamant that "there will be no war." Nevertheless, using an expression that would appear several months later in his Meniscus speech to the Presidium on January 8, 1962, he was convinced that "we must continue our game. We are not afraid, but we do not want war."[56]

While a Soviet show of resolve was necessary, it had to stop short of gunfire.[57] Neither Kennedy nor Khrushchev wanted the Checkpoint Charlie showdown to escalate: "The resolution of the Checkpoint Charlie stand-off showed the stark reality of superpower relations. Neither superpower leader was about to go to war over who showed what bit of paper to whom in the streets of Berlin."[58]

Khrushchev was amenable to delaying the peace treaty process with East Germany and allowing the American tanks to remain on the field of confrontation as the Soviet armor withdrew once he knew that the armored threat to the integrity of the Berlin Wall had been neutralized and that the Americans would thenceforward respect the local GDR authority at the border crossing.[59] In these circumstances he was willing to relinquish the more immediate but transient glamor of surface appearance.[60]

The fourth signature Kennedy diplomacy element—that of secrecy—was adhered to by both sides but coveted most by the American president. The president needed to come out looking like the winner, if in appearance only. In 1961 Berlin, border guard authorities were a prosaic matter, but the president's sensitivity to criticism for weakness was raw in the aftermath of the Bay of Pigs, the disastrous Vienna summit, and the shadow cast by the Berlin Wall. Kennedy needed tensions to end quickly, and he was willing to pay the price on substance, but only so long as the deal remained hidden from public view. He badly needed to project an image of strength and decisiveness, and this would be impossible if it were known that Americans had surrendered to the Soviets any significant concession the latter were seeking.

During the months that followed the October 1961 showdown at Friedrichstrasse Plaza, Kennedy stepped up his efforts to display US strength and his own decisiveness as the president. Yet in doing so he inadvertently planted in his adversary's mind seeds of fear and resentment that would yield the bitter harvest of another, and this time far larger, superpower crisis.

CHAPTER 3

Superpower Smackdown

Khrushchev's Boasting versus the Kennedy Brothers' First-Strike Innuendo and Caribbean War Games

In some circumstances we might have to take the initiative.

—PRESIDENT KENNEDY, APRIL 1962

KHRUSHCHEV INITIALLY RELIED on boasting to mask Soviet strategic inferiority. Khrushchev was famous for being "endlessly boastful about Russia's weapons of mass destruction."[1] The more colorful examples of his campaign to inflate Russian military prowess became familiar to a nervous public in the West due to wide press coverage. Perhaps most famously, Khrushchev seemed to threaten Western ambassadors when he told them at a meeting in Moscow on November 18, 1956, "We will bury you!"—a statement that many interpreted as the victory he hoped to achieve in a nuclear war.[2] A year later, when the Soviets became the "first in space" by launching *Sputnik* into orbit, indicating that their missile technology might be capable of delivering nuclear warheads to targets in the continental United States, the October 11, 1957, edition of *Pravda* quoted Khrushchev as bragging that Russian factories were producing missiles "like sausages."[3] In November 1959, Khrushchev told journalists, "We have such a stock of rockets, such an amount of atomic and hydrogen weapons, that if they attack us we could wipe our potential enemies off the face of the earth." He added that in a single year the assembly line of one Soviet factory he had visited produced "250 rockets with hydrogen warheads."[4] Khrushchev's boasting often involved efforts to undermine the NATO alliance by intimidating individual US allies. Thus, Khrushchev warned Italy's president, Amintore Fanfani, in August 1961 that, in any nuclear exchange, "the first two countries to be destroyed would be Italy and Great Britain, since they contain many missile bases."[5]

Soon after Kennedy took office, administration officials learned that Khrushchev's boasting was an exercise in strategic disinformation—known in Russian military parlance as *dezinformatsiya*. Far from having a lead in nuclear and rocket technology, the Soviets had fallen behind. In truth, Khrushchev and his Kremlin colleagues were vulnerable to a surprise attack. It was at this juncture that an inexperienced president, stung by criticism from political adversaries that he lacked the toughness to stand up against the Soviet chairman, found it a propitious time to publicly flex America's muscles, even to the point of hinting that he was actively considering that the United States might strike the first nuclear blow—the risk the Soviets feared most.

The missile gap and the fears of a Soviet lead in nuclear striking power had been heavily publicized during the US 1960 presidential race. As he waged his campaign, Kennedy "made the missile gap a central feature," and as late as the inauguration he was still stoking the public's anxieties; his State of the Union speech on January 30, 1961, contained multiple references to the Communist threat, including the dire warning that "each day we draw nearer to the hour of maximum danger, as weapons spread and hostile forces grow stronger."[6] The new president's dark pronouncement repeated the phrase "hour of maximum danger" that had been used in a National Security Council report issued more than a decade earlier warning of a feared Soviet capacity to effectively wipe out America's strategic military might by launching a devastating surprise "first strike."[7]

However, Kennedy soon became aware of the Soviet ICBM deficit and the overall US strategic nuclear advantage. The president began to appreciate the adverse impact the earlier erroneous public perceptions could have on deterrence. It was not hard to imagine how Khrushchev might exploit public concerns about America's supposed military inferiority by inflating the Kremlin's advantage, however illusionary, through aggressive moves in various theaters of superpower rivalry.

But there was a more powerful incentive for the president to set the record straight. His recent candidacy had benefited from the concerns of a misinformed public worried about the vulnerability of US defenses to the threat of a Soviet attack. Once Kennedy became president, responsibility rested on his shoulders, and it was the Republicans' turn to attack the commander in chief, this time for his inability to push back against Khrushchev's internationalist ambitions. Political attacks of this kind began almost as soon as the new administration took office in January 1961, and the Bay of Pigs fiasco only a few months later, followed by Kennedy's poor performance at the Vienna summit and the erection of the Berlin Wall, only added fuel to the fire. Thus, it is not surprising that the president would look for an early occasion to correct the public record regarding America's lead over its Soviet rival and to emphasize his own sure hand in using that advantage effectively. In doing so he overreached.

The messaging began almost immediately after he took office. During a meeting with journalists on February 6, 1961, Robert McNamara, the new secretary of defense, was asked about "the missile gap that Kennedy had so dramatized" during the campaign. McNamara responded, "in what he thought were off-the-record remarks," that after reviewing the classified evidence he had concluded: "There is no missile gap."[8]

Eight months later, Kennedy ordered that the same message be delivered, but in greater detail and in a venue that would reach a global audience. On October 17, 1961, Khrushchev had delivered a bombastic speech at the Twenty-Second Communist Party Congress announcing plans to test a 50-megaton hydrogen bomb, and he hinted at the existence of a 100-megaton bomb too powerful to test.[9] Just short of two weeks later the Soviets would indeed drop a 57-megaton "monster bomb," subsequently nicknamed *Tsar Bomba*, the "Tsar's bomb"—over a remote Arctic archipelago called Novaya Zemlya, which produced a five-mile-wide fireball that could be seen a thousand kilometers from the site.[10]

Kennedy responded to Khrushchev's Party Congress speech by directing Deputy Secretary of Defense Roswell Gilpatric to give a public and detailed presentation of US strategic nuclear superiority. Speaking at an October 21, 1961, business conference that was well publicized, Gilpatric provided a remarkably blunt and detailed recitation of the American advantage: US strategic forces were so massive that, even after absorbing an all-out surprise Soviet attack, they would be able to muster an overwhelming nuclear counterattack "at least as extensive as what the Soviets can deliver by striking first." This "second strike" retaliatory capability made the Kennedy administration "confident that the Soviets will not provoke a major nuclear conflict."

Gilpatric also hinted at the possibility of US nuclear first use. He stated that because the United States was intent on acquiring "flexibility rather than rigidity in the options open to us," it would not only strengthen conventional, nonnuclear capabilities but also consider "the use of tactical nuclear weapons in a limited war if our interests should so require."[11]

Kennedy may have believed that Gilpatric's speech would serve as a measured counter to Khrushchev's boasting. But he underestimated his rival's sense of vulnerability. As Michael Beschloss has observed, by authorizing the Gilpatric speech Kennedy "may have strengthened his own political standing and reassured American allies," but he also "provocatively undermined Khrushchev's position in the Kremlin and in the world."[12]

It wasn't hard to imagine that America's possession of an unquestionable second-strike defensive capability might raise apprehension in the Kremlin that the sheer number of nuclear weapons and weight of their striking power available to SAC might give the president the ability to launch a crippling, preemptive first strike on the Soviets—one so devastating it would extinguish Russia's ability to retaliate. According to Beschloss, the emphatic, public response Gilpatric had delivered, intensified by a thinly veiled brandishing of an American first-strike capability, likely prompted Khrushchev "to look for a quick, cheap way to remake the nuclear balance of power so that he could genuinely claim that the Soviet Union was the superior force in the world." This time, it was President Kennedy's boasting that had "provoked the adversary by exposing Soviet nuclear weakness to the world, and unwittingly caused the Soviets to fear that he was on the verge of exploiting American nuclear strength to settle the Cold War on American terms, perhaps even in a preemptive strike."[13]

The Defense Department's hubris did not stop with the deputy secretary's October 21 speech. Twenty days later McNamara made public remarks of his own that included even more pointed claims of US nuclear superiority. During a speech in Atlanta on November 11, 1962, in which he referenced Khrushchev's boast earlier in October that the Soviets possessed a 100-megaton bomb, the defense secretary called that claim a "transparent attempt[] to conceal his nuclear inferiority" and noted that the US retaliatory force able to survive a Soviet surprise attack would be as much as three times the magnitude of the Kremlin's all-out first strike.[14]

The US strategic nuclear superiority posturing went a dangerous step further when top officials in the Kennedy administration, including the president himself, began publicly discussing the twin red-hot issues of American nuclear first-use scenarios and first-strike capability. As will be seen, these audacious, even bombastic, hints that the new American president might be thinking of launching nuclear weapons against Soviet forces quickly caught the Kremlin's attention. Yet far from restoring calm after years of Khrushchev's disingenuous saber-rattling, the president's new talk of first nuclear use had the opposite effect on a Russian leader who was already acutely conscious that he had placed the Soviet Union, rather than the United States, in an "hour of maximum danger." The thought that the United States might now possess a first-strike capability and be thinking about using it set an impulsive Khrushchev to thinking that prompt and determined measures were needed to redress a military imbalance in which his country suddenly found itself vulnerable.

During the Eisenhower years US deterrence policy was based on a strategy of threatening to respond to any attack on the United States or one of its allies by so-called massive retaliation—"in essence, a threat to use nuclear weapons against Communist aggression wherever and whenever it might occur."[15] Yet Eisenhower kept silent about the circumstances under which he would actually order a nuclear strike. "Even in his most private councils," the president "remained vague about what he might or might not do in a crisis. His closest adviser, General Andrew Goodpaster, guessed Ike would never use nuclear weapons, but others weren't so sure, and Eisenhower wasn't about to tell them."[16] Thus, late in his second term of office Eisenhower resisted the temptation to answer critics who accused him of weakness and passivity in the face of the supposed "missile gap" controversy that arose during the 1960 presidential campaign.[17] Eisenhower knew from U-2 and satellite surveillance over the Soviet land mass that the missile gap was a myth, but he refused to expose the emptiness of his critics' charges because to have done so might have compromised the secrecy of the country's most sophisticated intelligence-gathering capabilities.

Deputy defense secretary Gilpatric's muscular October 21, 1961, speech may have signaled, intentionally or not, a US readiness to mount its own first-strike capability. The president had received his first briefing on America's nuclear war-fighting strategy and capabilities on July 20, 1961, when he attended a meeting of an obscurely named Net Evaluation Subcommittee of the National Security Council (NES/NSC). Generals Hickey and Lemnitzer set out the consequences of a nuclear exchange following a surprise attack by the Soviet Union, hypothesized to occur in late 1963 while the United States would still enjoy overwhelming strategic superiority. The projected US casualties resulting from "a general war" following the Soviet "first strike" were shocking: 39%–49% of the US population would be killed (sixty-eight million to ninety-three million dead) depending upon the weight of the attack.[18]

A summary of the July 20 NES/NSC meeting (apparently prepared by a military aide to Vice President Johnson) indicated that the president took an active part in the discussions, raising the question whether an assessment had ever been made "of damage results to the U.S.S.R. which would be incurred by a preemptive attack." The president also asked about "the probable effects" of a nuclear exchange "in the winter of 1962." General Lemnitzer confirmed that damage results studies had been made and told the president that he would bring them over at a later date "and discuss them personally with the President." At the conclusion of the meeting Kennedy directed that none of the participants ever divulge the contents or even the subject of the meeting.[19]

The planned meeting between the president and General Lemnitzer occurred on September 13, 1961, when Lemnitzer briefed the president on "Single Integrated Operational Plan-62," also referred to by its acronym, SIOP-62.[20] Lemnitzer projected that even after a US first strike, "there was the likelihood of a few Soviet nuclear warheads slipping through American defenses and detonating over American targets."[21] Lemnitzer told the president that while the Soviet Union "would pulverize Western Europe with short- and medium-range nuclear missiles," only twenty-five or fewer Russian missiles could strike the United States. The Soviet Union could also use roughly twenty-eight nuclear submarines and two hundred bombers in a first-strike attack, which would pose "a great threat to U.S. urban areas" but only "a more limited danger . . . to American nuclear striking forces." Nevertheless, "Even if the United States were to launch a first strike against the Soviet land mass," there would be some surviving portion of the Soviet long-range nuclear force that would be able to hit the United States, causing "perhaps two to fifteen million American casualties, not to mention European deaths in the 'low tens of millions.'" The Russians would suffer far greater damage, of course, as the American attack would leave "Soviet society . . . much destroyed."[22] But this did not provide comfort to the president, who earlier in the summer had given an interview to the *New York Post* "in which he said that only fools believed in victory in a nuclear war."[23]

It was official US policy at the time, publicly expressed by the president himself,[24] as well as by the deputy defense secretary,[25] that the United States would not be the first to launch a nuclear attack. But it was not long after the September 13 meeting that hints began to emerge in the press that the United States was prepared to be the first to use nuclear weapons, and might be contemplating a nuclear first strike against the Soviet Union, at least "in some circumstances" not specified. And those hints each time seemed to have the imprimatur of US government officials at the highest level.

There is, of course, a big difference, in theory at least, between nuclear first use and a nuclear first-strike attack. The former might involve dropping a single nuclear bomb or firing a small number of tactical nuclear weapons to blunt or forestall a large-scale conventional attack by the adversary. A nuclear first use of this kind would presumably be a response to a military attack launched by the opponent and would be intended to send a clear signal of the defender's resolution to act forcefully but with restraint, allowing the aggressor to stop and think. A first-strike attack, by contrast, would exploit overwhelming military advantage to eliminate the adversary's ability to mount a counterattack. A first strike would thus unleash a far larger nuclear onslaught using strategic weapons in numbers meant to destroy the adversary's nuclear retaliatory forces entirely.

As may be obvious, however, it might be difficult to parse with assurance an adversary's warning or threatening messages touching on these sometimes subtle distinctions when the messages are coming from multiple sources and using diverse and not always reconcilable verbal formulations. In these circumstances it can be human nature to fear the worst. That appears to have occurred when Khrushchev and his Kremlin colleagues began to notice the Kennedy brothers' unsettling repetition of first-use/first-strike language.

The first explicit public statement indicating that the president might be contemplating actual use of a nuclear weapon came from the attorney general on September 24, 1961, in an interview on *Meet the Press*. Robert Kennedy was asked to respond to concerns expressed by Senator Margaret Chase Smith that the president would refuse to use nuclear weapons even in a crisis. The attorney general responded that his brother would "use nuclear weapons" to "stand up" on Berlin.[26] The Soviets reacted immediately calling the attorney general's remarks an unacceptable provocation. On September 25, 1961, US undersecretary of state Chester Bowles reported that Soviet ambassador Mikhail A. Menshikov told him that Robert Kennedy's comment was "threatening and that it would undoubtedly require some response from Moscow."[27]

On February 2, 1962, journalist Joseph Alsop, a Kennedy intimate, wrote an article entitled "Responsibility Shifts on Military Rulings," in which he indicated that the administration's defense policy was moving toward consideration of a nuclear first strike as an option in "really desperate circumstances." The article gave no specifics but referred broadly to "the kind of circumstances in which Britain fought on against Hitler."[28]

On March 9 and 11, 1962, Khrushchev received two reports from the GRU "that days after the Vienna summit in June 1961, the Pentagon had given serious consideration to a first strike against the Soviet Union." Although the identity of the source has not surfaced, he was described as a member of "the US national security bureaucracy" who reported that a US first strike had only been averted because of "the US appreciation of Soviet power following the resumption of nuclear testing in September."[29]

Against this background, the fact that fifteen Jupiter IRBM missiles at the Cigli Air Force Base in Turkey achieved operational status between November 1961 and March 1962 may have contributed to the Kremlin's already overheated apprehensions about a US first strike.[30] These first-generation intermediate-range missiles, like the Soviet Union's ICBMs, used liquid fuel and therefore required time-consuming launch preparation. They also operated from above-ground, "unhardened" launch facilities, making them especially vulnerable to a surprise attack. As a counterintuitive consequence, the vulnerability of the Jupiter missiles in forward locations along the Soviet periphery made them an especially provocative weapon: because they could easily be destroyed by an initial enemy attack, "they could not retaliate," and so could logically be perceived as serving the sole purpose of "striking first by surprise." This being so, the Jupiters "might be a considerable provocation" that "would tend to provoke rather than to deter general war."[31]

Kennedy was made aware of this dilemma early in his presidency by a high-level task force he had created under former secretary of state Dean Acheson's leadership to review US policy regarding NATO. The task force's report, presented to the president in late March 1961, argued that efforts should be made to persuade the Turkish government to accept "the projected deployment and commitment of Polaris submarines in place of the first generation IRBM squadron now scheduled for Turkey." The report then underscored that cancellation of the Jupiter installation plan "would avoid the deployment of '*strike first*' weapons in a politically volatile country on the Soviet border."[32] The president nevertheless did nothing to stop installation work in Turkey out of concern that cancellation would be perceived as a "sign of weakness."[33]

A dangerous coincidence then occurred in March 1962. First, the president gave an interview in which he seemed to contradict his earlier public statements that the United States would not be the first to use atomic weapons. Speaking on the record with journalist and close friend Stewart Alsop (Joseph's brother), the president appeared to send exactly the opposite message. Published in the March 31, 1962, edition of the *Saturday Evening Post*, the president's statement seemed to suggest that he was giving active consideration to the possible utility of a first strike against the Soviet Union: "'Khrushchev must *not* be certain that, where its vital interests are threatened, the United States will never strike first.' As Kennedy says, 'in some circumstances we might have to take the initiative.'"[34] Coincidentally, it was at that same juncture that the last three Jupiter missiles in Turkey became fully operational. According to Fursenko and Naftali, Khrushchev was reminded of the nearby US missiles during his visit to Bulgaria in mid-May 1962; Soviet monitoring of the installation in Turkey two months later determined that seventeen Jupiter intermediate-range missiles there "were nearly operational."[35] Was that the reason Kennedy, in his public comments on March 31, referred to "strike first" weapons?

Just over two months later, on June 3, 1962, Robert Kennedy made another extraordinarily unwise comment along the same lines to his back-channel intermediary, Georgi Bolshakov, in the course of a casual meeting between the two at Hickory Hill, Kennedy's home in McLean Virginia. Responding to a general question from Bolshakov about the Pentagon's role in Washington, Kennedy told the GRU officer that "recently, the Chiefs [Joint Chiefs of Staff] offered the president a report in which they confirmed that the United States is currently ahead of the Soviet Union in military power and that in extremis it would be possible to probe the forces of the Soviet Union." Bolshakov promptly reported this astonishing piece of highly classified information to Moscow via a communication from Ambassador Dobrynin dated June 4, 1962.[36]

Finally, on July 26, 1962, a front-page article by *New York Times* columnist Hanson Baldwin revealed top-secret information, apparently from a national intelligence estimate, that the United States was aware of the Soviets' efforts to "harden" some of their ICBM missile sites against preemptive US attacks. This apparent leak was all the more sensitive because it also included disclosure of "the assessment of U.S. military experts that these defenses would be of little help against a U.S. nuclear first strike."[37]

It should be noted that the foregoing series of publicized comments by Kennedy administration insiders and the president himself are not models of clarity or consistency. Were these meant to denote a "nuclear first strike" in the sense of a preemptive attack against the Soviet Union? If so, did they signify hypothetical thinking, mere options development, or actual planning? Or did they reflect, rather, the administration's desire to send a limited signal of its willingness to consider first use of nuclear weapons, but only as a defense, and only as necessary to thwart a Soviet attack on Berlin or West Germany? Was the unclarity and ambiguity of these messages a product of sloppiness, or was it deliberate? It is impossible to answer these questions definitively. What can be said, however, is that the comments instantly caught the attention of Khrushchev and his advisers and left them with a distinct sense of unease.

President Kennedy did not limit his saber-rattling efforts to Defense Department speeches and hints of first-strike capability during interviews with journalists and Soviet officials. Rather, the president seemed intent on sending Khrushchev additional bellicose signals of his personal toughness on an altogether different subject—the Soviet Union's protégé, Fidel Castro, the "Commandante" in control of Cuba. Khrushchev might have held the stronger hand in the Cold War game being played in Berlin, which stood incongruously as a lonely Western outpost surrounded by occupying Soviet military forces in East Germany. But Khrushchev had his own vulnerable enclave to worry about, and it, too, was a distant outpost surrounded by hostile forces under the control of his rival. Here it was President Kennedy who seemed to hold all the cards. Out of the ashes of the Bay of Pigs fiasco, the young president seemed to have emerged with a fresh start and a winning hand, and he was determined to play it out.

A few illustrations stand out. On November 30, 1961, the president authorized Operation Mongoose, a covert action program aimed at overthrowing the Castro regime.[38] The project was placed under the direction of the CIA's Major General Edward Lansdale and William King Harvey, and they in turn were to report to an oversight committee of the White House called the Special Action Group (Augmented). The word "augmented" referred to the fact that the oversight committee would be led by the president's brother, Robert Kennedy. On January 19, 1962, the attorney general addressed members of the group, including the CIA's new director of operations, Richard Helms, who recorded Kennedy's statement that overthrowing Castro was "the top priority of the United States Government—all else is secondary—no time, money, effort, or manpower is to be spared."[39]

On January 30, 1962, the president made sure that Khrushchev would understand the depth of his determination to eliminate the Castro regime in Cuba. At his White House meeting on that date with Alexsei Adzhubei, and with Georgi Bolshakov serving as an interpreter, Kennedy stated emphatically that if he did not deal with Cuba before the 1964 presidential election, "then Cuba will be the main problem of the campaign, [and] we will have to do something."[40] Kennedy also drew a chilling parallel between his Bay of Pigs embarrassment and the violent precedent Khrushchev had established when he brutally suppressed the 1956 insurrection in Hungary. According to the meeting report prepared by Adzhubei, the president "hit his fist on the table" for emphasis and stated that he had "summoned" CIA director Allen Dulles and "rebuked him," telling him to "learn from the Russians. When they had a tough situation in Hungary [in 1956], they put an end to the conflict in just three days. . . . And you, Dulles, couldn't do a thing."[41] Adzhubei considered these remarks to be so sensitive and alarming that he excluded them from the formal postmeeting cable he sent back to Moscow, delivering the news personally and privately to Khrushchev when he returned home. According to Fursenko and Naftali, Adzhubei's report "that Kennedy was impatient with the status quo in Cuba shook the Kremlin and re-opened a debate over Fidel Castro's security."[42] It would not be long before Khrushchev would formulate his "gamble" to secretly ship Soviet ballistic missiles to Cuba.

Historians have disagreed about the extent to which the Kennedy administration was moving to oust the Castro regime during the months preceding the Cuban missile crisis. What cannot be doubted is that in the lead-up to the crisis the United States took four provocative steps against Khrushchev's Caribbean outpost that were each visible to the leaders in Moscow and Havana and could be seen as threatening. The first was orchestration of decisions by the Organization of American States (OAS) at its meeting in Punta del Este in January 1962 to isolate Cuba by excluding it from the inter-American system. This was followed by a US decree on February 7, 1962, establishing "a total embargo on trade with Cuba, except for medicines and similar supplies."[43]

The second step was a series of naval maneuvers simulating a US invasion of Cuba, including a military exercise in April–May 1962 called LANTPHIBEX-1-62, which was the "largest Atlantic-Caribbean military exercise ever conducted," involving "40,000 men aboard 84 ships."[44] Shortly thereafter, the US military conducted two other follow-on exercises code-named Quick Kick (which began on May 7) and Whip Lash (scheduled for May 8 to 18). These exercises "received significant notice at the time in the American press," were "designed to test procedures that would be used by CINCLANT during an actual invasion of Cuba," "presumably attracted intense scrutiny from Soviet intelligence analysts reporting to the Kremlin from embassies in Washington and Havana," and therefore "could indeed have heightened the suspicions of Khrushchev and Soviet military authorities concerning US intentions toward Cuba at precisely the moment when the Soviet leader is reported to have made up his mind to send the nuclear missiles."[45]

Third, in the weeks immediately preceding the Cuban missile crisis, two US marine and two airborne divisions were assembled in forty ships to conduct a full-scale invasion exercise on the island of Vieques scheduled to begin October 15, 1962. Dino Brugioni, who had served during the Cuba crisis as a senior official at the CIA's National Photographic Interpretation Center (NPIC), called this mock invasion, code-named PHIBRIGLEX-62, "one of the largest ever staged."[46] The exercise was said to involve liberation of the island from a fictitious ruler named Ortsac ["Castro" spelled backward], a verbal trick that James Hershberg later called a "sophomoric bit of psychological warfare."[47] Brugioni observed that "the Cubans were convinced this exercise was a prelude to an imminent attack on their island and began alerting their forces."[48] As it happens, however, the operation was postponed at the last minute due to adverse weather, and then put on standby after the president's October 22 address poised for possible use as the actual invasion force that the president could have launched against Cuba.[49]

The fourth and final step involved urgent efforts from August through early October 1962 to accelerate the Kennedy administration's Operation Mongoose program for subverting the Castro regime. By August the operation was not quite a year old and was receiving the highest level of White House attention. On August 23 the White House issued National Security Action Memorandum 181, containing several mandated action items on Cuba, the fourth of which read: "The line of activity projected for Operation Mongoose Plan B plus should be developed with all possible speed. (Action: General Taylor)."[50] It is not completely clear what the "line of activity" referred to entailed, and not all the relevant documentation can be found in the historical record.[51] But at least some of the activity involved sabotage, as indicated by the list of harassment and sabotage options set forth in General Lansdale's August 31 memorandum to the Special Action Group (Augmented).[52] In September, meetings of the group would consider a variety of proposals, such as "agricultural sabotage" (including "producing crop failures by the introduction of biological agents"), and "sabotaging airplane parts which are scheduled to be shipped from Canada to Cuba."[53]

On October 4, 1962, Robert Kennedy chastised the Special Action Group, all of whom were high-level officials of the Departments of Defense and State and the CIA. The attorney general told them the president was "dissatisfied" and wanted "massive activity." As Evan Thomas would later write, "Maybe a program of sabotage and subversion was not enough, and more 'direct action' was called for, said RFK. The attorney general demanded 'dynamic' and 'imaginative' solutions."[54] A week later, William K. Harvey of the CIA prepared a memorandum for General Lansdale providing a "response" to the Special Action Group's "stated desire for more aggressive sabotage action." Over eight pages Harvey listed a wide range of potential sabotage options, including maritime and land targets with indications of prioritization in terms of their economic importance in Cuba, as well as "Harassment Operations," "Minor Acts of Sabotage," and "Economic Denial Operations."[55]

The following week, on October 16, a matter of hours after the White House had learned of the Soviet ballistic missiles in Cuba, Robert Kennedy "was still seething" when he joined the weekly meeting of the Special Action Group and chastised them for having produced "no significant sabotage in Cuba." He told them that they would be receiving more of his "personal attention" and that the group would be meeting from that point forward "every morning at nine-thirty."[56]

President Kennedy may have hoped that by sending these signals of strength he would be sobering his adversary and constraining the latter's belligerence. In fact it appears that these messages had the opposite effect. As Michael Beschloss has observed, although the president "may have strengthened his own domestic political standing and reassured American allies" by authorizing the Gilpatric speech in October 1961, he also "undermined Khrushchev's position in the Kremlin and in the world" and "was playing with fire."[57]

Most chillingly, Khrushchev was angered by Kennedy's unsubtle hints about the American first-strike capability reported in Stewart Alsop's March 31, 1962, column. In a conversation with Anatoly Dobrynin in March 1962, he described the apparent American attempt to use its nuclear leverage as "particularly arrogant," and said, "It's high time their long arms were cut shorter."[58] Khrushchev also told Kennedy's press secretary, Pierre Salinger, at a meeting on May 10 that Kennedy's comments reported by Alsop were a "very bad statement . . . for which [Kennedy] would have to pay," and that "perhaps [the] Soviet Union would have to reassess its position."[59] As Michael Beschloss has written, the president's provocative comments and actions left Khrushchev feeling "trapped and deeply insecure," and with "an almost childlike feeling of spite and rage."[60]

Immediately after the appearance of the Stewart Alsop article, Khrushchev "ordered Soviet forces to heightened alert," and a *Pravda* editorial interpreted Kennedy's words as implying that the United States "was entitled to strike the first atomic blow, to become the initiator of a war of aggression"[61] and further stated: "It is incomprehensible what upside-down logic prompted [Kennedy] to make this rash and provocative statement about a possible preventive nuclear attack against the Soviet Union."[62]

Thus, the US deployment of Jupiter IRBM missiles in Italy and Turkey, which at least nominally had been designed solely to bolster the *defense* of these two allies, was being perceived in Moscow to pose an offensive threat to their homeland. From his vacation villa in Sochi during the summer of 1962, Khrushchev "seethed with resentment" over the presence of American nuclear missiles only a short distance away across the Black Sea in Turkey.[63]

Khrushchev had explained the asymmetry problem to the Soviet Presidium as early as December 1959, which was a critical juncture for the Soviet military. In a memorandum he prepared on December 8, 1959, for circulation to Presidium members in advance of their forthcoming meeting scheduled for December 14, Khrushchev noted that while the Soviets had indeed managed to assemble a small handful of first generation R-7A ICBMs, these missiles were relatively primitive and highly vulnerable due to their aboveground installations and their dependence on liquid fuel, which could not be placed in the missiles in advance, adding problematic delays for any ultimate launch decision. Further, the hoped-for deployment of the next-generation solid-fuel R-9 and R-16 ICBMs capable of being launched from underground "hardened" silos would not be possible for another six or more years. Khrushchev believed the Russian economy needed immediate urgent investments, and he didn't want to divert the country's limited available resources to inferior, stop-gap missile technology that was then available. Yet, in the meantime, there would be a significant period of vulnerability to superior US nuclear strike forces in which the Soviet Union might face a devastating first-strike attack leaving it no ability to deliver a retaliatory blow. Khrushchev's warning to his colleagues, later summarized by Fursenko and Naftali, was that "the missile gap favoring U.S. power would probably widen before the R-9 and the R-16 could be deployed."[64]

Soviet strategic inferiority persisted and even deepened during the first two years of the Kennedy administration. On January 8, 1962, Khrushchev delivered to the Presidium a secret speech about the uneven balance of military might existing between the two superpowers. The speech would remain unknown outside the Kremlin for forty years until it was unearthed from previously classified Soviet archives by historians Fursenko and Naftali and named Khrushchev's "Meniscus" speech. Looking back on the struggles over Berlin during the year just ended, Khrushchev admitted to his colleagues that he had misjudged Kennedy and the NATO member states, thinking that, being fearful of Soviet aggression, the Western powers would succumb and agree to the demands Khrushchev was making regarding the status of Berlin. But the Soviet leader admitted his hopes were misplaced, and he had reached a gloomy conclusion: "No, they won't agree."[65]

Despite resigning himself to Western intransigence on Berlin, Khrushchev was determined to stay the course: "We should still press on. . . . It's too early. So it's worthwhile playing the game."[66] The "game" required application of sufficient pressure on the United States so that the Kennedy administration would feel the heat of the Soviet Union's growing strength, but not to the point of precipitating military hostilities. Khrushchev asked his colleagues to consider the condition of a glass filled up to its very brim with liquid, but just barely short of overflowing: "We should increase the pressure. . . . But don't pour the last drop to make the cup overflow; be just like a meniscus, which, according to the laws of surface tension in liquid, is generated in order that the liquid doesn't pour out past the rim."[67]

Khrushchev cautioned, however, that the game needed to be played with extreme care, given the overshadowing menace of nuclear weapons, because a misjudgment could be calamitous. He drove his point home by switching from surface physics to dark peasant humor about games of chance: "We need to advance rationally, not to resemble a gambler, in this game, who bets whatever is left in his pocket and then grabs a pistol and shoots himself."[68]

Neither the Presidium nor Khrushchev could foresee how these mixed metaphors of "playing the game," obeying the "laws of surface tension in liquid," and avoiding the suicidal impulses of a gambler would actually play out later in the year. Yet as Khrushchev's signature method of "playing the game"—or, as will be seen, his and the president's reciprocally cunning and in some respects duplicitous "double game" played for high stakes—evolved from August 1962 through the end of October that year, the Soviet chairman's "meniscus" would indeed withstand the increased pressure his Operation Anadyr imposed on it, and he neither bet everything nor shot himself. As will be seen in the next chapter, Khrushchev would mount a major messaging campaign, at first privately in his communications with the president but increasingly in the public sphere, designed to justify his shipments of arms and other materials to Cuba as purely "defensive" measures. To the extent these shipments included missiles, these were consistently described using remarkably repetitive "party line" terminology: they were uniformly referred to as "defensive weapons" being provided for "defensive purposes."

CHAPTER 4

Both Sides Can Play Defense

Fidel totally failed to understand our purpose.

—NIKITA S. KHRUSHCHEV, MEMOIRS[1]

KHRUSHCHEV'S NOMINALLY DEFENSIVE objectives in ordering Operation Anadyr to defend a beleaguered ally and reduce the tremendous US strategic nuclear lead may seem naive and overreaching in retrospect. But there should be little dispute that moving the missiles to Cuba was a logical defensive step when one considers the Soviet disadvantage in strategic nuclear arms, the disturbing and repeated hints that the Kennedy administration was mulling over first-strike scenarios, and the ominous indications that plans were afoot for heightened US aggression against the Kremlin's only ally in the Western Hemisphere, perhaps including an invasion of Cuba.

Khrushchev doubtless had multiple reasons for placing MRBM and IRBM missiles in Cuba, close to the border of the continental United States. At least three were certainly defensive and deterrent—to match and thereby check the US installation of ballistic missiles in Turkey, close to the border of the Soviet Union; to reduce a US strategic nuclear advantage that had become so overwhelming that the American president was beginning to drop hints in the public media that he was considering circumstances under which he might mount a nuclear first strike against his adversary; and to deter a feared US invasion of Cuba.

Whether the message came through Khrushchev's personal letters to the president, or through Soviet government intermediaries, or via official Soviet news channels, in all cases the same locutions were used: the arms shipments were limited to "defensive weapons" that would serve only "defensive purposes."[2] That this was an instance of orchestrated *dezinformatsiya* must have been readily evident if only from the monotonous regularity of the flat and unvarying pronouncements. Listed in chronological order below are eight successive, official Soviet statements repeating the key "defensive" formulation that were made over the approximately six-week period from September 4 through October 18, 1962.

September 4, Dobrynin to Robert Kennedy. The Soviet ambassador and the American attorney general met privately on September 4 and had a detailed discussion of the Soviet equipment being shipped to Cuba. According to Dobrynin, he told the younger Kennedy that the equipment his country was sending to Cuba was "defensive in nature and did not represent any threat to the security of the United States."[3] As will be seen below, Kennedy confirmed these were Dobrynin's remarks in a report of the meeting he provided soon thereafter to Theodore Sorensen. According to Dobrynin, Kennedy asked him rhetorically whether the Soviets might not one day send to Cuba missiles capable of reaching the United States. Dobrynin, who would later insist he had no knowledge of the October shipments of ballistic missiles, claims he "neither confirmed nor denied" Kennedy's future speculations.[4]

September 6, Dobrynin to Sorensen. Dobrynin met with senior White House adviser Theodore Sorensen two days later and they, too, discussed the Soviet shipments to Cuba. According to Sorensen's account, recorded in a memorandum written that same day, Dobrynin stated that "all these steps were defensive in nature and did not represent any threat to the security of the United States." Notably, Sorensen's file memorandum also commented that Dobrynin's statement was "identical" to what Sorensen understood the Soviet ambassador had told the attorney general just two days before.[5]

September 7, Dobrynin to Stevenson. One day later, Dobrynin made the same assurance to US ambassador to the United Nations Adlai Stevenson: there were only "defensive" weapons being sent to Cuba.[6]

September 11, TASS statement. On September 11, 1962, the official Soviet news agency, TASS, carried a statement that "the arms and military equipment sent to Cuba are designated solely for defensive purposes"; there was "no need for the Soviet Union to shift its weapons for the repulsion of aggression, for a retaliatory blow, to any other country, for instance Cuba."[7] As Barton Bernstein has observed, "That statement was deceptive and undoubtedly so intended; it was not clearly a lie."[8]

October 7 or 8, Khrushchev to President Kennedy via Bolshakov through Robert Kennedy. Bolshakov had been back in Russia in September and had met with Khrushchev and Anastas Mikoyan, first deputy chairman of the

Council of Ministers, at the chairman's dacha in Pitsunda near the Black Sea in mid-September, most likely sometime between September 10 and 15. According to Bolshakov, Khrushchev "set forth a precisely worded message I was to convey to the President of the United States by word of mouth." Bolshakov subsequently returned to the United States, "proceeded to Washington on October 3," called the attorney general on the morning of October 4 to set up a meeting, and was invited to come to Kennedy's office "on the following day" (October 5) "after lunch." Bolshakov told the younger Kennedy he had an oral message from Khrushchev that he had been instructed to deliver to the president. Robert Kennedy said he would "tell [his] brother about that," and Bolshakov subsequently waited for further instructions, which came two days later when Robert Kennedy invited him "for a talk," once again in the attorney general's office. At that time—which would have been October 7 by Bolshakov's chronology, or October 8 by Dobrynin's official report of the meeting to Moscow,[9] the GRU agent delivered Khrushchev's message word for word. The portion related to the Soviet weapons shipments, according to Bolshakov's subsequently published notes, was as follows: "Premier Khrushchev is concerned about the situation being built up by the United States around Cuba, and we repeat that the Soviet Union is supplying to Cuba exclusively defensive weapons intended for protecting the interests of the Cuban revolution and not for perpetrating an aggression against any state on American continent, the US included."[10]

October 13, Dobrynin to Bowles. Bowles stated in his memoirs that he confronted Dobrynin on October 13 with the US finding that Soviet arms shipments to Cuba included "heavy IL-28 bombers." Dobrynin's response was to insist that these reports "must be untrue" and that the Soviets "were not shipping offensive weapons to Cuba." Bowles quipped that this would not be the first time in modern history when an ambassador had been deceived by his own government.[11]

October 16, Khrushchev to Kohler. On October 16 Khrushchev told the US ambassador that Soviet "purposes" in Cuba were "wholly defensive."[12]

October 18, Gromyko to President Kennedy. Soviet foreign minister Gromyko visited with President Kennedy at the White House for an official meeting on October 18 at which others were present and official notes were taken. Although Kennedy would later report that Gromyko told many "barefaced lies" at the meeting, the official notetaker's notes said only that the minister asserted that Soviet military aid "was by no means offensive" and assistance was being provided "solely for the purpose of contributing to the defense capabilities of Cuba."[13]

There is no dispute that five of the preceding statements parroted a strict form of Soviet party line that the arms were for defensive purposes only. The remaining three instances involved representations that Dobrynin and Bolshakov allegedly made to Robert Kennedy alone, and statements made by Soviet foreign minister Gromyko to the president at the official White House meeting on October 18. The attorney general would subsequently maintain that the Dobrynin and Bolshakov comments, made to him alone, provided specific false characterizations of the Soviet weapons that went beyond the party-line "defensive only" formulation. These statements were allegedly made during the attorney general's separate meetings with Dobrynin on September 4 (and allegedly reaffirmed by Dobrynin on October 23), and with Bolshakov on October 7 or 8 and October 17 (or October 22). On October 18, the president would later chime in that Gromyko uttered "barefaced lies" about the Soviet weapons in Cuba at their meeting in the White House on that date. All three of these episodes will be discussed in chapter 8.

One question that troubled President Kennedy at the height of the missile crisis was whether the US placement of Jupiter missiles in Turkey would be understood by the rest of the world as a contradiction of his essential argument that the Soviets had acted offensively and therefore unacceptably when they moved similar missiles to emplacements in Cuba. It is therefore instructive to reflect on the strikingly similar ways the Soviet Union and the United States each acted and reacted when the other took steps to install ballistic missiles at the borders of its adversary. The Soviets were first to face this challenge when they learned at the conclusion of the NATO Ministerial Conference in Paris on December 16–19, 1957, that the Eisenhower administration was offering to install Thor and Jupiter IRBMs on the territories of its NATO allies. Notable among the Americans' stated reasons for these deployments was the defensive aim of deterring Soviet aggression.[14] Citing the Soviet Union's mobilization of "the most modern and destructive weapons, including missiles of all kind," NATO announced in the communiqué issued at the conclusion of the NATO conference that "we have no alternative but to remain vigilant and to look to our defences." This would include the establishment of "stocks of nuclear warheads, which will be readily available for the defence of the Alliance in case of need," as well as "intermediate range ballistic missiles" to be deployed "in conformity with NATO defence plans."[15]

Deterrence remained a consistent theme as the Eisenhower administration sought to persuade first the United Kingdom[16] and later its other NATO allies[17] to accept the US missiles on their soil. The State Department issued a press announcement in November 1958 stating, "The IRBM program is best suited to strengthening that part of the free world's defenses which lie in Europe."[18] The missiles were considered to serve both as a deterrent to Soviet attack and as a check against pressure and threats by the Kremlin in order to "protect the NATO countries from Soviet missile blackmail."[19]

Soviet officials strenuously objected to the planned US deployments, which they characterized as acts of aggression. In 1958, Khrushchev complained to Adlai Stevenson that his country was "encircled by your bases," to which Stevenson replied that the American installations "were defensive—not aggressive."[20] Similarly, Vice President Richard Nixon, while on a visit to Moscow, attempted to reassure the Russian people in a talk broadcast over Soviet television on August 1, 1959, in which he stated that the US nuclear missile bases "were purely defensive, born of past Soviet provocations, massive Soviet defense spending, and NATO fears of Soviet intentions."[21] Nor was the vice president's comment a transient policy pronouncement confined to the unique circumstances of the moment. The US policy of "nuclear sharing" with its NATO allies has continued unabated up to the present moment, and NATO members still field "dual-capable aircraft" that are "equipped to carry nuclear bombs" and manned by "personnel [who] are trained accordingly." As recently as February 13, 2019, a spokesman for German chancellor Angela Merkel pronounced that her government continued to back "nuclear sharing" and "to fully support the defensive nuclear strategy of NATO." Simultaneously, the US Ambassador to Germany, Richard A. Grenell was quoted as saying, "NATO's nuclear forces are there for deterrence and defense. This is a commitment the alliance has made together."[22]

Ultimately, it fell to President Kennedy to authorize the completion of the Turkey missile installations. Philip Nash found no specific presidential statement confirming the defensive character of the Jupiter missile deployment. That point was made, however, by Dean Rusk, who said that "the president hoped that such resolute action would serve to restrain Khrushchev over Berlin."[23] On October 22, 1962, when President Kennedy raised the question of how he should distinguish the Soviet missiles in Cuba from the US missiles in Turkey if the question came up in conjunction with his address to the nation that evening, Rusk emphasized the Eisenhower administration's and NATO's defensive posture by noting that NATO's decision to introduce these weapons came only after the Soviets began "insisting upon having hundreds of these weapons aimed at Europe and none of these weapons pointed the other way. . . . That's the Turkey-Italy situation."[24]

Khrushchev was thinking the same way—only from the reverse angle. He had equated Soviet interests in Cuba with the US missiles in Turkey as early as June 1961 during the Vienna summit.[25] It seems clear from the record that his initial idea of deploying his own ballistic missiles in Cuba germinated in April 1962, a month after the last of the Jupiter missiles became operational in Turkey.

Khrushchev believed the White House would accept Soviet missiles in Cuba the same way the Kremlin had come to accept the US missiles in Turkey. As his biographer, William Taubman, would later write, Khrushchev hoped "to deploy the missiles 'very speedily' by September or October and then inform Kennedy, possibly in person at the United Nations, after the congressional elections in November. He expected Washington to accept the news calmly, 'as the Turkish missiles were received in the Soviet Union.'"[26] Responding to objections raised by his foreign policy aide, Oleg Troyanovsky, Khrushchev said that "he wasn't doing anything that Americans hadn't already done by deploying nuclear weapons along Soviet borders."[27]

The installation of the Jupiter missiles near the borders of the Soviet Union was surely a significant motivating factor in Khrushchev's decision at that same time to send MRBM and IRBM missiles to Cuba. As Philip Nash has noted, President Eisenhower had foreseen the danger of precisely this kind of reflexive reaction as early as June 1959. He expressed to his top advisers his misgivings about the consequences of deploying US ballistic missiles in another NATO country near the Soviet border. What would be our reaction, the president asked, if "Mexico or Cuba had been penetrated by the Communists, and then began getting arms and missiles from them?" Wouldn't the United States "look on such developments with the gravest concern" and find it "imperative for us to take positive action, even offensive military action."[28]

Khrushchev echoed Eisenhower's thinking when he was told that the missiles in Turkey had become operational, a process that had taken place in stages between November 6, 1961, and March 5, 1962.[29] Nash described Khrushchev's angry reaction to the growing threat while on a visit to his Black Sea villa in April or May 1962: "Why do the Americans have such a possibility? They have surrounded us with bases on all sides, and we have no such possibility and right to do the same." It didn't take long, however, for Khrushchev to come up with a logical counter. Addressing his defense minister, Rodion Malinovsky, Khrushchev cited an old Russian folk tale: "Rodion Yakovlevich, what if we throw a hedgehog down Uncle Sam's pants?"[30]

Later, when he described his thinking to the secret delegation he sent to Cuba to propose his missile scheme to Castro, Khrushchev emphasized that the weapons were meant to deter, not to strike. Fursenko and Naftali have described Khrushchev's May 27, 1962, farewell speech to the group: "'An attack on Cuba is being prepared,' he said. 'The correlation of forces is unfavorable to us, and the only way to save Cuba is to put missiles there.' . . . The American rockets in Turkey 'are aimed at us and scare us. Our missiles will also be aimed at the United States, even if we do not have as many of them. But if missiles will be deployed near the U.S., they will be even more afraid.'"[31]

The Presidium was also present at this meeting, and Khrushchev told the gathering that there was no danger of a conflict even if the United States were to discover the missiles prematurely. The American president was "intelligent," he reassured them, and would not "set off a nuclear war."[32] Khrushchev was not alone in these views in Moscow. KGB chairman Semichastny would later recall that the Soviet leadership "expected [Kennedy] to swallow the missiles as we accepted the missiles in Turkey."[33] Fursenko and Naftali found in the Kremlin's archives that a "growing consensus" had emerged in the Soviet government that "even if the United States learned about the missiles before they became operational, Anadyr would succeed because John Kennedy would swallow whatever he found in Cuba." There were also additional indications from "confidential sources" in the United States that the American president "was more concerned with Berlin and the congressional elections," so that even if he "had time to react to the missiles before they were fully operational, he would not do anything about them."[34]

On the other side of the Atlantic Ocean, ExComm advisers readily understood that the Kremlin might want to install missiles in Cuba as a defensive response to its "deficiency" against US strategic nuclear might.[35] During the ExComm deliberations, Dean Rusk perceived that the provocation of Jupiter missiles in Turkey could have prompted Khrushchev to attempt a similar move in America's backyard. Noting that the United States held "a substantial nuclear superiority," Rusk observed that Khrushchev would also be thinking "that we don't really live under fear of his nuclear weapons to the extent that he has to live under fear of ours," and he pointedly mentioned in this context that "we have nuclear weapons nearby, in Turkey and places like that."[36] The president seemed at first to be caught off guard by

Rusk's remarks. In a curious exchange with McGeorge Bundy and Deputy Undersecretary for Political Affairs U. Alexis Johnson, the president wondered aloud why Khrushchev had installed missiles in Cuba:

> KENNEDY: Why does he put these in there though? . . . It's just as if we suddenly began to put a major number of MRBMs in Turkey. Now that'd be goddamn dangerous, I would think.
>
> BUNDY: Well, we did, Mr. President.
>
> JOHNSON: We did it. We did it in England.
>
> KENNEDY: Yeah, but that was five years ago . . . that was during a different period then.[37]

The best that can be said about the president's initially confused and then defensive response is that he may have been referring to the fact that the initial arrangements that set in motion the stationing of US IRBM missiles as part of NATO forces in Europe had indeed begun under his predecessor some years before. The more salient fact that the president overlooked, however, was that the Jupiter IRBM missiles in Turkey and Italy were reaching operational status under his watch and with his approval just as Khrushchev was setting his own reciprocal, forward missile deployment in motion. Kennedy could have reversed the program, or placed it on hold, but he did not do either during the months immediately preceding Khrushchev's determination to launch Project Anadyr. On the contrary, these were months during which the president and his brother were making public comments about how the United States might need to consider nuclear first-use scenarios.

The president and his advisers were certainly aware of the dangerous provocation that the Jupiter missiles engendered in their adversary. As already noted, in their above-ground installations and with their laborious set-up procedures and dangerous liquid-fuel technology, these missiles were highly vulnerable to Soviet preemptive attack and even to being disabled by rifle fire from casual passers-by. They were thus clearly destabilizing because their very vulnerability meant they could logically be perceived by the Soviets as weapons useful only for first-strike purposes.[38] Nevertheless, Kennedy felt compelled to proceed with the deployment as a matter of US prestige and the president's own credibility. As Philip Nash has noted, despite having received "well-reasoned recommendations to cancel the Turkish deployment," the president felt he had to go forward; "like Ike, credibility made him do it":

"Facing Turkish resistance, and then alarmed by the Vienna summit and Khrushchev's reopening of the Berlin crisis, Kennedy and his advisers decided that cancellation would be a sign of weakness that would distress Ankara and encourage Moscow."[39]

A June 22, 1961, memorandum to McGeorge Bundy from George C. McGhee, the undersecretary of state for political affairs, supports this conclusion. Noting that he had been asked by the president to "study and report on the matter of Turkish IRBMs," McGhee told Bundy that the Turkish missile deployment should not be canceled "based primarily on the view that, in the aftermath of Khrushchev's hard posture at Vienna, cancellation of the IRBM deployment might seem a sign of weakness." McGhee stated that Rusk and General Norstad concurred with this conclusion.[40]

It is surely a matter of human nature and common sense that a weapon—any weapon—can simultaneously embody both defensive and offensive natures. Defensive, because a potential adversary who is aware that his rival possesses the weapon might be deterred, at least to some extent, out of fear that the weapon could be used against him with harmful effect. Conversely, the weapon has an offensive nature because having any weapon, whether simple or fearsome, can embolden its possessor, at least to some extent, to believe he could commit a successful aggression using that weapon to kill or disable his foe. And although the differing capabilities of weapons in the hands of two adversaries may affect their respective inclinations to attack, defend, retreat, or submit, this does not negate the essential truth that all weapons may be seen as having both defensive and offensive purposes and potentialities. As a leading expert in the field of strategic weapons has concluded: "The offensive or defensive character of a weapons system must be defined by both its intrinsic characteristics and the tactical doctrine which determines its use."[41]

Senator Keating would later use the same logic in an effort to mock the administration's inaction in the face of the Soviet arms buildup when he stated on October 5: "Who is to say whether a weapon is offensive or defensive? It depends on the direction in which it is aimed."[42] McGeorge Bundy later acknowledged that, while the Soviets repeatedly claimed their weapons were only "defensive," at least some of these assurances "were not without their ambiguities."[43] Theodore Sorensen made the same point in his memoirs of his longtime dealings with the president when he observed that the distinction between offensive and defensive capabilities was "not always clear-cut."[44]

The CIA readily appreciated during the Soviet military buildup in Cuba during the fall of 1962 that any weapon brought to the island nation, whether a handgun or a ballistic missile, could in theory serve both defensive and offensive purposes. Although the agency had identified only defensive weapons at the time, its Special National Intelligence Estimate 85-3-62, issued on September 19, 1962, observed that "the USSR might be tempted to establish in Cuba other weapons *represented to be defensive in purpose, but of a more 'offensive' character*: e.g., light bombers, submarines, and additional types of short-range surface-to-surface missiles (SSMs)."[45]

In the particular case of the United States and the Soviet Union during the Cuban crisis, it appears that a divergence of usage may have contributed to the confusion. As Khrushchev pointed out in his letter to President Kennedy on October 26, 1962: "Our conceptions are different on this score, or rather, we have different definitions for these or those military means."[46] Soviet ambassador Dobrynin would later write in his memoirs, "In our military jargon, the word 'defensive' meant that all the weapons were meant to be used 'for the defense of Cuba.'"[47] And as David Coleman has pointed out, "The Soviet Union emphasized the role of the weapons, whereas Western military planners stressed technical capabilities such as range and explosive yield."[48]

In comparing the US/NATO and USSR intermediate-range ballistic missile emplacements in Turkey and Cuba in terms of their "defensive" or "offensive" attributes, no meaningful differences can be identified since both deployments had a predominant deterrence objective. As Philip Nash has observed, the NATO deployment was meant "to protect its friends, to compensate for the adversary's enormous local conventional superiority, and to serve as stopgap ICBMs." The Soviet reaction in Cuba "was in part following the American precedent." And then, "considering such US policies as the Bay of Pigs invasion, the economic embargo, the anti-Castro covert action program (Operation Mongoose), and the repeated, large-scale military maneuvers staged nearby," the Kremlin had even more immediate defensive motivations since "it was not at all 'obvious' that Cuba was not under threat of attack."[49]

Khrushchev had made the same point on October 24, 1962, in his typically blunt way during a conversation with the president of Westinghouse Electric Corporation, who happened to be in Moscow: "If I point a pistol at you like this in order to attack you, the pistol is an offensive weapon. But if I am to keep you from shooting me, it is defensive, no?" Beschloss noted that the Soviet chairman added that "the United States claimed that its Turkish bases were defensive, but what was the range of the missiles there?"[50]

It was well known to US national security leaders at the time that there was no immutable distinction between "offensive" and "defensive" weapons. In a press interview on Sunday, October 14, 1962—coincidentally on the very day that a U-2 would take the first photographs of the Soviet MRBM installation being built near San Cristóbal in western Cuba—ABC reporter Edward P. Morgan asked McGeorge Bundy to explain how one could distinguish between offensive and defensive weapons. Bundy responded: "Now it is true that these words 'offensive' and 'defensive,' if you try to apply them precisely to every single item, mislead you. Whether a gun is offensive or defensive depends a little bit on which end you are on. It is also true that the MiG fighters which have been put into Cuba for more than a year now, and any possible additions in the form of aircraft, might have a certain marginal capability for moving against the United States." But then Bundy shifted to a more general response for the administration introducing the qualified term "major." He emphasized that the Soviets had placed no "*major* offensive capability" in Cuba and that the United States "is not going to be placed in any position of *major* danger to its own security in Cuba, and we are not going to permit that situation to develop."[51]

The ExComm were certainly aware of the argument that both the NATO missiles in Turkey and the Russian missiles in Cuba could be characterized as "defensive." At the ExComm meeting on October 18, Llewelyn Thompson explained that Khrushchev's "general line" would probably be that "these are not missiles other than defensive. They're much less offensive than your weapons in Turkey. You've got these armed with nuclear warheads. We haven't given any nuclear weapons to them. These are simply to deal with the threat to Cuba."[52]

Former secretary of state Dean Rusk would also subscribe to this view eight years later as he participated in the JFK Presidential Library's oral history project. Responding to questions about key moments during the Cuban missile crisis, Rusk discussed the president's October 18, 1962, meeting with Soviet foreign minister Gromyko, which occurred four days before Kennedy would reveal to the world during his momentous October 22 speech to the nation that US surveillance had photographed Soviet ballistic missile bases under construction in Cuba. The president had decided not to alert Gromyko to this shocking discovery, choosing instead to repeat his earlier warning to the Kremlin about the dire consequences that would follow any placement of Soviet offensive weapons in Cuba. Noting that Gromyko had responded by "simply repeating the formulation" that "only defensive weapons" were in Cuba, Rusk immediately acknowledged the obvious parallel posed by the contemporaneous deployment of US ballistic missiles on NATO military bases located close to the Soviet Union: "Of course, you can make the argument that offensive missiles are, in fact, defensive weapons, as would be true in the NATO countries, for example."[53]

It is useful to pause here and reflect on the fact that on August 29, 1962, six days before the president's September 4 "red line" pronouncement against any appearance of Soviet "offensive ground-to-ground missiles" in Cuba, US surveillance had detected exactly that type of weapon—ground-to-ground cruise missiles—near the town of Banes on the eastern coast of that island. When word of this finding reached the president on September 7, a mere three days after his momentous warning to the Soviets, he was predictably disturbed, and his reflexive response was to sequester the news. As Bundy would later report: "The president told [deputy director of the CIA] General Carter that this information should not be included in intelligence publications pending more exact determination; he directed that no reports on weapons which might be offensive should be published without his approval."[54]

We will return to the pivotal September 7 meeting below. But for present purposes, it should suffice to note that the distinction between "offensive" and "defensive" weapons was a highly diffuse and debatable matter of semantics in 1962, and this was understood by the president and his top advisers from the earliest moments of the lead-up to the Cuban missile crisis.

Why did Khrushchev order the secret delivery of strategic nuclear missiles to Cuba in mid-1962? From the Kremlin's point of view, the answer is obvious: this was a "defensive" initiative designed for deterrence on multiple grounds. Explaining his thinking to the Presidium on May 27, 1962, Khrushchev told his colleagues that "the only way to save Cuba is to put missiles there."[55] Decades later, a Russian historian attending a Belfer Center conference marking the fiftieth anniversary of the crisis argued that the Kremlin was mainly aiming for "deterrence to prevent the United States from staging a large-scale invasion that could overthrow the government of Fidel Castro and the Communist Party of Cuba." These concerns were said to justify treating the "Soviet nuclear warheads and associated delivery vehicles" in Cuba as "defensive weapons."[56]

The question of Soviet intentions and motivations behind the missile installation was a preoccupation of Kennedy and the ExComm throughout much of their deliberation in October 1962, and it has remained a key subject of speculation in succeeding years.[57]

The ExComm readily identified two possible rationales that could have led Khrushchev to make this aggressive move: (1) to bolster the defense of Cuba, a key ally, and (2) to redress the major US advantage in the strategic balance of power, by increasing the numbers of nuclear-armed missiles able to reach continental US targets. That the latter objective was understood in realistic terms to be modest and defensive rather than aggressive and offensive is illustrated by a later comment of McNamara's quoted by Beschloss: "As [McNamara] said years later, if Khrushchev in 1962 'thought he was numerically behind by seventeen to one or thereabouts, do you think an extra forty-two missiles in Cuba, each carrying one warhead, would have led him to think he could use his nuclear weapons? No way!'"[58]

Addressing this same question of Khrushchev's objectives with the benefit of hindsight bolstered by significant revelations from previously secret Soviet archival material and Khrushchev's own memoirs, modern scholars have not always agreed about specific prioritization but they have formed a consensus about a small number of key reasons for Khrushchev's Anadyr operation. Raymond Garthoff would neatly summarize in 1998 the three most likely motivations, and all were defensive in nature: "A need to shore up the strategic balance with the United States, a perceived need to deter an attack by the United States on Cuba, and a belief that a successful missile deployment in Cuba analogous to US deployments around the Soviet Union would give the United States a dose of its own medicine."[59]

While Allison and Zelikow still felt in 1999 that the question of Khrushchev's motivations "eluded [a] satisfactory answer[]," they focused on the three considerations mentioned by Garthoff and added a fourth rationale: Khrushchev's possible desire to gain leverage in pursuing his ambitions to push the United States and its allies out of West Berlin. Their conclusion was that "the missile power and Berlin hypotheses offer the most satisfactory explanation of the thinking behind the Soviet move to send nuclear missiles to Cuba."[60] Yet regardless of whichever assessment gets the prioritization of Khrushchev's reasons right, it seems beside the point given the fact, which most historians seem to accept, that there were multiple defensive and deterrent reasons, each one of which standing alone could have provided a rational "defensive" justification for Khrushchev's action. As summarized by Beth Fischer, "Although it is still unclear which of these motives carried the most weight, it is now generally agreed that Khrushchev's motives were largely defensive."[61] The key point for purposes of this assessment is that Khrushchev had rational, articulable reasons, including important defensive reasons; no specific plan of aggression was among them; he was able to prevail on his colleagues to accept his proposal; and the secret project for projecting Soviet strategic nuclear weapons into the Western Hemisphere moved forward.

During the 1962 crisis there were numerous indications the Soviets had determined it was necessary to place missiles in Cuba in order to defend against US aggression, which appeared to include a possible threat of invasion. Khrushchev made this prime objective clear to the Presidium in his explanation of the plan: official notes of the Presidium meeting of May 21, 1962, read: "On aid to Cuba. How to help Cuba, so that it holds on. (Khrushchev)."[62]

It is also telling that Khrushchev made a "no-invasion pledge" the centerpiece of both his original proposal for and his final acceptance of the settlement agreement that ended the crisis. In his report to the Supreme Soviet on December 12, 1962, Khrushchev explained, "Our purpose was only the defense of Cuba."[63]

With the declassification of US documentation of Operation Mongoose—the Kennedy administration's long-standing effort, launched on November 30, 1961, and led by Robert Kennedy,[64] to bring about the "overthrow" of "the Communist regime" in Cuba—it is no longer possible to argue that Khrushchev's "defense of Cuba" justification was a makeweight. In truth, Fidel Castro was facing numerous US threats to his regime's existence in mid-1962, including political and economic subversion, physical sabotage, assassination plots, and advanced planning for an outright invasion.[65] As stated in an October 11, 1962, status report to the Special Action Group (Augmented) through which Robert Kennedy monitored Mongoose's progress: "At your October meeting, it was your desire that Mongoose be stepped up. The Operational Representatives were so tasked, promptly, and we can expect a series of proposals in the near future (with sabotage given priority attention.)"[66]

President Kennedy acknowledged that "defense of Cuba" was the main line of Soviet justification on October 19, 1962, when he reported to the ExComm, then meeting with the Joint Chiefs of Staff, that Soviet foreign minister Gromyko had used exactly this "defensive" characterization during a discussion just the evening before: "Well, he talked tough about Berlin. On Cuba he really just talked about their defensive aspirations. He said, 'We're only sending defensive weapons in.' Of course, that's how they define these weapons, as defensive."[67]

Khrushchev's memoirs mentioned numerous justifications for his missile gambit, including defense of Cuba, strategic considerations, political sensitivities raised by his country's rivalry with Communist China, and matters of prestige and credibility. Nevertheless, Khrushchev tried hard to demonstrate that his main concern was defense of his ally against US aggression. That was also the view of Oleg Troyanovsky, who had served as an assistant and interpreter for Khrushchev. In an interview with a journalist for *Peter Jennings Reports*, ABC News, in 1992, Troyanovsky offered two main defensive reasons for Operation Anadyr: "One reason obviously was to prevent a new invasion of Cuba after the Bay of Pigs. . . . The second was, of course, to try to redress, in a way, the balance between the two countries as far as nuclear capability was concerned."[68]

As already discussed, the Kennedy administration's efforts through Project Mongoose to subvert the Castro government, combined with active military exercises during the same period that were thinly veiled simulations of a full-fledged invasion of Cuba, caused the Kremlin to fear that its only ally in the Western Hemisphere was in peril. Although Christopher Andrew has disparaged these efforts as "farcically inept American efforts to topple or assassinate Moscow's Cuban ally," he also saw these as "actions ideally calculated to exacerbate the paranoid strain in Soviet foreign policy."[69]

Meanwhile, planning was underway for large amphibious assault exercises in the Caribbean simulating an invasion of Cuba. Original planning for a rapid response amphibious invasion of Cuba was begun in February 1962 under contingency operational plans (OPLAN) 314-61 and 316-61, involving an assault by two Army Airborne divisions followed by two Marine Corps divisions with further armored support units to arrive later.[70]

The Kennedy administration lost no time in considering the Soviet arms deliveries in defensive terms, at least in the sense of the Kremlin's likely desire to diminish the missile gap that favored the United States. During the first day of ExComm discussions, President Kennedy asked rhetorically: "What is the advantage? Must be some reason for the Russians to set this up. Must be that they're not satisfied with their ICBMs."[71] The president and his brother's multiple dropped hints about active US first-strike or first-use thinking during the period from mid-1961 through mid-1962 have already been mentioned. Khrushchev was fully aware of these reports and considered them to be deadly serious, whether stated in blunt first-strike language or more restrained or vague formulations like first use, only in "really desperate circumstances," or to "probe the forces of the Soviet Union." This suggests that Operation Anadyr was launched at least in part to address and potentially neutralize the US first-strike advantage or first-use threat. The Presidium voted to approve Operation Anadyr based upon a report authored by Soviet defense minister Rodion Malinovsky, which was formally presented on June 10, 1962, a time when the implicit threats of the president's and attorney general's public statements were top-of-mind within the Kremlin. Considering the array of weapons Khrushchev's plan would be delivering to Cuba, especially the land-based ballistic missiles, with ballistic missile submarines soon to follow, the Presidium was likely seeking a more favorable strategic weapons balance where "no general in the Pentagon would again dare consider a nuclear first strike against the Soviet Union or an attack on Cuba."[72]

Thomas Patterson summed up the Soviet Union's predominant *defensive* strategic motive best in concluding that "the emplacement of missiles in Cuba served the Soviet strategic objective of catching up in the nuclear arms race. . . . The Soviets hoped to enhance their much weaker deterrent power in the Cold War and save a threatened ally."[73]

Taking into account the thinly veiled signals that the US president might be considering a preemptive first strike, the Jupiter deployment in Turkey, and the sword-brandishing maneuvers in Operation Mongoose and OPLAN, Sheldon Stern, the longtime historian of the John F. Kennedy Presidential Library, rightly concluded the Kennedy administration must bear "significant responsibility" along with Khrushchev for provoking the Cuba crisis.[74] Yet, paradoxically, a foreign policy crisis was the very last thing the president wanted during the fading days of summer 1962. His primary concern at that time was the upcoming midterm elections on November 6, 1962, which would provide an all-important first report card sent by the public on his presidency. The stakes were high for two reasons. First, a president traditionally fares poorly in his first midterms due to the American public's notorious habit of experiencing a reflexive letdown after the euphoria of electing a new president. And second, that new president's own personal reckoning with the electorate would be coming a mere two years later when the 1964 presidential election would determine whether the young president would be granted a second term. Given Kennedy's concern that a poor midterm showing for Democrats would hurt his chances for securing congressional passage of his signature domestic legislative priorities, as will be shown in the next chapter, there was ample reason for a feeling of acute vulnerability.

As will be seen in chapters 5 and 6 below, Kennedy made every effort to ease tensions with Khrushchev during the lead-up to the midterm elections. He initially took these steps in an effort to stave off growing criticism from Republicans of his handling of the Soviet challenge to Western occupation rights in the city of Berlin. As the summer of 1962 wore on, however, and as growing numbers of Soviet cargo ships believed to be carrying military supplies were discovered heading for Cuba, the president broadened his communications with Khrushchev to include his desire for a pause in tensions surrounding both Berlin and Cuba in order to provide the breathing room he needed to attend to midterm electioneering. These efforts would reach a level of reckless double-gamesmanship that threatened to undermine US national security interests.

CHAPTER 5

A Devil's Bargain and a President's Word

Khrushchev and other Soviet leaders . . . hope that President Kennedy will keep his word.

—MESSAGE FROM KHRUSHCHEV TO PRESIDENT KENNEDY, TRANSMITTED BY GEORGI BOLSHAKOV

THE SUMMER OF 1962 was troubled for President Kennedy in terms of his prospects for reelection. As a first-term president he faced the inevitable challenge of midterm elections, to be held on November 6, in which the incumbent's party historically does poorly.[1] The Democrats held a majority of seats in both houses of Congress, but this did not mean the president could get his way, because many Democratic legislators from southern states voted with the Republicans against liberal administration programs. At a news conference on June 27, 1962, the president quipped that "some of the Democrats have voted with the Republicans for 25 years, really since 1938," and this made it "very difficult to secure the enactment of any controversial legislation. . . ." The president concluded that "this election in November is an important one, because if we can gain some more seats, we will have a workable majority."[2]

Less than a month later, Kennedy would feel his domestic political vulnerability even more sharply. The president suffered his "Blackest Week in Congress," according to the *Los Angeles Times*, when his proposed legislation for providing medical assistance to the elderly was defeated in the Senate on July 21 "despite an overwhelming Democratic majority in that body."[3]

Adding to Kennedy's anxiety about his lack of a workable majority on his signature domestic programs were growing concerns about his fitness for leadership in foreign policy, where the president's record in dealings with Khrushchev was held in low regard. The president's public approval rating had slipped from a high of 78 percent at the beginning of 1962 to 62 percent by early October.[4]

In these worrisome circumstances, the president tried to concentrate the public's attention on his "New Frontier" domestic policies (like Medicare), which were his strength, and keep foreign policy as much as possible in the background. Republicans tried "to make Cuba, not Medicare, the leading topic of the congressional elections." Kennedy took the opposite tack: campaigning in the Midwest on October 5–7, "The president barely mentioned foreign policy."[5] On October 11 Kennedy told an ABC interviewer that if his party's midterm election results tracked average outcomes dating back to 1930, "it would make it virtually impossible for him to get his legislation through Congress."[6]

Looking warily at foreign policy as a possible spoiler of his political ambitions, the president's main concern was Berlin, which appeared to be America's greatest Cold War vulnerability. Kennedy was determined to avoid any new confrontation with Khrushchev over Berlin in advance of the midterm elections, lest the ensuing rise in tensions cause his domestic standing further erosion. Khrushchev was aware of the president's vulnerability, and he tried to exploit it. Khrushchev met with departing US ambassador Llewelyn Thompson on July 25, 1962, and offered to help the president. In an "eyes only" cable to the secretary of state on that date, Thompson wrote: "Khrushchev suggested that when I got home I personally ask President—not through State Department—whether it would be better for him if Berlin question brought to a head before or after our Congressional elections. He did not want to make things more difficult for President—and in fact would like to help him."[7]

It is not clear why Khrushchev thought Kennedy might welcome a Soviet offer of help in pursuit of the president's domestic political objectives. Research has not uncovered a preceding request by the president for this offer of foreign assistance. Nevertheless, the Soviet chairman's gesture found a willing recipient, and the private and official correspondence between the two leaders returning to this subject would pervade their discussions, from Khrushchev's initial proposal on July 25 to the president's meeting with Gromyko in the White House on October 18, two days after Kennedy had learned of the missiles in Cuba. The message that the Soviet leader "would like to help him" in America's "congressional elections" ultimately had the reverse effect, facing Kennedy with acute and potentially career-threatening embarrassment that would bedevil him after the missile crisis erupted.

But in late July 1962, with his hopes set on the November 6 midterm elections and his worries fixed on the threat posed in Berlin, the president initially viewed the events in Cuba as an unwanted political nuisance but not a serious provocation. And while some others, especially among his Republican adversaries but also within his own administration, would begin to express alarm over the Soviet arms buildup on America's doorstep, these Cassandras at first simply hardened Kennedy's view that Cuba posed mainly an incipient political problem for his administration rather than a national security threat. His immediate response was therefore to downplay the Kremlin's ambitions in Cuba and to deflect the public's attention from events in the Caribbean, at least until after the midterm elections. The president nevertheless made a mistake in his calculations: he shared his hopes for a pause in tensions with Khrushchev via their personal back-channel messenger, GRU officer Georgi Bolshakov. Perhaps not surprisingly, the Kremlin attempted to take full advantage of this intelligence windfall.

There were numerous instances beginning in late July 1962 and extending throughout the ExComm deliberations in late October where Kennedy's reactions to the Cuba developments appear to have been driven more by his anxiety over the potential political fallout he was facing than by apprehension about a national security threat. The Kennedy-Khrushchev exchanges on this subject began with Khrushchev's July 25 offer to "help" by delaying the Berlin question until after the elections. This offer produced one and possibly two private White House meetings between the Kennedy brothers and their confidential Soviet emissary, Georgi Bolshakov, held on July 31 and (perhaps) August 31, 1962. The fragmentary record confirms that the president proposed a specific deal at the July 31 meeting and then gave his "word" as part of a "conciliatory message" to Khrushchev via multiple messages possibly including a follow-up White House meeting with Bolshakov on August 31. However, a degree of confusion is attributable to Bolshakov's later and somewhat inconsistent versions of events, which warrant additional archival exploration.

The US National Security Agency (NSA) began to pick up indications of a major increase in Soviet arms shipments to Cuba as early as mid-July, at the commencement of Operation Anadyr.[8] Soviet cargo ships, many of which were closely monitored as they passed out of the Black Sea through the Dardanelles Strait, raised suspicions as their captains provided "false declarations to Turkish authorities in Istanbul" and "lied about the cargoes' weight," clearly indicating to NSA analysts at Fort Meade that the ships "were secretly carrying military cargoes."[9]

As Llewellyn Thompson was preparing to leave Moscow, Khrushchev asked him to convey a second personal message to President Kennedy supplementing his July 25 proposal that the "Berlin question" might best be "brought to a head . . . after . . . Congressional elections." In this second message, conveyed by Thompson in a separate "EYES ONLY SECRETARY" telegram sent on July 26 based on the same July 25 meeting with Khrushchev, the ambassador reported that the Soviet chairman had also made a personal appeal that, in order to ease tensions, the president should order the cessation of "harassment" of Soviet shipping by the US military. Khrushchev "cited both air inspection and one case where American ship had commanded Soviet ship stop or be fired on." Thompson reported that Khrushchev had conveyed his request with unusual "heat," calling these tactics "virtually acts of war" and threatening that if they continued, "Soviets would have to reply in kind but wished [to] avoid war like actions."[10]

Coincidentally, the president's secret White House taping system was installed within a few days after the arrival of Thompson's telegram.[11] It was at this juncture that Georgi Bolshakov met privately in the White House with the president and Robert Kennedy, on July 31, 1962, a meeting that is confirmed by entries in the president's desk calendar and the attorney general's desk diary for that date.[12] There is no evidence that the president activated his taping system to record the meeting.

The Kennedys must have learned of Khrushchev's personal requests conveyed by Thompson's cables prior to this meeting, because President Kennedy reportedly told Bolshakov to inform Khrushchev that he had already on that same day ordered the cessation of all US air reconnaissance of Soviet shipping "over open waters." The president told Bolshakov that he expected to receive in exchange the Kremlin's assurance, confirming Khrushchev's July 25 offer, that tensions over Berlin would be placed "on ice" until after the US midterm elections, which were scheduled to take place about nine weeks later, on November 6, 1962.[13] The president did not activate the White House taping system for this meeting, though he had used it to record five meetings just the day before. Fursenko and Naftali have located in Kremlin files undated instructions to Soviet ambassador Dobrynin sent in response to the July 31 meeting directing the ambassador to use the Bolshakov channel to underscore Khrushchev's request that the reconnaissance flights over Soviet ships be stopped. Notably, Bolshakov and Robert Kennedy apparently had met on no less than six occasions during the month of July 1962 alone.[14]

Why would Kennedy have made a direct request of the Soviet chairman to help his domestic political fortunes in a US election? And why did he offer as an inducement for this personal favor a presidential order letting down the nation's guard, if only slightly, on a matter of potentially consequential national security? Seeking a favor from a foreign government to help the president's interest in a US election may have been a dubious use of diplomacy for self-serving purposes, but it was not unprecedented. Franklin Delano Roosevelt had done much the same thing almost two decades earlier in his dealings with Stalin.[15] And it appears that neither president faced later criticism of any serious kind for having done so. John Lewis Gaddis would later describe FDR's petition to Stalin as merely a "peculiar conversation." Kennedy's more audacious offer to make a military concession in exchange for a domestic political favor has scarcely raised an eyebrow among scholarly commentators: Evan Thomas noted Kennedy's promise ("I've ordered those flights stopped today") but left out the requested quid pro quo that Berlin tensions be abated until after the midterms. Thomas's verdict, that "the United States had been blinded and deceived," placed no explicit blame on the president. Taubman simply observed noncommittally: "A concession like that implied that Kennedy was trying to avoid trouble."[16] Yet the price paid was potentially high. On its face, Kennedy's offer to eliminate low-level air surveillance of Soviet military shipping could have delayed exposure of the true danger the United States was facing from the ships' lethal cargoes. And the implicit message the offer seemed to convey—that the president was willing to limit intelligence gathering for Soviet arms shipments to Cuba—could have led the Kremlin to believe it was being given a green light, at least for the period up to the midterm election campaign, to ship weapons of its choosing to its ally in Cuba.

Barrett and Holland believe that the president saw Berlin as the only serious foreign policy threat the United States was facing at the time, and he considered Cuba to be mainly a political problem that Kennedy's Republican adversaries were attempting to exploit. After an October 5 meeting with the president's top foreign policy adviser, McGeorge Bundy, CIA director McCone became convinced "that the White House still viewed the military build-up as primarily a domestic, not a foreign policy, crisis." Bundy left McCone with the impression that the president's top national security adviser "thought he was expertly steering the president clear of a needless crisis that might prove as politically damaging as the Bay of Pigs invasion had been."[17]

The president's willingness to do a deal found favor in Moscow. The Soviet Presidium approved of Kennedy's assurances and authorized Bolshakov to tell the Kennedys: "N. S. Khrushchev is satisfied with the president's order to curtail the U.S. planes' inspections of Soviet ships in open waters."[18] The Soviets wished to know, however, what Kennedy meant by putting Berlin matters "on ice," and they also asked Bolshakov to "speak to the Kennedys about the test ban issue."[19] The GRU officer dutifully reported this response and questions back to Robert Kennedy, most likely on August 2, based on the attorney general's desk diary entry that day, which read: "5:00–7:00 Georgi Bolshakov was in."[20]

It remains unclear, however, what actually happened in terms of US air surveillance during the month of August. Timothy Naftali would later opine, but without providing substantiation, that Kennedy elected not to follow through on his promise because "nothing came" of the quid pro quo the president had asked for in Berlin.[21] But that explanation makes little sense, since there were no notable developments in Berlin one way or the other either just before or during the first few weeks after the president made his July 31 commitment. Evan Thomas, on the other hand, presumed that the president was telling the truth when he instructed Bolshakov to inform Khrushchev that his surveillance-cessation order had been issued "today." This would have meant that "the United States had been blinded and deceived. . . . To ease Cold War tensions, the Kennedys had acceded to the Kremlin's request to stop American spy planes from flying over Soviet ships bound for Cuba; now, it appeared, the Americans had been snookered."[22] Like Naftali, however, Thomas provided no source substantiation for what appears to have been his speculative appraisal of what happened after July 31. What is clear, however, is that the pace of cargo ships carrying Soviet arms continued unabated, and the US intelligence community continued to report on this information to the president.[23]

Curiously, an otherwise inexplicable rift in the joint reporting of the Soviet cargo ships occurred at just this time between two US intelligence agencies. The views of the Defense Department's intelligence arm—the Defense Intelligence Agency (DIA)—diverged sharply from the CIA reporting and the NSA's signals intelligence gathering, referred to as SIGINT. Viewing the underlying intelligence community's analysis when it was declassified years later, Matthew Aid discovered that the DIA unaccountably refused to accept the NSA's SIGINT findings that the Soviet ships carried military cargo, and "blocked an attempt by the CIA to insert an item in the August 3, 1962, edition of the *Central Intelligence Bulletin* noting that 'an unusual number of suspected arms carriers were en route to Cuba.'" The CIA/NSA-proposed message was replaced by "a watered down version," and "DIA blocked four more attempts by CIA analysts to publish reports that the Russians were shipping weapons to Cuba," with DIA analysts expressing the view that the "high volume of shipping probably reflects planned increase in trade between USSR and Cuba." Even as late as the end of August, the president's military adviser, General Maxwell Taylor, told him that "the surge in Soviet shipping traffic to Cuba 'reflected an increased flow of economic aid.'" The CIA would later use a harsh word to describe the DIA's performance during this critical period: "disgraceful."[24]

From Khrushchev's standpoint, however, US intelligence agencies continued their aggressive low-level air surveillance maneuvers (which the Soviets referred to as "buzzing") throughout August 1962 in an effort to determine what the Soviet ships were carrying to Cuba. On September 28, 1962, in a lengthy letter to Kennedy covering a number of topics, Khrushchev lectured the president in a tone bordering on mockery about the intrusive US air surveillance being conducted without interruption throughout August, despite the president's July 31 assertion to the contrary: "I was pleased to receive from you, Mr. President, your assurance that you had given strict instructions not to allow buzzing of our ships. But whether you know it or not the assurance you gave me is not being kept. Your planes even now go on buzzing our ships. I can tell you: in August there were 140 cases of such buzzing."[25]

There is no indication that anyone in the Kennedy administration who would likely have been shown Khrushchev's September 28 letter to the president ever inquired about or even called attention to this passage about the president's "assurance" to the Soviet leader or his "strict instructions" that US surveillance aircraft should stop "buzzing" Soviet cargo ships. Nor have historians made any serious attempt to unravel this mystery: Did the president really give Khrushchev this assurance on July 31, 1962, as Kremlin records unearthed by Naftali and Fursenko seem to document? If the president did this, was his order disobeyed by the US military, as Khrushchev insinuated? Or did the president give the order and then rescind it, although no documentation of this has ever surfaced? Or was the president intentionally not telling the truth when he gave his "assurance" to Khrushchev? That last potential explanation, perhaps impossible to confirm or refute given the passage of time and dearth of documentation, presents a conundrum. If Kennedy knowingly fed an untruth ("flat lie"?) into the Bolshakov back channel on July 31, 1962, meant to be passed along as his personal message to Khrushchev, that would introduce an interesting irony for consideration as the subject turns in chapter 8 to the question whether Khrushchev "flatly lied" to the president in the messages he transmitted through Bolshakov and others regarding the "defensive" nature of the Soviet weapons being sent to Cuba.

During the closing days of August 1962, President Kennedy learned of several minor yet disturbing developments in Berlin that threatened to raise exactly the kind of tension he had been trying to avoid through his assurance to Khrushchev on July 31. Rather than putting Berlin tensions on ice during the lead-up to the US midterm elections, as the president had proposed, Khrushchev seemed once again to apply heat to his peace treaty proposal to the GDR. At the same time, Kennedy was receiving news of highly troublesome discoveries made by American surveillance aircraft that the Soviets were including sophisticated weapons among the military materials they were sending to Cuba. As the pace of "bad news" reports reaching the White House began to accelerate in late August and early September, the president's hopes for abatement of Cold War tensions in return for his July 31 offer to stop low-level air surveillance of Soviet cargo ships headed for Cuba began to fade.

On August 22, 1962, the president received the 1962 report of the Net Evaluation Subcommittee of the National Security Council (NES/NSC), which included evaluation of US casualties if the United States were to launch a preemptive first strike against Soviet military targets in a scenario that was set in 1965, and in which the Russians would strike back with their surviving strategic forces. Based on the assumption that the Soviets would hit urban-industrial targets in retaliation, the NES/NSC predicted massive US civilian casualties. Despite the United States being left "superior militarily," America "would have lost 45 percent of industry and suffered almost 55 million casualties."[26] Thus, only one year after Kennedy had listened to General Lemnitzer's September 1961 prediction that there would be two to fifteen million US casualties in a hypothetical 1962 US first-strike scenario, those alarming American civilian death projections had more than tripled in a comparable scenario set in 1965.

That same day the Kremlin eliminated the position of Soviet commandant in Berlin, seemingly signaling a further step toward the eventual transfer of governance authority to the GDR. This was taken by the White House to be an ominous development.[27] McGeorge Bundy saw the Soviet move as a harbinger of renewed problems in Berlin, and he shared this concern with Theodore Sorensen by memorandum on August 23, preparing the president's political adviser for a meeting that day with Soviet ambassador Dobrynin and telling him what to say.[28]

Sorensen met with Dobrynin on August 23, and their discussion of the Berlin development and its impact on the president's domestic political prospects foreshadowed Kennedy's preoccupation with the political costs that unsettling developments in Cuba might inflict on him. Sorensen's write-up of his meeting with Dobrynin noted the ambassador's "agreement and understanding when I stressed on two different occasions (both relating to the fall elections, which seemed to be his principal topic of interest) that the President could not possibly lay himself open to Republican charges of appeasement in his response to any buildup in Berlin pressures between now and November 6 [election day]."[29]

Despite Sorensen's plea, Khrushchev seemed to be gingerly advancing rather than backing off. On August 28 the Soviet leader publicly informed UN acting secretary-general U Thant that the Soviet Union would soon enter into a "peace treaty" with the GDR terminating the latter's status as a territory under a "state of war" (i.e., dating from World War II), whereupon the "Western powers will lose their rights as occupiers to have occupation forces in West Berlin and therefore they will have to withdraw them from there."[30]

Khrushchev's treaty idea had been a bone of contention with the United States and its NATO allies for years, but the controversy had cooled after the resolution of the Berlin tank standoff of October 1961. For Khrushchev to suddenly raise the temperature at this juncture may have been a response to indications that Kennedy was reneging on his promise to terminate low-level surveillance flights over Soviet cargo ships bound for Cuba during August. Khrushchev's son, Sergei, emphasized the connection with Cuba when he later described his father's late August decision to revive the GDR peace treaty issue, although "the date for concluding the agreement was prudently not indicated. . . ." Sergei noted that "the Berlin splash was intended by Father as a diversion. Washington had begun focusing its attention too intently on Cuba." His father's "craftiness" worked when, "through already tested private channels," the White House "sent a request not to aggravate the situation in Europe until the election was over. Father agreed with alacrity—all right, let it be after the election."[31] Was Sergei's mention of activating "already tested private channels" a reference to the secret White

House meeting(s) Georgi Bolshakov had with the two Kennedy brothers? The historical evidence strongly suggests this.

On August 29, 1962, Republican Senator Homer Capehart of Indiana made a speech attacking the administration's Cuba policy and asking how long the United States should "continue to 'examine,' as President Kennedy has promised, the Soviet intervention in Cuba—the establishment, in fact, of a Communist beachhead 90 miles from American shores." A reporter subsequently cited Capehart's criticism in questions he posed to Kennedy at the president's news conference later that day.[32]

Also on August 29, an American U-2 overflight of Cuba produced startling news. U-2 surveillance of Cuba began after the Bay of Pigs calamity and had been increased to two per month in May 1962 in response to signs of "increased Soviet activity in Cuba." The first August overflight, mission 3086 on August 5, detected no Soviet military construction activity, but the second, mission 3088—initially scheduled for August 8 but postponed to August 29 because of bad weather—"revealed at least eight surface-to-air missile (SA-2) sites in the western half of Cuba."[33] As NPIC official Dino Brugioni would later note, "All of us at the Center were convinced that something extraordinary was happening, involving an exceptionally large amount of Soviet military hardware and manpower, and that additional SA-2 sites would probably be found on subsequent missions."[34]

The August 29 overflight also discovered other missiles, which needed more time for identification. Two follow-up U-2 flights on September 5 and 17 confirmed these were ground-to-ground cruise missiles of the type the Soviets referred to as *Sopka*, which may or may not have been capable of being configured with nuclear warheads. Hilsman opined in his first published account of the missile crisis released in 1967 that these weapons were of short range (thirty-five to forty miles) suitable for coastal defense against ships. Three decades later, however, his appraisal was more detailed and alarming; these Soviet cruise missiles "normally carry nuclear warheads and have a range of several hundred miles," and their "most likely" targets would have been US "troop concentrations in Florida if the United States started preparing for an invasion."[35] The president learned of the cruise missile findings at a tense meeting with CIA officials on September 7 described below.

Robert Kennedy subsequently referred to the troubling developments of August 29 in handwritten notes he prepared for himself three weeks later to outline the options facing the administration as of October 22, the day the president presented his televised address to the nation. The attorney general wrote: "Do Invasion or Strike," "Do Nothing," "Do Something," and then at the end of his notes he added the following illuminating expression of concern that he and his brother might later face criticism about "why we did not [take action] earlier." After listing a number of arguments emphasizing the administration's careful deliberations, the attorney general addressed the initial discovery of SAM-2 missiles by noting there was no evidence of *ballistic* missiles either in what was found on August 29 or in relation to Cuban sources on the ground as of that date: "2. Surveillance of island did not reveal missiles until last wk . . . August 29 Nothing present . . . won't allow Cubans on sites"[36]

The attorney general's last notation—"won't allow Cubans on sites"—referred to a clear but largely unheeded sign of danger. On September 15 US intelligence received a letter with "secret writing" from an informant on the island that Cubans had created a large restricted area in the Pinar del Rio province of western Cuba near the city of San Cristóbal. The area was reported to be "heavily guarded by Soviets with the assistance of Peruvian and Colombian nationals," with security "enforced to prevent access to the finca (plantation) of Dr. Cortina, at La Guira, where very secret and important work is in progress, believed to be concerned with missiles."[37] That area later turned out to be the site of the first Soviet ballistic missile installation to be discovered by a U-2 flight on October 14, 1962.

On August 30, 1962, two Cuban patrol boats fired on a low-flying US Navy antisubmarine search-and-attack bomber conducting a training mission over international waters approximately fifteen miles off the coast of Cuba. The president was informed immediately, but his alarm was not directed at the unlawful Cuban action, as might have been expected, but at the composition of the American air crew. As reported by Brugioni, the president asked: "What in the hell are reservists doing training so close to Cuba?" Sensitive to Republican attacks on the administration's Cuba policy and the demands by even Democratic senators for a more aggressive response by the administration, the president "asked that before news of the incident was released to the press, a protest be drafted and presented to the Cubans."[38]

Also on August 30, Republican congressional leaders accused the Kennedy administration "of following a course of fumbling and retreat in foreign policy and nuclear test negotiations."[39]

Kennedy's mounting concern that Cuba developments spelled domestic political trouble was validated on August 31. Curiously, the president did not activate the White House taping system for any of his meetings on August 31, although he had taped five of his conversations just the day before.

The CIA's August 31 "President's Checklist," provided to the White House that morning, informed President Kennedy that the August 29 U-2 overflight of Cuba had discovered "at least seven SA-2 sites on the western half of the island" and "seven or eight Soviet missile-equipped torpedo boats." The checklist described the vessels as converted PT boats of the *Komar* class "mounting two surface-to-surface missiles with an estimated range of 35 nautical miles."[40]

At one or more points during the day on August 31, President Kennedy conferred about surveillance measures concerning Cuba with at least four members of his White House national security advisory team: McGeorge Bundy, Carl Kaysen, General Ted Clifton, and Tazewell Shepard.[41]

Bundy sent the president a memorandum on August 31 recommending that Khrushchev's "present actions in Cuba do not justify" a US military operation in response. Interestingly, Bundy's memorandum attempted to articulate a principle that would call for a military response only in the face of a challenge to the country's "elemental national security." In Bundy's view, this meant something more threatening than a mere violation of the Monroe Doctrine. Posing the issue from the point of view of the Soviets, Bundy asked the president to consider what such a threat to their "elemental national security" would be. This was "not the same as [US] missiles in Turkey," but rather, in the national security adviser's opinion, was more "like the Soviet attitude toward the Black Sea or the Baltic states." Bundy concluded by focusing on the ramifications for US "domestic politics." He emphasized that "in domestic politics, again, we need to draw this same sharp distinction between what is now going on and what we would not tolerate. This will require a careful exposition from you, and it is the only reason for thinking that a press conference toward the end of next week may be important."[42]

The president's domestic political challenges also intensified on August 31. Press reports that day described an impending, coordinated Republican initiative focused on Cuba developments: "Determined to make inroads into the Democratic congressional majority, the Republican leadership met on August 31 and set the theme for the upcoming campaign. The Republicans would assail the administration's foreign policy as being one of making concession to and retreat from that of the Russians. . . ."[43] Sorensen reported similarly that "the Republican Senatorial and Congressional Campaign Committees announced that Cuba would be 'the dominant issue of the 1962 campaign.'"[44]

After acting CIA director Marshall Carter had given Bundy and Lemnitzer a "readout of U-2 flights showing SA-2 sites" based on photographs taken by a U-2 surveillance aircraft on August 29, the president "called General Carter at 1300, asked how many people had this information, and told General Carter that he wished it put back in the box and nailed tight."[45] Kennedy wanted the information to be strictly controlled and asked: "How many people know about it?" As Fursenko and Naftali would later observe: the president "did not even want the information to be shared with the working analysts at the CIA, for fear of leaks."[46]

At about 4:00 p.m. on August 31 Robert Kennedy received a briefing on the SAM installations from Arthur Lundahl, founder of the NPIC facility at the CIA, William A. Tidwell, the CIA's deputy director of intelligence (planning), and William Harvey. The meeting took place at the Justice Department and lasted until sometime before 4:45. The attorney general promptly set in motion the drafting of a warning to the Soviets that would later become the first White House "red line" statement released on September 4, which will be discussed in further detail below.[47]

New York Republican senator Kenneth Keating addressed the Senate at approximately 4:30 p.m. on August 31,[48] delivering a sharp attack on the administration's handling of the Soviet arms buildup in Cuba. He asserted that the Soviet personnel being transported to Cuba were "troops" and not "technicians," as the president had been claiming, that "in all probability" they were stationed "near a missile base," that "five Soviet torpedo boats" had been delivered to the island, and that a nighttime convoy including "closed vans" transporting "concave metal structures supported by tubing" had been detected "moving toward an installation . . . in a closely restricted area believed to contain a rocket installation."[49] Keating charged that the president's "look-the-other-way policy in Cuba depends to a large extent on popular ignorance of the facts," and that "the Soviet stronghold which is being established at this minute on the island of Cuba is undoubtedly a loaded gun that can be aimed directly at our military and space efforts."[50]

Commenting on the Keating speech, Richard Reeves observed that the New York senator possessed "the power to make the build-up, and the White House's calm reaction, evidence that John Kennedy just did not have the guts to stand up to the Communists even when they were only ninety miles away." These were "precisely the charges that Kennedy believed were his greatest political problem." Just as problematic, Kennedy believed that Keating was being fed the information for his speech by antiadministration officials in the Central Intelligence Agency, calling them "those CIA bastards." Kennedy then muttered a threat: "I'm going to get those bastards, if it's the last thing I ever do."[51]

It is known from a September 1 transmittal note by Carl Kaysen, deputy special assistant to the president for national security affairs, that the president also met with three other members of the White House national security team on August 31. Thus, Kaysen's September 1 note stated that the president "asked Gilpatric, Shepard and me [Kaysen]" several questions "before leaving yesterday" (i.e., August 31) for his weekend vacation in Newport, Rhode Island. Kaysen provided a "partial response" to those questions in a September 1 memorandum he wrote to the president, which was attached to his transmittal note and which covered three topics.[52]

First, Kaysen's memorandum attached a further memorandum on "Rules of Engagement for Aircraft in the Area of Cuba" prepared by the Joint Chiefs of Staff (JCS) "via Max Taylor's office." While the JCS paper has not been found, a cover memorandum prepared by Julian J. Ewell, their executive assistant to Clifton, summarized the paper, beginning with this highly illuminating statement: "Reconnaissance or other flights near Cuba will be conducted in a non-provocative manner, which is interpreted as generally flying parallel to the coast." The summary also listed three additional nonprovocative precautions that were to be taken: if unarmed US boats or aircraft were "harassed or attacked," they "will take evasive action"; "hot pursuit into Cuban air space" would be "authorized" but "may not be prolonged" and no "pursuing force" was to be organized; and finally, if armed US aircraft were to be harassed by Cuban aircraft, they were under instructions to merely "attempt to shoulder them off and shepherd them back into Cuban air space or waters."[53]

Second, Kaysen referred to an ongoing review the president had asked for "all our reconnaissance operations in the neighborhood of Cuba." Kaysen reassured the president that Gilpatric was taking steps to "see that we don't do anything this weekend that might lead to another incident"—presumably referring to the August 30 attack by a Cuban patrol boat on a US antisubmarine surveillance plane flying over international waters. Kaysen also told the president that all but one of the military's reconnaissance flights were "well without the range of antiaircraft capability," the one exception involving "electronic intelligence," which was "possibly within the range of Cuban based missiles," was being "carefully reviewed" and would not "present[] any hazard" the next time it was flown on September 4. U-2 overflights of Cuba were not specifically mentioned in Kaysen's September 1 memorandum to the president but, as will be seen, they, too, would soon be affected, and indeed would be severely curtailed.

Third, Kaysen referred to "routine patrol missions" flown by air units subordinate to the commander in chief of the Atlantic fleet that conducted "low level reconnaissance of shipping," a tactic Kaysen called "a routine part of antisubmarine operations" that "does not contravene international law." Kaysen added that "we are now in process of examining orders under which such flights operate in considering the extent to which they are useful and should be run in similar aircraft." This third topic may well have been raised by the president as he pondered the assurance he had given to Khrushchev through Bolshakov at their White House meeting on July 31, possibly repeated at their second meeting on August 31, that he was terminating surveillance of Soviet ships by low-flying military aircraft—what Khrushchev referred to as unlawful (also "piratical") "buzzing" of cargo ships headed to Cuba.[54]

Might the president have known at this time that the Soviet arms shipments to Cuba included ballistic missiles? There is some fragmentary evidence, as yet unconfirmed, that as early as July 1962 President Kennedy may in fact have been expecting the Soviets to send ballistic missiles to Cuba. That evidence appears in the form of a statement by Lieutenant Commander Gerry McCabe, who had served throughout 1962 as the president's assistant naval aide and duty officer for the Situation Room at the White House. McCabe had been "cleared for special and compartmented intelligence" and was "in everyday contact with both the president and McGeorge Bundy." He attended Bundy's daily morning staff meetings and "act[ed] as a courier for sensitive information." McCabe, who "recorded his observations in a diary that he kept during his years with Kennedy," later told US Naval Academy scholar Robert Beer that the "president became aware of the planned introduction of Russian nuclear missiles into Cuba sometime in early July," having "learned that Raul Castro had agreed with Khrushchev that the Russians could install nuclear missiles in Cuba and that they could start doing it . . . in the fall." Although McCabe was unable to pinpoint the source of the intelligence, Beer speculated that it was from "communications intercepts or a highly placed spy"—data that would have been the most highly classified and tightly held within the US government, perhaps provided to the president alone.[55]

Georgi Bolshakov remembered receiving an unexpected early call from the attorney general on the morning of August 31 inviting him to come by later that same day. When the Soviet agent dutifully appeared late that afternoon, the attorney general "announced the President was waiting for me" and said, "He knows you are leaving for Moscow, and he'd like to hand over his message to Khrushchev right upon your arrival there." The two thereupon "got into a black executive Lincoln and set off for the White House."[56]

The president's secretary, Evelyn Lincoln, recorded many of Kennedy's White House meetings on a daily desk calendar. The entry for August 31, 1962, showed that Kennedy met with Dean Rusk and the attorney general from 4:40 to 5:20 p.m., and Lincoln's "Day at a Glance" placed the attorney general's arrival at 4:45 p.m.[57] No record of the subjects discussed at this meeting has been found, nor do White House records available to historians indicate that Georgi Bolshakov, too, would be present at the White House with the president and the attorney general.

Although no record of Bolshakov's arrival for the meeting could be found in the available White House security logs, this should not be surprising; a similar covert visit to the White House would have been within the recent memory of the GRU colonel, who would most likely have accompanied Khrushchev's son-in-law Alexei Adzhubei on a similar secret visit to the president earlier in 1962. As described by Adzhubei in his lengthy report of his private meeting with President Kennedy on January 31, 1962, "Through Bolshakov, [Presidential Press Secretary Pierre] Salinger agreed that at 6:00 that evening he would send a car for me from the White House, in which I would ride around the city so that journalists would not discover the president's new meeting with a Soviet editor." After a circuitous journey "down some long streets," the car eventually arrived "at the White House at the president's private entrance," where "the gate opened quickly, we were asked for no documents, and the car went immediately through the entrance."[58]

According to Bolshakov's account of his August 31 visit to the White House, published in February 1989, twenty-seven years later, the attorney general accompanied him from the Justice Department to the White House, where they were immediately ushered in to see the president. No one else was present. Bolshakov's 1989 account confusingly states that the president provided the assurance that Kremlin records confirm he had conveyed to Bolshakov exactly one month earlier, during the July 31 private meeting in the White House: that the president had on that day ordered the termination of low-level surveillance flights over Soviet vessels. Here is how Bolshakov recounted Kennedy's August 31, 1962, comments, almost three decades after the fact:

> I'd like you to do me a favour and communicate to Premier Khrushchev the following: Llewellyn Thompson, our Ambassador in Moscow, informs me Khrushchev is concerned over our planes flying low over Soviet Cuba-bound ships. Tell him I've ordered these flyovers stopped today. . . . I believe that the outlook for American-Soviet relations is good. I am profoundly convinced of that. To my mind, the signing of a treaty on banning nuclear tests will be the next milestone along the road to their improvement. The signing of such a Treaty could mark the initial stage of our two countries' disarmament, and we would spare our children and grandchildren the war threat. . . . Tell Khrushchev I hope seeing him again in the near future.[59]

Bolshakov seems to have conflated the president's comments at the two sequential White House meetings held one month apart. The president's reference to "our ambassador" Llewellyn Thompson, and the air surveillance issue, clearly referred to what the president had told Bolshakov at the White House meeting *on July 31*, not August 31, as can be seen by considering two fairly obvious flaws in Bolshakov's 1989 *New Times* account. First, Thompson had returned from Moscow in July, not August, having had his farewell dinner with Khrushchev on July 25.[60] He carried Khrushchev's request for abatement of US close-in air surveillance of Cuba-bound ships back to the White House in late July, not late August. Moreover, Khrushchev would later remind the president of his July 31 assurance that he had "that same day" ordered cessation of the complained-of buzzing overflights in a private letter he would have Dobrynin deliver to Kennedy in late September. Khrushchev made clear that the president's assurance had been transmitted in July, since the Soviet chairman's letter chided the president for having broken his word, as evidenced by 140 violations of the commitment in August alone.[61]

Second, because Thompson had given up his ambassadorial post in July and been replaced in that position by Foy Kohler, the president would not have referred to Thompson as "our Ambassador in Moscow" more than a month after he had ceased being ambassador. When one then considers the Kremlin records placing the air surveillance assurance on July 31, it becomes clear that Bolshakov was mistaken in his dates.

On the other hand, Bolshakov's recollection that the president had mentioned the test ban treaty squares well with the Kremlin's instruction to Bolshakov *after* the July 31 White House meeting that he should "speak to the Kennedys about the test ban issue.[62] Moreover, the specific steps taken in response to President Kennedy's directives on August 31—that is, curtailment of US surveillance near and over Cuba, with such flights to "be conducted in a non-provocative manner, which is interpreted as generally flying parallel to the coast," and a reevaluation of "low level reconnaissance of shipping" and the extent to which that tactic was "useful and should be run in similar aircraft"— were certainly consistent with a renewed presidential assurance that could have been given to Bolshakov on the evening of August 31 to the effect that "these flyovers" would be "stopped today." On balance, it seems likely that Bolshakov's 1989 recollection of his private conversation with the president and attorney general at the White House on August 31, 1962, is at least partially accurate, even if not complete, and even if the much later recounting may have inadvertently conflated some features of two discussions of the same topic at the same location one month apart.

As Bolshakov left his meeting with the president, accompanied by the attorney general, Robert Kennedy gave vent to one of the most alarming expressions of fear and frustration that history has attributed to him. According to Bolshakov's account, the attorney general "burst out suddenly" saying: "Goddamn it, Georgi, [d]oesn't Premier Khrushchev realize the President's position? Doesn't the Premier know that the President has enemies as well as friends?" Assuring Bolshakov that "my brother really means what he says about Soviet-American relations," the younger Kennedy complained that "every step he takes to meet Premier Khrushchev halfway costs the brother a lot of effort. If the Premier just took the trouble to be, for a moment at least, in the President's shoes he would understand him." Then he offered this chilling warning about the president's enemies: "In a gust of blind hate, 'they' may go to any length. . . ." The timing of the attorney general's outburst certainly fits with the escalating partisan accusations that were being made by Republican leaders in Congress and the increasingly alarming Soviet arms shipments that were observed almost daily in Cuba on August 31 and the days immediately preceding. It is harder to imagine the attorney general being so exercised on July 31, when things were far more quiet unless the source of his anxiety was looming trouble in his dealing with Bolshakov further afield—over Laos for example.[63]

As demonstrated above, it seems most likely that Bolshakov was simply confused in his assignment of the buzzing-cessation statement to the August 31 meeting, rather than to the meeting a month earlier when it was demonstrably made, or both meetings. But might there have been no White House meeting on August 31? Could there have been only a single Bolshakov meeting with the Kennedy brothers at the White House, which occurred on July 31? Bolshakov's two articles place him in the White House with the president on August 31. Further, both versions of Bolshakov's report on his August 31 meeting at the White House contain details that seem to corroborate the August 31 timing of the meeting even if one seems mistaken as to the range of topics discussed.

Thus, the logistical details Bolshakov provided in his recounting of the August 31 meeting square with several known facts about what was happening at the end of August and early to mid-September. These include the fact that Bolshakov reported the substance of his August 31 White House meeting when he met with his superiors in Moscow, and he was then directed to meet with Khrushchev in mid-September at the latter's vacation retreat in Pitsunda on the Black Sea.[64]

Finally, Bolshakov described this precise sequence of events to Robert Kennedy only a few weeks after his Pitsunda visit with Khrushchev and Mikoyan when the GRU agent met with the attorney general at the latter's office in early October on a date that has been variously placed on October 5, 7, or 8. In his two published recollections, Bolshakov reported to Robert Kennedy in early October what Khrushchev (and Mikoyan) had told him in mid-September to relay to the Kennedys: that the Soviet leaders "welcome the President's moves aimed at reducing tensions and bringing the relations between our two countries back to normal," "hope President Kennedy will keep his word and prevent things from taking a dangerous turn," believe "it is necessary to make every effort to reduce tensions instead of stepping them up by interfering in other countries' internal affairs as the United States appears to be doing with regard to Cuba," and "are perfectly well aware of President Kennedy's position, and will not take any action with regard to the United States before the elections to Congress due in November 1962 and hope that after the elections we shall get down to a new round of active negotiations."

There is also the curious incident Bolshakov described as the younger Kennedy agonizing about the president's enemies, who might "go to any length" in "a gust of blind hate." The attorney general's outburst would most plausibly have occurred on August 31 in the immediate aftermath of Khrushchev's mischievous message to the UN secretary-general on August 28 renewing the GDR treaty fight, the CIA's discovery on August 29 of SAM-2 missiles among the Soviet arms shipments, and Senator Keating's August 31

Senate speech charging the president and his administration with "willful neglect" for their failure to detect Soviet missile bases in Cuba. By contrast, it is hard to see how Robert Kennedy would have been anywhere near as upset on July 31 when none of these aggravating events was occurring.

There is some fragmentary evidence that might rule out an August 31 meeting however. FBI files on Bolshakov's movements include informant statements that the GRU colonel left the United States for his vacation in Russia on August 3, and that this was meant to be a vacation of "approximately one month" duration. FBI files that have been released thus far contain no indication of his return before October 2.[65] Might Bolshakov have taken a two month vacation during this critical juncture?

No tape recording or other documentation of the August 31 White House meeting with Bolshakov has yet been uncovered, apart from the GRU officer's own published reminiscence published in 1989. The White House taping system apparently was not activated for the meeting, and no notes by either the president or his brother have been found. Did the president follow up the August 31 oral message he transmitted through Bolshakov by a *written* statement? Here again, Commander Gerry McCabe told his 1989 interviewer that some time before September 4, 1962, "Dean Rusk gave the president a draft letter to be sent to Khrushchev" and that "so far as I [McCabe] know, the letter was sent." Robert Beer speculated that the letter was probably delivered by the attorney general to Soviet ambassador Dobrynin at their meeting on September 4.[66]

The undocumented word of a single White House staffer, no matter how well placed, would not be sufficient to prove the truth of assertions as provocative as early presidential knowledge of secret intelligence that Soviet missiles were being shipped to Cuba, and transmission of the president's private word to Khrushchev in conjunction with that early knowledge. Nevertheless, the sequence of documented events that followed is at least consistent with these details. Within a few short weeks after the July 31 White House meeting with Bolshakov, McGeorge Bundy on August 23 would issue National Security Action Memorandum (NSAM) 181, which ordered two illuminating action items directed to the possibility that Soviet ballistic missiles might be placed in Cuba. Number 5 was "an analysis . . . of the probable military, political, and psychological impact of the establishment in Cuba of either surface-to-air missiles or surface-to-surface missiles which could reach the U.S.," and number 6 was "a study . . . of the advantages and disadvantages of making a statement that the United States would not tolerate the establishment of military forces (missile or air, or both?) which might launch a nuclear attack from Cuba against the U.S."[67] NSAM 181 will be discussed at greater length below.

Then, at a meeting between the president and his top foreign policy advisers on September 4, the matter of Soviet surface-to-surface nuclear missiles in Cuba came up in the discussion directly and without generating much alarm. McNamara said: "And I further feel that [the Soviets will] be adding to what could be interpreted as offensive strength in the months ahead." The president asked, "The missiles really are what are significant?" and Bundy responded, "Surface-to-surface missiles are the turning point." McNamara then added: "They can, they may well put surface-to-surface missiles or missile launchers, artillery or missile launchers in there. . . . Is it equipped with a nuclear warhead or isn't it equipped with a nuclear warhead?" The underlying issue before the small group on September 4 was how to draft the public message that would ultimately be sent at the end of the day warning the Soviets not to place offensive weapons in Cuba.

But should the message refer specifically to nuclear armed missiles? McNamara worried that even mentioning such hot-button weapons would overly inflame the already troublesome commentary coming out of Congress: "I just worry about the President having made a statement which can be used as a lever by elements of the Congress and of the public, unless we know exactly what we're going to do under those circumstances." Rusk would later echo this concern: "Well, if we designated ground-to-ground missiles or we specified the nuclear weapon, I think we would create a kind of panic that the facts themselves don't now justify." Bundy chimed in, "That's correct," and Rusk followed with the suggestion that "it would be better to get a warning to the Soviets in more general terms. . . ."

When McNamara had offered his initial "I just worry . . ." comment, Bundy responded with an extraordinary statement about what the administration would need to do if the United States discovered Soviet nuclear ballistic missiles in Cuba: "Our preliminary analysis of the consequences for us, Bob, of the establishment of a surface-to-surface nuclear capability gives me at least the feeling that we wouldn't have to act." Rusk disagreed ("I think we'd have to act, Bob . . ."), and McNamara made an elliptical comment (". . . If we do it then, why wouldn't we do it today?"). President Kennedy then stepped in and provided his own thinking in line with Bundy—that the United States would not be required to act in the face of nuclear missiles in Cuba because of the escalating threat to Berlin: "The reason we don't is that, is because we figure that they may try to blockade Berlin and we would then try to blockade Cuba. But I think that the reason we don't today is the [*unclear*] is that it wouldn't do them that much harm for quite a while . . . and then Berlin would be the obvious response."

As Philip Zelikow and Ernest May stated about President Kennedy in their preface to volume 2 of the *Presidential Recordings*, the tapes "make abundantly clear that his preoccupation was not with Cuba or the immediate threat to the United States." Rather, his fear was that "if he did not insist on removal of the missiles," Khrushchev "would be emboldened to try to take over West Berlin" and the president would be left with a painful choice between "abandon[ing] two and a half million West Berliners" or "use nuclear weapons against the Soviet Union.[68]

Although the president's September 4 comments about Berlin are not a model of clarity, it is evident he would not have been especially troubled to learn the Soviets were installing nuclear missiles in Cuba, and that his chief concern even in that scenario would have been to avoid giving Khrushchev justification for a move on Berlin, leading to a choice between passive US acquiescence or the extreme danger of a nuclear response. Indeed, the president's thinking was still focused on Berlin rather than Cuba as late as September 30, 1962, when he privately shared with his longtime friend British ambassador David Ormsby-Gore, that Khrushchev "was trying to goad him to invade Cuba, thus giving the Soviets a pretext to seize West Berlin."[69]

In the event, the public message that the White House would issue at the end of the day on September 4 would be a compromise: an acknowledgment that there was "no evidence" yet of "the presence of offensive ground-to-ground missiles or of other significant offensive capability" in Cuba, and a warning that "were it to be otherwise, the gravest issues would arise."[70] No specific mention was made of nuclear weapons.

Kennedy activated the White House taping system five times on September 4, and all five involved Cuba. After that date, however, the number of times the taping system was activated dropped precipitously. The tape was turned on during parts of only thirteen of the forty-one days between September 5 and October 15 (September 5, 10, 13, 25, 28, 29, and 30 and October 1, 2, 3, 8, 9, and 10), and on only three of those occasions (September 5, 13, and 29) did Cuba come up as a direct subject of any discussion. Then, once again, beginning on October 16, the first day of the Cuban missile crisis, and for weeks thereafter the taping system was in nearly continuous use, and Cuba was the predominant topic of the recorded discussions. Interestingly, the almost continuous five-week gap in use of the White House taping system for Cuba-related discussions was almost exactly coincident with a five-week gap in U-2 overhead surveillance of Cuba, a subject to which we will turn in chapter 6.

It was not long before officials at the CIA ("those bastards") felt the president's burning anger at the apparent leaks to his Republican critics of the Intelligence Community's mounting findings of Soviet weapons systems showing up in Cuba. The intense heat first appeared at a September 7 meeting between the president and agency officials during which the president was informed of the discovery of Soviet surface-to-surface cruise missiles in Banes, Cuba—apparently a direct violation of the president's red-line "gravest issues" warning against such weapons, issued on September 4. Then, just three days later, the CIA was treated to an even darker exhibition of the president's wrath in the form of a written question McGeorge Bundy handed to CIA acting director Carter on September 10, giving him thirty minutes to refute White House suspicions that someone in the agency's "operations or planning" bureau might intentionally "provoke" an incident disclosing US intelligence collection methods involving U-2 aircraft overflying Cuba. In both instances, the president's harsh message led to curtailment of the gathering and dissemination of intelligence information concerning the Soviet buildup in Cuba.

Much would later be made of the fact that Khrushchev attempted to conceal the true nature of his arms buildup in the Caribbean and supposedly lied to the president both directly and through intermediaries about the specific types of weapons that were being sent to Cuba (see chapter 8). Yet no scholar of the crisis appears to have seriously pursued the question why the president never used his frequent correspondence with the Soviet chairman or their back-channel messages to directly ask Khrushchev the specific $64,000 question: "Do your arms shipments include any ballistic missiles or nuclear weapons?" As will be seen below, there were indications Khrushchev believed that Kennedy either knew about the Soviet missiles in early October or preferred not to learn the true facts while the midterm elections were hanging over him.

President Kennedy had additional reasons to doubt that the Soviets would intentionally provoke an armed conflict. He had learned shortly after taking office that the United States held a commanding lead over the Soviets in strategic nuclear weapons, that the lead would be growing larger in the coming years, and accordingly that there seemed to be little likelihood that Khrushchev would expect to come out ahead if he engaged in open aggression, at least for the foreseeable future. Conversely, he was also convinced that, because the Soviets already possessed ICBM missiles that could reach the United States, an adequate deterrent effect against the Americans was already in place and it would make little difference if more Soviet missiles in other locations might be added to the equation.

It is clear in retrospect that the president's oral message to Khrushchev via Bolshakov proposed confirmation of a mutual understanding emerging between the two leaders whereby both sides would exercise reciprocal restraint in their actions regarding Berlin and Cuba until after the US midterm elections. This can be demonstrated by reference to four important, documented messages from Khrushchev to Kennedy during the forty days between September 6 and October 16, 1962, and by comments made by Anastas Mikoyan to the Cuban leadership on November 4, 1962, in an effort to explain Khrushchev's thinking in the lead-up to the crisis.

The first important documentation of the emerging deal arrived at the White House on September 6, 1962. In an oral message conveyed by Ambassador Dobrynin to Kennedy aide Theodore Sorensen, Khrushchev confirmed that he would suspend his GDR treaty initiative and do nothing further regarding Berlin—until after the midterm elections—that would "complicate the international situation or aggravate the tension in the relations between [the] two countries," including "a German peace settlement and West Berlin." Khrushchev expected that Kennedy would in turn take "no actions . . . on the other side which would change the situation." Kennedy's "other side" of that bargain clearly referred to Cuba.

The foregoing remarks that I have placed in quotation marks are found in the meeting memorandum Sorensen prepared following his encounter with Dobrynin on September 6, 1962, just one week after Bolshakov's reported August 31 White House meeting. Sorensen noted that Dobrynin read the message slowly so that it could be transcribed exactly and relayed to the president word for word.[71] Sorensen reported further on this remarkable exchange in his "Memorandum for the Files" written that same day. After noting that Dobrynin said "he had received a personal message from Chairman Khrushchev directing him to make known directly to [Sorensen]" the following specific message intended to be read slowly so that Sorensen could take notes as the message was read to him, Sorensen committed the following to his file memorandum using quotation marks to confirm wording precision: "First, 'nothing will be undertaken before the American Congressional elections that could complicate the international situation or aggravate the tension in the relations between our two countries. We shall follow this course, provided there are no actions taken on the other side which would change the situation. This includes a German peace settlement and West Berlin.'"[72]

Note Khrushchev's specific assurance that a GDR peace settlement would be put on hold. This would have been top-of-mind for President Kennedy on August 31 and would certainly have been a condition he would have been insisting on as part of any agreed reciprocal stand-down in superpower tensions before the midterm elections. But the Cuba situation was becoming increasingly problematic for the president. Sorensen thus responded to Dobrynin that he "appreciate[d]" the message, but he conveyed the president's "feeling that the recent Soviet actions in Cuba"—presumably referring to Sorensen's description of the arms buildup as including "Soviet military personnel, electronic equipment and missile preparations"—"had already caused considerable turmoil" and "a far more difficult problem for the administration politically," and that the president "regarded the Cuban action, therefore, as something of a deliberate and personal affront." Sorensen reported Dobrynin's response to this rejoinder on the Cuban issues as follows: "He repeated several times . . . that they had done nothing new or extraordinary in Cuba—that the events causing all the excitement had been taking place somewhat gradually and quietly over a long period of time—and that he stood by his assurances that all of these steps were defensive in nature and did not represent any threat to the security of the United States. He neither contradicted nor confirmed my reference to large numbers of Soviet military personnel, electronic equipment and missile preparations."[73]

In effect, what Khrushchev proposed on September 6 was a reciprocal understanding that both sides would refrain from taking actions that might "complicate the international situation" at least up until the November 6 midterm elections. This meant that the Soviets would temporarily stand down from their announcement regarding "a German peace settlement and West Berlin" provided that the Kennedy administration would in return take "no actions" that would "change the situation" either in Berlin or in respect of the Kremlin's "defensive" arms buildup in Cuba.

Mark White noted that Republican senator Keating seemed to have suspected the presence of an emerging Berlin-Cuba reciprocity deal, and the secretary of state tried to stifle this speculation: "Dean Rusk, for example, telephoned on 11 September to berate [Keating] for charging that Kennedy and Khrushchev had made an arrangement whereby the Soviets would limit their involvement in Cuba in return for American restraint over Berlin."[74]

Beschloss seems to have drawn this same conclusion that a kind of Cold War armistice was in play, even though he was apparently unaware of Bolshakov's reported August 31 White House meeting. Referring to Dobrynin's September 6 message read to Sorensen, Beschloss concluded that "by signaling the President that the Soviet Union would not do anything to harm him until after his elections, Khrushchev was not only trying to throw Kennedy off guard but he may have been encouraging the President, if the missiles were found before November, to explain them away to his own generals as purely defensive and conceal them from the public until the balloting was done."[75]

A curious "leaking" incident occurred at just this moment with strikingly adverse consequences for the US intelligence community's ability to keep track of Soviet arms shipments to Cuba. According to an internal CIA memorandum from the assistant director for research and reports to the deputy director (intelligence), dated September 11, 1962, the State Department had a week before leaked the CIA's reporting of Soviet arms-carrying cargo ships to journalists, leading to a *Washington Post* article appearing a mere twelve hours after the CIA report had reached the department. This led, according to the CIA's assistant director for research and reports, to "a regrettable experience of loss of sources in this area through unbridled use of the material by persons for whom research has been performed." The memorandum listed three categories of information sources that had been lost to NSA surveillance.[76] Matthew Aid would later describe the consequences of this State Department leak as "devastating" and a "disaster" for intelligence collection: "By mid-September, NSA had lost its ability to provide the U.S. intelligence community with details concerning what weapons Soviet merchant ships were carrying to these countries."[77]

Dobrynin delivered a second "oral message" from Khrushchev to the president via the attorney general on September 18, 1962, according to the Soviet ambassador's memoirs. The new document, which was in the form of a fifteen-page English translation of Khrushchev's message for the president that Dobrynin had prepared himself for hand-delivery to Robert Kennedy, was, according to Dobrynin, "the most detailed and significant statement of the Soviet leadership's views about relations with the Kennedy administration shortly before the Cuban crisis."[78] Remarkably, many historians have neglected to call serious attention to what Dobrynin called his "strictly unofficial but complete translated text of this 'oral' message," which "officially did not exist."[79]

Dobrynin's memoirs, published in 1995, revealed that he followed a practice in transmitting Khrushchev's long messages of "translating these messages into English beforehand." He would then "give the addressee a brief oral account and hand over a strictly unofficial text of this 'oral' message"—which was a practice that "suited Rusk, Robert Kennedy, and the president fine."[80] Dobrynin's memoirs provided a revealing summary of the September 18 message's key points, and of Robert Kennedy's reaction to the message upon hearing it and receiving the "strictly unofficial"—that is, officially deniable—copy. According to Dobrynin, Khrushchev began by disavowing responsibility for problems in Soviet-American relations, which he blamed on the "unnatural situation" in Berlin, where he promised again "to freeze matters until after the election." Then, after citing his pleasant recent discussions with Secretary of Interior Stewart Udall, Khrushchev contrasted his own forbearance regarding Berlin with America's aggressive moves on Cuba. Thus, the Soviet chairman complained about Kennedy's unexpected September 7 decision "to ask Congress to call out 150,000 reservists" at a time when "the Soviet Union was doing nothing to provoke tensions while the United States was making 'piratical demands' to inspect Soviet ships heading for Cuba."

Dobrynin said that he fully expected an "unpleasant and probably stormy conversation" after Robert Kennedy read Khrushchev's message, but that he was "surprised" at what occurred next: "[RFK] contented himself with saying, somewhat gloomily, that he was going to pass the message to his brother on the same day. He refrained from discussing any specific questions apart from saying that it would be a good idea for both countries to refrain from any action, including action in Berlin, that could aggravate the situation before the congressional elections."[81] This was the third time the Kennedy administration had explicitly asked for a stand-down in tensions through the US midterm elections: the first occurring at the president's meeting with Bolshakov on July 31, the second during Sorensen's meeting with Dobrynin on August 23.

The attorney general's specific reference to the midterm elections seems to provide definitive evidence that domestic politics was still uppermost in the president's mind on September 18, and this despite the known presence in Cuba of Soviet surface-to-air antiaircraft missiles and surface-to-surface cruise missiles threatening US naval vessels as far as forty miles offshore in international waters. Of course the September 18 comments were made by the attorney general and not by the president himself. Yet Robert Kennedy would underscore the same point the next time he met with Ambassador Dobrynin, this time in the fraught circumstances of October 23, the day after the president had publicly announced the discovery of Soviet ballistic missiles in Cuba. Once again, Robert Kennedy's comments were memorialized by Dobrynin, this time in his telegrams back to the Kremlin. As reported by William Taubman in his biography of Nikita Khrushchev, Robert Kennedy called on Dobrynin at the latter's office that same evening of October 23 in a state of extreme agitation: "According to Dobrynin, the attorney general was 'obviously upset; he kept repeating himself and going off on tangents.' Kennedy said his brother had 'staked his political career' on Soviet assurances about Cuba."[82]

It is possible that the September 18 oral message Dobrynin described in his memoirs is the same document—though given a different date by the White House—as the lengthy message from Khrushchev to Kennedy that historians have accepted as having been transmitted ten days later on September 28, 1962.[83] Although the first half of this important letter covered nuclear test ban treaty matters not mentioned in Dobrynin's memoirs, the last half provides an extensive discussion of tensions over Berlin and Cuba, and of the connection between hostile acts in each region and conditions in the other. This fact, combined with the appearance in the September 28 letter of several notable words and phrases mentioned in Dobrynin's summary of the September 18 letter,[84] suggest that the two documents are likely the same one.

In the second half of the September 28 letter Khrushchev turned abruptly to the topic that had been discussed at Dobrynin's meeting with Robert Kennedy on September 4: "During his meeting with Ambassador Dobrynin Robert Kennedy referring to you, Mr. President, confidentially touched upon the problem of Soviet-American relations." Khrushchev began this discussion by citing the problems over West Berlin, and he emphasized that his side was blameless for any increase in tensions attributable to this long-standing point of tension. But then the Soviet chairman shifted from the situation in West Berlin to the president's domestic political challenges in the run-up to the "congressional elections," and he observed that he was aware of "traditions" in the United States that in the course of election struggle politicians get "carried away by passions," take leave of "common sense and begin playing with fire, competing in saying more and louder absurd things that sow danger of world war. . . ." He cited in this context President Kennedy's September 7 request for congressional authorization to call up 150,000 reservists, which he linked to "threats against Cuba" and labeled an "inconceivable step" that made "the atmosphere red-hot" and forced "the other side to respond in kind."

Khrushchev reminded the president of the deal he thought the two of them had reached back on July 31 when Kennedy claimed to have ended close-in air surveillance on Soviet shipping in exchange for Khrushchev putting Berlin tensions on ice until the US midterm elections. The Soviet chairman then noted, "We had in mind that after elections we would resume the dialogue. We were under the impression that we would meet an understanding on the part of the American side. . . ." The Soviet chairman referred to the two leaders' bilateral stand-down in terms that seemed to echo the similar call for mutual restraint made by Robert Kennedy to Dobrynin earlier in September: "If there were no statement by you on Cuba, we, naturally, as Ambassador Thompson and Mr. Udall were told, would not say anything on West Berlin. Your statement forced us to do so."

Khrushchev closed his letter by asking Kennedy to abide by their reciprocal tension-reducing arrangement in the two areas of conflict: "Therefore I would ask you to correctly understand our anxiety and not to do anything that could further aggravate the atmosphere and even expose the world. We on our part again say to you that we will do nothing with regard to West Berlin until the elections in the U.S."[85]

It is perhaps noteworthy that there is evidence the Soviets believed at this time that the United States, or at least the president, may have known about the Soviet missiles in Cuba by as early as mid-September, and that the Kremlin believed he planned to take no action before the congressional elections. Garthoff noted that the evidence stemmed from an "intriguing datum" from conversations in November 1962 in which Mikoyan had informed Castro of the Soviet leaders' belief "that the Americans had learned of the transport of 'Soviet troops and strategic missiles' to Cuba by mid-September." According to Mikoyan, "'Kennedy didn't want to speak [publicly] about Soviet missiles in Cuba until after the congressional elections' but his hand was forced by the public disclosure by Republican senators (not named, but Senators Kenneth Keating [R-NY] and Everett Dirksen [R-IL]. Mikoyan added that we, the Soviet leaders, 'had no information on how he intended to act.' They believed, however, according to Mikoyan, that Kennedy had intentionally been holding back because of the election campaign and therefore that he presumably was inclined to acquiesce in the deployment."[86]

The White House taping system recorded a meeting between the president and two of his top Soviet experts, Llewellyn Thompson and Charles Bohlen, beginning at 11:00 a.m. on September 29, at which the September 28 letter was discussed at some length. Thompson noted Khrushchev's comments about "our buzzing their ships," but the former ambassador's reaction was merely to the fact that this had caused the Soviet leader some "annoyance"; Thompson said nothing about Khrushchev's assertion that the president had agreed to stop the close-in air surveillance.[87]

As noted, President Kennedy apparently failed to provide any official response to Khrushchev's observations about the interrelated East-West problems in Berlin and Cuba despite having told the Soviet chairman in his October 8 responding letter that he would do so. While Kennedy chose to respond on October 8 only to Khrushchev's views on test ban treaty matters and ignore his rival's provocative rendition of the tensions raised by the two men's dealings on Berlin and Cuba, Dobrynin did just the opposite, electing to pass over the entire subject of a test ban and record instead only Khrushchev's comments on Berlin and Cuba.

It would appear that the mutual forbearance deal was reconfirmed yet again in a third documented message Khrushchev sent to President Kennedy. The messenger this time was Bolshakov, who met with Robert Kennedy on October 7 or 8, 1962, to deliver an oral message from Khrushchev meant for the president. Told that the president was too busy to see him, the GRU officer slowly dictated to the attorney general a precisely worded message he said had been dictated to him by Khrushchev in mid-September with directions that he "was to convey to the President of the United States by word of mouth."[88] Bolshakov would later repeat this message in two 1989 articles he published in Soviet journals:

> In mid-September . . . , I was received by Khrushchev and Mikoyan, who listened carefully to President Kennedy's oral message of 31 August, presented to me in your [Robert Kennedy's] presence. . . . The Soviet leaders . . . positively assess the President's steps aimed at reducing tensions and at the normalization of relations between our nations. However, they must point out to the President that the situation has recently worsened mainly because of hostile actions by the American government in the area of the Caribbean Sea, around Cuba. Khrushchev and other Soviet leaders are disappointed with this development of events and hope that President Kennedy will keep his word and not permit events to develop in a dangerous direction. . . .
>
> Premier Khrushchev is concerned about the situation created by the

> United States around Cuba, and we repeat once again that the Soviet Union is sending only defensive weapons to Cuba and not weapons for aggressive purposes against any state on the American continent, including the United States. The Soviet leaders understand President Kennedy's situation well and will not undertake any actions regarding the United States before the congressional elections in November 1962, and they hope that we can begin a new round of active talks when the elections are over.[89]

The Bolshakov message made clear that there was a coalescing Khrushchev-Kennedy understanding based on the president's "steps aimed at reducing tensions," and his keeping "his word" not to "permit events to develop in a dangerous direction." The pact was meant to be reciprocal, it included abatement of tensions on both the Berlin and Cuba fronts, and it was meant to last at least through the November 6 congressional elections.

A fourth documented message from Khrushchev along these lines was given personally by the Soviet chairman to US ambassador Kohler on October 16. Reported in Kohler's cable 133 on that date, Khrushchev said in pertinent part that "US elections will take place . . . and then we'll try to renew dialogue and reach agreement. Soviets won't sign peace treaty immediately; they know unilateral signing would be aggravation. . . . For time being, Soviets would do nothing and make no statements until elections. [Khrushchev] had given his word on that. . . . Khrushchev repeated that they would not undertake anything to worsen relations. He regretted that things had not worked out in accordance with his discussion with Ambassador Thompson. It was regrettable that Cuban question had blown up right in the middle of election campaign."

Further evidence of the existence of an agreement between Kennedy and Khrushchev may be found in the fact that each leader (or his surrogates) complained on several occasions that the other side had not carried through on its side of the bargain. Thus, as noted previously, there was the White House meeting that included Robert Kennedy's outburst as he accompanied Bolshakov on their way out of the meeting demonstrated his frustration with Khrushchev's insensitivity to the need for full compliance: "Every step [President Kennedy] takes to meet Premier Khrushchev halfway" involves political "costs," and this may mean that the president's enemies "in a gust of blind hate" may "go to any length." Later, as will be seen below, on October 22 President Kennedy would complain to Prime Minister Macmillan that Khrushchev was playing a "double game": "You remember that he kept saying he was coming over here after the election and would do nothing to disturb the situation until after the election. He said that the weapons were defensive, that they weren't moving any missiles there and all the rest. And obviously he has been building this up in order to face us with a bad situation in November at the time he was going to squeeze us on Berlin."[90] And then on October 27 Robert Kennedy would refer to this same perceived perfidy on Khrushchev's part as a "double-cross."

Khrushchev, for his part, complained to the president in his September 18/28 "oral message" that Kennedy was acting inconsistently with his commitments when American aircraft "buzzed" Soviet cargo ships on more than 140 occasions in August, thereby breaking the president's July 31 pledge, and again when the president called up 150,000 reservists at a time when "the Soviet Union was doing nothing to provoke tensions while the United States was making 'piratical demands' to inspect Soviet ships heading for Cuba." Referring to Kennedy's September 4 public warning about Soviet arms shipments to Cuba, Khrushchev also complained in the September 18/28 "oral message" that "if there were no statement by you on Cuba, we, naturally, as Ambassador Thompson and Mr. Udall were told, would not say anything on West Berlin. Your statement forced us to do so."

Of course, the foregoing theory of a reciprocal superpower deal based on the president's July 31 and (possibly repeated) August 31 proposals and the Soviet premier's four responsive messages involves a degree of speculation based upon circumstantial evidence. Nevertheless, what followed the September 6 message delivered by Dobrynin to Sorensen, the September 18/28 "oral message" from Khrushchev to Kennedy, the October 7/8 Bolshakov message read to the attorney general, and the days leading to the October 16 Kohler cable 133 was a sequence of actions and inactions by the president and his top advisers that indicated a determination to restrict, slow down, or outright block the further gathering of information on the Soviet military buildup in Cuba that might complicate the president's political plans for the November 6 elections. And at the same time, whenever troubling new intelligence nevertheless managed to work its way up to the president's attention, he and his close advisers consistently downplayed its importance and confined its circulation while candidly acknowledging that the president's intention was to prevent further ammunition from coming into the hands of his political adversaries.

Shortly after the October 28 settlement of the acute phase of the crisis, Khrushchev sent Mikoyan to Cuba in an effort to rebuild confidence and trust between the two Communist allies. Addressing Castro and the Cuban leadership at a tense gathering on November 4, 1962, Mikoyan attempted to explain the understanding that had emerged between Khrushchev and Kennedy at the outset of the crisis. The key to that understanding, according to Mikoyan, was the domestic political problem Kennedy was facing against fierce Republican criticism of his weakness in dealing with Khrushchev on Berlin and other foreign policy challenges: "It was known through diplomatic channels that Kennedy did not want to make matters more serious and asked us not to move on the issue of Berlin before the elections. We told him that we agreed to this." Mikoyan added that the Kremlin "thought it was convenient to please him," especially since "We did not intend to act on Berlin."

When the Americans discovered the surge of arms-laden Soviet ships headed for Cuba, the Kremlin leadership "were surprised that Kennedy only made reference to technicians and not to our troops. At first, it seems that is what he thought." They later concluded, however, that the president "knew more than he was saying, but he was not revealing it [so as] not to hinder the electoral campaign." Ironically, according to Mikoyan, it was expedient for Kennedy no less than for Khrushchev to keep the focus on Berlin though Cuba was the more pressing problem: "When the North Americans learned about the transports to Cuba, they also concentrated their campaign on Berlin. Both sides had their principal interest in Cuba, but appeared as if concentrated on Berlin."[91]

Kennedy's July 31 proposal that the Kremlin put tensions on ice through the US midterm election must have struck Khrushchev as an unimaginable windfall. After all, the Kremlin needed to maintain the secrecy of its Anadyr operation only through early November, because that was the time frame projected for completion of the Soviet IRBM and MRBM installations and bringing the missiles to operational status.[92] It was only after the new missile bases had become a fait accompli that Khrushchev planned to sign and publicly announce "a formal Soviet-Cuban military accord" during a "triumphant visit by the Chairman to Cuba in November after the missiles were installed."[93] And now, here was the US president offering to, in effect, abate American aerial intelligence surveillance of the Soviet transportation of those very missiles, and to do so based on a time horizon exactly matching the Kremlin's need for secrecy. Could any offer have been better calibrated to accommodate the Soviet chairman's most ambitious wishes? As Jonathan Haslam has observed: "[Khrushchev's] throwaway comment that 'out of respect for your President we won't do anything until November' again looks alarmingly pointed in retrospect given the simultaneous timing of missile readiness and the congressional elections."[94]

There are indications that Khrushchev kept his part of the bargain by reducing tensions over Berlin, at least until the August 22 announcement eliminating the position of Soviet commandant of Berlin. Indeed, the US Intelligence Community was able to connect the dots between these positive Berlin developments and Cuba. Thus, in the CIA's special assessment of the Soviet military buildup in Cuba, issued on September 19, 1962, the agency made the following observations: "Further, in their 11 September statement, the Soviets implied that US action against Cuba would be countered by Bloc moves elsewhere in the world and for the first time publicly linked the Berlin and Cuban crises. The Soviets are also aware that a drastic heightening of tension over Cuba is an important factor in their general relations with the US and has an impact on various other issues. Thus developments in the Cuban situation probably influenced the recent Soviet decision to let the Berlin situation simmer, rather than boil, for the time being."[95]

Based on their own research of Soviet archives, Fursenko and Naftali found that "initially, Khrushchev's ploy seemed to have worked. In early August the Presidium authorized Bolshakov to tell the Kennedys, 'N.S. Khrushchev is satisfied with the president's order to curtail U.S. planes' inspections of Soviet ships in open waters.'"[96] Bolshakov most likely conveyed Khrushchev's message back to Robert Kennedy on August 2, since the attorney general's desk diary includes the following entry on that date: "5:00–7:00 Georgi Bolshakov was in."[97]

It remains uncertain whether, and if so to what extent, Kennedy stood behind his commitment to terminate air surveillance over Soviet shipping. Naftali has opined that the president did not in fact follow through on his commitment to Khrushchev because he saw no sign of a quid pro quo from the Kremlin on the Berlin front.[98] Yet that explanation seems unsatisfactory given Khrushchev's claim in his September 28, 1962, letter to the president that there had been numerous "buzzing" incidents throughout the month of August. If that was true, and Kennedy seems never to have denied it, then the president did not give Khrushchev a chance to provide a quid pro quo in relation to Berlin.

In the end, Kennedy's July 31 assertion that he had halted low-level air surveillance—whether true or not—would have made no difference on the critical issue of ballistic weapons because the Soviet MRBM and IRBM missiles were stowed in the holds of large-hatch cargo ships and therefore were invisible to surveillance from the air. The first units of these missiles were off-loaded in Cuba, always at nighttime, beginning in mid-September.[99]

Khrushchev did, in fact, keep his side of the bargain. There would be no significant Soviet military or border provocations in or around Berlin during the summer and fall of 1962, bringing tensions there down to a simmer. And although Khrushchev briefly reminded Kennedy of the GDR peace treaty stick he still held by making public comments to the UN secretary-general on August 28, that appears to have been simply a public relations gesture that quickly faded after Kennedy delivered his conciliatory message to Khrushchev through Bolshakov. This explanation of the somewhat murky events that unfolded during this period finds strong support in what the two leaders said to one another at this juncture. Kennedy, for his part, directed Theodore Sorensen to tell the Soviet ambassador, Anatoly Dobrynin, that the president needed a period of calm through the November 6 midterm elections and was willing to deal in reciprocal foreign affairs concessions to make this happen. According to Dobrynin's memoirs, Sorensen had delivered this message initially at a private meeting in "late August" (evidently their August 23 meeting) at which he informed Dobrynin that his "main duty" as the president's "personal assistant" was "monitoring political feeling to promote the president's personal appeal, win support for his policies, and develop the president's strategy for supporting the Democratic Party in the congressional election campaign that was just getting into high gear." Sorensen went on to say, "The Soviet Union . . . could potentially influence the outcome of the campaign by increasing pressure on Berlin. In this case, regardless of the president's actions, the result would be some additional points for the Republicans. He implied that Kennedy would prefer the Soviet Union to stay neutral during the election. This could pave the way toward another meeting with Khrushchev after the election, unless the prospects for an agreement on some specific issue arose in the meantime."[100]

Dobrynin considered this appeal "clearly unusual and could not but attract Moscow's attention," so he reported it back to Khrushchev promptly. What followed from the Soviet side was a clear message from Khrushchev spelling out the two leaders' reciprocal assurances to one another using the same Dobrynin-to-Sorensen channel. The ambassador met with Sorensen again on September 6, 1962, as previously noted, and read Khrushchev's quid pro quo message slowly, word by word, so that Sorensen could write it down and no actual document would need to pass from one country to the other. Here is what Sorensen conveyed to the president: "Nothing will be undertaken before the American Congressional elections that could complicate the international situation or aggravate tension in the relations between our two countries . . . provided there are no actions taken on the other side which would change the situation."[101]

There then followed a cascade of assurances by the Soviet chairman, through letters and oral statements by intermediaries, that the Soviet Union would suspend aggravating foreign policy tensions in order to give the president an untroubled campaign season. The idea of a pause until the November midterm elections had been hatched by Khrushchev in late July[102] and encouraged by Kennedy through his meeting with Bolshakov on July 31 and his messages to Dobrynin conveyed through Sorensen on August 23 and September 6. But Khrushchev's initial assurance of accommodation to the president's domestic political concerns truly became a barrage during the run-up to the Cuba crisis, ultimately amounting to ten separate, private and public communications issuing from Khrushchev over a forty-four-day period beginning on September 4 and extending to October 18. These messages passed through no fewer than nine Soviet and American middlemen: Soviet ambassador Dobrynin, US attorney general Robert Kennedy, Secretary of the Interior Udall, Kennedy special assistant Theodore Sorensen, GRU officer Georgi Bolshakov, Dobrynin's assistant Alexander Zinchuk, American journalist Charles Bartlett, US ambassador Foy Kohler, and Soviet foreign minister Gromyko. The sheer number, consistency and exaggerated repetition of this outpouring of friendly stand-down assurances is one of the most striking yet least commented-upon features of the missile crisis historiography.

September 4, 1962, Khrushchev message to Kennedy via Dobrynin to Robert Kennedy. ". . . Khrushchev would do nothing to disrupt the relationship of our two countries during this period prior to the election."[103] In his biography of Khrushchev Taubman focused on a more personal note that the Soviet leader wished to convey to the president through Ambassador Dobrynin: "He liked President Kennedy and did not wish to embarrass him."[104] On October 16 Khrushchev would tell Ambassador Kohler that he was "most anxious not to do anything that will embarrass the President during the campaign."[105] As will be seen shortly (see chapter 7), Khrushchev's somewhat condescending concern not to "embarrass" the president in the run-up to the American midterm elections would stick in Kennedy's mind and reappear at a critical juncture six weeks later as a goad that Kennedy would consider an infuriating and insulting lie. But by that time this particular lie was one that could not be publicly revealed or acknowledged because it would cause the president political embarrassment in its most acute form.

September 5, 1962, Khrushchev message to Kennedy via Udall at a meeting between the two in Pitsunda. "Out of respect for your President we won't do anything until November."[106]

September 6, 1962, Khrushchev message to Kennedy via Dobrynin, who read to Theodore Sorensen a message from Khrushchev to JFK. "Nothing will be undertaken before the American Congressional elections that could complicate the international situation or aggravate tension in the relations between our two countries."[107]

September 11, 1962, Khrushchev statement in interview with the New York Times. The Soviet leader would do nothing in Berlin that would interfere with the US midterm elections.[108]

September 18, 1962, Khrushchev message to Kennedy via Dobrynin's delivery of a transcribed fifteen-page "oral" message to Robert Kennedy. "It would be a good idea for both countries to refrain from any action, including action in Berlin, that could aggravate the situation before the congressional elections."[109]

Late September 1962 Khrushchev message to Kennedy via the Soviet embassy's counselor, Alexander Zinchuk, to Charles Bartlett. Beschloss noted that Khrushchev's message through the embassy counselor was "that he [Khrushchev] understood the problems of the congressional elections. He understood that the President would be preoccupied . . . and wanted him to know that he would do nothing during this period that would in any way divert him or create problems for him."[110]

September 28, 1962, letter from Khrushchev to President Kennedy. The letter mentioned Kennedy's offer to discontinue air surveillance of Soviet ships and repeated what he had told US ambassador Thompson: "We are ready to take into consideration the circumstances that you are finding yourself in in connection with preparation for congressional elections. . . . in order not to play in such conditions a role of some third force breaking from outside into this struggle between the competing parties we decided to put the German problem, so to say, on ice until the end of the elections. . . ." Khrushchev noted the reciprocal obligation of the president "not to do anything that could further aggravate the atmosphere and even expose the world."

October 7 or 8, 1962, Khrushchev message to Kennedy via Bolshakov. Bolshakov met with Robert Kennedy on a day "3 dramatic weeks" before their next meeting on October 23, most likely referring to a meeting on October 7 or

8.[111] As noted above, in conveying Khrushchev's response to President Kennedy's "oral message of 31 August," Bolshakov recounted Khrushchev's message as he conveyed it to the attorney general: "The Soviet leaders understand President Kennedy's situation well and will not undertake any actions regarding the United States before the congressional elections in November 1962, and they hope that we can begin a new round of active talks when the elections are over."[112]

Interestingly, when the president provided his response to Khrushchev's September 28 letter, the midterm elections were highlighted as a point of concern. The message was conveyed to the Soviet chairman through the well-traveled back-channel route of Robert Kennedy to Georgi Bolshakov. According to a memorandum by Dobrynin, reported by Fursenko and Naftali, Robert Kennedy met with Bolshakov on October 8, 1962, after the latter had returned to the United States from a visit of "a few weeks" in Russia. Bolshakov wished to convey "a special message for the president from Khrushchev." Robert Kennedy, in turn, wanted to provide the president's response to Khrushchev's September 28 letter. Bolshakov stated on behalf of Khrushchev that "in order to resolve the issues in a reasonable fashion we must proceed from the real correlation of forces, to respect the sovereign right of other countries, not interfering in their domestic affairs." Robert Kennedy told Bolshakov that Soviet arms shipments to Cuba "have angered the president," that his brother was "especially sensitive to these changes because of the midterm election," and that the United States could not agree "to remove all Western troops from West Berlin" or to a "five-year moratorium on underground testing in return for an atmospheric test ban."[113]

October 16, 1962, Khrushchev message to Kennedy via US ambassador Foy Kohler. Khrushchev intended to "come to New York latter part of November," and he would "take no action before meeting which would make situation more difficult." Khrushchev regretted that an announcement about a Cuban fishing village "had been published during electoral campaign in US which was due to his own absence from Moscow."[114] Khrushchev also said he was "most anxious not to do anything that will embarrass the President during the campaign."[115]

October 18, 1962, comment by Soviet minister of foreign affairs Andrei Gromyko to President Kennedy during their meeting in the White House. The Soviet government had "already indicated that it would do nothing with regard to West Berlin before the US elections. . . ."[116]

That ten sequential messages from one head of state to another focused on the recipient's personal political standing in his own country is extraordinary for multiple reasons. First, of course, is the sheer number of these pointed messages. Beschloss observed that Khrushchev seemed to "be taking extraordinary care to ensure that his message reached Kennedy."[117] Why was Khrushchev repeating himself so many times on the topic of his rival's domestic political concerns? Why was he so determined to get across that particular assurance of support through noninterference? Did the sheer multitude of these messages promising a period of calm so that the president could achieve success in the midterm elections confirm that the two leaders were trading on the concern that was uppermost in the president's mind?

Second, what did President Kennedy, or for that matter any of the numerous intermediaries, take away from the Russian leader's proffered stand-down from provocations? What did Khrushchev's assurances imply about what would occur in the days immediately *following* the midterm elections? Was he saying, in effect, "The trouble I have in store for you is surely coming, but I will do you the personal favor of waiting until after your precious elections." Was Khrushchev unsubtly setting up a situation in which Kennedy would feel compelled to conclude he owed his adversary for this important personal accommodation?

Third, what did the US government officials who saw these messages make of the implicit deal that bound the Soviet premier to provide a personal, partisan, political favor that was linked to the timing of an imminent international confrontation. It is clear from the ExComm deliberations that the president's advisers had taken note of Khrushchev's assurances about a period of calm during the lead-up to the midterm elections. As the ExComm considered, on October 18, whether the president should inform Soviet foreign minister Gromyko at a meeting scheduled for the end of the day that US surveillance had located Soviet ballistic missile installations in Cuba, Robert Kennedy suggested a less frontal approach designed to see whether Gromyko would flatly deny what he must surely have known. At that point, Theodore Sorensen stated: "Actually, I think the Attorney General's suggestion is a pretty good gambit, to say to him: 'Well, Khrushchev was not going to do anything before our election.' But look what he's doing in Cuba and so on."[118] None of the ExComm participants asked what Sorensen meant by his reference to Khrushchev's promised forbearance, presumably because they were already well aware of the premier's repeated assurances. Did this odd link between superpower tensions and domestic political aims create a conflict of interest for the American president?

Fourth and, perhaps, most amazing, why hasn't the sheer magnitude and persistence of this parade of Khrushchev messages and the questions they raise about the president's preoccupation with domestic politics ever attracted the attention or engaged the focused interest of historians of the Cuban missile crisis?

It may be useful to summarize the more important dimensions of Khrushchev's response to President Kennedy's back-channel diplomacy as matters stood in early September 1962. Soviet-chartered cargo ships continued to ply their way to Cuban ports, and multiple assurances continued to issue from Soviet spokesmen that any weapons being shipped were defensive in nature and intended to accomplish only defensive objectives. Some on the American side, especially Republicans, were questioning these inherently vague assurances, but the president seemed unconcerned. Berlin quieted down with no further upgrading of East German prerogatives or Soviet statements about the urgent need for a separate treaty. And Khrushchev took great pains to ensure that his soothing message to Kennedy of a pre-midterms stand-down was unmistakable. Through both private and public channels the key assurance was reiterated: nothing would be done to increase tensions or otherwise cause trouble for the president while he tended to his domestic political affairs in the lead-up to the midterm elections.

So then how did the Kennedy administration respond? As will be seen in the next chapter, the administration's surveillance efforts aimed at the Soviet military buildup in Cuba during the weeks that followed August 31 were a catalog of drawing-backs exhibiting extreme caution, coupled with aggressive efforts to sequester all new and potentially contrarian intelligence findings within a small circle of officials at the highest White House level with no dissemination allowed without the approval of the president himself. Echoing the Soviet chairman's stated rationale for his cooperative gestures on Berlin, Kennedy administration insiders explained that surveillance abatement and secrecy measures were needed to avoid incidents that might provide fodder for partisan criticism of the president during the final, critical weeks of midterm election campaigning.

CHAPTER 6

Keeping the Lid On

The President was prepared to consider any initiatives of the Soviet government aimed at relaxing tensions in that part of the world.

—MESSAGE DELIVERED ON BEHALF OF PRESIDENT KENNEDY TO KHRUSHCHEV VIA CHARLES BARTLETT TO BOLSHAKOV[1]

THROUGHOUT THE CRITICAL MONTH of September 1962 and on into early October, as evidence mounted that worrisome Soviet armaments were present in Cuba, the president and his inner circle seemed to meet every new piece of news with skepticism. Rather than sharpening surveillance, they took steps to stand down, especially in the case of the most fruitful source of valuable information: U-2 overflights of the Cuban interior. A steady stream of Kennedy administration actions after August 31 confirms that the president wished to avoid bad news even if this meant curbing American intelligence-gathering. Domestic politics and avoidance of further damage from Republican attacks were frequently mentioned as the reason a reduction in international tensions was needed, and this view was expressed by Kennedy insiders no less than by the president's political opponents.

Roger Hilsman later commented that the attacks by Kennedy's Republican critics were "always a factor to be taken account of in policy discussions—and policy was at times either adjusted to accommodate some element of their view so as to disarm them or presented in such a way as to forestall them."[2] It is hard not to perceive the president's secret mutual accommodation with Khrushchev—that nothing would be done on either side that might exacerbate tensions surrounding either Berlin or Cuba until after the US midterm elections—as a kind of "invisible hand" influencing the administration's actions.

Eight administration decisions in particular over the six weeks that followed the momentous events of August 31, 1962, show a pattern of the Kennedy administration's diffidence in the face of developments in Cuba.

September 1, 1962,"new" orders regarding military reconnaissance flights around Cuba. As noted, Kaysen sent to the president on September 1 a paper from the Joint Chiefs of Staff reflecting the Pentagon's new "Rules of Engagement, particularly in the vicinity of Cuba." In the future, the defense officials assured the president, "Reconnaissance or other flights near Cuba will be conducted in a non-provocative manner, which is interpreted as generally flying parallel to the coast." If unarmed US aircraft were "harassed or attacked," they should "take evasive action"; "hot pursuit into Cuban air space" was "authorized" but "may not be prolonged," and no "pursuing force" was to be organized; and finally, if armed US aircraft were harassed by Cuban aircraft, they were under instructions to merely "attempt to shoulder them off and shepherd them back into Cuban air space or waters."[3]

September 7, 1962, Kennedy's anger at the CIA upon learning of the agency's discovery of Soviet surface-to-surface cruise missiles in Cuba. Brugioni described a tense meeting held at the White House on September 7 where CIA and DIA officials Marshall Carter, Ray Cline, Art Lundahl, and John McLauchlin briefed the president and his top national security officials, including Bundy, Rusk, and McNamara, on the discovery of Soviet surface-to-surface cruise missiles at the Banes site in Cuba on August 29. The president would have first seen this news on his August 31 "President's Checklist" provided by the CIA. On September 7 he expressed displeasure, especially because the missiles appeared to be able to reach any US ships within forty miles of the Cuban coastal area: "The president snapped, 'That would make it an offensive weapon, wouldn't it?' Cline again explained that the site seemed designed to defend possible landing beaches. The president, growing impatient, said, 'You've explained that before.'"[4]

Lundahl tried to address the president's concern by noting that the cruise missile site "was located in the eastern part of Cuba with the launchers oriented eastward, away from the continental United States." But the intelligence officers' admission that they still had only limited knowledge about the precise characteristics of these new Soviet weapons irritated the president: "I want no further reporting until the missile site has been completely evaluated and you can report back to me." The president asked how many people had received this information and was told by Lundahl that "a rather large number of intelligence organizations and military commands" were in the routing list. The president was "obviously angry" and said, "We have to be very careful about any evidence of offensive weapons in Cuba. If such evidence is found, it must be kept very restricted and I want to be the first to know about it."[5]

Upon General Carter's return to his office at the CIA in Langley, he instructed Huntington Sheldon, the agency's assistant deputy director for intelligence, to institute "as a presidential directive" a new security system "that would absolutely safeguard the dissemination of highly sensitive information derived from the Cuban overflights should offensive missiles be found."[6] That new system, introduced by the president's order on September 7, 1962, would become known by the code name PSALM.[7] May and Zelikow noted that establishment of the PSALM system for restricting information about possible offensive weapons in the Soviet arms buildup in Cuba was in part a response to domestic political criticism the president was facing over his handling of the buildup; it was critically important that the information "not leak out into the ongoing, volatile domestic debate over his response." The new PSALM classification system "was thereupon created—with a tightly restricted distribution—for future reports on Soviet deployments in Cuba."[8]

In a postcrisis report by the CIA, approved as final on January 3, 1963, and provided by the DCI to the President's Foreign Intelligence Advisory Board (PFIAB) recounting the agency's intelligence gathering during the Cuban crisis, the CIA noted that the "restriction on publishing intelligence on offensive weapons in Cuba was discussed in USIB executive sessions on 7 and 13 September," and was then "established just a few days before reports of actual sightings of offensive missiles began to come in from ground observers in Cuba." Yet the PFIAB focused on the fact that it was not until October 11 that a "special" US Intelligence Board (USIB) meeting "put this verbal order into effect by establishing the so-called PSALM system effective 12 October."[9]

According to Barrett and Holland, the SA-2 missiles discovered by the August 29 U-2 overflight raised not so much a foreign policy concern from the president's standpoint as a "domestic political one." Citing Sorensen's memoir, these two historians noted: "With a midterm election fast approaching, pressure to 'do something' about Cuba was bound to mount and would have to be managed carefully."[10]

In her compilation of key documents related to the Cuban missile crisis in CIA files, Mary McAuliffe included a "Memorandum for the Record" dated September 1, 1962, which she listed as the source for her statement that "by early September President John F. Kennedy had instructed the intelligence community to strictly limit the internal dissemination of information on missiles to Cuba." The memorandum was prepared by William A. Tidwell, the CIA's deputy director of intelligence (planning) to reflect a telephone conversation between President Kennedy and acting CIA director Carter. In his report of this conversation to the CIA's deputy director for intelligence, Ray S. Cline, Carter stated that the president had instructed that "the clamps were to remain on the release of certain information concerning Cuba except for the barest minimum access on a need-to-know basis for the purpose of preparing a comprehensive briefing for the President Tuesday morning September 4."

Cline's memorandum went on to state that a certain "report concerning Cuba" needed for the September 4 meeting with the president could be disseminated to "OCI" and a "single copy to State, Army, Navy, Air and DIA" but with instructions that "there is to be no further dissemination except on a minimum need-to-know basis" and that "no actions were to be taken on the basis of the information."[11]

September 10, 1962, Special Action Group meeting resulting in decision to curtail further U-2 surveillance of SAM-protected Soviet military sites. Separately, the safety of US surveillance overflights of Cuba was becoming a matter of concern. On August 31 a U-2 had strayed into Soviet airspace, drawing a protest. Then, on Saturday September 8, a U-2 piloted by a Taiwanese pilot was shot down over China. The White House feared that a similar loss over Cuba could be highly problematic. A "standdown of U-2 overflights until 16 September" was ordered as a result of the September 8 shoot-down.[12] Robert Kennedy felt "an overwhelming concern for the effect on the president's image," and he "asked that not only the Chinese U-2 program but also the U.S. Cuban U-2 overflights be reviewed at the scheduled meeting of the Special Action Group on Monday, September 10."[13]

Barrett and Holland in *Blind over Cuba* and Brugioni in *Eyeball* have extensively examined what happened next. On Monday morning September 10, Bundy sent an urgent memorandum to the chairman of the Committee on Overhead Reconnaissance (COMOR), which was responsible for recommending the Cuba overflights to a National Security Council "Special Group" for ultimate authorization.[14] Bundy's memorandum strongly signaled a decision to back off had already been made: it demanded responses to three questions within thirty minutes: "How important is it to our intelligence objectives that we overfly Cuban soil? . . . How much would our intelligence suffer if we limited our reconnaissance to peripheral activity utilizing oblique photography? . . . Is there anyone in the planning of these missions who might want to provoke an incident?"[15]

If the first two questions from the national security adviser sounded outcome-determining, the third question was downright strange. The president's strained relations with the CIA after the Bay of Pigs fiasco had become well known, and his anger displayed at the meeting over the cruise missile findings only a few days earlier was not a good sign. But had the president or his closest advisers reached the extreme point of fearing that intelligence officers might actually wish to put a secret surveillance operation in jeopardy and a U-2 pilot's life at risk in order to embarrass the administration? As will be seen below, that toxic concern led CIA officials a few weeks later to enlist their Defense Department rivals, the newly created Defense Intelligence Agency (DIA), to assume responsibility for recommending to COMOR the flight path for the next U-2 overflight after September 5—a surveillance mission that ultimately would cross western Cuba on October 14, 1962, and detect the Soviet MRBM base at San Cristóbal in Pinar del Río province.

The Special Action Group gathered in Bundy's office at 5:45 p.m. on September 10 to discuss the upcoming U-2 schedule for Cuba. In addition to the president's national security adviser, those present according to a file memorandum written much later included James Q. Reber (chairman of COMOR), Robert Kennedy, Dean Rusk, CIA deputy director General Marshall ("Pat") Carter, General Edward Lansdale (chief of operations for Mongoose), James A. Cunningham (deputy director of the CIA's U-2 program), and Dr. Herbert Scoville (CIA deputy director for research).[16] Shortly before the meeting began, Bundy made it clear where the White House stood by "abruptly rescind[ing] presidential approval of the remaining [U-2] overflight."[17] At the meeting Bundy and Rusk argued that the overflights were vulnerable to the SAM-2s and that an incident of this kind would damage US prestige and foreign policy objectives more generally. Carter argued for continuation of the overflights. While the meeting had ostensibly been arranged to review "a CIA proposal to run two long overflights that would cover the entire island," it had turned into "a policy meeting on further U-2 missions over Cuba."[18] When Rusk and Bundy held fast, Carter was compelled to acquiesce.

Later commentators, including Dino Brugioni in his 1991 book *Eyeball to Eyeball*, have stated that Robert Kennedy joined Carter in arguing for continued overflights based on a report that the attorney general derisively said to Rusk: "What's the matter, Dean, no guts?" (or "What's the matter, Dean, you chicken?" in Brugioni's rendering). But Brugioni did not attend the meeting, and he cited no sources for his detailed description of the discussion in his *Eyeball* account published twenty-nine years later.[19] The more contemporaneous documentary source for Robert Kennedy's unusually demeaning comment was a CIA file memorandum dated February 28, 1963, which was based on statements by Reber and Cunningham and the postcrisis Lehman report presented to CIA director McCone on November 14, 1962. It, too, was prepared by another nonparticipant after the fact, but at least appeared within six months of the event. The CIA file memorandum is brief, but it indicates that Rusk's initial comment to which the attorney general's "riposte" was directed had referred only to the difficulty Rusk faced in his ability to "negotiate on Berlin" in the midst of potential U-2 incidents, not on any particular fear he had of the Soviet SAM-2s in Cuba. And the memorandum's observation that Rusk's comment was said "half joshingly" at the outset of the discussion further suggests that Kennedy's riposte may similarly have been nothing more than an attempt at humor or insult. Most tellingly, the file memorandum mentions only General Carter as the proponent of continuing the U-2 overflights, and contains no suggestion that Kennedy or anyone else at the meeting spoke out in support of Carter's position. It is hard to imagine that the president's younger brother would first call for an urgent Special Action Group meeting out of concern for harm to the president's image in the wake of a U-2 shoot-down in China, then quixotically throw his support behind the CIA (which was under White House suspicion for disloyalty) in its battle against Bundy, who moments before had unceremoniously canceled the next U-2 overflight, only to change his allegiance again at the end of the meeting, and all with no mention in the CIA file memorandum of the attorney general's strange zigzag performance.[20]

The September 10 meeting ended with the group agreeing to a plan calling for four surveillance flights during the remainder of September: two peripheral flights that would stay over international waters and two "quick 'in-and-out' operations" across the narrow width of the island "with the 'additional precaution' that flightpaths would be laid out to avoid known SAM sites."[21] As a result, the in-and-out flights that were selected traversed only "small portions of central and eastern Cuba. Western Cuba, the known location of the Soviet SAMs, would be left unsurveilled."[22] And even the scaled-down plan was cut back when Bundy called Carter in the late afternoon of September 10 to announce that one of the four substitute flights "had been rescinded" and that "all future requests for a mission had to be sent through him to the president."[23]

Notably missing from reports of the September 10 discussion itself, and from subsequent commentaries, was any discussion of the fact that US electronic and signals intelligence surveillance allowed monitoring of the operational status of the Soviet SAM-2 sites and even their readiness to fire at overflying US aircraft. The latest U-2 overflight had occurred only a few days before, on September 5, and US intelligence surveillance should have been aware of the reaction of the SAM-2 sites through their active monitoring by both sea and air outposts.[24] Brugioni included no mention of this key fact in his otherwise detailed account of the crisis.

Although Bundy, Rusk, and Robert Kennedy could not read the minds of their Soviet adversaries, they should surely have sought and considered the evidence of whether the SAM missiles were fully operational, whether their target acquisition radars had been switched on at the approach of the September 5 U-2 overflight, and whether the multiple SAM-2 sites in Cuba had been electronically connected into an integrated system. These facts were detectable by US surveillance and should have been known at the latest by the time the September 5 overflight had occurred without apparent incident. As will be seen, a serious U-2 vulnerability analysis would be prepared by a CIA official, air force colonel Jack Ledford, for a Special Action Group meeting held just one month later, and the relatively low risk of a U-2 shootdown provided in that report resulted in the abrupt resumption of the U-2 overflight program at that time and the immediate discovery of Soviet ballistic missiles in San Cristóbal. Why wasn't a vulnerability analysis such as this solicited before U-2 overflights of Cuba were precipitously suspended on September 10?

A later review of the crisis chronology prepared for the Joint Chiefs of Staff on January 4, 1963, noted that the president's Daily Intelligence Summary for September 20 reported indications "that at least one of the 12 SA-2 sites would soon be operational."[25] Two weeks after that report, CIA director McCone would raise questions at a Special Action Group meeting held on October 4 whether the U-2 flight restrictions that had blocked island overflights since September 5 were "a reasonable restriction at this time, particularly since the SAM's were almost certainly not operational."[26]

October 5, 1962—McCone-Bundy discussion of restrictions on U-2 overflights. On October 5, 1962, McCone met with Bundy to discuss Soviet policy in Cuba. McCone wrote a "Memorandum of Discussion" in which he recorded his and Bundy's exchange. After noting his expressions of concern about a notable reduction in momentum behind the Operation Mongoose activities, and the administration's abatement of U-2 overflights of Cuba territory posing the highest risk of possible missile installation construction, McCone warned Bundy that "the decisions to restrict U-2 flights had placed the United States Intelligence Community in a position where it could not report with assurance the development of offensive capabilities in Cuba." McCone felt it "most probable" that the Soviets would end up with an offensive capability in Cuba, "including MRBMs." Bundy disagreed based on his belief that the Soviets "would not go that far," and to McCone he "seemed relaxed over the fact that the Intelligence Community cannot produce hard information on this important subject."[27]

Robert Kennedy would later flatly deny in his oral history that McCone ever communicated his concerns about possible Soviet missiles in Cuba to the president "or to anybody else."[28] Yet that statement by the attorney general was demonstrably false, as later historians have demonstrated citing documentation of McCone's multiple warnings directly to the president and his top advisers beginning in August 1962.[29] Once McCone learned of the Soviet SA-2 missile installations in Cuba, it was his intuition, which he conveyed to White House officials, that "the Soviets wished to hide something of extreme importance," and he concluded "this must mean that they were deploying strategic nuclear missiles."[30]

There is a further curiosity in the historical record about whether Bundy should have anticipated that the Soviets might "go that far" and place medium-range ballistic missiles in Cuba. Bundy's apparent doubt echoed an important judgment in the US Intelligence Community's special national intelligence estimate dated September 19, 1962, that the Kremlin most likely had not decided to deploy MRBMs or IRBMs in Cuba because "the establishment on Cuban soil of a significant strike capability with such weapons would represent a sharp departure from Soviet practice, since such weapons have so far not been installed even in Satellite territory."[31] But that statement was flatly erroneous, as the US State Department clearly was aware at the time, and the CIA doubtless would have known as well. Just a few years before in 1958–59 the Soviets had secretly installed a battery of R-5M (SS-3) Shyster medium range ballistic missiles with nuclear warheads near the towns of Vogelsang and Furstenberg in East Germany. Although these missiles were withdrawn shortly thereafter, in August 1959, there can be no doubt that for a significant period covering most of 1959 the Soviets had indeed built and maintained a nuclear ballistic missile installation in satellite territory. The CIA was aware of the Soviet missile installation in the GDR, having learned of it from multiple sources, including its most valuable intelligence asset within the Soviet Union, Oleg Penkovsky.[32]

October 6 or 8 or 9, 1962, message from President Kennedy to Khrushchev conveyed through Charles Bartlett to Bolshakov. Bolshakov met for lunch with Charlie Bartlett a day after the GRU agent's October 5 (or 7 or 8) meeting with Robert Kennedy[33] in order to dictate to the journalist the same Khrushchev message for the president that he had reported to the attorney general the day before. Khrushchev's message was the Soviet leader's response to the president's giving of his "word" regarding a reciprocal reduction of tensions before the US midterm elections. In his *New Times* article describing his lunch meeting with Bartlett, Bolshakov recorded an additional conciliatory message Kennedy had asked Bartlett "some days previously" to convey to Khrushchev through Bolshakov so that the Soviets would not "misinterpret[]" the president's actions in the Caribbean: "He stressed that by taking certain measures in that region the President by no means intended to build up tensions; on the contrary, those measures, such as the imposing of economic embargo, were supposed to prevent the situation there from getting dangerous, and the President was prepared to consider any initiatives of the Soviet government aimed at relaxing tensions in that part of the world."[34]

October 9, 1962, meeting of Special Action Group (Augmented) to consider COMOR recommendation for resumption of U-2 overflights of Cuba. At a follow-up Special Action Group meeting on October 9 attended by President Kennedy, McCone was accompanied by Colonel Jack C. Ledford, director of the CIA's Office of Special Activities (OSA), who provided "a vulnerability analysis that estimated the odds of losing a U-2 over Cuba at 1 in 6."[35]

Ledford is one of two little-known US military colonels who were involved in the pivotal October 9 Special Action Group meeting and thereby became true unsung heroes of the missile crisis. A long-serving air force officer, Ledford had flown under General Curtis LeMay's command during World War II. He had expected to be given a SAC assignment in mid-1962, but learned that LeMay had recommended him for a good assignment in Washington whose details were highly classified and required a polygraph exam. He passed all qualifying requirements and was assigned to the 1040th USAF Field Activity Squadron, which served as "an administrative office for Air Force personnel assigned to the CIA, NSA and other intelligence agencies."[36]

Ledford and his team had concluded that the Soviet SAM sites "were still not functioning as an integrated SAM system."[37] Notes taken at the October

9 meeting by Roswell Gilpatric indicate that the president was told "there were no indications as yet that the SA-2 antiaircraft emplacements had reached operational stage, although it had been nearly 2 months since their first installation."[38] The meeting concluded with a decision by the president to allow the U-2 mission over the suspect San Cristóbal site to go forward, and the result was production of the first photographic evidence of the presence of Soviet ballistic missiles in Cuba. Parenthetically, the Special Action Group also discussed the president's abiding desire to keep incoming intelligence findings of Soviet offensive military units in Cuba within a tight circle. JCS chairman Maxwell Taylor's handwritten notes taken during this period cited October 9 as the date when "JFK put restrictions on circulation of Cuba info and particularly info ref. offensive missiles."[39]

As it happened, although the Kennedy administration did not know this on September 10, Khrushchev had prohibited the SAM-2 batteries from firing on US surveillance aircraft. Soviet general Gribkov would later confirm that all of the Soviet SAM sites had been instructed that their mission was "to defend against air attack, not aerial espionage." So long as no invasion was thought to be imminent, "The SAM commanders were not even allowed to use their radars to track the spy planes overhead."[40]

As a fallback, acting DCI Carter requested approval for use of "tactical low-level reconnaissance," not vulnerable to the SAM-2 missiles, to overfly the Banes missile site "and other targets along the coast that would be suitable for such missions." Defense secretary McNamara agreed to consider the request, but he later "demurred" based on his seemingly non sequitur conclusion that "he preferred the continued use of the U-2 against Cuba."[41] Those decisions proved to be the precipitating actions (or more precisely, inactions) that produced what would become a five-week hiatus in surveillance overflights of the critical area in western Cuba near the town of San Cristóbal where a secret Soviet missile launch site was being built. The next U-2 overflight of this area would not take place until October 14, 1962, and it was this mission that discovered the Soviet missiles. The five-week blackout of US intelligence from aerial surveillance over western Cuba would later be referred to as the "photo gap."

Holland and Barrett later drew the link between the September 10 rejection of Carter's request for continued U-2 overflights of Cuba and the president's midterm election concerns: "The SA-2 deployment did not signal a foreign policy crisis in [Kennedy's] eyes as much as it marked the onset of a domestic one. With a midterm election fast approaching, internal political pressure to 'do something' about Cuba was bound to mount and had to be managed."[42] Skeptics of the administration's SAM-threat rationale for suspending all U-2 overflights might well ask the question: if the SAM missiles were truly thought to be a serious problem from September 10 to October 14, why did this problem suddenly disappear overnight, ushering in a furious campaign in which "there was hardly an hour of daylight that did not see a U-2 over some part of Cuba"?[43]

Each side's passivity might have been intended as a signal to the other that a mutual stand-down would be observed. Khrushchev would have known that the U-2 overflights were being curtailed, indicating the Americans' lessening anxiety about Cuba. And President Kennedy might have interpreted the absence of radar readiness signatures from the SA-2 sites as an indication that Khrushchev was not looking to create an incident. Notably, a postcrisis report by the staff of the CIA's deputy director of intelligence observed that curtailment of U-2 overflights of the Cuba land mass would probably have been detected by the Soviets and might well have been taken by Khrushchev as a signal of American acquiescence in the arms buildup: "Khrushchev might have concluded that the President, after stating that developments in Cuba were 'under our most careful surveillance,' had in fact decided to alter the pattern of surveillance in such a way as not to keep himself well informed: in other words, just as the United States had been indirectly invited to accept the build-up under the formula of defensive purpose, the United States might now be indirectly replying that it would acquiesce in the build-up by declining to discover the character and scope of it."[44]

Taubman echoed this same conjecture in his biography of the Soviet chairman, noting that Khrushchev's messages concerning standing down until the midterm election during September 1962 may have been intended to encourage the president "to do what [Khrushchev] assumed the president wanted to do anyway—namely, look the other way so as to avoid a preelection crisis and pave the way for a postelection summit."[45]

Ironically, the key evidence pointing to the Soviet installation of an MRBM missile site in western Cuba had been available to the US intelligence community in U-2 photographs from overflights that had already occurred on August 29 and September 5. General William Y. Smith, aide to General Taylor, would later reveal that a Defense Intelligence Agency analyst serving on the Mongoose project named Colonel John R. Wright Jr., had performed a "careful review of the films" from those two flights and "found patterns of Soviet equipment and construction pointing to preparations for a missile site." Wright was the second unsung hero of the missile crisis. Having served as chief of the DIA's (one-man) Latin American Division in the Estimates Office, Wright was enlisted in January 1962 to become the DIA's liaison to Mongoose and deputy chief of the JCS's working group for the operation.

It was Wright who first asked the NPIC in August 1962 to follow up on reports from Cuban refugees claiming to have sighted large equipment arriving in Cuba with a shape that appeared to resemble that of a surface-to-air missile. The report back from the agency describing "'long, slim objects' and their transport vehicles in convoy formation" persuaded Colonel Wright that these were indeed Soviet SA-2 surface-to-air missiles. On September 21, Wright received further reports of refugee sightings of "a convoy of twenty objects measuring between sixty-five and seventy-five feet, far too large to be SA-2s." By late September 1962, Wright had put the pieces together and concluded from intelligence photographs that "at least three of the SA-2 sites in Pinar del Rio province in western Cuba had no obvious reason for being there." He later wrote, "Thus, the pattern of the SA-2 sites, the reported presence of MRBMs, and the large restricted area in Pinar del Rio when put together led to the hypothesis that the Soviets could be setting up strategic missiles in Cuba." His conclusions convinced Secretary McNamara and JCS chairman Taylor at a meeting on October 1.[46]

Wright's pattern recognition was likely corroborated by a combination of overhead surveillance photos of missile installations in the Soviet Union and highly classified intelligence received from Oleg Penkovsky, a Soviet agent operating as an American spy, who was serving in the Chief Intelligence Administration of the Soviet General Staff. That Wright had consulted Corona or U-2 photos showing the configuration of Soviet bases in the homeland is indicated by notes JCS chairman Taylor made at the time which read: "By Oct. 1, possibility of MRBM's might be in the Pinar del Rio area . . . First MRBM—San Cristobal area in N. Cuba, no missile launchers, similar to Sov photo."[47] Similarly, Penkovsky had provided to his handlers both official operations manuals for Soviet MRBMs and IRBMs and his own handwritten diagrams of the standard configuration of Soviet missiles sites, including their surrounding array of SAM missile emplacements.[48] Information provided by Penkovsky was given the code name IRONBARK.[49]

Wright had been specifically enlisted by his intelligence analyst counterparts at the CIA to get involved in the overflight advocacy effort. This uncharacteristic exercise in interagency cooperation emerged, according to Holland and Barrett, after the CIA's combative September 10 meeting with Bundy and

Rusk. Following this meeting, "A degree of defensiveness had developed within the agency over the U-2 flights," causing the CIA's key staff official, Sam Halpern, to become concerned that any request emanating from the CIA "would be immediately discounted as the product of a politicized, unruly, or overly aggressive agency."[50] Wright's correct interpretation of the San Cristóbal photographic evidence, coupled with Colonel Ledford's opinion that the Soviet SAM sites posed a relatively low risk of a shoot-down, led the Kennedy administration to belatedly conduct what would turn out to be the pivotal U-2 overflight of the key target area at the critical eleventh hour.

October 10, 1962, first photographs of crates suspected of containing disassembled parts of IL-28 bombers shown to the president. The president requested that they be withheld and "future information be suppressed" until after the elections. Six weeks after Bolshakov's reported August 31 White House meeting, the presidential nondisclosure directive was still in effect, and the reason remained the same: Kennedy's concern over the potential adverse impact on the midterm elections. At a meeting on October 10, 1962, between the president, Bundy, and McCone, the CIA director showed the president air surveillance photographs of disassembled IL-28 bombers. These were offensive weapons under any practical definition since they had a combat radius of six hundred miles and were capable of carrying nuclear bombs.[51] According to McCone's contemporaneous file memorandum of the meeting, the president requested that this evidence "be withheld at least until after the elections as if the information got into the press, a new and more violent Cuban issue would be injected into the campaign and this would seriously affect his independence of action." When McCone demurred "that these particular photographs could not be restricted as they had been disseminated to the Intelligence Community and several joint and specified commands," the president requested that the report "be worded to indicate a probability rather than an actuality because in the final analysis we only saw crates, not the bombers themselves." McCone agreed to do this. But when the president went further and "requested that all future information be suppressed," McCone responded that this would be "extremely dangerous."[52]

It should be noted that the DCI report submitted to PFIAB in January 1963 gave an incomplete and somewhat misleading summary of the president's October 10 decision about dissemination of the IL-28 findings. Thus, the DCI's report noted at paragraph 21 that one result of the dissemination restriction put into place in early September was that "none" of the ensuing information "indicative . . . of a qualitative change in the nature of the arms build-up" appeared in the "President's Checklist." This was bound to leave an impression that even the president himself might have been denied early access to important new findings. The DCI report then stated at paragraph 22 that the "White House" gave permission for publication of the October 10 IL-28 findings on October 11, suggesting that the president had acted promptly as soon as he learned of this ominous new development. The report thus failed to record two highly illuminating elements of the president's earlier directives restricting dissemination of incoming intelligence: (1) that any new information suggestive of the presence of offensive Soviet weapons in Cuba had to be provided to the president himself before being shown to anyone else, and (2) that the president had tried unsuccessfully to order DCI McCone to keep all such information from other government officials "at least until after elections." The report was also somewhat misleading given that the purported October 11 White House permission to publish the IL-28 findings was a reference to the new intelligence sequestration program PSALM, which, as noted, was designed to maintain a highly secretive closed system of dissemination.

October 15, 1962, president wants no military action in Cuba over the next three months, or at minimum next thirty days. At a meeting on October 15, 1962, between Secretary of Defense McNamara and JCS chairman Maxwell D. Taylor, McNamara told Taylor that the president had directed that there should be no military action against Cuba during the next three months. Notes taken by the official recorder at the meeting were later produced under the Freedom of Information Act: "President wants no military action within the next three months, but he can't be sure because he does not control events. For instance aerial photos made available this morning show 68 boxes on ships that are not believed to be IL-28s and cannot be identified. However, the probabilities are strongly against military action in the next 30 days."[53]

SUMMARY

The historical record is reasonably clear that beginning on July 31, 1962, and for almost two and a half months thereafter President Kennedy actively solicited from Khrushchev a pact of mutual restraint so that the president could turn his full attention to advancing his domestic political agenda during the run-up to the crucial US midterm elections in early November 1962.

The president wanted protection from attacks by his domestic political opponents, who were charging that his administration was weak in its dealings with the Soviets over Berlin and Cuba. Khrushchev attempted to exploit Kennedy's vulnerability by offering his rival an arrangement based on mutual assurances of reciprocal accommodation. When the president accepted the deal, Khrushchev used the ensuing period of relative calm to continue Operation Anadyr under cover of a continuous stream of public and private assurances that he would do his part to preserve superpower tranquility through November 6. When the October 14 U-2 overflight discovered Soviet MRBM missiles in San Cristóbal, Cuba, President Kennedy concluded Khrushchev was guilty of playing a double game, and his brother would use a closely similar expression of opprobrium, calling it a double cross.

Yet the president had started the convoluted game and been a willing participant. It is true that he had been taken advantage of. But, as will be seen in the next chapter, the president was not naive about private deals of this kind, and he had taken steps to protect himself from at least some of the risks that were inherent in dealing with the Soviets, whom he knew to be masters of disinformation (*dezinformatsiya*) and military deception (*maskarovka*). The president and his brother would soon learn, however, that the most prominent step they had taken to protect themselves against deception—a highly publicized "red line" announcement by the administration on September 4, repeated on September 13, that the United States would not tolerate any installation of "ground-to-ground missiles" or other "significant offensive capability" or Soviet bases in Cuba—turned out not to be an insurance policy but rather a belated and excessive self-imposed constraint on their freedom of action.

CHAPTER 7

Painted into a Corner

Last month I said we weren't going to [allow it]. Last month I should have said that we don't care.

—PRESIDENT KENNEDY, EXCOMM, OCTOBER 16, 1962

Why would the president have agreed to an arrangement that seemed to let down the nation's guard in exchange for the president's domestic political interests? The most plausible answer is that Kennedy was persuaded that he wasn't giving away anything important; he saw no significant national security concern in the Soviet buildup in Cuba and felt that the bad publicity it was causing him was unfair partisan gamesmanship. He was convinced that the real Cold War threat emanated from Berlin, not Cuba.

The president's apparent thinking was punctuated by the unusual proposal he made to Khrushchev through Bolshakov on July 31. But was the president mindful at that time of the possibility that the Soviet arms shipments to Cuba might include ballistic missiles with nuclear warheads? Certainly officials responsible for national security would be expected to give some consideration to that possible danger in the circumstances, and strong suspicions were early aroused in the minds of CIA director John McCone, as already noted, as well as a number of high officials in the Pentagon.[1] And there is indeed some evidence in the historical record, provided by Commander Gerry McCabe based on his eyewitness experience as duty officer in the White House's Situation Room, that in early July 1962, President Kennedy was himself aware that the Soviets were likely sending ballistic missiles to Cuba.

Before the Soviet missile installations were photographed in western Cuba, it appeared, on the surface at least, that Soviet behavior was largely consistent with the conclusion that no new dangers were at hand. The Soviets had not undertaken any meaningful acts of aggression during 1962, there had been no serious cutoff of Western access to Berlin during that period, and, although the arms buildup in Cuba was troublesome from a domestic political standpoint, it did not overly concern the president as a matter of any real national security consequence threatening the Western Hemisphere. Rather, it seemed evident to President Kennedy and his team of national security advisers in September and early October 1962 that the stakes in Berlin and Cuba, the two major zones of friction, were matters of political concern rather than strategic or military consequence.

Surprisingly, the president did not change his basic opinion about this even after he learned of the U-2 photographs of the Soviet missiles on October 16, 1962. And his national security adviser, McGeorge Bundy, and his secretary of defense, Robert McNamara, both seemed to share this view.

How much did the forthcoming midterm elections claim the president's attention as he observed the Soviet arms buildup in Cuba during the late summer and early fall of 1962? If anyone would have had an insightful opinion on that issue, it would have been the president's top political advisers, Theodore Sorensen and Kenneth O'Donnell. Sorensen recalled that "politics was an ever-present influence in the Kennedy White House, not as the sole subject of many meetings in his office, but as a criterion for trips, visitors, appointees and speeches, and as an unspoken force counterbalancing the unrealistic, checking the unreasonable, occasionally deterring the desirable and always testing the acceptable." Members of the president's staff "automatically assumed" that "part of our role was to weigh the effect of every move and statement, large and small, on various voter groups, on Congress, on national unity and on the 1962 and 1964 elections."[2]

O'Donnell added that, while some in the White House believed the president "should remain aloof from party political fights while in office," O'Donnell and other "Irish partisan politicians in his circle" felt that the president "was urgently needed in the off-year campaign because our party desperately needed to increase its slim majority in Congress." According to O'Donnell Kennedy "loved to campaign and mix with the crowds" and "required little or no urging from us when the time came to hit the trail." While the president was campaigning on "the rise in employment and our need for more Democrats in Congress to push our social programs, particularly Medicare," the Republicans' "number one issue . . . was the Soviet buildup of weapons and military aid in Cuba."[3]

On October 16, the first day of ExComm meetings triggered by discovery of the missiles, McGeorge Bundy asked a key question: "What is the strategic impact on the position of the United States of MRBMs in Cuba?" McNamara responded that installation of Soviet missiles in Cuba did not change the strategic balance, which at the time strongly favored the United States, and McGeorge Bundy and CIA acting director Marshall Carter agreed:

BUNDY: But the question that I would like to ask is, quite aside from what we've said, and we're very hard locked on to it, I know: What is the strategic impact on the position of the United States of MRBMs in Cuba? How gravely does this change the strategic balance?

MCNAMARA: Mac, I asked the Chiefs that this afternoon, in effect. They said, "Substantially." My own personal view is: Not at all.

BUNDY: Not so much.

MCNAMARA: And I think this is an important element here. But it's all very . . .

BUNDY: Doesn't improve anything in the strategic balance.

CARTER: Doesn't improve anything. That was what the estimators felt, and that the Soviets would not take the risk.[4]

President Kennedy immediately picked up on this reaction, revealing his own impression of the critical issue in play: "What difference does it make? They've got enough to blow us up now anyway. I think it's just a question of . . . After all, this is a political struggle as much as a military."[5] McNamara echoed the president's views two days later, using almost the same words: "Speaking strictly in military terms, really in terms of weapons, it doesn't change it at all, in my personal opinion. . . . This doesn't really have any bearing on the issue, in my opinion, because it is not a military problem that we're facing. It's a political problem." The secretary of defense further explained that "the problem of holding the [NATO] alliance together, the problem of conditioning Khrushchev for our future moves, the problem of dealing with our domestic public, all requires action that, in my opinion, the shift in military balance does not require."[6]

On October 17, the second day of ExComm meetings, the president absented himself to make a campaign visit to Connecticut in support of a Democratic senatorial candidate. He rejoined the ExComm meeting at 11:00 a.m. on the morning of October 18 and that evening attended his prescheduled meeting with Soviet foreign minister Gromyko. The president then promptly headed west for further campaigning. The conventional narrative of this decision is that the president headed out on the campaign trail solely in order to "keep up appearances" in order to maintain the secrecy of the ExComm deliberations, and that when his brother called him on October 20 and "told him to come home," he feigned a cold and returned to the meetings with his top advisers.[7] While there is doubtless some truth to this narrative, a fuller and more candid explanation of the president's political imperatives in making the campaign swing west—especially the visit to Chicago at the behest of Mayor Richard Daley, Kennedy's key patron there—was again provided by his political adviser, Kenneth O'Donnell, who had given Daley "our firm promise that the President would appear on Friday [October 19] in Chicago to speak for Congressman Sid Yates, the Mayor's Democratic candidate in the Illinois Senatorial race that year against Everett Dirksen, the Republican leader in the Senate." There had been "much speculation in the press and in political circles about whether Kennedy might refrain from giving Yates his sincere support because Dirksen was friendly with the President."[8] Thus, at a minimum, the president was not simply "keeping up appearances" on the campaign trail; he was keeping vital campaign commitments that he considered to be of possibly greater importance than his participation in the ExComm meetings.

Some historians have imagined that the president had to reach into his reserves of strength and endurance to weather the psychological demands of the thirteen-day Cuban crisis. These commentators consistently cite Robert Kennedy's anecdote about a "pained" president, his face "drawn," putting his hand to his mouth in apparent shock when he learned that the navy was dropping mock depth charges in an effort to warn Soviet submarines to surface.[9] Two of the president's close associates, Kenneth O'Donnell and Dave Powers, who were in position to observe the president's state of mind during the crisis, provided a sharply different characterization: "Our outstanding memory of the two weeks of strained suspense in the White House during the Cuban missile crisis is the President's calmness and cool relaxation throughout the whole hectic period. The discovery of the Soviet offensive weapons in the Caribbean brought a kind of peace to his mind because now Khrushchev had crossed the Rubicon and the guessing game was over."[10]

In a comprehensive study of the US domestic political backdrop to the Cuban missile crisis published in 1986, Thomas G. Paterson and William J. Brophy concluded that President Kennedy and his domestic political advisers were intensely concerned about the upcoming midterm elections on November 6, 1962. Although the Democrats had comfortable majorities in both houses of Congress, midterm elections during a new president's first term were usually a setback for the incumbent's party. Moreover, in Kennedy's case, his apparent Democratic Party strength was weakened by the fact that many of the Democratic representatives and senators from the South were not aligned with the president's domestic policy agenda, especially on civil rights and social welfare programs like Medicare that were high priorities for the president's reelection. In this setting, the Soviet arms buildup in Cuba "took on serious political dimensions" when Republican leaders made it an effective midterm campaign issue "that probed one of the administration's most vulnerable spots." This also had the effect of "divert[ing] attention from Republican vulnerabilities stemming from their opposition to popular New Frontier programs." Republicans thus "strove to make Cuba, not Medicare, the leading topic of congressional campaigns."[11]

In his biography of Kennedy, Theodore Sorensen recalled that Fidel Castro's continued presence in 1962 as a Soviet client state just one hundred miles off the US mainland, and the Kennedy administration's seeming inability to do anything about it, became "the political Achilles' heel at which the President's opponents aimed." In the lead-up to the midterm elections, "The Republican Senatorial and Congressional Campaign Committees announced that Cuba would be 'the dominant issue of the 1962 campaign.'"[12]

Against this backdrop, Paterson and Brophy nevertheless reached the conclusion that Kennedy did not allow his domestic political interests to influence his handling of the foreign policy crisis in Cuba. But in reaching this conclusion, they were looking the wrong way. They assumed that if such influence existed, it would necessarily have been evidenced by presidential efforts "to manufacture or dangerously manipulate a confrontation with the Soviet Union"[13]—as a means to rally the country to the president's side against a foreign danger. They found no such evidence of what has more recently been referred to colloquially as a "wag the dog" tactic. But by thus focusing their attention, the authors were missing the real story. For if a heightening of Cuban tensions would shore up the Republican narrative that the president was weak, and thus divert attention from Democratic domestic policy strengths, it would have been in the president's interest to downplay the Cuba confrontation, not amplify it. And indeed that appears to have been the president's determined course of action. When leading Republican critics in the late summer and early fall of 1962 began to conduct almost daily attacks against the Kennedy administration for not paying close enough attention to what they claimed was a serious Soviet military threat in the nation's backyard, the president's consistent response was to deny the threat and diminish the significance of each new bit of evidence his critics cited.

When the president learned on October 16 that a U-2 mission had photographed a Soviet ballistic missile installation in Cuba two days before, he instantly recognized the harsh political repercussions. He told O'Donnell: "We've just elected Capehart in Indiana and Ken Keating will probably be the next President of the United States."[14] And he spoke even more despairingly with his brother: "The campaign is over. . . . This blows it—we've lost anyway. They were right about Cuba."[15]

The White House had issued a public statement on September 4 regarding the Soviet arms buildup in Cuba that was intended to be simultaneously reassuring to the American public and an emphatic red-line warning to the Soviet Union. The announcement, released on President Kennedy's instructions by Pierre Salinger, made it clear that, while there was no specific evidence that Soviet offensive missiles were in Cuba, the Kremlin should consider itself placed on notice that the Americans were watching and would not accept any significant offensive capability. A U-2 flight six days before the president's September 4 statement had detected the presence of a Soviet ground-to-ground cruise missile at the Banes site in Cuba, and this information had been included in the "President's Checklist" provided by the CIA on August 29. McGeorge Bundy would later confess that the president's September 4 statement was not deemed necessary for any serious foreign policy concern, but was issued "because of the requirements of domestic politics."[16] He would also later assert that "we did not expect Khrushchev to put missiles in Cuba, which accounts for the relatively untroubled way in which we wrote our warnings in September."[17] But Bundy's comment was at best an oversimplification. While the president may not have expected the Soviets to put missiles in Cuba at that moment on September 4, 1962, he and his advisers had in fact been expecting that Soviet surface-to-surface missiles would be sent to Cuba in the near future, and they were discussing that concern at a meeting only eleven days earlier, leading to the previously mentioned NSAM 181 and its call for a study of "the probable military, political, and psychological impact of the establishment in Cuba of . . . surface-to-surface missiles which could reach the U.S." Moreover, when the anticipated event arrived, the president made it clear that he did not consider the missiles to be of any military concern to him. When he learned of the U-2 photos showing the missiles being installed in western Cuba, he expressed regret that he had made his red-line pronouncements against them on September 4 and 13 when he told his advisers: "Last month I said we weren't going to [allow it]. Last month I should have said that we don't care."[18] Sorensen underscored this point years later when he acknowledged that "if we had known that the Soviets were putting forty missiles in Cuba, we might under this hypothesis have drawn the line at one hundred, and said with great fanfare that we would absolutely not tolerate the presence of more than one hundred missiles in Cuba."[19]

There were other indications that the September 4 warning was politically charged. Senator Keating had appeared on a political talk show with Martin Agronsky earlier that day, prompting "a livid Pierre Salinger" to call Agronsky and complain to the NBC commentator that he should not have given the senator this public platform to air his "inaccurate statements": "'We can't stop a Senator from saying whatever he wants to,' Agronsky replied. 'In what respect was it inaccurate?' 'Well, the President will deal with those inaccuracies,' replied Salinger. 'He'll have a statement later today.' The president's 4 September message was to a considerable degree, then, a direct reply to Keating's charges."[20]

It was no coincidence that President Kennedy met with congressional leaders on that same day, September 4, in an effort "to quiet the clamor," and that he thereafter issued the press statement quoted above. But the statement did not placate the administration's critics. Reacting the next day to the president's red-line warning about offensive missiles, Senator Keating said, "Who is to say whether a weapon is offensive or defensive? It depends on the direction in which it is aimed."[21] Dean Rusk made the same point in late September in an interview with the ABC State Department correspondent: "Now, I don't think that we ought to play with words on this question of defensive and offensive weapons. Any weapon is offensive if you are on the wrong end of it."[22]

The Kremlin responded to the president's September 4 message with its own counterstatement published on September 11 in TASS, an official government press organ, which denied there was any need for the USSR to place offensive weapons overseas. As noted earlier, the TASS statement then repeated the Soviet disinformation that the arms buildup in Cuba was "solely for defensive purposes."

It is evident that the president considered the Cuba developments to be largely a *political* distraction rather than a national security problem. As the drumbeat of Senator Keating's speeches about the administration's weak response on Cuba began to mount, McGeorge Bundy urged the president on September 13 to issue a strong rejoinder, stating that "the Congressional head of steam on this is the most serious that we have had." Bundy feared that the administration "may appear to be weak and indecisive," and he urged the president to speak out with "a very clear and aggressive explanation" of US policy to establish that the Cuban problem was "within our control."[23]

The president followed this advice by opening his press conference that day with a formal statement that if Cuba were to become "an offensive military base of significant capacity for the Soviet Union," then he would do "whatever must be done" to protect the nation's "security and that of its allies."[24] He made no mention of nuclear weapons. The president remained convinced that much of the talk about Cuba was politically motivated. As his political aide Kenny O'Donnell later wrote, Kennedy believed that "the possibility of Soviet offensive missiles being installed in Cuba seemed so unlikely in the early days of October, 1962," that he "assumed that the charges of Keating and Capehart were merely Republican campaign talk."[25]

The White House pronouncements of September 4 and 13—amounting to a red-line declaration that the United States would not allow the Soviets to place offensive missiles in Cuba—created a problem of major proportions for the president. First, the rigid red-line feature of the declarations severely limited his options if the Soviets chose to defy the US mandate.[26] But second, and perhaps even more problematical for Kennedy given his concerns about an adverse reaction to his foreign policy stewardship in forthcoming elections, the declarations eliminated the president's option of doing nothing dramatic in response to direct Soviet disobedience of the mandate.

Michael Beschloss neatly summed up the magnitude of the mistake: "Kennedy now knew he had erred badly by brushing aside McCone's numerous warnings" and by making "an unambiguous pledge" to "do whatever must be done" if Khrushchev introduced ground-to-ground missiles into Cuba. Instead, he should have "phrased his September pledge more vaguely or not at all," leaving his administration "the option of explaining to Americans that they had little to fear from the missiles in Cuba."[27]

Khrushchev had explained to the Presidium nine months earlier in his Meniscus speech that the superpowers were playing the Cold War game across a vast global landscape. The Soviet leader ultimately concluded that he had allowed the surface tension to become disturbed to overflowing and thus he had to pull back. Kennedy, too, recognized that he was in a high-stakes game with Khrushchev, and he learned on October 16, 1962, that he had suffered a humiliating setback. He had been tricked into thinking he and Khrushchev had agreed to a kind of armistice through the midterm elections. As he confided to British prime minister Harold Macmillan, Kennedy felt he had been fooled by his rival's double game. Robert Kennedy would subsequently use a similar but more prosaic expression: Khrushchev had "double-crossed us." President Kennedy's instant, hapless reaction of deep personal affront on October 16 when he learned about the Soviet missiles—"He can't do this to me!"—was what courts refer to as an "excited utterance"—a statement deemed to be reliable because it was spoken spontaneously at the scene of an alarming event without affording the speaker time to formulate a deception.[28]

The president's initial view of the Soviet buildup was closely aligned with the Kremlin's disinformation campaign about defensive weapons being deployed for defensive purposes only. As Barrett and Holland concluded in their study of the "photo gap," the president shared the view "held by the overwhelming majority of senior officials in his administration" that the military aid being sent to Cuba "was for the purpose of ostentatiously defending" the Castro regime and "setting up the island as a model of socialist development and bridgehead for subversive activities in the region." Thus, the discovery of Soviet surface-to-air missiles "did not signal a foreign policy crisis as much as a domestic political one. With a midterm election fast approaching, pressure to 'do something' about Cuba was bound to mount and would have to be managed carefully."[29]

As the president's political adviser, Kenneth O'Donnell, later wrote in his memoirs: "President Kennedy never felt that the installation of the missiles really changed the balance of military power. He knew we possessed overwhelming military superiority."[30] Kennedy himself made this point on the first day of the ExComm deliberations, observing, in effect, that possession of ICBMs already gave the Soviets all the threat they needed:

> You may say it doesn't make any difference if you get blown up by an ICBM flying from the Soviet Union or one that was 90 miles away. Geography doesn't mean that much. . . . I agree, what difference does it make? They've got enough to blow us up now anyway. I think it's just a question of . . . After all, this is a political struggle as much as military.[31]

McNamara made the same point more bluntly a few minutes later: "I'll be quite frank. I don't think there *is* a military problem there. . . . This is a domestic political problem. In the announcement [on September 4]—we didn't say we'd go in and not [that] we'd kill them. We said we'd *act*. Well, how will we act?"[32]

McGeorge Bundy had been one of the earliest among the members of the president's group of top advisers to express *lack* of concern about a possible Soviet insertion of ballistic missiles in Cuba. As early as September 4, when the White House was drafting the message the president would issue later that day warning the Russians about grave consequences that would attend any discovery of offensive weapons in Cuba, McNamara cautioned the drafting group that it would be a mistake to include in the warning specific weapons like surface-to-surface missiles "unless we know exactly what we're going to do under those circumstances." It was at that point that Bundy observed, "Our preliminary analysis of the consequences for us, Bob, of the establishment of a surface-to-surface nuclear capability gives me at least the feeling that we wouldn't have to act."[33] Six weeks later, on October 17, 1962, Bundy prepared a memorandum for the president in which he stated that it was "generally agreed" that the Soviet missiles in Cuba "even when fully operational, do not significantly alter the balance of power" or "significantly increase the potential megatonnage capable of being unleashed on American soil, even after a surprise American nuclear strike."[34]

On October 18, in a self-dictated summary of discussions during the day that had not been recorded by the White House taping system, President Kennedy noted that he had spoken with Robert Lovett, who told the president that while "he was not convinced that any action was desirable," he feared "a Soviet reprisal against Berlin . . . that . . . would divide our alliances," and he was concerned the United States would "be regarded [by its European allies] as having brought about the loss of Berlin with inadequate provocation, they having lived with these intermediate-range ballistic missiles for years." The president also dictated for the record Bundy's recommendation "against any action" and in doing so returned to the theme that he and Khrushchev were engaged in a high-stakes game. According to the president's recording, Bundy's view, echoing his own and that of Robert Lovett, was that "we would be better off to merely take note of the existence of these missiles, and to wait until the crunch comes in Berlin, and not play what he thought might be the Soviet game."[35]

There is an intriguing hint in the early drafting of what would become the president's October 22 address to the nation that Kennedy's view of the Soviet missiles continued to be placid even at that critical juncture. Thus, Theodore Sorensen's second draft of the speech, dated October 20, 1962, and distributed to JCS chair Taylor for comment, contained the following statement: "Nevertheless, American citizens have become adjusted to living daily on the bull's eye of Soviet missiles located inside the USSR or in submarines. In that sense, our danger today has not yet been greatly increased." General Taylor recommended that the entire section containing that statement should be deleted because it "can be turned to our disadvantage" and "will not bear careful scrutiny."[36]

One of the most extraordinary portions of the secret taping system that President Kennedy maintained at the White House is a fragment of the tapes recorded during the evening of October 23, 1962. That fragment, which preserved for posterity a private conversation in the Oval Office between the president and his brother, is unique in the historiography of John F. Kennedy's presidency and crucial to a clear understanding of the president's thinking about how the crisis arose and his strategy for bringing it to an end. Yet this densely packed segment of the White House tapes has garnered scant interest from missile crisis scholars, who have taken note of the Kennedy brothers' private moment pondering the risk of impeachment,[37] but have given this arresting exchange little more than brief attention.

The passage is the only recording in existence that captures Kennedy in a private moment of candor[38] discussing his unvarnished views about three underexamined mysteries of the Cuban missile crisis: why Kennedy felt that the naval quarantine was the only politically palatable option available to him in the partisan cauldron his Republican adversaries had created; how he planned to launch his secret missile trade offer through the Bolshakov back channel in an effort to bring a quick end to the crisis; and how Khrushchev had double-crossed him by flouting the mutual forbearance deal the two leaders had struck in the lead-up to the crisis.

Here is the full transcribed text of the brief, private, Cabinet Room conversation between the president and the attorney general at approximately 7:00 p.m. on the evening of October 23, 1962. Accommodation must be made for the president's Delphic and frequently elliptical and "rapid-fire shorthand" way of speaking,[39] and for the attorney general's "inarticulateness," as is abundantly clear to any reader of the White House tape transcripts.[40]

ROBERT KENNEDY: How does it look?

PRESIDENT KENNEDY: Ah, looks like hell—looks real mean, doesn't it? But, on the other hand, there is no other choice. If they get this mean on this one, it's just a question of where they go about it next.[41] No choice. I don't think there was a choice.

ROBERT KENNEDY: Well, there isn't any choice. I mean, you would have been, you would have been impeached.

PRESIDENT KENNEDY: That's what I think. I would have been impeached. I think they would have moved to impeach. I wouldn't be surprised if they didn't move to impeach right after this election, on the grounds that I said . . . and didn't do it and let . . . I mean, I'd be . . .

ROBERT KENNEDY: I don't think that [unclear]. You know that's a . . . if we'd gone in and done something else, or taken some other step that wasn't necessary, and then you'd be . . .

PRESIDENT KENNEDY: Yeah.

ROBERT KENNEDY: Yeah. But now, the fact is, that you couldn't have done any less. The fact that you got all those South American countries to vote unanimously [in the Organization of American States]. When they've been kicking us in the ass for two years, and they vote unanimously for this. And then to get the reaction from the rest of the allies, you know like [British ambassador] David Ormsby-Gore and everybody else. Saying that you had to do it. You calculate . . . I mean, if it's going to come at you, it was going to come as something you couldn't have avoided. I think I just probably had—could get somebody that kept in communication with them [the Soviets]. It's too bad. [unclear].

PRESIDENT KENNEDY: What is?

ROBERT KENNEDY: You know.

PRESIDENT KENNEDY: Take Georgi [unclear]

ROBERT KENNEDY: No, he had lunch today with—

PRESIDENT KENNEDY: What's he [Bolshakov] saying?

ROBERT KENNEDY: He said they are going to go through [the blockade].

PRESIDENT KENNEDY: The ships are going through?

ROBERT KENNEDY: He [Bolshakov] says this is [chuckles slightly], this is a defensive base for the Russians. It's got nothing to do with Cuba.

PRESIDENT KENNEDY: Why are they lying about that? Khrushchev's horseshit about the election. In any event, it's the sickening thing that [unclear] to be getting very mad about . . . they revealed about [sarcastically] this *horror* that [this] would embarrass me in the election.[42] Who saw Georgi? Holeman? While we were there? But he's not with us in this.

ROBERT KENNEDY: Well, as you know, he [Bolshakov] is very hurt about the fact that I hadn't seen him. And then he came back to see me, and he said Khrushchev had a message for you. And I followed it up. The ambassador [Anatoly Dobrynin] kept telling me: "Don't pay attention to Georgi." So I don't know if there's something going on.

PRESIDENT KENNEDY: But did any of them tell you that they were going to put missiles there?

ROBERT KENNEDY: No. Remember, when I told you that.[43]

First, this private exchange between the president and his brother makes it clear that the president's preference would have been to do nothing, or next to nothing, in response to the discovery of Soviet ballistic missiles in Cuba, but that course would have been too politically dangerous. The president opened by saying: "There [was] no other choice . . . no choice . . . I don't think there was a choice." His brother emphatically agreed, explicitly identifying domestic politics as the problem: "Well, there isn't any choice. I mean, you would have been, you would have been impeached." The president concurred: "That's what I think. I would have been impeached. I think they would have moved to impeach."[44]

Most of the ExComm participants had favored more aggressive military options, including air strikes and invasion. What did Robert Kennedy mean when he said, "You couldn't have done any *less*" (emphasis added)? The only less aggressive choices that ExComm had seriously discussed were to do nothing or merely apply "diplomatic pressures and warnings." Here the president was agreeing with his brother that he would have faced impeachment if he had opted for an unnamed lesser strategy that he had "no choice" but to discard. That could only have been the option of doing nothing. Stated differently, Kennedy's preference would have been to do nothing, but he was compelled by domestic political pressure to do something or face impeachment, even if that something was the relatively minimal step of a quarantine.

Kennedy had made the same point to his friend David Ormsby-Gore, the British ambassador to the United States, only two days before when the president had asked him "to come unseen" to meet with the President "alone, just before lunch" on October 21. In his first cable (on October 22) to Prime

Minister Macmillan summarizing their discussion, the ambassador revealed the president's concern about political pressures that were weighing on him: "The President explained that he and his colleagues had also decided on the blockade. At this point he alluded to other options, including a full-scale invasion, for which 'they might never have a better opportunity'; they could also 'do nothing at all and go on as before, but he thought that this was not only politically impossible but was in any case too dangerous.'"[45]

In his second and more detailed October 23 cable to Macmillan—coincidentally transmitted at almost exactly the same time as Robert Kennedy's "you couldn't have done any less" comment to his brother—Ormsby-Gore offered his leader the opinion "that Americans of every persuasion regard the President's action as the *absolute minimum* required to meet what all see as a deliberate Russian challenge to test the will and resolution of the United States."[46] In doing so the ambassador was almost surely conveying something Kennedy had said to him; the close linkage between the Ormsby-Gore and Robert Kennedy comments is underscored not only by the similarity of the two formulations but also by the fact that the British ambassador and his wife had dined with the president at the White House just a few minutes after Kennedy concluded his private conversation with the attorney general that was picked up by the White House taping system.

In hindsight, it seems implausible that a "do nothing" choice would have been a credible option for the president. But in fact, as indicated by Ormsby-Gore's cable to the British prime minister, the president had rejected the "do nothing" option because it was "politically impossible" as well as "too dangerous." And, notably, the "do nothing" option was exactly what the Kremlin firmly expected: the president "would swallow whatever he found in Cuba" because, Soviet leaders believed, he "was more concerned with Berlin and the congressional elections and was not about to reopen the debate in his own government over using military forces in Cuba."[47]

The do-nothing option, and its marginally more assertive variant of pursuing only "diplomatic pressures and warnings," were the first and second alternatives listed among the ExComm's six major options at the outset of their deliberations, and "both [were] seriously considered" in the lead-up to the actual quarantine decision, as confirmed in Theodore Sorensen's biography of Kennedy: "As some (but not all) Pentagon advisers pointed out to the President, we had long lived within range of Soviet missiles, we expected Khrushchev to live with our missiles nearby, and by taking this addition calmly we could prevent him from inflating its importance. All the other courses raised so many risks and drawbacks that choice No. 2 [diplomacy and warnings] had its appeal. All of us came back to it at one discouraged moment or another; and it was advocated to the President as a preferable alternative to blockade by one of the regular members of our group in the key Thursday night [October 18] meeting."[48]

Sorensen stated in his 1965 *Kennedy* biography that the president rejected the two minimalist options "from the outset," not so much out of concern for their "military implications" but rather because of "their effect on the global political balance," especially considering the "political and psychological effect on Latin America."[49] When Sorensen was writing his biography of Kennedy, however, he did not have the benefit of the ExComm transcripts, which allow modern readers to examine much of what the president actually said each day of the crisis, ranging from his initial, almost panicked assertion on October 16 that a prompt air attack on the missile sites would "certainly" be necessary ("We're certainly going to do number one; we're going to take out these, uh, missiles"),[50] to his later comments, presumably during calmer moments, about the do-nothing option. When Sorensen recounted the Cuban crisis in his later memoirs, written in 2008, he was more forthcoming about the saliency of the do-nothing option in the president's and Bundy's thinking at later stages of the ExComm deliberations. Sorensen noted, for example, that on Thursday, October 18, "Mac Bundy (possibly at the president's urging) was insisting that the 'sit-tight and do nothing' option be discussed again." Bundy was making the facially persuasive point that "our European allies had learned to live in the Soviet nuclear bull's-eye and maybe we could do so as well." But the president's aide observed that the do-nothing option was foreclosed by domestic politics: Kennedy would "surely" have incurred the "domestic political wrath from hard-line superpatriots (by doing nothing)" and this would have led to "their take-over of the U.S. government," which, in Sorensen's view, would have "made world war even more likely."[51]

The president's comments captured on the White House taping system indicate that Kennedy would have preferred to take no aggressive action in response to Khrushchev's missile gambit—because the Soviet missiles in Cuba did not materially change the strategic balance. Nevertheless, he felt compelled to "do something" lest he suffer political criticism from NATO allies and even the risk of impeachment in Congress, as the following transcripts show.

Tuesday, October 16, 1962, 6:30–8:00 p.m.

PRESIDENT KENNEDY: I said we weren't going to [allow it].
BUNDY: That's something we could manage.
PRESIDENT KENNEDY: Last month I said we weren't going to [allow it]. Last month I should have said that we don't care. But when we said we're *not* going to, and then they go ahead and do it, and then we do nothing, then I would think that our risks increase.[52]

Thursday, October 18, 1962, 11:10 a.m.–1:15 p.m.

PRESIDENT KENNEDY: On holding the alliance. Which is going to strain the alliance more: This attack by us on Cuba, which most allies regard as a fixation of the United States and not a serious military threat? I mean you'd have to . . . an awful lot of conditioning would have to go in before they would accept, support our action against Cuba, because they think we're slightly demented on this subject.
So there isn't any doubt that whatever actions we take against Cuba, no matter how good our films are, or going to cause [problems] in Latin America. A lot of, a lot of people would regard this as a mad act by the United States, which is due to a loss of nerve because they will argue that, taken at its worst, the presence of these missiles really doesn't change the . . . if you think that, they're going to, certainly. With all the incentives to think the other way, viewing this as you do as an American, what's everybody else going to think who isn't under this gun. . . .[53]
PRESIDENT KENNEDY: Let me ask you. It seems to me we have been talking about the alliance, you've got two problems. One would be the problem of the alliance when we say to them that the presence of these missiles requires a military action by us. There's no doubt that they will oppose that, because they'll feel that their risks increase, and this is a risk to us. They'll argue what is Secretary McNamara's point.
If we don't take any action, then of course there will be a more gradual deterioration, I suppose. . . .[54]
After my statement, and then, I mean . . . Somehow we've got to take some action because we couldn't. . . . Because the Alliance would disintegrate. . . .[55]

PRESIDENT KENNEDY: Well, let me ask you this. Is there anyone here who doesn't think that we ought to do something about them?[56]

Friday, October 19, 1962, 9:45–10:30 a.m.

PRESIDENT KENNEDY: Well, it is a fact that the number of missiles there, let's say . . . no matter what they put in there, we could live today under. If they don't have enough ICBMs today, they're going to have them in a year. They obviously are putting in a lot of . . .[57]

PRESIDENT KENNEDY: Well, the logical argument is that we don't really have to invade Cuba. That's not really . . . That's just one of the difficulties that we live with in life, like we live with the Soviet Union and China.

That problem, however, is after . . . for us not to do anything, then wait until he brings up Berlin. And then we can't do anything about Cuba.

But I do think we ought to be aware of the fact that the existence of these missiles does add to the danger but doesn't create it. The danger is right there now. They've got enough to give us, between submarines and ICBMs, or whatever planes they do have, I mean now they can kill, especially if they concentrate on the cities, I mean they've pretty well got us there anyway.[58]

October 22, 1962. As noted above, Robert Kennedy's handwritten list of options mirrored the president's statements in ExComm meetings that NATO allies would wonder why the United States could not accept "living under the gun" since for years they had become accustomed to being within range of Soviet MRBM and IRBM missiles. Kennedy included in his options list the entry: "Do Nothing—Argument that we have been living under the gun . . . Argument that we are [crossed out] have been living under gun anyway and we can't guarantee getting them out."[59]

The president recognized that if he was in danger of impeachment proceedings, he had only himself to blame. This was because he had painted himself into a corner by broadcasting his highly specific red-line pronouncement on September 4 that the "gravest issues" would arise if the Soviets placed any offensive missiles in Cuba. There can be no doubt that Kennedy himself recognized that his unqualified public commitment that a Soviet installation of offensive missiles in Cuba would be a matter of grave concern was a serious tactical mistake that severely constrained his options.

Did Kennedy really mean to say to his ExComm colleagues that a wiser course in early September would have been for him to communicate to the Soviets that the United States *"didn't care"* about their Cuban arms buildup, even if it included MRBMs and IRBMs? Would the reason for this expression of disinterest have been because the United States maintained such a great strategic lead that even a hostile missile installation close to the US border would make no difference? Or was the president simply expressing a view, shared by leaders among his NATO allies no less than by Khrushchev himself, that the United States should simply accept the presence of hostile missiles close to its borders as a fact of modern life that all of its Western European allies and the Soviet Union had long since been compelled to get used to?

Yet having drawn such an explicit red line over the consequences that would follow should Soviet missiles appear in Cuba, Kennedy was virtually compelled by political necessity to follow through with at least some action even though his preference would have been to say, in effect, "We don't care." He was acknowledging the same "I said it but then didn't do it" problem, albeit using highly elliptical words, in his private October 23 conversation with his brother, when he said: "I wouldn't be surprised if they didn't move to impeach right after this election, on the grounds that I said . . . and didn't do it and let . . . I mean, I'd be . . ."[60]

McNamara later acknowledged that "right from the beginning, it was President Kennedy who said that it was *politically* unacceptable for us to leave those [Cuban] missile sites alone."[61] Barton Bernstein remarked on the irony that "what dominated the ExComm discussions was the political, not the military, significance of the MRBMs and possible IRBMs in Cuba." Bernstein also saw the obvious connection to "the earlier deployment of the Jupiters in Turkey and Italy," an action by the United States that "had been shaped by political, not military considerations."[62]

The president was not the only one in the ExComm sessions who had domestic politics in mind. Richard Lebow has observed that there was good reason for ExComm members to avoid explicit references to domestic political concerns, noting that "the president was an astute enough politician to be sensitive to the possibility that any comment he made about the election might later be used against him or even leaked by ExComm members opposed to the blockade." Nevertheless, Lebow pointed to domestic political considerations that were discussed on the first and last days of the ExComm meetings, including McNamara's statement on October 16 that the missiles were "primarily a domestic political problem," and the president's mordant observation on October 27 that "when the blood starts to flow," public opinion would turn against a president who allowed this to happen because of concern for obsolescent missiles in Turkey.[63] Lebow failed to mention another intrusion of domestic politics into the ExComm deliberations. Theodore Sorensen reported in his biography of Kennedy that Douglas Dillon, a Republican member of the president's ExComm advisers, handed him a note during one of the ExComm sessions stating: "Have you considered the very real possibility that if we allow Cuba to complete installation and operational readiness of missile bases, the next House of Representatives is likely to have a Republican majority? This would completely paralyze our ability to react sensibly and coherently to further Soviet advances."[64]

Turning back to the private conversation between the president and his brother on October 23, the president's mention of the journalist Holeman was followed by this mysterious question posed as a querulous statement: "But he's not with us in this." The "he" was clearly Holeman, but who was the "us" that the president was referring to? Then, even more important, what was the "this" that the "us" were pursuing? The answers seem fairly clear given that a main subject of the brothers' private conversation on the evening of October 23 was use of the Bolshakov back channel to send a message to Khrushchev that withdrawal of the NATO missiles in Turkey might be part of a deal to resolve the Cuba crisis. The president did not bother to ask his brother whether Charles Bartlett was "with us" even though he had mentioned Bartlett immediately before Holeman. But then the president already knew that Bartlett was on board in advancing the missile swap-out deal because Kennedy himself had disclosed the possibility of such a deal to Bartlett only two days before, on October 21, and he had also specifically instructed Robert Kennedy to have Bartlett meet with Bolshakov on that very day, October 23, to further that purpose.[65] So the "us" clearly referred to the small group of Kennedy intimates who knew about the president's decision to offer Khrushchev a US missile exchange concession—including at least Bartlett and the attorney general—and the "this" was most logically the terms of the concession itself—an offer of the Turkey missiles in exchange for the Cuba missiles. The president evidently had been unaware that his brother had invited Holeman to join the missile swap-out inner circle, but so great was his trust in the attorney general and in Holeman that this addition did not seem to generate any concern.[66]

A modern observer might wonder at the notion of a president using journalists as his private intermediaries in a highly sensitive diplomatic transaction in which protecting the details from public scrutiny was vital. But then Frank Holeman and Charles Bartlett were no ordinary journalists. They were trusted insiders within the president's and his brother's back-channel operation. Frank Holeman had introduced Georgi Bolshakov to the attorney general in 1961, and the *New York Daily News* reporter had been "worked" as a source of useful information by successive Soviet agents working undercover in the United States.[67] Bartlett enjoyed an even closer Kennedy connection. A longtime personal friend of the president, Bartlett was the one who introduced Jack and Jackie to each other at "a small dinner party in May 1951" at the journalist's Georgetown home. As noted in his obituary in the *New York Times*, Bartlett was "well aware of the conflict he faced" in reporting for his newspaper on the presidency of his close friend. He would later tell writer Sally Bedel Smith, "Nothing mattered to me more than to have Jack Kennedy succeed as president. . . . It did compromise my role as a journalist."[68]

The president's meaning in this tangled part of his private conversation with his brother on the evening of October 23 can be decoded by focusing on the key words "lying," "election," and "embarrass."

"Lying" and the "election." First, the president seemed to be indicating in his October 23 remarks to his brother that he was angered not simply by Bolshakov's disingenuous comment that the Soviet arms shipments were "defensive" but also by the separate notion the Soviets were conveying that the arms were not being given to the Cubans but rather remained under the control of the Soviets.

In response to the president's question, "What's he [Bolshakov] saying?" Robert Kennedy provided two of the GRU officer's comments: that the Soviet ships would try to penetrate the blockade (which proved to be incorrect), and then this statement, which Robert Kennedy delivered with a derisive chuckle: "He [Bolshakov] says this is [chuckles slightly], this is a defensive base for the Russians. It's got nothing to do with Cuba." Bolshakov's reference to "defensive" is plain enough; it parroted the Soviet party line about the defensive nature of the arms shipments. But why did Bolshakov emphasize, as if to placate the Kennedys, that the bases being built in Cuba were "for the Russians" and had "nothing to do with Cuba"?

The most likely possibility, though this is speculative, is that the Kremlin understood the president would be more comfortable with the Soviet arms shipments—whatever their nature—if he could be assured that all such arms would remain under the exclusive control of Soviet military leadership and would not be placed into the hands of the Cubans. This notion makes sense, given the view, shared by both White House and Kremlin officials, that the Cubans were "hot-headed" and would be unpredictable in a crisis. It is therefore plausible that an assurance that Soviet commanders would maintain tight control over the weapons would have been an integral part of Khrushchev's back-channel messaging to Kennedy. But if such a confidential communication was in fact being transmitted by Bolshakov and with that purpose, it seemed to have lost some of its significance in the translation, to Robert Kennedy at least, since the attorney general's reaction appears to have been a derisive chuckle.

There is fragmentary evidence in the historical record that maintenance of Soviet control over their weapons in Cuba may in fact have been one of the subjects that was discussed in the Kennedy/Khrushchev back-channel exchanges. The evidence, which is unconfirmed, consists of comments Anastas Mikoyan later made to Fidel Castro shortly after the Cuban missile crisis had abated and the Soviets were trying to patch up their frayed relationship with their Cuban protégé. In his conversation with Castro, Mikoyan evinced what appears to have been his government's purported knowledge in the lead-up to the crisis that the Kennedy administration's main concern was not so much the missiles themselves as the question of whose military—Russian or Cuban—would control them. At a meeting on November 22, 1962, for which a contemporaneous detailed summary was prepared, the following exchange occurred:

> F. CASTRO: It all began with the Soviet Marshal of the Rocket Forces [Sergey Biryuzov], promising us the missiles. We believed that the missiles were delivered to Cuba not in the interest of Cuba, because we did not need them. Then I gave my consent, thinking that we were fulfilling our duty to the socialist camp. We took the risk, believing that the socialist camp would also take the risk for us. We were even prepared for a nuclear war in the event if the Soviet Union was attacked. Now I can see that the Soviet government was not prepared to do the same for us.
>
> A. I. MIKOYAN: We were also prepared to make sacrifices for Cuba. The Americans were not as much afraid because we deployed our missiles in Cuba as they were afraid that we would transfer them to you.
>
> F. CASTRO: Doesn't the Soviet Union transfer nuclear weapons to other countries?
>
> A. I. MIKOYAN: We have a law prohibiting the transfer of any nuclear

> weapons, including the tactical ones, to anybody. We never transferred it to anyone, and we did not intend to transfer it. The nuclear weapons, remaining in our hands, would be used in the event of a war to defend the entire socialist camp.[69]

"Lying . . . horseshit . . . election . . . embarrass . . . election." The president asked a question that appears in the flow of the brothers' conversation to be a non sequitur: "Why are they lying about that? Khrushchev's horseshit about the election." This was evidently a reference to the Soviet chairman's cascade of promises directly and through intermediaries that he would give the president a period of relative calm allowing him to campaign without foreign disturbance for his party's candidates in the US midterm elections. It is apparent the president was angry and worried that the long line of Khrushchev's election stand-down assurances could create problems for him: "In any event, it's the sickening thing that [unclear] to be getting very mad about . . . they revealed about [sarcastically] this horror that [this] would embarrass me in the election."[70]

What did "embarrass me in the election" signify for the president? The vivid language ("sickening," "horror") and the sarcastic tone suggest that what bothered the president was the Soviet leader's assurances, now shown to be a double cross or double game, that he would keep tensions between the superpowers on hold until after the midterm election. And what angered Kennedy even more, to the point of uttering a vulgar expression, was Khrushchev's condescending desire to do this in order to spare the president embarrassment in his domestic political affairs.

Kennedy felt that he had fallen victim to the Soviet chairman's duplicity, which he had characterized as a "double game" in a telephone conversation with British prime minister Harold Macmillan just the day before. As memorialized on October 22 by the official notetaker: "Khrushchev, Kennedy thought, had 'played a double game. You remember that he kept saying he was coming over here after the election and would do nothing to disturb the situation until after the election. He said that the weapons were defensive, that they weren't moving any missiles there and all the rest. And obviously he has been building this up in order to face us with a bad situation in November at the time he was going to squeeze us on Berlin.'"[71]

At a minimum, the president seemed to be conveying to Macmillan his resentment, verging on anger, about having been encouraged to think that Khrushchev was being truthful when he provided multiple repeated assurances that the Soviets would be doing nothing during the months of July through October to cause tensions between the superpowers, whereas in fact Khrushchev had been using this time to secretly place ballistic missiles right next to the American homeland.

The president's reference to "embarrass" as "the sickening thing" about Khrushchev offering to save him from being "embarrass[ed] . . . in the election" was foreshadowed by messages Kennedy had received from Khrushchev through Soviet ambassador Dobrynin on September 4 ("he liked President Kennedy and did not wish to embarrass him"), Alexander Zinchuk, a Soviet embassy official, on October 12, (Khrushchev "expressed regret that their [Soviet technicians in Cuba] arrival had been a political embarrassment to [the president]"),[72] and US ambassador Kohler on October 16 (Khrushchev was "most anxious not to do anything that will embarrass the President during the campaign"). It seems likely that what mainly "sickened" President Kennedy was consideration of what might befall him if Khrushchev's many stand-down-through-the-election messages were opened to public scrutiny, especially if considered in conjunction with Khrushchev's simultaneous offer of political assistance to the president and his duplicitous campaign to sneak ballistic missiles into Cuba. Would this not painfully reveal the magnitude of the president's own naivete, imprudence, and politically self-serving indifference to mounting evidence of a national security threat that seemed so obvious to his Republican adversaries?

As it happened, President Kennedy was spared having to deal with any fruition of this unsettling thought. That is because neither the president's Republican adversaries in Congress nor any member of the press or the public would learn of Kennedy's July 31 promise to attenuate air surveillance in exchange for putting Berlin tensions on ice until after the midterm elections, nor of the fact that the president gave his word to Khrushchev through assurances made to Bolshakov and Dobrynin regarding a mutual stand-down in tensions both in Berlin and on the president's side, nor of Khrushchev's communicated desire to spare the president embarrassment in the domestic political arena, nor of the remarkable accumulation of Khrushchev's repeated assurances that the arrangement would remain in place through the midterm elections, all premised on the quid pro quo that the president would "keep his word" and "not permit events to develop in a dangerous direction."

Nevertheless, the impact of Khrushchev's numerous assurances to the president that the Soviets would observe a stand-down in international tensions until after the US midterm elections did engage the ExComm participants on a number of occasions and in a number of different ways. On Thursday, October 18, at a morning meeting in the Cabinet Room, Khrushchev's stand-down promise was mentioned by Ambassador Thompson, the attorney general, and Theodore Sorensen as the three considered the various scenarios that might unfold if the United States were to institute a quarantine on Soviet military shipments to Cuba. Responding to comments by Alexis Johnson and Dean Rusk about the impact of a "blockade," Thompson speculated, "Seems to me that one point on this—there are a lot of little signs—but I was always curious as to why he [Khrushchev] said he would defer this [a renewed confrontation over Berlin] until after the election. It seems to me it is all related to this."

The attorney general picked up the same point a few minutes later when the discussion turned to whether the administration should give the Soviet leaders a private warning about the US discovery of the ballistic missiles in Cuba before any disclosure would be made to the public. Robert Kennedy suggested that the president could finesse this during a meeting that had been scheduled with Soviet foreign minister Gromyko later that same day. Might Kennedy be able to bait Gromyko into a direct discussion of the missiles, which were proving to be "embarrassing in this election": "I suppose the other way is to do it rather subtly [with Gromyko] with me saying 'What are you doing in Cuba? It's embarrassing in this election. What kind of missiles are you sticking down there?'" Sorensen concurred, once again mentioning the upcoming US elections: "Actually, I think the Attorney General's suggestion is a pretty good gambit, to say to him: 'Well Khrushchev was not going to do anything before our election. But look what he's doing in Cuba, and so on.'"[73]

In the end, none of these discussions about a Khrushchev agreement to stand-down until after the US elections, or about sparing the American president embarrassment, would become public or cause political damage for the president. Rather, as will be discussed in chapter 8, the Kennedy brothers deftly created an alternative and attention-deflecting narrative of Soviet duplicity by claiming the administration had been the victim of the most egregious form of deception—the "flat lie"—emanating from three Soviet officials who had purported to speak for Khrushchev himself.

CHAPTER 8

Composing Flat Lies

It seems to me, Mr. President, . . . your hand is strengthened somewhat if the Soviets have lied to you.

—ROSWELL GILPATRIC TO PRESIDENT KENNEDY, TUESDAY, OCTOBER 16, 1962

THE TWO KENNEDY BROTHERS grasped that the administration was vulnerable to Republican accusations that the White House had allowed the Soviets to covertly install ballistic missiles in Cuba. The Kennedys asserted that top Kremlin officials had not simply disseminated ambiguous misinformation but had told the president "flat lies." But that left a key question: what exactly were those "lies"? The president could not point to the Kremlin's defensive weapons and purposes propaganda campaign because, as Republican critics had pointed out, that terminology was inherently ambiguous.[1] And Kennedy could not cite Khrushchev's false promise to relax tensions until after the US elections as a favor to the president's political standing, especially if it came out that the quid pro quo was the president's determination to relax his country's intelligence surveillance over Cuba. That left the Kennedy brothers with one alternative: finding a way to embroider—or in modern parlance to "sex up"[2]—Soviet statements about the arms shipments above and beyond the ambiguous "defensive" formulation. They needed something more to show blatant lies not merely deceptive generalizations.

There was one problem. The president had not managed in any of his direct communications with Khrushchev to ask his counterpart the simple question point blank: would the chairman assure him personally, leader to leader, that none of the Soviet arms being shipped to Cuba were nuclear weapons or surface-to-surface missiles or other weapons similarly capable of causing mass destruction in the United States? There was thus a yawning gap that needed to be bridged. The attorney general went to work.

According to Robert Kennedy's later reconstruction, two Soviet officials had given him private assurances containing more specific and detailed information about the nature of the weapons being sent to Cuba: namely, that they did not include any surface-to-surface or ground-to-ground missiles, nor did any such weapons have a range capable of reaching the continental United States. By coming up with these specific Soviet assurances by high-level Kremlin officials believed to be trustworthy sources, Robert Kennedy hoped the president would be able to avoid charges of naiveté and inexperience that would otherwise have been leveled by his critics. If, by contrast, trusted, high-level Soviet officials were shown to have been flatly lying in specific, unambiguous ways, then hopefully the moral calculus would shift, leaving the Americans responsible, at most, for honorable reliance on the good faith of top-level diplomats, whereas the Soviets would be guilty of blunt, calculated dishonesty.

However, there are numerous reasons to be skeptical about the reliability of Robert Kennedy's ex post facto accounts of his conversations with the two Soviet officials in question, which have never been corroborated by any contemporaneous documentation prepared either by Kennedy himself or by any other American official. A close review of the record demonstrates with reasonable clarity that Robert Kennedy's version of his conversations with Dobrynin and Bolshakov was the product of the attorney general's outright distortion of the true facts.

President Kennedy faced a serious dilemma. His administration had begun receiving the Soviet party line generalities about defensive weapons and defensive purposes as early as September 4, 1962. Although they were wary of a foe who was known to put out misleading messages, administration officials had largely been satisfied by the Soviet statements that there was no imminent danger. Kennedy knew that when word of the Soviet missiles became public, the American people would be shocked and the Republican Party would try to take advantage of the administration's negligence in trusting the Soviets and allowing the threat to grow so close to American shores.

The president also worried that world opinion would likely side with the Soviets, since a plausible argument could be made that all Khrushchev had done was to match the American justification for having installed Jupiter missiles near the shores of the Soviet Union. Kennedy's closest allies among leaders in Europe had as much as told him so, and these sentiments persisted in the European press even after proof of the Soviet missile sites was displayed to the world.[3]

A solution emerged from a discussion at the ExComm meeting on October 16 of whether to use an upcoming meeting between the president and the visiting Soviet foreign minister, Gromyko, scheduled for October 18, to privately alert the Soviets that the United States had discovered their missile installation in Cuba. That idea produced no consensus. Attention then turned to an alternative option: might it be better to remain silent about the US discovery in hopes that Gromyko could be induced to make exploitable, flatly false statements about the arms buildup that could later be used to America's public relations advantage? Roswell Gilpatric first raised this idea, which received McGeorge Bundy's immediate endorsement:

Tuesday, October 16, 6:30–8:00 p.m.

PRESIDENT KENNEDY: I'm going to see Gromyko on Thursday and I think the question that I'd really like to have some sort of a judgment on is whether we ought to do anything with Gromyko, whether we ought to say anything to him, whether we ought to indirectly give him sort of an ultimatum on this matter, or whether we just ought to go ahead without him. . . .

GILPATRIC: It seems to me, Mr. President, in your public presentation simultaneous or subsequent to an action, your hand is strengthened somewhat if the Soviets have lied to you, either privately or in public.

BUNDY: I'll agree to that.

ALEXIS JOHNSON: And therefore, without knowing, if you ask Gromyko, or if Bobby asks Dobrynin again, or if some other country could get the Soviets to say publicly in the UN: "No, we have no offensive" . . .[4]

As it turned out, the president adopted this course when he sat down with Gromyko on October 18. Kennedy never mentioned his evidence of the Soviet missiles in Cuba, and he listened quietly as Gromyko repeated the Soviet party line that all military shipments to Cuba were defensive in nature. When Gromyko left, the president told Robert Lovett, "Gromyko . . . told more barefaced lies than I have ever heard in so short a time."[5]

In fact, however, the president's takeaway from the meeting was mistaken wishful thinking. The notetakers at the meeting had carefully taken down Gromyko's statements, which did not depart in any material respect from the Soviet formula about defensive purposes. Indeed, the CIA's postcrisis report assessing the "flat lie" narrative concluded, "We cannot judge whether the Soviet aim in this interview was deceptive."[6] Here is the pertinent meeting summary provided by the official US notetakers:

> As to Soviet assistance to Cuba, Mr. Gromyko stated that he was instructed to make it clear, as the Soviet Government had already done, that such assistance, pursued solely for the purpose of contributing to the defense capabilities of Cuba and to the development of Cuba toward the development of its agriculture and land amelioration, and training by Soviet specialists of Cuba nationals in handling of defensive armaments were by no means offensive. . . .
>
> Mr. Gromyko continued that Cubans and the Cuban Government had before them the vital question of whether they should remain unprepared to resist attack or to take steps to defend their country. He said . . . as far as armaments were concerned, Soviet specialists were training Cubans in handling certain types of armaments which were only defensive . . . and he wished to stress the word defensive in character, and thus such training could not constitute a threat to the United States. . . .
>
> Mr. Gromyko stated the Soviet Union proceeded from the assumption that on the basis of Soviet Government's statements and his own today the US Government and the President had a clear idea of the Soviet policy on this matter and of the Soviet evaluation of US action in relation to Cuba. He said he had nothing to add to what he had already said.[7]

Later, questions were raised about the fairness of the president's silence, and about the wisdom of denying the Russians a timely confidential notification of the US discovery and an ensuing private discussion that could have led to an earlier resolution of the crisis. Soviet ambassador Dobrynin raised the issue when he met with the attorney general on the evening of October 23. According to the ambassador's telegram to Moscow the next day, he asked Robert Kennedy "why the President—if he had some sort of doubts—had not negotiated directly and openly with A.A. Gromyko . . . but rather had begun actions, the seriousness of the consequences of which for the entire world are entirely unforeseeable. Kennedy provided two reasons: first, the president had been put off by the 'very harsh tones' Gromyko was using in his opening remarks blaming the United States for rising tensions; and, second, the president had listened as Gromyko had once again offered the misleading 'defensive' characterization of the Soviet arms buildup and felt that the Russians had 'deceived him again.'"[8]

Theodore Sorensen provided a different explanation in his biography of Kennedy, emphasizing that the US information was still incomplete, that the White House was still "not yet ready to act," and that an early warning to the Kremlin might lead to "all the delays, evasions, threats and other disadvantages of a diplomatic warning."[9] Sorensen's view has been accepted by most historians. These commentators have not considered the alternative explanation offered by Gilpatric's sly proposal and confirmed by the administration's subsequent management of Republican criticism: that the president needed stronger evidence than was readily available that Soviet leaders had engaged in flat lying.

In his October 22 message to the nation, President Kennedy emphasized that the Russians had engaged in duplicity, calling the missile deployment a "secret swift and extraordinary buildup" and a "sudden, clandestine decision" that "contradict[ed] the repeated assurances of Soviet spokesmen, both publicly and privately delivered, that the arms buildup in Cuba would retain its original defensive character."[10] Six weeks later, the Soviet deception campaign became a central feature of the Alsop-Bartlett insider account of the crisis based on their privileged access to the president.[11] Calling the Soviet operation "a systematic attempt to dupe the American leaders," Alsop and Bartlett singled out Dobrynin, Gromyko, and Bolshakov (though not mentioning the GRU officer by name) as the miscreants. Dobrynin was charged with having "flatly assured a Cabinet officer" in early October, and Chester Bowles on October 13, "that no missiles capable of reaching the U.S. would be placed in Cuba."[12] Similar assurances were said to have been "conveyed in an official statement of the Soviet government, and by Andrei Gromyko to the President on October 18."[13] Finally, Bolshakov was accused of passing along to the president a false assurance by Mikoyan that "only air-defense missiles, incapable of reaching American targets, were being provided." Importantly, Alsop and Bartlett noted that the Bolshakov message did not reach the president until after he "already knew that Mikoyan's promise was false."

Robert Kennedy wrote in *Thirteen Days*, his posthumous memoir of the missile crisis, that he personally received direct, specific, and unambiguously false assurances from two Soviet officials, Ambassador Anatoly Dobrynin and another unnamed "important official in the Soviet Embassy" (clearly a reference to GRU officer Georgi Bolshakov), that Khrushchev and the Kremlin had authorized them to confirm more pointedly that there were in fact no "ground-to-ground missiles" (reputedly Dobrynin's words), or surface-to-surface missiles (reputedly Khrushchev's words conveyed by Bolshakov) among the Soviet arms sent to Cuba.[14] Notably, the attorney general made no mention of any statements by Mikoyan.

Other US officials later wrote that Bolshakov conveyed to Robert Kennedy yet another false statement of particularity about the Soviet weapons—that Mikoyan had told him (Bolshakov) to tell the American president that the only missiles being sent to Cuba were "antiaircraft missiles . . . which could not reach American targets."[15] Beschloss speculated that Mikoyan may have chosen his words carefully to preserve at least a veneer of truth. If he had said only antiaircraft missiles were being sent to Castro, then "he might have argued that he was not lying: the MRBMs and IRBMs were being sent to Cuba, but since they remained in Soviet possession they were not being sent to Castro."[16] Further research now makes clear that the source for this story was a journalist who enjoyed the president's intimate trust, and who developed the story after October 22 when the presence of Soviet missiles in Cuba were already well known to the president and indeed to the world.

Administration officials during and after the crisis would claim that all of the foregoing more specific assurances about missile characteristics or capabilities that had allegedly been served up by Soviet officials had been "flat lies," or "barefaced lies," but a closer examination of the record casts doubt on whether any of these specific assurances were ever in fact made.

Before addressing the evidence, however, it is important to consider whether the distinction between Soviet statements that were merely misleading and those that were flat lies made any meaningful difference during the crisis. In this instance the distinction did indeed make a difference, and the Kennedy administration was acutely aware of that difference. The Soviet formulaic statements about the defensive nature and purposes of the arms being delivered to Cuba were inherently self-serving and ambiguous, as Kennedy critics like Senator Keating were quick to point out. The language matched in tone and rhetorical intent Khrushchev's repeated claims that the Kremlin stood for "peace-loving peoples" everywhere.[17] While many skeptical observers in the West automatically discounted "peace-loving" statements of this kind as propaganda, Kennedy was on record as having credited these similar statements about defensive aims. It was therefore necessary, even urgent, for the White House to identify a more serious act of deception to demonstrate that it had been the victim of flat lies by top Soviet officials about the weapons being sent to Cuba. Only then would the administration's acceptance of Soviet assurances stand a chance against charges in the political arena of naivete and ineptitude.

Two years after the Cuban missile drama had abated, the CIA's deputy director for intelligence (DD/I) issued a staff working paper analyzing the crisis that devoted a full section to the Soviet Union's apparent "Use of the Flat Lie" as a means to preserve the secrecy of their plans. The agency found it hard to understand why Khrushchev would have made this almost "incomprehensible" and "remarkably stupid" blunder in diplomacy given the fact that "when the lie was exposed, as it surely would be sooner or later, this would destroy in advance the credibility of future Soviet assurances on any matter."[18] The agency engaged in speculation about why Khrushchev might nevertheless have ventured on such a foolish course.[19]

Most important, in contrast to the Kennedy brothers' identification of numerous Soviet "lies" and "barefaced lies" propagated by at least three official Soviet spokesmen, the CIA's nine-page analysis of Khrushchev's purported "flat lie" campaign found only a single conversation that would actually qualify for that label—the episode that supposedly took place on October 5 based on Robert Kennedy's report that Bolshakov had relayed to him a statement by Mikoyan that only antiaircraft missiles were involved and they could not reach American targets.[20] Yet despite finding it "incomprehensible" and "remarkably stupid" that Khrushchev would have engaged in blatant lying of this kind to the attorney general, the agency staff suspended their disbelief by failing to consider the possibility that that particular alleged falsehood had not been conveyed. And they did so notwithstanding four circumstances they should have found suspicious: (*a*) this was the only instance they found of a Soviet statement that qualified as a flat lie, (*b*) the alleged transmitter of the supposed lie was not a recognized official of the Soviet government but rather a GRU officer working under cover, (*c*) the attorney general had not provided a contemporaneous written record of what he claimed to have been told, nor had anyone else in the government to whom Kennedy would have reported the conversation done so, and (*d*) there was and remains considerable confusion about when the conversation in question took place.

The combination of all these red flags should counsel against accepting at face value any feature of the administration's early flat-lies narrative. Indeed, even the president's first authorized account of the missile crisis, written by journalists Stewart Alsop and Charles Bartlett, reported that the Mikoyan comments did not come to the president's attention until after he had already learned from U-2 surveillance that Soviet ballistic missiles were being installed in Cuba. So how could the administration have been misled by flat lies?

As noted, any effort to assess the credibility of "flat lie" accusations needs to distinguish between Soviet representations made before the president's speech to the nation on October 22, and those made after the speech when the true facts had become known and Kennedy insiders were trying to strengthen their claim that they had been lied to beforehand.

Dobrynin's remarks to Robert Kennedy on September 4. In his memoir of the Cuban missile crisis, *Thirteen Days*, Robert Kennedy placed his meeting with Dobrynin on the same day, September 4, that the president issued his first warning to the Soviets that the "gravest issues" would arise if the United States were to discover "offensive ground-to-ground" missiles or Soviet bases in Cuba.[21] The attorney general claimed that Dobrynin had on that date given him a specific assurance about the missiles: "He told me I should not be concerned, for he was instructed by Soviet Chairman Nikita S. Khrushchev to assure President Kennedy that there would be no ground-to-ground missiles or offensive weapons placed in Cuba."[22]

Michael Beschloss, Dino Brugioni, and James Hansen have all relied upon Robert Kennedy's account for the assertion that Dobrynin lied to Robert Kennedy in that initial conversation.[23] Curiously, although Kennedy noted in *Thirteen Days* that he promptly conveyed Dobrynin's remarks to the president as well as to Secretary of State Dean Rusk and Secretary of Defense Robert McNamara, while at the same time recalling that he "relayed my own skepticism,"[24] no contemporaneous documentation of these supposed conversations with any of the three mentioned officials has yet been identified. Elie Abel, whose early account of the missile crisis in 1966 appeared to reflect extensive access to the principal actors, had only one thing to say about Dobrynin's September 4 comments to the attorney general conveying "a message from Khrushchev for the President." Abel reported: "It boiled down to a promise that the Soviet Union would create no trouble for the United States—in Berlin or Southeast Asia—during the election campaign."[25]

Historians have long had access to the taped transcript of the meeting Robert Kennedy attended in the White House with the president, Rusk, and McNamara, as well as others from 4:00 to 4:50 p.m. on September 4, 1962, which would have been shortly after the attorney general had left his meeting with Dobrynin. Because the White House meeting was organized for the specific purpose of drafting the administration's official public message warning the Soviets not to place any significant offensive weapons in Cuba, this would have been the occasion for Robert Kennedy to inform his colleagues of any more precise message from Dobrynin denying surface-to-surface or ground-to-ground missiles in Cuba. But the president's brother conveyed no such message. Commenting on this lapse, Naftali and Zelikow stated in *Presidential Recordings—Miller Center* that "the Attorney General had made use of the meeting [with Dobrynin] to mention Cuba, but the Soviet ambassador said nothing to deter Kennedy from his belief that it was only a matter of time before Moscow put nuclear missiles on the island."[26]

Tellingly, while Brugioni accepted the *Thirteen Days* account at face value, he stated without editorial comment or explanation that the content of Dobrynin's supposed falsehood "never reached down to the intelligence community."[27] Similarly, Roger Hilsman's 1967 and 1996 descriptions of what Dobrynin told the attorney general did not support the flat-lie notion but rather closely mirrored the Soviet formula about defensive weapons and contained nothing of Robert Kennedy's more precise "ground-to-ground" specificity: "In early September, Soviet Ambassador Anatoly Dobrynin on separate occasions told both Robert Kennedy and Theodore Sorensen, the President's special assistant, that the equipment they were sending to Cuba was 'defensive in nature and did not represent any threat to the security of the United States.'"[28]

Similarly, Dobrynin's recollection of the September 4 conversation contradicts Robert Kennedy's version. In his memoirs, which tracked his diary, Dobrynin recalled that it was Robert Kennedy who mentioned the matter of missile capabilities, and that Dobrynin had provided no direct response, since he lacked any information about particular Soviet weapons being sent to Cuba.[29] As a result Dobrynin said in his memoirs that he could only demur:

> But what would happen, Robert Kennedy said, after [Soviet surface-to-air missiles] were passed into the hands of "impulsive Cubans?" A much more serious question would arise for the security of the United States itself, he added, if events continued along a logical path: Wouldn't still more powerful missiles arrive, capable of reaching U.S. territory from Cuban soil? And wouldn't they carry nuclear warheads? . . . In response, I pointed out that Cuba had a right to defend itself. As far as nuclear warheads were concerned, the Soviet Union fully favored the expeditious conclusion of a nuclear nonproliferation treaty. At the same time I avoided the subject of missiles in gen-

eral and military personnel. I neither confirmed nor denied the reports, since I had no information about them whatsoever until the very beginning of the Cuban crisis only about six weeks later.[30]

Although Dobrynin had no specific information to impart on the subject of Soviet missiles in Cuba, he recognized this was a potentially important concern in the minds of Kennedy administration officials, so he "urgently asked Moscow for instructions." The Kremlin's response was provided "curtly": "In talking to the Americans you should confirm that there are only *defensive* Soviet weapons in Cuba." That was clearly the Soviet party line and no exceptions would be tolerated. Indeed, Dobrynin said in his memoirs that "Bolshakov, who had just returned from his vacation, had been instructed to tell Robert Kennedy the same thing and invoke Khrushchev's name."[31] It is simply not conceivable that either Russian official would independently stray from these instructions by the Soviet chairman when they had no independent knowledge of the underlying facts.[32]

Interestingly, Theodore Sorensen's contemporaneous file memorandum, recording his own September 6 conversation with Dobrynin on the same subject just two days after the Dobrynin meeting with Robert Kennedy, corroborates Dobrynin's version of his conversation with the attorney general. Echoing Dobrynin's "neither confirmed nor denied" assertion about the key question of Soviet missiles, Sorensen reported: "He repeated several times, however, that they had done nothing new or extraordinary in Cuba—that the events causing all the excitement had been taking place somewhat gradually and quietly over a long period of time—and that he stood by his assurances that all of these steps were defensive in nature and did not represent any threat to the security of the United States. He neither contradicted nor confirmed my reference to large numbers of Soviet military personnel, electronic equipment and missile preparations."[33]

In Sorensen's 1965 biography of Kennedy, the president's former top assistant corroborated Dobrynin's version of the Robert Kennedy/Dobrynin September 4 exchange. On the key subject of Dobrynin's characterization of the Soviet arms buildup to Robert Kennedy, which the attorney general had in turn reported at the time to Sorensen, Sorensen wrote: "The reassurances given me by Dobrynin on September 6 were identical to those he gave to the Attorney General and others in the same period." Here is how Sorensen described the "identical" message Dobrynin delivered to both himself and Robert Kennedy, which in his own case Sorensen had "dictated that same afternoon": "He [Dobrynin] neither contradicted nor confirmed my reference to large numbers of Soviet military personnel, electronic equipment and missile preparations. He repeated several times, however, that they had done nothing new or extraordinary in Cuba—that the events causing all the excitement had been taking place somewhat gradually and quietly over a long period of time—and that he stood by his assurances that all these steps were defensive in nature and did not represent any threat to the security of the United States."[34] Sorensen's statement that Dobrynin "neither contradicted nor confirmed" his references to "missile preparations" almost exactly mirrored Dobrynin's statement: "I neither confirmed nor denied the reports."

Finally, it is noteworthy that in the CIA's postcrisis assessment of the alleged Soviet campaign of "flat lies," the agency determined that the campaign was initiated following a decision by Khrushchev made "toward the end of September" and arrangements were made to put it into operation "in late September and early October."[35] The agency found no flat lie by Dobrynin or Bolshakov or anyone else in early September. In fact the CIA ultimately identified only a single example of a purported flat lie: a statement reported in a Washington journalist's column that was attributed to Bolshakov, who was referred to not by his name or his military rank but as a Junior Soviet official."[36]

Robert Kennedy's October 5, 7 or 8 conversation with Bolshakov. The single example of a flat lie accepted by the CIA supposedly occurred at a meeting between Robert Kennedy and Bolshakov in which the GRU officer reportedly said that he met recently with Khrushchev and Mikoyan and that Mikoyan had told him to assure the president that only antiaircraft missiles were being sent to Cuba and these were incapable of reaching the United States. But the agency report did not name the individuals involved, or the actual date of the conversation, saying only that the "flat lie" was conveyed by a "junior Soviet official stationed in Washington" to "American officials" on an unspecified date "during October." The agency admitted to being "uncertain as to the date of actual transmission." Perhaps most surprisingly, given the apparent importance of the event, the CIA report authors acknowledged that they were relying on a newspaper article for this key portion of their report, stating in a footnote that their account was "drawn from Mr. Joseph Alsop's column of 5 November 1962." The intelligence agency's reliance on a source of this low degree of substantiation and without further cross-checking is more than puzzling. As Beschloss would later conclude, citing similarly questionable renditions of the flat-lie claim by Sorensen and various news journals of the time, "exactly what NSK and Mikoyan said, exactly what was reported, by whom and to whom has been obscured by the fog of history."[37]

The Robert Kennedy–Bolshakov meeting most likely occurred on either October 7 (as indicated by the chronology contained in Bolshakov's *New Times* article)[38] or October 8 (as reported by Soviet ambassador Dobrynin),[39] but has been variously reported as having occurred on September 11, or October 4 and 6, or October 17, or October 24.[40] As will be seen below, the historical record existing as of October 5/8 and shortly thereafter provides no hint of the alleged Mikoyan assurance. That bit of missile crisis lore appeared only after the president's speech, and it came from a Kennedy insider journalist.

No contemporaneous written confirmation prepared by Robert Kennedy or any other US official or by Bolshakov has been identified as the source for the Mikoyan "flat lie" that Bolshakov supposedly conveyed to Robert Kennedy at what will hereafter be referred to as the October 7/8 meeting. Those circumstances alone should give historians pause before concluding with confidence that any such lie was actually imparted at the meeting.

Of all the dates various commentators have proposed for the pertinent Robert Kennedy–Bolshakov meeting, only October 5, 7, and 8, 1962, are supported by documentation, of which either October 7, supported by Bolshakov's detailed memorialization, or October 8, supported by Dobrynin's cable to Moscow, is most likely to be the actual date. First, Bolshakov reported in his subsequent 1989 articles describing the event that he met with Robert Kennedy shortly after his return to the United States from his Pitsunda meeting with Khrushchev and Mikoyan. That meeting had occurred in mid-September "between September 10 and 15" at Khrushchev's dacha in Pitsunda, and Bolshakov had thereafter returned to Moscow "the following morning" and boarded a "plane for the States a few days later." After a "brief stopover in New York" he "proceeded to Washington on October 3," and met with Robert Kennedy two days later.[41] Robert Kennedy's daily diary reveals that the attorney general had a meeting with Bolshakov on October 5.[42] Bolshakov's *New Times* article went on to report, however, that he was not able to convey Khrushchev's oral message at that meeting but did so after another two-day delay, which would have put him back in the attorney general's office on either October 7 (or according to Dobrynin's official report of Bolshakov's meeting on October 8). Although Bolshakov did not provide a precise date for this meeting, he said it occurred "3 dramatic weeks" before the October 27 meeting he would later have with Robert Kennedy shortly after Kennedy had left Ambassador Dobrynin with his missile trade proposal.[43]

It is remarkable, given the salience of this October 7/8 meeting, and the wide attention it has drawn from historians attempting to reconstruct what the Kennedy administration had been told by the Soviets about their Cuba military buildup in the weeks before the October 14 U-2 photographs, that no written memorandum or notes prepared contemporaneously by Robert Kennedy or any other US government official have ever surfaced providing a description or even a summary of what Bolshakov supposedly told the attorney general on October 7/8. Neither the December 8, 1962, magazine article purporting to describe the Kennedy/Bolshakov meeting written by two journalists who enjoyed privileged, inside access to the president nor the first published work of history that mentioned the meeting (Sorensen's 1965 biography of President Kennedy) provided a date for the meeting or a source for reporting the episode.

Robert Kennedy's *Thirteen Days* never mentions Bolshakov by name. There is a single vague reference, however, that likely refers to the Bolshakov meeting, although it says nothing about Mikoyan or whether any Soviet weapons in Cuba would be able to "reach the United States," and it inaccurately placed the meeting sometime around September 11 or "during this same period of time." Thus, Kennedy wrote in his memoirs: "During this same period of time, an important official in the Soviet Embassy, returning from Moscow, brought me a personal message from Khrushchev to President Kennedy, stating that he wanted the President to be assured that under no circumstances would surface-to-surface missiles be sent to Cuba."[44]

In the portion of his oral history recorded on February 29, 1964, Kennedy stated that, "unfortunately, stupidly," he "didn't write many of the things down" when he had conversations with Bolshakov.[45] In fact, Kennedy did prepare file memoranda when he felt he needed to create an official record for his own purposes, including his October 24 and 28 memoranda of conversations he had with Ambassador Dobrynin on October 23 and October 27, respectively. On each occasion, his file memorandum distorted the record in self-serving ways, as will be shown below.[46]

Only Bolshakov, among the eyewitness participants at the October 7/8 meeting, has left a detailed written version of what transpired. Bolshakov evidently kept the notes he used at the meeting, which he referred to in his 1989 *New Times* and *Secret Channel* articles. The relevant portion of the

Khrushchev/Mikoyan message that Bolshakov said he delivered to Kennedy at a meeting in the attorney general's office held during the first week of October 1962 is the following: "Premier Khrushchev is concerned about the situation being built up by the United States around Cuba, and we repeat that the Soviet Union is supplying to Cuba exclusively defensive weapons intended for protecting the interests of the Cuban revolution and not for perpetrating an aggression against any state on American continent, the U.S. included."[47]

Bolshakov noted that Kennedy asked him to repeat the portion of the message containing Khrushchev's assurance about "defensive weapons only," whereupon the attorney general "got behind the desk and jotted down this part of the message which I slowly dictated to him." Kennedy then handed his secretary the sheet of paper and told her, "Angie, type this as fast as you can." He then said to Bolshakov, "I shall pass Premier Khrushchev's message on to the President, and he will communicate his reply through me, if necessary." No copy of the attorney general's jottings or of his secretary's transcription has surfaced.[48]

Bolshakov then recounted that the journalist Charles Bartlett invited him to meet the next day and told him that Robert Kennedy wanted Bolshakov to "dictate Khrushchev's message" to Bartlett, supposedly because "the President would like to have it in detail in writing, not in his brother's wording of it." And so Bolshakov "retold him, word per word, what I had communicated to Robert Kennedy on the previous day."[49]

Recent research by this author has located two Bartlett versions of the message allegedly dictated by Bolshakov on October 23 or 24, 1962, after the president knew about the Soviet missiles, not on October 6, 8 or 9. Bartlett evidently sent one of these versions to the attorney general on October 26, 1962, and the other to President Kennedy on November 5, 1962.

Note that Bolshakov's version of the Khrushchev message he delivered to Robert Kennedy on October 7/8, 1962, contained no statement attributed to Mikoyan, no mention of antiaircraft missiles, and no denial of "surface-to-surface" missiles. Bolshakov's version of his statement to the attorney general is indistinguishable from the Soviet party line and contained no specifics about the nature of the Soviet weapons themselves. Like Dobrynin, Bolshakov had no personal knowledge of the Soviet deployment of missiles in Cuba,[50] and thus he could not have added any credible additional information about weapons characteristics.

As noted, the CIA's analysis of the Kremlin's alleged effort to deceive the

White House by conveying a flat lie to the president accepted the attorney general's version of events even though the agency found the Soviet action to be "remarkably stupid." Yet there are several reasons why the agency should have been skeptical about the notion that Khrushchev would tell the president a "flat lie" at this critical juncture beyond the fact that this would dangerously compromise the Kremlin's credibility in future dealings with the White House. First, agency officials must have been concerned about having to reach conclusions based solely on a journalist's newspaper column, especially one so lacking in details. Despite the paucity of identifying information, the CIA could only have been referring to the Bolshakov meeting with Robert Kennedy on October 7/8, 1962. The agency gave as its source "Mr. Joseph Alsop's column of 5 November 1962."[51] Further, the agency recognized there was a further plausibility deficit in their story: if Khrushchev had indeed concluded from the president's September 13 press conference remarks that a flat lie would be needed to lull the United States into passivity, why did he wait until early October to transmit the lie? The answer they gave to this question—"We suppose that he needed some time to think, and to find the right channel for delivery of the lie"—does not seem very persuasive.[52]

Finally, if the Soviets had actually decided that a lie was necessary, despite the long-term negative repercussions, why would the particular lie they chose—no surface-to-surface missiles—have been both too limited to achieve the desired effect of quieting US concerns, and at the same time so specific that it would not be able to withstand even minimal scrutiny and still remain believable? Thus, the fact that surface-to-surface missiles might be excluded would not eliminate US concerns about introduction of an offensive Soviet capability, since medium-range bombers (like the IL-28s that were discovered on October 10), and nuclear weapons of any kind, however delivered, could still present a significant offensive threat to the United States. Similarly, any denial of the presence of surface-to-surface missiles could be readily contradicted by discovery of any one of the numerous surface-to-surface cruise missiles that the Soviets had delivered to Cuba, many of which had already been discovered by US surveillance as early as August 29 and were thus well known to Robert Kennedy at the time he had his conversation with Bolshakov in early October.

Dino Brugioni has provided the most detailed description of what allegedly transpired at the October 7/8 Bolshakov/Kennedy meeting in his 1990 book, *Eyeball to Eyeball*, where he noted that Robert Kennedy himself "misdated" that particular meeting as taking place in the vicinity of September 11, 1962, whereas "records show it to have been in October" and Brugioni's narrative placed it in "early October."[53] Brugioni reported that Bolshakov recited at this meeting a message Khrushchev and Mikoyan had given him when the three met "in Moscow on October 1." This is not a promising opening to Brugioni's account, however, because in fact Bolshakov had met with Khrushchev and Mikoyan in mid-September, not October 1.[54] Brugioni went on to state that Bolshakov referred during the meeting to notes he had recorded in a "blue notebook" he carried with him and used when he conveyed the Soviet leaders' message to Robert Kennedy in early October.[55] By Brugioni's account Bolshakov stated that Mikoyan had told him that "the missiles were for anti-aircraft purposes and could not reach the United States."[56] Surprisingly, Brugioni provided no source for his version of this story. He claimed that "information from this meeting was circulated throughout the intelligence community," but he provided no time frame for when this occurred, no specification of what particular information was disseminated, and no documentary evidence or other sources demonstrating the provenance of this narrative.[57]

In his biography of Robert Kennedy published in 2000, Evan Thomas placed the meeting between Bolshakov and Robert Kennedy as likely to have occurred on October 5, 1962, but he characterized the GRU officer's comments quite differently than Brugioni. Thomas reported that the GRU officer "repeated a promise from Chairman Khrushchev that the Soviets were only putting defensive weapons in Cuba—'exclusively defensive weapons intended for protecting the interests of the Cuban revolution.'" This was precisely the Soviet party line. Thomas reported that "Kennedy anxiously asked Bolshakov to repeat the part about defensive weapons, and then took careful notes while the GRU officer spoke."[58] Yet no such Kennedy notes have been unearthed.

Subsequent investigation by this author has now made it possible to positively identify the originator of the Mikoyan story as Charles Bartlett, the president's close friend, and to more closely pinpoint the date when the story arose: October 23 or 24, 1962. October 23 was the day the two Kennedys would launch their multipronged effort to resolve the Cuban crisis by offering Khrushchev a Turkey-for-Cuba missile swap-out deal, and one of the ways they would communicate this idea to the Kremlin was by sending a message through Bartlett to Bolshakov for transmittal to Khrushchev (see chapter 9). At Robert Kennedy's instigation, Bartlett also took this opportunity—either on October 23 or the next day—to buttress the administration's "flat lie" story by asking Bolshakov to recount the statements he had made to the attorney general during their October 7/8 meeting regarding the earlier Khrushchev assurance about the limited scope of his missile deployment in Cuba.[59]

On October 23, 1962, the day after the president's televised address informing the American people about the Soviet missiles in Cuba, the attorney general organized two key meetings that he hoped would create a stronger record for arguing that the Soviets had engaged in a campaign of lies during the lead-up to the missile crisis. The first was the Bartlett-Bolshakov meeting on October 23 or 24 mentioned above. The second was the attorney general's arrangement to meet with Soviet ambassador Dobrynin on October 23.

Investigation has uncovered in the papers of former journalist Edward Weintal what appear to be copies of two communications written by Charles Bartlett: the first is a "Memo to the Attorney-General" dated October 26, 1962, and the second is a letter addressed to "Mr. President" dated November 5, 1962. Each describes a conversation Bartlett had with Georgi Bolshakov on the subject of the latter's September meeting with Khrushchev and Mikoyan. Curiously, however, the memo and the letter conflict in several important ways in their description of the Bolshakov encounter, and both contain obvious errors.

First, the memo to Robert Kennedy states that Bartlett tried to reach Bolshakov by phone on the afternoon of October 23, was unable to do so, finally got through to him on the morning of October 24, and arranged to have lunch, where Bolshakov ultimately relayed Khrushchev's message in person. By contrast, the November 5 letter to President Kennedy stated that Bartlett had spoken by phone with Bolshakov on October 23, indicating that Khrushchev's and Mikoyan's comments were relayed to him over the phone rather than in person. The conflict in dates and method of transmission between the two versions is surprising enough, but the evident error in at least one of them becomes all the more suspicious when one considers that Bartlett failed to mention in either document the fact that he had met with Bolshakov on October 23 for the separate purpose of transmitting the Kennedy administration's secret Turkey-for-Cuba missile swap-out proposal to Khrushchev. How can the fact of that actual October 23 meeting be squared with Bartlett's reported inability to contact Bolshakov by phone on that same date?

Second, both the October 26 memo and the November 5 letter state that

Bolshakov gave October 1 as the date of his meeting with Khrushchev and Mikoyan in Russia, and "mid-October" as the date of Bolshakov's return to the United States. Of course, Bolshakov would not have given either of those dates; as demonstrated from historical records summarized above, Bolshakov's meeting with Khrushchev and Mikoyan had occurred in mid-September (not on October 1), and the GRU officer had returned to Washington by October 3, not in mid-October.

Third, Bartlett's November 5 letter to the president suggests that Bolshakov had not been able to communicate his message from Khrushchev and Mikoyan to anyone earlier than October 23 due to Robert Kennedy's "failure to make the arrangements." How could that assertion be squared with Robert Kennedy's statement in *Thirteen Days* that Bolshakov's lie had been communicated to him on September 11 or in the vicinity of that date?

Finally, when it comes to the substance of Khrushchev's and Mikoyan's remarks, there is a curious divergence between the memo and the letter. The October 26 memo to the attorney general cites Bolshakov as stating that Khrushchev "said they were only giving Castro defensive weapons"—which was an essentially verbatim rendition of the Soviet party line.[60] The memo then reports that Mikoyan interrupted his boss: "At this point Mikoyan interjected to Bolshakov that he should tell the President that they were only giving Castro short-range missiles to be used against airplanes."[61] The letter to the president, by contrast, cited Mikoyan rather than Khrushchev as the one who referred to "purely defensive missiles": "At this point, according to Bolshakov, Mikoyan interrupted to direct him to tell you that the missiles they were putting in Cuba were purely defensive missiles with only a capacity for striking at airplanes."[62]

As already noted, Bolshakov's later article reporting on this meeting did not mention any interjection by Mikoyan and contained no reference to antiaircraft missiles.

Many historians have delivered against Bolshakov a guilty verdict for the purported crime of delivering the flat lie, and accepted the story that the GRU agent was unceremoniously dropped by the Kennedys, outed by the president's friendly news media, and recalled by the Kremlin in disgrace.[63] But if that was an accurate narrative of the demise of Bolshakov's role as trusted intermediary, how does one explain the multiple Kennedy outreaches to Bolshakov after the purported flat lie was uncovered: for example, the deputizing of Bartlett and Holeman to meet with the Russian agent on October 23 and transmit the missile-trade proposal to Khrushchev, Bartlett's display of the classified U-2 photographs of the Soviet missiles for Bolshakov's personal perusal at the request of the president, and the postcrisis messages delivered by Robert Kennedy personally on November 9 and 19, 1962, enlisting Bolshakov's services as trusted intermediary once again to persuade the Kremlin to include the IL-28 bombers among the "offensive" Soviet weapons that would have to be removed from Cuba?[64] Above all, how does one account for the fact that Robert Kennedy paid a personal visit to Bolshakov on the night of October 27 shortly after his crucial meeting with Dobrynin, formally making the offer on the president's behalf to trade the US missiles in Turkey for the Soviet missiles in Cuba? According to Bolshakov's later reconstruction of his last personal visit from the attorney general: "Having parted with Dobrynin, Robert Kennedy phoned me and suggested we met [*sic*] near my house and had a talk in his car. He repeated to me what he had told Dobrynin and stressed that upon imposing the blockade the President had become a prisoner of his own actions and would find it next to impossible to restrain the military within twenty-four hours from then if no positive answer came from Moscow."[65]

Parenthetically, Bartlett's November 5 letter to the president also covered, at the president's specific request, a lunch meeting between Bartlett and another Soviet embassy official in Washington, Alexander Zinchuk, which Bartlett said had taken place on October 12. Bartlett's report of the Zinchuk meeting is mainly important for the message it conveyed from Khrushchev about a proposal to settle the looming Cuba crisis via a presidential assurance that there would be no invasion of Cuba—a proposal that would be repeated by Khrushchev. Yet Bartlett also inserted into his recital of the Soviet official's comments the assertion that on October 12 Zinchuk "was extremely emphatic and precise in asserting that the missiles were purely defensive and designed to operate only against aircraft." It is hard to accept the veracity of this retroactive effort to add another Soviet official to the list of prevaricators, especially since Bartlett had stated in an earlier letter to the president, written on October 29, that Zinchuk told him that day that "he knew nothing about the missiles." Bartlett's October 29 letter contained no suggestion that he found this statement to be untrustworthy or in conflict with anything Zinchuk had said earlier.[66]

As noted earlier, Robert Kennedy paid a visit to Dobrynin on October 23 and attempted to resuscitate what the two had spoken about in early September regarding the nature of the Soviet arms being sent to Cuba. Dobrynin reported on this meeting in telegrams he sent to the Kremlin describing the attorney general's state of high agitation and his concern about the fate of his brother's presidency after the president had "staked his political career" on his trust in the messages that Khrushchev had been conveying.[67] Robert Kennedy, for his part, had a distinctly different purpose in visiting the ambassador. After leaving the meeting, the attorney general prepared a memorandum for his brother, dated the next day, which purported to outline the supposed "lie" the Soviet ambassador had told him on September 4. Reciting what he had told Dobrynin the evening before, Kennedy wrote: "When I had met with him some six weeks before, I said, he had told me that the Russians had not placed any long-range missiles in Cuba and had no intention to do so in the future. He interrupted at that point and confirmed this statement and said he specifically told me they would not put missiles in Cuba which would be able to reach the continental United States."[68]

The foregoing confession that Robert Kennedy's memorandum attributed to Dobrynin on October 23 seems suspect, at best, for several reasons. First, it appears to be an effort by Robert Kennedy to belatedly plant in the written record his own self-serving version of an earlier conversation he had not recorded. Second, as has been shown above, Dobrynin was careful to note in his memoirs that he had neither confirmed nor denied any specific facts about the Soviet weapons in his September 4 conversation with Kennedy, since he possessed no information about them, and Sorensen had contemporaneously confirmed Dobrynin's version of what he had said to both Kennedy and himself on September 4 and 6, respectively. Third, Kennedy's recitation of an alleged Dobrynin confession two months later is all the more hard to believe because, coming as it did a day after the president of the United States had presented evidence to the world that demonstrated the earlier statement being attributed to Dobrynin to have been incorrect, it seems highly unlikely that Dobrynin would have been so eager to confirm his own mendacity to the very man he had allegedly lied to. Fourth, Robert Kennedy's later description of Dobrynin's September 4 statement in *Thirteen Days* contained yet another version of what Dobrynin supposedly said, attributing to the Soviet ambassador a denial that there were any "ground-to-ground" missiles,[69] whereas the attorney general's October 24 memorandum had the Soviet ambassador confirming he had denied the presence of missiles "which would be able to reach the continental United States." Remarkably, Kennedy's two post hoc versions of the same alleged Dobrynin statement didn't even match one another.

Further evidence supporting Dobrynin's contrary version of both his

September 4 and his October 23 statements to the attorney general appears in the ambassador's lengthy October 24 cable back to Moscow describing the October 23 conversation with Kennedy. Dobrynin's summary of the two men's discussion provides a far more realistic and therefore more credible account of what most likely transpired on October 23—one not dependent upon a spontaneous, inculpatory confession by Dobrynin emulating Kennedy's self-serving reconstruction of a lie Dobrynin had supposedly told during their prior conversation. Thus, Dobrynin wrote:

> "From the very beginning," continued R. Kennedy, "the Soviet side—N.S. Khrushchev, the Soviet government in its pronouncements and the Soviet ambassador during confidential meetings—have stressed the defensive nature of the weapons which are being delivered to Cuba. You, for instance," said R. Kennedy to me, "told me about the exclusively defensive goals of the delivery of Soviet weapons, in particular, the missile weapons, during our meeting at the beginning of September. *I understood you then as saying* that we were talking only about /and in the future, too/ missiles of a relatively small range of action for the defense of Cuba itself and the approaches to it, but not about long range missiles which could strike practically the entire territory of the USA. I told this to the President, who accepted it with satisfaction as the position of the Soviet government. There was a TASS declaration in the name of the Soviet government in which it was clearly stated that all military deliveries to Cuba are intended exclusively for defensive goals. The President and the government of the USA understood this as the true position of the USSR."[70]

The words I have placed in italics for emphasis—"I understood you as saying"—provide a far more credible corroboration of what had apparently happened: Robert Kennedy had understood the various Soviet party line statements using the expression "defensive" as having meant "short range" missiles, and he concluded in his own mind that this must surely have excluded the possibility of missiles capable of reaching the United States. In short, there is strong reason to conclude that Kennedy had not been exposed to any privately communicated false specification about the Soviet missiles amounting to a flat lie. Rather, he had been naively taken in by the repeatedly disseminated Soviet disinformation/party line statements using the term "defensive," which the attorney general had facilely interpreted to have a more specific meaning. Dobrynin's further mention of Robert

Kennedy's reference to the September 11 TASS statement, echoing the president's equivalent citation of the TASS statement as evidence of Soviet duplicity, seems to confirm this interpretation. This is because the TASS statement also mentioned only the party line generalizations about defensive weapons meant to serve defensive purposes, and thus contained no obvious falsehood.[71]

In summary, the tangled record of the alleged campaign of flat lies supposedly told by Bolshakov, Dobrynin, and Gromyko appears to be so hopelessly burdened by mischaracterization, lack of documentation, exaggeration, and inconsistencies as to dates and message content, that no reliance can be confidently placed on this part of the Cuban missile crisis narrative. Perhaps most remarkably, the president's angry comment that Gromyko had told barefaced lies before a crowd of witnesses at their October 18 White House meeting was demonstrably at odds with the official White House summary of what Gromyko actually said. Indeed it was the State Department's contemporaneous view that Gromyko's remarks to the president and Khrushchev's earlier comments of the same nature to Ambassador Kohler were actually temperate. In a report by the Department's Bureau of Intelligence and Research (INR) that was issued a short time after the Kennedy-Gromyko session, INR concluded: "We believe that the tenor of the Gromyko and Khrushchev conversations suggests an attempt to avoid a direct confrontation with the United States over the issue of missile deployments in Cuba. . . . Moscow may well hope to avoid being overly committed to counteractions which it may not wish to take in response to vigorous US response to the Cuban buildup, and thus leave its hands free for negotiation and, if faced with extreme danger of war, for withdrawal with the least loss of face."[72]

CHAPTER 9

Pawn Trading

The president can't say anything public in this regard about Turkey.

—ROBERT KENNEDY TO SOVIET AMBASSADOR DOBRYNIN, OCTOBER 27, 1962

IN NEGOTIATING A RESOLUTION to the Cuba crisis, Kennedy was so concerned about domestic political fallout and so averse to military action that might escalate to war with the Soviets that he was prepared to agree to the most ambitious demands the Soviets were making on substantive issues, so long as his concession would be kept secret. As was the case a year earlier in Berlin, Khrushchev reciprocated by accepting secrecy even though that would expose him to charges of defeat and retreat.[1]

Both leaders' conviction that they must avoid armed conflict was so strong that they almost immediately signaled their readiness to make major concessions to keep the peace in Cuba, and the core deal points were quickly agreed to in each instance. Khrushchev was willing from the outset to settle for a noninvasion pledge. Kennedy went his adversary one better: by floating an offer so generous (at least from Khrushchev's perspective) that the Soviet chairman himself had not yet even thought of it—dismantlement of America's Turkey-based IRBMs as a trade for removal of the Soviet missiles in Cuba. Kennedy insisted only that his concession be kept secret to spare himself political fallout. It turns out that Khrushchev's infamous October 26/27 last-minute public demand for withdrawal of US missiles from Turkey was actually an opportunistic embrace of Kennedy's secret initiative. The temporary embarrassment of a public withdrawal was far preferable on each occasion when compared to the longer-lasting damage the Soviets would have suffered if Khrushchev's Anadyr gamble had led to an outbreak of fighting.

At the heart of the matter was the fact that President Kennedy did not think the Cuba missile crisis was worth fighting over. Max Frankel emphasized this point, noting that the president's reluctance to authorize any bombing campaign against Cuba was based on Kennedy's "fundamental view of the crisis: Much as he wanted the Russians out of Cuba, he could not get past the thought that they had as much right to be there as the United States had in Turkey."[2]

KENNEDY'S OFFER THAT KHRUSHCHEV COULD NOT REFUSE

One of the enduring memes of the Kennedy decision-making process during the thirteen days has been that the president was far more than a "rational actor"; he was a paragon of wisdom and restraint in the face of fevered calls for immediate military action. He was measured where others were impulsive, a consensus-builder rather than an antagonist. Much of this wise-hero narrative emerged from administration insiders like historian Arthur Schlesinger Jr., who wrote about the "superb" way the president guided his experts on the ExComm, challenging them to deliberate carefully, sort thoughtfully through all the options, and take the time necessary to germinate the wisest possible counsel for the president's ultimate decision.

Yet there is another way of accounting for the president's actions during the crisis that conforms to what actually transpired and, perhaps most importantly, to the things the president actually said and did at each critical juncture. In short, President Kennedy's demonstrated preference throughout the crisis was to delay US action long enough to see the fruition of his secret missile-swap proposal, especially since the ExComm seemed to be moving relentlessly toward a strong military response. The president's consistently contrary preference, after his momentary reaction of shock and confusion in the face of Khrushchev's unexpected double cross, was to prolong deliberations, preserve strict secrecy to stave off the predictable domestic political uproar that would ensue once the public learned that Soviet missiles had been installed just offshore, and try to formulate a US concession so generous that Khrushchev would be unable to refuse it. However unheroic this delay-and-concede strategy may seem in comparison to the hero meme that has persisted for so long, it matches not only what President Kennedy actually said when speaking with the people he trusted most, but also what he actually did.

The Kennedy administration first learned of the major escalation in Soviet arms shipments to Cuba in July 1962. It did not take long before top administration officials began to imagine that the Kremlin might be planning to build an offensive missile capability within easy striking distance of the US homeland, and to begin developing options for dealing with any such contingency. The proximity of the missiles was not the only cause for alarm. There was also an important geographic factor. A missile attack originating from the southeastern coast of the continental United States would take the United States by complete surprise because the Ballistic Missile Early Warning System (BMEWs) and its associated strategic missile defense measures that had been built in the late 1950s were arrayed along the northern reaches of Alaska and Canada as well as in Greenland and England, and aimed north and west toward the anticipated path of incoming missiles launched from the Soviet-Asian landmass. No similar defenses protected against a missile attack from the south. The White House thus began a review of options for eliminating this threat in its incipiency by various military means. More interesting were the diplomatic options that were also examined at the very outset of this "Top Secret & Sensitive" exercise, and in particular the seemingly incongruous option of "get[ting] Jupiter missiles out of Turkey."

One of the earliest administration officials who saw a serious national security threat in the Cuba arms buildup was John McCone, director of Central Intelligence. McCone appears to have been the first among top Kennedy administration officials to "raise the specter of offensive missiles being placed on the island," first at a meeting of the Special Action Group (Augmented) on August 10, 1962, and then repeatedly at later meetings, including one in Dean Rusk's office on August 21 and then with the president in the White House on August 22 and 23.[3] During the August 23 White House meeting, McCone drew the potential connection between Cuba and Turkey and then "took this opportunity to voice his long-held doubts about the Jupiters. Secretary McNamara 'agreed they were useless' but declared them 'difficult politically to remove.'"[4]

Although McCone then abruptly left Washington on August 24, 1962, for a planned overseas honeymoon, and would remain largely out of the picture until his return on September 23,[5] the wheels of White House planning for a possible showdown with the Soviets over their arms shipments to Cuba began to turn. As previously noted, the president issued National Security Action Memorandum 181 (NSAM 181) over McGeorge Bundy's signature on August 23, 1962, containing eight action items bearing on the Cuban arms buildup, with a follow-up meeting to brief the president scheduled for September 1, 1962. Items 7 and 8 of NSAM 181 addressed potential military responses, including an "outright invasion" of Cuba. Bundy asked that five of the eight action steps, including both military items, be conducted if practicable by "senior officers already informed of MONGOOSE," the code name for the administration's covert program of subversion aimed at facilitating a regime change in Cuba.

Curiously, NSAM 181's first action item, placed under the responsibility of the Department of Defense, read: "What action can be taken to get Jupiter missiles out of Turkey?"[6] A September 1, 1962, memorandum prepared by the Department of Defense in response to this item was submitted by Carl Kaysen, the president's deputy special assistant for national security affairs, to the president's military representative, General Ted Clifton. Unfortunately, the Defense Department's three-and-one-half page discussion of the Turkey Jupiters issue remains classified.[7]

Later, when the ExComm discussions commenced in mid-October, it was President Kennedy who first raised and then continuously and repeatedly reiterated the option of a negotiated trade whereby the United States would remove its Jupiter missiles from Turkey in exchange for Khrushchev's removal of Soviet missiles from Cuba. He brought the subject up first on Thursday October 18 at a morning meeting in the Cabinet Room on Day 3 of the ExComm discussions:

> PRESIDENT KENNEDY: If we said to Khrushchev that: "We have to take action against it. But if you begin to pull them out, we'll take ours out of Turkey." . . .
>
> PRESIDENT KENNEDY: The only offer we would make, it seems to me, that would have any sense, according to him, would be the . . . giving him some out, would be our Turkey missiles.[8]

The president repeated the missile trade idea during a meeting of the National Security Council in the Oval Office on Saturday, October 20, 1962, and in doing so added the Jupiters in Italy to the possible deal. Although there was no live taping of that meeting, the official notetaker reported that "the President made clear that in the United Nations we should emphasize the subterranean nature of the missile buildup in Cuba. Only if we were asked would we respond that we were prepared to talk about the withdrawal of missiles from Italy and Turkey. In such an eventuality, the President pointed out that we would have to make clear to the Italians and the Turks that withdrawing strategic missiles was not a retreat and that we would be prepared to replace these missiles by providing a more effective deterrent, such as the assignment of Polaris submarines."[9]

The president returned to the subject on several occasions at ExComm meetings on the morning and afternoon of Monday, October 22:

> PRESIDENT KENNEDY: This gives us an excuse to get them out of Turkey and Italy. . . .
>
> I think maybe this is just a political problem. But I think we ought to be looking to the day when they are removed from Cuba, Italy and Turkey. Now maybe that's two or three days from now, or a week. But that proposal can be made after this one's been accepted [the United States will announce today]. . . .
>
> In other words, what is the distinction between these missiles and the missiles which we sent to Turkey and Italy, which the Soviets put up with, which are operational, and have been for 2 to 3 years.[10]

On Friday morning, October 26, Kennedy posed the choice facing him in stark terms in his discussion with ExComm. Assuming that the quarantine alone would not force the Soviets to remove their missiles from Cuba, "We've only got two ways of removing the weapons. One is to negotiate them out—in other words trade them out. Or the other is to go in and take them out. I don't see any other way you're going to get the weapons out."[11]

The next day, Saturday, October 27 at meetings throughout the day, the president and ExComm attendees at the White House received Khrushchev's public message, broadcast over Moscow radio, proposing an agreed swap-out of the Soviet missiles in Cuba for the US missiles in Turkey. Kennedy was displeased with the public nature of this negotiating step—complaining that Khrushchev had "put this out in a way to cause maximum tension and embarrassment"—but he nevertheless made clear his own view that "to any man at the United Nations or any other rational man, it will look like a very fair trade. . . . Because most people would regard this as not an unreasonable proposal. . . . As I say, you're going to find a lot of people who will find this a rather reasonable proposal. . . . Let's not kid ourselves. They've got a very good proposal, which is the reason they've made it public. . . . Emotionally, people will think this is a rather even trade and we ought to take advantage of it . . . this is a pretty good play of his. . . . Now [the Turks are] not going to want to do it, but we may just decide we have to do it in our interest. . . . We can't very well invade Cuba, with all this toil and blood it's going to be, when we could have gotten them [the Soviet missiles] out by making a deal on the same missiles in Turkey."[12]

In view of the president's repeated suggestions that a missile trade would be a logical and perhaps an unavoidable way to resolve the crisis, it is hard to fathom why it seemed so hard for the ExComm to catch the hint. The president's consistent comments failed to produce any significant ExComm consensus favoring the trade. As Marc Trachtenberg has noted, the president "was opposed on this issue by all of his chief advisers."[13] Apart from a few isolated expressions of what appeared to be polite but fugitive approbation by Bundy and McNamara, the president's idea was essentially adrift. It might also be asked why the president failed to press his point harder or insist on a full discussion and possibly an informal poll or even a vote. Did he not think it important to secure consensus around the idea he would subsequently transform into a settlement proposal? Or did he want his idea to become the final plan only behind closed doors?

There appears to be no way to answer that question. Yet the important thing is that the president's idea lived on in the only mind that really mattered. And he had actually put his idea into play several days before when he launched back-channel negotiations with Khrushchev on October 23 using an odd assortment of bit players in the Cuban missile drama: two American journalists, two Russians, and two Englishmen. The process had actually begun two days earlier when the president tested his idea in a private discussion with his close friend, the British ambassador.

As noted, Ormsby-Gore had been invited to join the president for a private meeting at the White House just before the lunch hour on Sunday morning October 21. In his first cable to Macmillan reporting on the meeting, not sent until October 22, the ambassador stated that the president had started the meeting by saying "that no one else outside the United States Government was being informed of what was going on." Kennedy then briefed Ormsby-Gore on the US discovery of Soviet missiles, posed various options for a response—do nothing, all-out air strike, invasion, blockade, or going to the United Nations—and asked the ambassador for his preference between the two leading options of air strike or blockade. Ormsby-Gore opted for the blockade, taking the occasion to observe that he "could not believe that the missiles so far landed constituted any significant military threat to the United States," and that "very few people outside the United

States would consider the provocation offered by the Cubans serious enough to merit an American attack."

The British ambassador reported these comments to Prime Minister Macmillan by cable sent on the evening of October 22: "Even then, Ormsby-Gore chose not to impart to Macmillan some of Kennedy's more private and highly significant views, which included consideration of a missile trade."[14] Thus, it wasn't until his second cable on October 23 that Ormsby-Gore informed the prime minister that Kennedy was considering a Turkey-for-Cuba missile swap-out: "He also said that intermediate range missile bases in Turkey and elsewhere had become more or less worthless. He was not doubtful whether they had been a good plan in the first place. Whether political developments would enable him to do a deal on the reciprocal closing of bases it was hard to tell at the moment, but certainly from a military point of view he could see no objection."[15]

Curiously, the president simultaneously shared his thinking on this highly confidential matter with another close friend, also outside the US government—the journalist Charles Bartlett. As reported by Fursenko and Naftali based on their interview of Bartlett: "Sometime on October 21 Kennedy reviewed for [Charles] Bartlett the choices that the Soviet move to Cuba had presented to him. As he had for his British friend, Kennedy expressed his preference for a diplomatic solution and admitted that the United States would probably have to sacrifice the Turkish missiles to maintain peace."[16]

One of the most convoluted yet ultimately the most effectual negotiating exchanges between the US and Soviet leaders during the Cuban missile drama covered a five-day period beginning on October 23, 1962, and culminating on October 27. During this period Kennedy and Khrushchev were simultaneously proposing deal terms to the other that were *more generous* than those the adversary was proposing or even expecting. In this seemingly backward bidding process, the two leaders were each revealing the weak or even empty hand they held in the high-stakes game they were playing.

President Kennedy opened the negotiations on October 23, 1962, by allowing (and probably directing) Robert Kennedy to enlist as back-channel intermediaries two of their favored journalist friends, Frank Holeman of the *New York Daily News* and Charles Bartlett of the *Chattanooga Times*. Robert Kennedy asked each journalist separately to approach Bolshakov, and both did so.[17] In their separate meetings with Bolshakov in Washington, DC, that day, the two journalists floated the president's idea that the Cuba crisis might be resolved on the basis of a Soviet withdrawal of their offensive missiles from Cuba in exchange for the United States removing its Jupiter IRBM missiles from Turkey and possibly from Italy as well.

The historical record makes it reasonably clear that the two journalists were specifically operating at the behest of the attorney general that day, and presumably of the president as well.[18] The Holeman approach came first. As reported by Fursenko and Naftali based on revelations they unearthed from Soviet archives: "The hoped-for telephone call came the day after Kennedy's speech. It was the journalist Frank Holeman who called to suggest a meeting."

> Holeman had grave business to conduct. Someone in the attorney general's office, possibly Robert Kennedy himself, wanted to use Bolshakov to sound out the Kremlin on a possible diplomatic solution to the crisis. Robert Kennedy and his people believed, Holeman explained, that the missiles in Cuba were the Soviet Union's way of responding to U.S. Jupiter missiles in Turkey. "In connection with this [the assumption about Soviet motives]," Bolshakov noted for his superiors, "Robert Kennedy and his circle consider it possible to discuss the following trade: The U.S. would liquidate its missile bases in Turkey and Italy, and the USSR would do the same in Cuba."[19]

Charles Bartlett was also coordinating his actions that day with Robert Kennedy, as indicated by the entry in the attorney general's desk diary for that date: "Charlie Bartlett called."[20] Michael Beschloss initially revealed the simultaneous Bartlett approach, based in part on oral histories provided by Robert Kennedy and Charles Bartlett, but he had only part of the story: "After the President's Monday night speech, the Attorney General called Charles Bartlett: 'Get ahold of Georgi and tell him how he betrayed us and how we're very disappointed.'"[21] Unfortunately, the oral histories provided by Robert Kennedy and Charles Bartlett left out the real reason for the meeting, which would only appear after Fursenko and Naftali gained access to the same archives of Bolshakov's messages back to Moscow from his earlier meeting with Holeman: "Apparently Bolshakov received confirmation of Holeman's story from a second journalist with inside information. Whether at the request of President Kennedy or on his own initiative, Charles Bartlett also passed word to Bolshakov in the first, tense hours of the crisis that the White House was thinking about a trade involving the Jupiter missiles."[22]

Evan Thomas provided additional information about the October 23 Bartlett-Bolshakov contact, noting that it was by telephone and at the attorney general's behest. There was also this further startling detail: Robert Kennedy telephoned Bartlett back barely a few minutes after the Bolshakov call ended to playfully chide the journalist about the tone he had used: "That wasn't very subtly done . . . I hope you can be a little more subtle." Kennedy apparently had personally overheard Bartlett's conversation with the GRU officer, presumably because he had accessed an FBI wiretap of the call! It is not clear whether the wiretap was placed on Bartlett's or Bolshakov's telephone line, though the latter seems the more likely.[23]

Although Fursenko and Naftali expressed uncertainty over whether the Bartlett initiative actually carried the president's knowing blessing, the Kennedy tapes leave little doubt on this score. They include the extraordinary private exchange on Tuesday evening October 23 between the president and attorney general, discussed earlier,[24] that was caught on the president's secret White House taping system as the two spoke for several minutes in the Oval Office after the ExComm meeting had concluded and before the president joined a dinner party he was hosting that included British ambassador David Ormsby-Gore and his wife.[25] Although the audio clarity of the tapes is uneven, so that there are gaps where words are undecipherable, portions of the conversation clearly reveal that both the president and his brother were aware of the interactions that had occurred earlier in the day involving Holeman, Bartlett and Bolshakov:

> PRESIDENT KENNEDY: Who saw Georgi? Holeman? While we were there? But he's not with us in this. . . .
>
> ROBERT KENNEDY: I said to tell Chuck, tell Charlie Bartlett to get hold of Georgi.
>
> PRESIDENT KENNEDY: Today? . . .
>
> PRESIDENT KENNEDY: You said this [for Bartlett] to tell Georgi?
>
> ROBERT KENNEDY: I told him so.[26]

The veiled comments exchanged between the brothers do not clearly lend themselves to any single, intelligible story. Nevertheless, their fragmentary references to Holeman, Bartlett, and Bolshakov provide the needed degree of validation that the clearer official report that Bolshakov submitted to his superiors in Moscow that same day regarding what he was told by Holeman and Bartlett bore the official imprimatur of at least Robert Kennedy and, most probably, the president as well. Robert Kennedy had personally launched the two journalists on their parallel, confidential missions, and he presumably would not have done so without the president's explicit or implicit delegation of authority.[27] In fact, Bartlett would be reporting back to the president personally later that same day, as indicated by the entry on the president's secretary's "Day at a Glance" calendar, which shows "Charles B." at the White House at 7:30.[28]

According to Fursenko and Naftali: "Kennedy was floating a trial balloon. If, as he expected, Khrushchev ignored the blockade, he needed to find a political exit. Aware of no military grounds for keeping the Jupiter missiles in Turkey, Kennedy informed Ormsby-Gore that he would have to see 'whether political developments would enable him to do a deal on the reciprocal closing of bases.'"[29]

The president's plan to transmit his missile trade proposal to the Soviets had not been disclosed to ExComm and in fact would never be shared with the full group of his top crisis advisers. As of the evening of October 23, 1962, only a matter of hours after the various back-channel overtures had been launched, the small circle of key insiders in the United States who were privy to President Kennedy's brainchild—the single most closely held secret of the president's handling of the Cuban missile crisis—included just four people in addition to the president and the attorney general, and none of the four was a US government official. The four were two journalists, Charles Bartlett and Frank Holeman; Ormsby-Gore; and a Soviet GRU officer, Georgi Bolshakov.[30]

Shortly after Kennedy's missile swap-out initiative was quietly relayed by his two Washington journalist friends to Bolshakov for retransmission to Khrushchev, the president took things up a notch. He instructed his brother to present the idea directly to Soviet ambassador Dobrynin at one of their almost daily meetings. The ensuing private discussion between Robert Kennedy and Dobrynin at the Soviet embassy in Washington would not become publicly known until twenty-five years later, when it was mentioned first by Georgy Shakhnazarov, personal aide to General Secretary Gorbachev, at a 1987 conference on the Cold War in Cambridge, Massachusetts, and then confirmed by Dobrynin at a conference on the Cuban missile crisis held in Moscow two years later.[31] According to Dobrynin, when he made the point that the Soviet deployment of missiles in Cuba was no different than the US installation of similar missiles in Turkey, Robert Kennedy asked to be excused for a moment to make a call to the president. When he returned to the room he told Dobrynin: "The President said that we are ready to consider the question of Turkey, to examine favorably the question of Turkey."[32]

The date of the RFK-Dobrynin meeting has been variously reported as October 24, 25, or 26. Yet whichever of the three dates the meeting actually occurred, the main revelation is not in dispute: the president wished to make clear to Khrushchev "that he was prepared to pull the Jupiter missiles out of Turkey."[33]

Sergei Khrushchev later recorded his father's information about what transpired at the Soviet ambassador's meeting with the attorney general:

> In the course of the conversation about possible conditions for the withdrawal of our missiles, [Dobrynin] only hinted at possibilities concerning "a state adjacent to the Soviet Union."
>
> Robert Kennedy's reaction was unexpected. He didn't answer, and simply asked to make a call from the next room, without witnesses. The ambassador was accustomed to such calls. The conversation was brief. Returning, Robert Kennedy relayed the words of the person to whom he had been speaking: "The president said that we are prepared to examine the question of Turkey. Favorably."[34]

News of the Holeman/Bartlett feelers reached Khrushchev in Moscow midday on October 25 at approximately the same time the Soviet chairman learned of a "Today and Tomorrow" column written by Walter Lippmann, another prominent American journalist who enjoyed privileged White House access. Lippmann's column, entitled "Blockade Proclaimed," also raised the idea of a missile trade.[35]

It is possible that the president or one of his top advisers could have planted the idea with Lippmann. After all, the journalist was close to Kennedy and had generous access to the president.[36] Only two weeks before, Lippmann had published an October 9 column, based in part on private conversations with unnamed administration officials, confirming that US surveillance of Cuba was "elaborate."[37] Historians later surmised that his source might have been McGeorge Bundy at the president's behest.[38]

On Monday morning October 22, as members of the ExComm planned for the press coverage that would accompany the president's address to the nation later that evening, Kennedy asked: "Now what do you do about Lippmann, Reston, and all those? Which one do they go to?" George Ball, who was serving as undersecretary of state, responded, "I'll get Walter in, and Scotty [Reston] [unclear], and the others."[39] The next morning, October 23, as the Kennedy brothers were in the process of deputizing Holeman and

Bartlett to transmit their missile swap-out proposal through Bolshakov to Khrushchev, Ball informed the president that he would be having a private meeting with Lippmann later that same morning.[40]

It is not clear whether Ball met or spoke with Lippmann on October 23. The columnist's diary for that day made no mention of Ball. The two did meet for lunch, however, on October 24 at Ball's State Department office, with the department's counselor, Abram Chayes, and Edward Martin, the assistant secretary of state for Latin American affairs, also in attendance. Lippmann's engagement book for that date mentioned the meeting ("1. Geo Ball"), and his diary contained a lengthier description that began with a reference to his forthcoming column—"Article: BLOCKADE PROCLAIMED"—and followed with identification of the participants, placement of the venue ("Lunched at George Ball's office at the State Dept."), and description of the subject of discussion ("We talked about Cuba").[41]

At that lunch, Ball would have had the president's Turkey-for-Cuba missile swap proposal fresh in his mind. Earlier that morning, Ball had drafted a telegram that Rusk sent to US ambassador Finletter in Turkey seeking his "assessment [of] political consequences" if the United States were to enter into a "negotiated solution for removal Cuban offensive threat" by an exchange involving "dismantling and removal Jupiters."[42]

The next day, Lippmann published his October 25 "Blockade Proclaimed" column—noting that he had written it the day before—which proposed the idea of a Turkey-for-Cuba missile swap-out. The column included criticism of the president's failure to engage in private diplomacy with the Soviets beforehand, so that Khrushchev might have received "what all wise statesmen give their adversaries—the chance to save face." Lippmann then proposed a missile swap-out, pointing out that neither side's distant missile base had any real value: "The Soviet military base in Cuba is defenseless, and the base in Turkey is all but obsolete. The two bases could be dismantled without altering the world balance of power." Lippmann closed with a carefully qualified prediction of the prospects for the missile trade ("an agreement of this sort may be doable") using words that closely resembled how Ormsby-Gore had described for Macmillan just two days before, on October 23, what Kennedy had told him (whether "political developments" would allow a deal involving the Turkish missiles "was hard to tell at the moment").[43] The columnist also simultaneously invoked historian Barbara Tuchman's warning about the way the world seemed to slide uncontrollably into World War I ("there may exist a way out of the tyranny of automatic and uncontrollable events"), which lined up with her best-selling book that is said to have been at the top of the president's mind during the crisis.

The provenance of the Lippmann column remains something of a mystery. Lippmann apparently told Soviet ambassador Dobrynin on November 1, 1962, that he had "caught it hot" for writing his column about a missile swap and thereby supposedly "suggest[ing] to N.S. Khrushchev the idea of raising such a question," whereas Lippmann stated he was simply writing some ideas he had come up with on his own based on information he had received from the US Arms Control and Disarmament Agency.[44] Despite these comments, it seems likely that the president had acted to plant his idea of a missile trade in the thinking of a respected columnist whose article would rapidly reach the Kremlin, and that he deputized George Ball to do so.[45] Ball would be the most likely intermediary for conveying the president's idea to the famous columnist given the undersecretary's knowledge of the president's interest in the notion of a missile swap, Ball's having informed Kennedy on October 22 and 23 that he would soon be meeting personally with the journalist; his having drafted the State Department's October 24 morning telegram to the US ambassador in Turkey addressing the subject of a missile trade; his having hosted Lippmann in his State Department office for a lunch meeting that same day, which occurred simultaneously with the columnist's drafting of his "Blockade Proclaimed" article; and Ball's and his lunch guests' having "talked about Cuba."

Soviet officials were used to seeing the well-known American columnist in settings reflecting his privileged access to the highest levels of government.[46] Michael Dobbs has observed that Khrushchev very probably assumed the Lippmann article was intended to be a message to him from the American president because the "Soviets knew the columnist had excellent sources in the Kennedy administration" and it therefore "seemed unlikely that he was speaking only for himself." It thus stood to reason that "Khrushchev understood the Lippmann column as an unattributable feeler from Washington."[47]

While it remains unclear whether Lippmann was acting directly on Kennedy's behalf, or exactly which Turkey-for-Cuba swap-out message—Bolshakov's or Lippmann's—first came to Khrushchev's attention, and whether one was more persuasive than the other,[48] it cannot be doubted that Kennedy, rather than Khrushchev, was the prime author of the swap-out proposal, and that Kennedy's overture was known to Khrushchev through any or all three of the Bolshakov, Dobrynin, and Lippmann channels. That conclusion finds some support from Soviet sources. Anastas Mikoyan told Fidel Castro at their meeting on November 4, 1962: "Speaking frankly, we were not thinking about bases in Turkey at all . . . but during discussion of the dangerous situation we received information from the United States of America, including an article by Lippmann, where it was said that the Russians could raise the question of liquidating the USA bases in Turkey."[49] Sergei Khrushchev recalled that his father had said much the same thing:

> Father became absorbed in reports that had come in during the night about Turkish missiles. It seemed that yesterday [October 25] everyone, both in the United States and Europe, had been talking about them. There were Lippmann's article and Kreisky's proposals, and intelligence reports about discussions of this question at the highest level in Washington and consultations with the Turks and NATO. Father later told me that someone close to high-level U.S. officials openly hinted that such a proposal coming from Moscow would get a favorable reception.[50]

The idea of a missile trade or swap-out had received scant attention from ExComm participants (other than the president) as most of the president's advisers were focused on various gradations of military responses, and the notion of a quick settlement did not hold center stage until nearly the end. As the news of escalating military confrontation grew more dire on Saturday, October 27, however, with confirmation that a U-2 aircraft had been shot down, and as the president's advisers began to press for an immediate retaliatory strike and a follow-up invasion involving hundreds of bombing sorties, President Kennedy's own comments in the ExComm meeting in the Cabinet Room that afternoon (4:00–7:45 p.m.) revealed that his initial instinct for compromise had evolved to a more fixed determination:

> I'm just thinking about what we're going to have to do in a day or so, which is 500 sorties, and seven days, and possibly an invasion, all because we wouldn't take missiles out of Turkey. We all know how quickly everybody's courage goes when the blood starts to flow, and that's what is going to happen to NATO. When they start these things and they grab Berlin, everybody's going to say, "Well, that was a pretty good proposition."[51] . . .
>
> "It seems to me what we ought to . . . To be reasonable, we're not going to

get these weapons out of Cuba, probably, anyway—but I mean, by negotiation. We're going to have to take our weapons out of Turkey."[52]

The president thus set in motion that same evening a bold, two-track plan for resolving the crisis by expressly offering Khrushchev an agreed, mutual, Turkey-for-Cuba missile extraction. The first track, which quickly succeeded and rendered the backup plan moot, involved a secret approach to Khrushchev whereby Robert Kennedy would reach out to Dobrynin and convey the US offer to remove US IRBM missiles from Turkey, and perhaps Italy as well, in exchange for removal of the Soviet missiles in Cuba. Then, in case the Dobrynin channel did not succeed, the president also set in motion a backup plan—the so-called Cordier ploy described below—whereby the United Nations secretary-general, U Thant, would serve as a neutral peace broker by publicly proposing the Cuba/Turkey missile exchange in order to bring international pressure to bear on the two sides to preserve world peace. This latter approach would also incidentally provide political cover for Kennedy by advancing the president's own proposal by means of an independent, irreproachable proxy.

Khrushchev had told his Presidium colleagues in his Meniscus speech in January 1962 that the great Cold War game had to be played aggressively but not foolishly lest the surface tension between the two superpowers spill over to armed conflict. Khrushchev warned against acting like the gambler "who bets whatever is left in his pocket and then grabs a pistol and shoots himself." Khrushchev had indeed been playing exactly this game of thrust and restraint by launching his audacious Anadyr missile transfer thrust in the first place, and he abided by the restraint step of his self-imposed rules after his secret maneuver had been discovered.

This, too, was an illustration of Khrushchev's double game. Within moments after learning that his adversary would not accept the presence of Soviet ballistic missiles on Cuban soil, the Russian leader recognized he had no choice but to give in and soon issued an order to stop the Cuba-bound ships still outside the zone of quarantine. Yet while these and other actions preparatory to a Soviet retreat were being put into effect, Khrushchev and the Kremlin also stepped up the belligerence of their statements in response to the US naval quarantine, mentioning threats of a "big war," "catastrophic consequences for world peace," and "the abyss of a world nuclear-missile war" if the US Navy were to attempt to interfere with Cuba-bound ships on the high seas.[53]

KHRUSHCHEV'S OPENING OFFER TO RETREAT IN EXCHANGE FOR A NO-INVASION PLEDGE

The first Soviet peace feeler came as early as October 12, 1962—well before President Kennedy disclosed the US discovery of Soviet ballistic missiles in Cuba. American journalist Charles Bartlett asserted in a later report he wrote to the president that Alexander Zinchuk, a Soviet embassy official, met with him at the National Press Club and "talked almost solidly for an hour," covering, among other things how the two sides could "work[] out the Cuban matter." Zinchuk reportedly told Bartlett that "the Soviets had no interest in Cuba beyond protecting it from an invasion. He said he thought that if you [President Kennedy] assured Khrushchev there would be no such invasion and if you agreed to take some steps towards at least formal relations with Castro's government, the Russian technicians could be quickly removed. He expressed regret that their arrival had been a political embarrassment to [the president]."[54]

The second Soviet approach occurred on October 26, when Aleksander Feklisov, also known by his alias Alexandre Fomin, the KGB's top agent in Washington, DC, arranged to have lunch with John Scali, an ABC correspondent, who was known to be friends with Roger Hilsman, the director of the Bureau of Intelligence and Research at the State Department. As Hilsman recalled: "The Soviets knew that Scali and I were friends, and Fomin asked Scali if he could find out from me if the highest levels of the US government would be interested in the following solution of the crisis: 1. The Soviets would withdraw the missiles in Cuba. 2. UN inspectors would be allowed to supervise and verify the removal. 3. The Soviet Union would promise not to reintroduce missiles to Cuba—*ever*. 4. The United States would pledge publicly not to invade Cuba."[55]

Scali reported the proposal to Hilsman, who in turn discussed it with Rusk and the president. Thereafter, Rusk prepared the US response "on a piece of yellow paper in his own handwriting," which Scali was instructed to deliver orally to Feklisov/Fomin: "I have reason to believe that the USG [United States Government] sees real possibilities and supposes that the representatives of the two governments in New York could work this matter out with U Thant and with each other. My impression is, however, that time is very urgent."[56]

As revelations from secret Soviet archives have emerged, it has become clear that Khrushchev had simultaneously reached his own decision to back down and was developing an exceptionally generous proposal to settle the matter. The first sign that the Soviet leader would be in retreat came almost immediately after the president's October 22 speech announcing discovery of the missiles. By 12:00 noon on October 23, US Navy "direction-finding stations began reporting to NSA that their tracking data indicated that some of the Russian merchant ships had stopped dead in the water, and that it seemed that at least eight of the ships had reversed course and were headed back towards Russia."[57] For Khrushchev the reverse-course step solidified into a full pullout decision early in the morning of October 25, when he told his Presidium colleagues that it would be necessary "to dismantle the missile sites" in order to prevent the crisis from coming "to the boil."[58] Later that day he received Kennedy's letter making it unmistakably clear that the United States was determined not to allow the Soviets to deploy offensive missiles in Cuba. He also learned that the US military was raising its alert level to Defense Condition-2 (DEFCON-2), which was only one step short of war. Khrushchev's biographer William Taubman described how these two events galvanized Khrushchev's decision to back down and pull out under cover of the softest imaginable quid pro quo—a US no-invasion pledge: "When the Presidium met after lunch [on October 25], Khrushchev rejected further 'caustic' exchanges with Kennedy, favored having ships carrying missiles turn around, and indicated that he wanted to resolve the crisis. 'We must dismantle the missiles to make Cuba into a zone of peace,' he told his colleagues. He proposed saying to Kennedy, 'Give us a pledge not to invade Cuba, and we will remove the missiles.'"[59]

Khrushchev did not come close to actually considering defending his distant missile emplacements militarily, though his private and public statements bristled with frightening references to war and the nuclear abyss. As his son Sergei reported: "Father felt trapped. If Soviet missiles in Cuba were attacked, he had no retaliatory actions in reserve. Such an attack must be averted at all costs. Not for a moment did he contemplate a nuclear strike on the United States. The atomic bomb was fine for newspapers. Father considered any action in Berlin to be unduly dangerous. Against his wishes, it could lead to a great war. He ruled out war as a way of resolving quarrels."[60]

Khrushchev searched for a face-saving compromise, and his initial idea, explained to the Presidium at an early afternoon meeting on October 25, was the proposal that had come from the October 23 Kennedy/Bartlett/Holeman/Bolshakov back channel and the Lippmann October 25 article: "a quid pro quo, the Cuban missiles staked against the Jupiters based in Turkey and

Italy." Gromyko was directed to have the Soviet Foreign Ministry prepare a letter making this proposal for the Presidium's consideration at its meeting scheduled for the morning of October 26.[61]

By the morning of October 26, however, news arrived from Soviet sources in Washington that rumors abounded of an imminent US invasion of Cuba. Khrushchev panicked and decided to put aside the missile trade proposal in favor of the softer, more lenient no-invasion pledge mentioned to the Presidium on October 25 and conveyed in the Fomin-Scali meeting in Washington the next day. Khrushchev told his Presidium colleagues, "We have been warned that war could start today. . . . We have to concentrate on the main point: if the United States, their president, pledges not to attack Cuba, we will withdraw our missiles, despite the unpleasantness. Otherwise the situation becomes too dangerous."[62] The Presidium agreed and a letter from Khrushchev to Kennedy presenting the no-invasion offer was drafted, revised, finalized, and sent to the US Embassy in Moscow, where it arrived at 4:43 pm on October 26 Moscow time. Because of further transmission delays, mainly at the Moscow International Telegraph office, the soft letter would not reach the White House until Friday evening, October 26, Washington time.[63]

Then began a period of conflicting messages, roller-coaster emotions, and exasperating confusion. When Khrushchev's soft letter reached Kennedy and his top advisers on Friday evening October 26, the reaction, as Beschloss described the scene, was enormous relief at the modesty of the Kremlin's demand and a sense that the crisis was nearing its end: "After reading the letter, Kennedy gave it to O'Donnell, who was 'deeply moved' by it. Sorensen found the letter 'long, meandering, full of polemics, but in essence appearing to contain the germ of a reasonable settlement." Kennedy must have been surprised and pleased that Khrushchev's proposal contained no hint of the more generous missile swap-out offer the president had floated through backchannels three days before: "That evening at ten, the President met with ExComm in the Cabinet Room. The ten days of pressures had depleted neither his sense of humor nor, evidently, his libido. Late in the second week of the crisis, he spotted one of the secretaries brought from the Commerce Department to cope with the increased White House workload and quietly told McNamara, 'Get her name. We may avert nuclear war tonight.'"[64] But the president's feeling of relief would be short-lived as he faced Khrushchev's first-drafted and more demanding proposal—which accepted the president's own missile swap-out idea—when he woke up the next morning.

KHRUSHCHEV'S REACHING OUT FOR THE RICHER KENNEDY OFFER

Khrushchev changed his mind once again on Saturday morning. October 27, Moscow time. He had come to believe that US invasion planning was proceeding more slowly than he had thought the day before, and so he finalized and transmitted the first of his two settlement proposals to President Kennedy—the one that had been drafted with the missile swap-out demand included but that had been put aside. This message, which was also publicly broadcast over Moscow Radio to give it more momentum and urgency, stated in relevant part: "We are willing to remove from Cuba the means which you regard as offensive" so long as the United States "will remove its analogous means from Turkey."[65] Fursenko and Naftali describe how Khrushchev persuaded his Presidium colleagues to accept the abrupt change of approach:

> Khrushchev discouraged any grand analysis of Operation Anadyr. "Did we make a mistake or not? It will be possible to determine that later." Instead, he wanted to discuss an idea that he had for dramatically improving the Soviet Union's situation in the crisis. "If we could achieve additionally the liquidation of the bases in Turkey we would win." Turkey had never been a highlight of any previous presidium discussion in this crisis. However, for a day at least, Khrushchev had been sitting on feelers from the Kennedy camp implying the possibility of exchanging U.S. missiles in Turkey for the Soviet missiles in Cuba. Now it was time to act on them. What had not been a determinative issue at all for Khrushchev, the Jupiter missiles in Turkey, now presented the Kremlin with a means of snatching a victory from the jaws of defeat.[66]

When Khrushchev's tougher missile swap-out letter arrived at the White House on the morning of October 27, the ExComm had already begun meeting and its participants were getting ready to discuss the soft Khrushchev letter that they had briefly seen the evening before. To say that the late-arriving missile swap-out letter came as an unwelcome surprise would be an understatement. The new Khrushchev demand left some ExComm members incredulous. McGeorge Bundy said, "It's very odd, Mr. President," and "We are in a very difficult position."[67] Robert Kennedy said at one point that day, "We can have an exchange with him [Khrushchev] and say: You double-crossed us, and you—and we don't know what deal to accept."[68]

President Kennedy must have felt uncomfortable when the tougher letter arrived, especially since it contained the very same missile swap-out proposal that he himself had put before Khrushchev through back channels just a few days before without having first informed his ExComm advisers. Perhaps not surprisingly, but certainly disingenuously, the president said nothing to his colleagues about his own role in the provenance of the new proposal. What is notable, however, is that Kennedy expressed no objection to the missile trade proposal on its merits. To the contrary, the president immediately launched into a steadfast defense of Khrushchev's new demand. And what is most striking about the arguments the president used is that they focused solely on how things would look, how others would regard the United States, and what others would *say* about the US leaders if they were to reject Khrushchev's missile-trade proposal. He apparently did not count it important enough to reflect on what the Soviets would do if their offer were rejected, or what would become of negotiations in those circumstances. Here are the arguments Kennedy advanced:

Saturday, October 27, 10:05–11:55 a.m.

> We're going to be in an unsupportable position on this matter if this becomes his proposal. In the first place, we last year tried to get the missiles out of there because they're not militarily useful. Number one. Number two, it's going to—to any man at the United Nations or any other rational man, it will look like a very fair trade. . . .
>
> Well, *this* is unsettling *now*, George, because he's got us in a pretty good spot here. Because most people would regard this as not an unreasonable proposal. . . .
>
> I think you're going to find it very difficult to explain why we are going to take hostile military action in Cuba, against these sites, what we're here thinking about, when he's saying, "If you'll get yours out of Turkey, we'll get ours out of Cuba." I think you've got a very touchy point here.[69]

Most historians and other commentators have focused mainly on the ultimate outcome, which was the president's secret acceptance of Khrushchev's new demand via the Saturday evening meeting between Robert Kennedy and Soviet ambassador Dobrynin, a denouement that at the time was known only to a small, handpicked group of Kennedy's advisers and was not revealed to the rest of the ExComm, far less to the public. Less attention has been paid, however, to the fact that in demanding absolute secrecy regarding his acceptance of Khrushchev's terms, Kennedy was also concealing the uncomfortable fact that the pivotal bargain in question, which a majority of his ExComm advisers had found to be unacceptable, was the president's own proposal.

Khrushchev had not stood by his soft proposal because he still hoped that events might yet allow the Soviets to bargain for a richer concession.[70] But this period of hopeful procrastination ended abruptly when he was awoken from sleep at about 1:10 a.m. early on the morning of October 28 (6:10 p.m., October 27, Washington, DC, time) and given an urgent and emotional message from Fidel Castro that an American invasion was imminent and that this was "the moment to eliminate such danger forever through an act of clear legitimate defense." Castro darkly requested that "the Soviet Union must never allow circumstances in which the imperialists could launch the first nuclear strike against it."[71] Khrushchev interpreted these comments to mean that Castro was proposing a preventive Soviet nuclear first strike against the United States.[72] But far from inspiring the Soviet premier, this request "appalled" him.[73] Already aware that Soviet troops manning a SAM missile site in Cuba had acted against orders and shot down an American aircraft without specific authorization, the shocking message from Castro evidently drove home in Khrushchev's mind the absolute peril the world might be facing if his control over Soviet forces in Cuba might be slipping, and galvanized his determination to stop looking for a better deal but rather immediately seek the Presidium's approval for a unilateral Soviet retreat.

Khrushchev was ready to settle immediately for a limited no-invasion pledge, but moments after he had begun delivering this message to the Presidium, news arrived of President Kennedy's back-channel offer made by Robert Kennedy to Dobrynin the night before to trade the US Jupiter missiles in Turkey so long as this exchange would be kept secret. That proposal and its secrecy proviso were immediately accepted even though the disappearance of any public mention of the missile trade would leave an impression that the Soviets had buckled under the pressure of US demands.

In the end, both sides' desperation to end the crisis peacefully, by whatever means necessary, was demonstrated by the remarkable generosity of the reciprocal demands. Allison and Zelikow succinctly summarized this curiously upside-down bargaining dynamic in the second edition of *Essence of Decision*: "To end this crisis, Kennedy was prepared to pay more, and Khrushchev to accept less, than the other required or understood. Kennedy offered the Turkish missiles, but before Khrushchev learned that Kennedy had sweetened his offer, he had chosen to withdraw Soviet missiles from Cuba in exchange for a noninvasion pledge alone."[74]

One of the president's most pressing concerns, evident on the first day of the ExComm deliberations, was the need to maintain a cloak of secrecy over the looming crisis. Many early commentators emphasized the administration's explanation that secrecy was needed to give the administration time to decide on its course of action and to avoid any opportunity for Khrushchev to confuse public perceptions about the confrontation and thereby gain time needed to bring the missiles to operational status before the United States could take action. But the president's additional political reasons for insisting on secrecy were also evident from the very beginning of the crisis, as indicated by his and Secretary McNamara's first exchange on the subject:

Tuesday, October 16, 11:50 a.m.–1:00 p.m.

PRESIDENT KENNEDY: How long do we estimate this will remain secure, this information, until people have it? . . .

MCNAMARA: Mr. President, I think, to be realistic, we should assume that this will become fairly widely known, if not in the newspapers, at least by political representatives of both parties, within, I would say, I'm just picking a figure, I'd say a week.[75]

Barton Bernstein underscored the importance President Kennedy ascribed to keeping his missile swap-out deal secret for political reasons relating both to voters and to key NATO allies: "Secrecy also meant that the president, as well as the administration and the Democratic party, did not have to face problems with voters. The claims of a great triumph, as opposed to the reality of a victory with compromise, greatly helped the president and his administration both at home and abroad."[76]

Robert Kennedy confirmed that the need for secrecy was driven by domestic political concerns in a conversation with Dobrynin a few days later when the ambassador attempted to deliver a letter confirming the Turkey missile swap-out arrangement. Kennedy refused to accept the letter, saying, according to Dobrynin's report of the meeting, "Who knows where and when such letters can surface or be somehow published—not now but in the future. . . . The appearance of such a letter could cause irreparable harm to my political career in the future."[77]

The president also hoped that "concealing the Jupiters" would allow the administration to "avoid[] problems in NATO." Indeed, Kennedy considered cohesion within the NATO alliance to be so critical that he chose secrecy to avoid a single member's objection even though, in Bernstein's estimation, many other members "would undoubtedly have endorsed the deal as a comparatively small price to pay for settling the crisis peacefully."[78]

The compromise deals that the rival leaders ultimately struck regarding border-crossing protocol in Berlin and the Soviet missiles in Cuba would likely have been unobtainable if their terms had been open to public scrutiny and exposed to criticism by the president's political enemies. Fortunately, however, Khrushchev and Kennedy found ways to achieve their shared peaceful objectives on these two occasions hidden from public view. In both cases, the American president followed his personal crisis avoidance method, and it delivered a workable agreement to stand down, as distilled in table 1.

SWEETENING THE DEAL BY SUCCESSIVE GESTURES OF GENEROSITY

As it turned out, both sides were willing to be generous in order to get the deal done.

US unilaterally adds Italy missiles to deal package. The initial US offer, conveyed to Georgi Bolshakov on October 23 by journalist Frank Holeman, provided that the United States might consider removing its Jupiter missiles from Turkey and Italy in exchange for removal of the Soviet missiles in Cuba.[79] Bolshakov thereafter received two visits that same day from Charles Bartlett, who "confirmed the offer to 'trade' the Jupiter missiles in Europe for the Soviet weapons in Cuba." However, it is not clear whether he specifically mentioned both Turkey and Italy, or only Turkey.[80]

Khrushchev's positive response to the Kennedy administration's missile swap-out proposal, contained in his second publicly broadcast letter to Kennedy, which arrived in Washington on October 27, referred only to the US missiles in Turkey,[81] and Robert Kennedy's follow-up offer, communicated to Ambassador Dobrynin, was in response to Dobrynin's question, "And what about Turkey?" Robert Kennedy's response, as memorialized in Dobrynin's contemporaneous cable to Moscow, was that the United States would remove its missiles from Turkey, with no mention of Italy:

Table 1.

	Berlin	Cuba
Show of force	Display US M-48 Patton tanks	Declaration of DEFCON-2
Back-channel negotiation	JFK RFK Bolshakov Khrushchev	JFK RFK Holeman/ Bartlett Bolshakov/Dobrynin Khrushchev
Give Soviets what they want on substantive terms[1]	Acquiescence in GDR/VOPO border control	No-invasion pledge; agreed withdrawal of US missiles from Turkey
Soviets must visibly be the first to retreat	Soviet tanks began withdrawal from Friedrichstrasse Plaza first, followed by reciprocal withdrawals of American tanks	Soviet missiles were withdrawn from Cuba first, while the US missiles were withdrawn from Turkey (and Italy) several months later
Deal must be kept secret	There was no US government acknowledgment that any kind of bargain had been arranged to resolve the tank standoff.	The bargain reached to withdraw US missiles from Turkey in exchange for withdrawal of Soviet missiles from Cuba was kept secret for twenty-seven years, until Sorensen disclosed it at an international conference in 1989.
No formal US record of deal	No written version of RFK's October 27, 1961, proposal to Khrushchev through Bolshakov has been found. RFK: "Stupidly, I didn't write many of the things down. I just delivered the messages verbally to my brother."[2]	Robert Kennedy refused to accept the bargain memorialization letter from Khrushchev tendered by Dobrynin.
Robert Kennedy subsequently acknowledged only the deal terms that were favorable to the United States.	RFK: "I . . . got in touch with Bolshakov and said the President would like them to take their tanks out of there . . . in twenty-four hours."[3] "I kept telling Georgi Bolshakov that we'd fight."[4]	RFK memorandum for the Secretary of State, October 30, 1962: "[Dobrynin] then asked me about Khrushchev's other proposal dealing with the removal of missiles from Turkey. I replied that there could not be any quid pro quo—no deal of this kind could be made."[5]

1. Cf. *Kennedy Tapes*, p. 29. Referring to President Kennedy's dealings with Khrushchev on Laos, May and Zelikow provided a strikingly similar description of Kennedy's signature crisis resolution diplomacy: "*Time* magazine took Kennedy to task at one point. Predicting that Laos would soon disappear behind an iron curtain, the magazine's editors wrote: 'Kennedy declared he would "pay any price to assure the survival of liberty." But the price in Laos seemed too high.' In the end, however, Kennedy got his way. He managed to seem uncompromising while in reality seeking and obtaining an accommodation that averted a genuine crisis" (May and Zelikow, *The Kennedy Tapes*, p. xlv).

2. RFK 1964 confidential oral history, cited in Thomas, *Robert Kennedy*, pp. 134–35.

3. Robert F. Kennedy Oral History, JFKL, vol. 1, March 1, 1964, p. 69.

4. Hilty, *Robert Kennedy*, p. 436.

5. Memorandum for the Secretary of State from the Attorney General, October 30, 1962, RFK Papers, JFKL, reprinted in Jim Hershberg, "More on Bobby and the Cuban Missile Crisis," *Cold War International History Bulletin*, nos. 8–9 (Winter 1996–97).

> "However, President Kennedy is ready to come to agree on that question with N.S. Khrushchev, too. I think that in order to withdraw these bases from Turkey," R. Kennedy said, "we need 4–5 months. This is the minimal amount of time necessary for the US government to do this, taking into account the procedures that exist within the NATO framework. On the whole Turkey issue," R. Kennedy added, "if Premier N.S. Khrushchev agrees with what I've said,["] we can continue to exchange opinions between him and the president, using him, R. Kennedy and the Soviet ambassador. "However, the president can't say anything public in this regard about Turkey," R. Kennedy said again. R. Kennedy then warned that his comments about Turkey are extremely confidential; besides him and his brother, only 2–3 people know about it in Washington.[82]

In subsequent accounts of the White House meeting on October 27 where the president instructed his brother on the message to be delivered to Khrushchev through Dobrynin, Bundy (in 1988), Rusk (in 1990), and Sorensen (in 1989) mentioned only Turkey, and not Italy.[83] And as noted above, Dobrynin mentioned only Turkey in the cable he sent to Moscow relaying Robert Kennedy's offer. Subsequently, Khrushchev prepared a private confirmatory letter to President Kennedy on October 28 for delivery by Dobrynin as a means to seal the secret deal. The confirmatory letter referred solely to Turkey, not Italy. The letter was delivered by Dobrynin to Robert Kennedy on October 29, and was then shown to the president, but was rejected and handed back, not because of any dispute over its summary of the terms of the missile swap, but rather because it might increase the risk that secrecy would one day be compromised.[84]

Beschloss noted that some later Soviet accounts suggested that Robert Kennedy had also mentioned the US missiles in Italy.[85] It seems improbable that the attorney general would have spontaneously and unilaterally added the Jupiter missiles based in Italy to his offer to remove the missiles based in Turkey. But even if he had done so, this would have been a gratuitous gesture, since neither Khrushchev's letter nor Dobrynin's comments had mentioned any missiles other than those installed in Turkey.[86] Yet whatever the sequence of bargaining, there can be no doubt that the Kennedy administration threw in the Italy Jupiters to the already sweetened bargain.

The United States moved forward with its plans to remove the Jupiter IRBMs from Italy as well as Turkey, and to achieve this step by the agreed April 1963 deadline. The Italian government acquiesced when promised that the better-protected and more potent missile-carrying Polaris submarines would be substituted in the Mediterranean and that Italy would receive additional military upgrades.[87] It seems likely that Kennedy removed the Italy missiles both because their shortcomings matched those of the Turkish Jupiters and because the parallel removals characterized as both modernization and upgrades would provide further cover shielding the quid pro quo nature of the Turkey missile trade.[88]

USSR agrees to add IL-28 bombers to deal package. Kennedy's October 22, 1962, speech to the nation focused on the installation of Soviet "offensive missile sites" in Cuba. The president "call[ed] upon" Khrushchev "to halt and eliminate this clandestine, reckless, and provocative threat to world peace and to stable relations between our two nations," and he urged the Soviet leader "to move the world back from the abyss of destruction—by returning to his government's own words that it had no need to station *missiles* outside its own territory, and withdrawing these weapons from Cuba."[89]

Khrushchev's initial settlement offer, delivered in his first offer letter to Kennedy received at the White House on the evening of October 26, stated that if the United States would make a no-invasion pledge, then "the necessity of our military specialists in Cuba would disappear."[90] Kennedy's letter effectively accepting the framework of a proposal set forth in Khrushchev's "first" letter, delivered to Dobrynin on October 27, stated that the Soviets would be required to remove "all weapons systems in Cuba capable of offensive use."

Khrushchev's October 28 response, sealing the parties' agreement, stated that work on the missile sites would cease and that a "new order" had been given "to dismantle the arms which you described as offensive, and to crate and return them to the Soviet Union."[91] But that left the Soviet IL-28 bombers, which were capable of delivering nuclear bombs to targets in large parts of the United States and then returning to Cuba for reload. With Khrushchev's publicly acknowledged agreement to remove the missiles already settled, Kennedy was emboldened to insist on more. Khrushchev soon acquiesced on November 20 when he "agreed also to withdraw the IL-28 bombers," whereupon "the crisis was really at an end."[92]

The negotiating process that led to Khrushchev's agreement to remove the IL-28 bombers has been well documented elsewhere.[93] It is noteworthy that Bolshakov continued to play an intermediary role between the president and attorney general and Khrushchev, given the acceptance by many historians of the notion, disseminated by administration insiders, that the GRU agent had been excommunicated due to his supposed propagation of flat lies. In fact, Robert Kennedy met with Bolshakov twice after the active phase of the crisis had ended, on November 9 and 19, each time to pass along to Khrushchev messages meant to underscore the deep seriousness with which the president was pressing his demand that the bombers be removed and that "conflict on this point threatened to liquidate all the agreements reached earlier."[94] Khrushchev grudgingly complied on November 20, although he couldn't resist stating in his letter to the president that Kennedy's demands during October had not included "a single mention of bomber aircraft," and that the IL-28s "cannot be classified as offensive types of weapons."[95]

In sum, both leaders urgently wanted a quick settlement above all else and were prepared to be exceedingly generous to get the deal done. In October and November 1962, peace was their driving ambition, and war their greatest fear.

CHAPTER 10
Who Plays the Berlin Card?

They might be more reluctant to fire them if they've already grabbed Berlin than they would be if we suddenly go in there.

—PRESIDENT KENNEDY, EXCOMM MEETING, OCTOBER 24, 1962

While the Cuban crisis witnessed high-level deliberations involving experts on both sides, and elaborate efforts of many intermediaries engaged in public diplomacy, in reality, Kennedy and Khrushchev were at all times effectively the sole determiners of the ultimate course of events. There is always a risk that unplanned, ad hoc hostilities might break out in isolated places, and that risk could not have been completely eliminated in October 1962 any more than it could today, even by the strongest precautionary measures. It also stands to reason that normal military operations must inevitably provide some measure of predelegated authority both to lower-level commanders and to forces on the front line to pull the trigger at their discretion in exigent circumstances, such as when defending themselves against sudden, unprovoked attack, or to apply other necessary force in extreme situations when contact with higher authority has been lost. Yet even accepting these qualifications, it was the case throughout the Cuban missile crisis that neither side's military could have initiated determined and consequential hostilities without having first requested and received the approval of its leader, and each leader's commitment to avoiding a nuclear exchange, let alone open war, was so strong that he was prepared to reject such requests. And in the event, as he exercised his unchallenged power in October 1962, each leader opted for generous concession to his rival as the price to keep the peace, and in doing so each leader rejected contrary advice from his more hawkish subordinates, expert advisers, and allies.

There was much speculation during the crisis and afterward that any outbreak of fighting between US and Soviet forces would inevitably escalate to just such an apocalyptic nuclear exchange. And it has become almost an article of faith among later historians that, had a US invasion of Cuba led to the discharge of one of the many tactical nuclear weapons the Soviets had placed on the island, this would have prompted the United States to respond in kind. As will be seen from the fuller ventilation of previously secret internal US and Soviet decision-making records, however, it now seems probable that neither of the two leaders would have taken the monumental step of escalating to a strategic nuclear campaign even if there had been a first use of tactical nuclear weapons by the other side in the Caribbean theater.

The historical record makes clear that the Soviets never had any intention of allowing the contest over Cuba to escalate. While Khrushchev engaged in some bluster in his correspondence with Kennedy, the true test of his intention to avoid armed conflict was provided by his determination that Soviet offensive forces would not be placed on a heightened state of strategic readiness at any time during the crisis despite the highly provocative US move to DEFCON 2, which could easily have been interpreted as a prelude to a first-strike attack.[1] As a 1995 NSA history of the missile crisis concluded, although Soviet forces were put on an "extraordinarily high state of alert" following the president's October 22 televised address, "defensive forces were primary" owing to a perceived threat that Russia might be subject to imminent attack. By contrast, "Offensive forces [of the USSR] avoided assuming the highest readiness stage, as if to insure that Kennedy understood that the USSR would not launch first."[2]

Most tellingly, the Soviet Union's most advanced missile-carrying submarines remained stationed at their Asian bases throughout the crisis, while US Polaris submarines left port for battle stations. Russian medium- and long-range bombers were never ordered to their arctic forward bases—the only locations from which they could credibly have mounted an attack on the continental United States—while SAC B-52s began their predesignated SIOP attack-mode sequences.[3] As the NSA historical study concluded in relation to Soviet strategic air forces: "Long-range aviation units continued normal training, although some precautionary steps were taken, such as insuring that the Arctic bases could be used. (Bombers were not deployed to the Arctic.)"[4] And Khrushchev maintained this state of down-scaled readiness for his nuclear strike forces throughout the crisis, despite the fact that the

United States had quickly and publicly upgraded its own strategic forces to an alert status just short of all-out war.

The Kremlin's decision to demur and defer is all the more striking when one considers the hyperaggressive American maneuvers the Soviets were observing just beyond their horizons. On Monday October 22, 1962, in conjunction with the president's address to the nation, the Joint Chiefs of Staff (JCS) raised the alert level for US strategic forces to DEFCON-3 over open (*en clair*) communications channels, and directed SAC, commanded by General Thomas Power, to initiate a one-eighth airborne alert for B-52 bombers[5] and to begin sending 183 B-47 Stratojet bombers to their predesignated dispersal sites at military air bases and civilian airports.[6] The American news media and the public thus learned of this ominous change in US military preparedness almost immediately. B-47 bombers had been moved from their US Air Force bases to civilian staging areas alongside commercial aircraft at metropolitan airports. Major population centers would thereby become possible targets in an enemy attack.[7]

Two days later, at 10:00 a.m., Washington time, on October 24, General Power received a second *en clair* order from JCS upgrading the strategic alert level a further step, to DEFCON-2. Power then addressed his commanders over an open communications channel that was also accessible to Soviet monitors.[8] Although some commentators later accused Power of unauthorized freelancing in his decision to speak to his commanders over an open communications channel, the predicate *en clair* DEFCON-2 order he had received from the JCS would seem to debunk that criticism, and, in any event, the highly public appearance of B-47 Stratojets at civilian airports under dispersal orders belied any supposed need for secrecy.[9] Indeed, there was an obvious value to transparency in the move to DEFCON-2 as a means to deter or at least temper Soviet armed resistance to whatever US action would be forthcoming. In the words of SAC commander Power: "This action by the nation's primary war deterrent force gave added meaning to the President's declaration that the U.S. would react to any nuclear missile launched from Cuba with a full retaliatory response upon the Soviet Union itself."[10]

US Air Force General Burchinal made this same point more bluntly in his subsequent oral history: "All these moves were signals the Soviets could see and we knew they could see them. We got everything we had, in the strategic forces, nuclear forces, counted down and ready and aimed and we made damn sure they saw it without anybody saying a word about it."[11] Contrary to later reports, the moves first to DEFCON-3 on October 22 and then to DE-

FCON-2 on October 24 were not the unilateral decision of a rogue general but rather were made under authority of the White House, secretary of defense, and Joint Chiefs of Staff. As recorded in volume 8 of the *History of the Joint Chiefs of Staff*, during lunch on October 22, "Secretary McNamara talked with [General] Taylor and decided that DEFCON-3 should be delayed to 1900 [7:00 p.m.], when President Kennedy would be addressing the nation. Generating SAC toward maximum readiness also would await a presidential decision." SAC remained at DEFCON-3 for only thirty-nine hours. McNamara transmitted White House approval of the upgrade to DEFCON-2 in a message to the JCS on October 23, and late in the day "the JCS directed SAC to begin generation of its forces" on October 24, thereby effecting "establishment of Defcon 2."[12]

The state of active readiness of US strategic air power was impressive: "With Defcon 2, 1,436 bombers and 134 ICBMs were on constant alert; one eighth of the bombers were in the air at all times, and air crews were waiting near the rest of the bombers, prepared for takeoff on a moment's notice. The SAC missiles also were ready for launching."[13] There was a similar prestaging of the US fleet of nuclear missile-carrying Polaris submarines. As would be documented by crisis scholars: "The Joint Chiefs' situation report to the White House and State Department for 25 October showed that 112 Atlantic Command SLBMs were on alert, indicating that all seven available SSBNs were on station."[14]

The Soviets were alarmed by these moves: "The Russians did not even have a ballistic missile early warning system to detect and track incoming missiles until the mid-sixties. They were so intimidated that 'they did not increase their alert; they did not increase any flights, or their air defense posture. They didn't do a thing, they froze in place.' Although Malinovsky proposed mobilization, Khrushchev ruled it out. The most he did was to cancel leave."[15]

The reason for the Kremlin's high state of anxiety in the face of DEFCON-2 becomes clear when one considers what it actually meant to have US strategic bombers "in the air at all times." These aircraft were not merely circling and waiting for instructions. Rather, they were proceeding in sequence toward Soviet landmass targets along predesignated Chrome Dome attack pathways established in 1961. At the height of the crisis twenty-eight B-52s were following SAC's northern route to the USSR "in a counterclockwise rotation that included an overflight of the Canadian polar regions"; thirty-six were taking the southern route "over the southern tip of Spain and into the

Mediterranean"; and two were taking the Thule monitor pathway up through Greenland.[16] The northern route took the B-52s "over the Northeast Corridor to be refueled off Labrador by tankers at a rendezvous known as 'Black Goat,'" where they then "circled across the Arctic to Alaska" to be refueled a second time if necessary by tankers out of Eilson AFB near Fairbanks, Alaska. The southern route "went from the United States to a refueling over northern Spain, after which the bombers wove a path through international air space over the Mediterranean to a turnaround over the Aegean." Finally, bombers on the Thule monitor route flew from "northernmost Greenland" and then "circled the Polar regions, being refueled as necessary."[17] This enhanced level of airborne firepower "required 150 aerial refuelings per day."[18]

Curiously, the ExComm expressed no interest about whether the decision to escalate the nation's strategic attack readiness to DEFCON-2 was a prudent move, or whether such an action would be a dangerous provocation that might frighten the Soviets into thinking they would soon face a first-strike attack, warranting their own reciprocal escalatory reaction. Secretary McNamara mentioned the issue of raising the SAC alert level in order to deter "a Soviet military response" at two ExComm meetings—the first on October 16 and again on October 22[19]—but these comments did not provoke any ExComm member to ask for an explanation, nor did they prompt any discussion of possible risks this action might have for maintaining the peace.

Deployment of so many bombers carrying nuclear weapons on a continuous airborne posture at hair-trigger readiness for intercontinental attack was a decision that "inescapably increased risks of provocation, accident, or other unintended consequences."[20] Each B-52 bomber "carried three or four thermonuclear weapons assigned to SIOP targets."[21] As a consequence, if as many have worried, the Cuban missile crisis posed for mankind a serious danger that a nuclear weapon might be detonated or an unprovoked nuclear war triggered by mistake, accident, or equipment malfunction, that risk was posed disproportionately by American forces on trigger alert under DEFCON-2, and not by any precipitous staging of Russian strike forces, since there was none.[22]

Richard Betts has astutely observed that "the only palpable signals in the crisis of readiness for nuclear war were American, not Soviet."[23] And, by all known accounts, the ExComm participants were either oblivious to the potentially extreme risk the Kennedy administration itself had engendered by assuming a superheightened readiness posture, or they were insufficiently troubled to even ask questions. An illustration of that heightened risk arose a little over three years later when a US B-52 bomber armed with hydrogen bombs crashed over Spain on January 17, 1966, following an in-air collision with its refueling tanker. Several of the aircraft's nuclear bombs fell into the sea, and several more landed in the vicinity of the Spanish town of Palomares. There were nonnuclear detonations of the warheads' conventional explosive triggering devices, which spread radioactive material over Spanish farmlands, but fortunately the safeguards that were designed to prevent a nuclear explosion performed effectively.[24]

Parenthetically, it is evident that SAC under General Power's leadership did an effective job of managing the nation's nuclear striking forces under the extreme pressures of DEFCON-2 throughout the missile crisis without interruption, accident, or loss of control. Consider that "SAC put in 109,000 hours of flight time, including 2,088 B-52 Chrome Dome missions that required 4,076 aerial refuelings" without significant incident.[25] President Kennedy stated shortly after the crisis ended that SAC's contribution was "unparalleled by any country in the history of air power."[26] It is thus unfortunate that some missile crisis scholars continue to portray General Power in one-dimensional terms as a dangerous or even unstable character in the drama.[27] There is certainly anecdotal evidence that, in Fred Kaplan's description in *Wizards of Armageddon*, "Power was a brutal easily angered man who struck Air Staff officers outside SAC as dim-witted and insensitive to the dilemmas that the bomb raised."[28] Yet Power also deserves considerable credit for the steady hand he displayed in performing a critical leadership role in a time of national crisis.

The president for his part—notwithstanding the "noisy" DEFCON-2 alert upgrade—similarly had every intention to contain the Cuban incident within the Caribbean theater and not allow it to escalate more broadly. Nor was this simply a matter of wishful thinking. In his first direct message to Khrushchev on the crisis—a cover letter transmitting a predelivery copy of his October 22 address to the nation—President Kennedy took care to reaffirm the critical importance of maintaining their mutual commitment to keeping the peace and his own determination to proceed by "minimum necessary" steps rather than more aggressive measures:

> In our discussions and exchanges on Berlin and other international questions, the one thing that has most concerned me has been the possibility that your Government would not correctly understand the will and determination of the United States in any given situation, since I have not assumed that

> you or any other sane man would, in this nuclear age, deliberately plunge the world into war which it is crystal clear no country could win and which could only result in catastrophic consequences to the whole world, including the aggressor. . . .
>
> At the same time, I wish to point out that the action we are taking is the minimum necessary to remove the threat to the security of the nations of this hemisphere. The fact of this minimum response should not be taken as a basis, however, for any misjudgment on your part.[29]

There was thus an overriding restraint in play on both sides—the inherent human recoil from the prospect of use of nuclear weapons due to their immense destructive power. An interesting illustration of this has been provided by Fred Kaplan in his reporting of war games conducted by the Pentagon during the fall of 1961, a time when the United States held "unquestionable superiority" over the Soviet Union in strategic military might. Under the direction of Thomas Schelling, a war game theorist and Harvard professor, separate "Blue" and "Red" teams consisting of selected high US government officials were engaged at Camp David over the weekends of September 8–11 and September 29–October 1 in exercises designed to simulate escalatory superpower confrontations over West Berlin. How would such contests of "threats and counterthreats" play out? When the two teams initially proved reluctant to escalate, Schelling "turned up the heat," creating ever more "provocative scenarios" over three days, but to no avail. It turned out that "all the players, Blue and Red, civilian and military, did all they could to clamp things down, to defuse the kegs of dynamite that Schelling had lit and thrown their way." Try as he might, the professor "simply could not get a war started, could not get either side to consider seriously the use of nuclear weapons."[30]

In sum, it seems more realistic to understand that "Armageddon thinking" of the type that naturally arose in October 1962 among the public and media who were in the dark about key deliberations of the two leaders, and that continued to entertain movie audiences and readers of doomsday novels thereafter, was greatly out of proportion to what was warranted by the facts. And while this same "one minute to midnight" and similar brink imagery[31] has been kept alive ever since by historians and other commentators, this may well be a consequence of the schadenfreude drama that such cataclysmic imagery conveys, more than a conclusion warranted by the factual record that has become available. The most salient truth of the matter was perceived clearly by Roger Hilsman: "In the Cuban missile crisis both the American and the Soviet leaders gazed down the gun barrel of nuclear war and shrank from the holocaust they saw there."[32]

And, most important, both leaders held effective control over their militaries and managed to keep it that way.

CONTROL MAINTAINED BY KHRUSHCHEV

Khrushchev held unquestioned command over Soviet decision-making throughout both the Berlin and the Cuba crises. In full control of Soviet military power, Khrushchev demonstrated that the Soviet Union under his leadership would not pull the nuclear trigger under any foreseeable circumstances. He showed this in four ways: (1) by making it clear to the Presidium at critical moments that the USSR could not survive a nuclear conflict with the United States, (2) by keeping his SLBM submarines in port and refraining from prepositioning his long-range bombers in their Arctic advance staging bases, the only locations from which they would have a reasonable chance of reaching targets within the continental United States (albeit in many cases on one-way missions), (3) by his insistence that the nuclear warheads sent to Cuba were not to be placed on missiles without further orders but rather were to be stored a considerable distance from the missile launch sites, and (4) by his conscious withholding of needed preapproval authority for the use of even the limited-range tactical nuclear weapons with which Soviet forces in Cuba had been equipped.

Most historians agree that Khrushchev was in charge of Soviet decision-making at all times during the two crises, and that there was no significant counterweight in the Kremlin's leadership that could hold back the chairman's initiatives, whether to advance or retreat. Typical of modern scholarly opinion on the subject is this conclusion by Len Scott and R. Gerald Hughes: "We sometimes use the name of the leader as shorthand for the country, but when we talk about the Soviet decision to deploy missiles to Cuba it really *was* Khrushchev's decision. This complicates the search for motives because while we have his and his son's recollections, the deliberative records that could be useful are unavailable not because they remain sealed but because there were no deliberations. Although the fact that it took two meetings before the Presidium may show some resistance (the records are too sparse to reveal this) there is no doubt that Khrushchev was in charge."[33]

In his biography of Khrushchev, Taubman described the Soviet leader's unmatched authority over the Soviet Union at the time of the Twenty-Second Party Congress in October 1961 as a "sole stewardship": "Khrushchev delivered both the Central Committee's general report and an equally prolix explication of the party program; altogether the two speeches took more than ten hours. . . . Before the congress closed, Leonid Brezhnev hailed Khrushchev's 'indefatigable energy and revolutionary passion [that] inspire all of us to fighting deeds,' while Nikolai Podgorny, who joined Brezhnev in the anti-Khrushchev conspiracy two years later, extolled Khrushchev's 'indissoluble bond with the people, humanity and simplicity, his ability to learn constantly from the masses and to teach the masses.'"[34]

Similarly, Fursenko and Naftali characterized Khrushchev's authority on Saturday, October 27, 1962, the pivotal day of the Cuban missile crisis, as "complete control": "One definition of leadership is the capacity to make decisions that run counter to conventional wisdom or current trends. Despite many reasons to do otherwise, Khrushchev chose to ignore the alarming information from Washington and Havana [about an imminent attack on Cuba by US military forces]. Then as later, analysts of the Soviet scene assumed that at this crucial moment in his life Khrushchev faced pressure from hard-liners in government. In fact, he was a free man in complete control of the Soviet leadership."[35]

It is true that there was one striking difference between the crisis management posturing of the two sides. President Kennedy opened the crisis with an order bringing the full array of US strategic nuclear forces to their highest state of alert short of war, and in doing so he sent the Soviets a message that they faced an existential threat from American strategic bombers, fully loaded and preprogrammed to reach and destroy specific targets in the Russian homeland, which would be sequentially launched and set on their attack routes on a continuous, round-the-clock cycling pattern, subject only to contingent callback orders as the crisis unfolded. Khrushchev, by contrast, knowing the mortal hazard to which his country was exposed by this massive US demonstration of force, confined his bellicose gestures to the realm of rhetoric. The Soviet leader recognized almost immediately after the president's October 22 speech that his only recourse in the circumstances would be to retreat, so he wisely refrained from ordering any military alert in kind. Yet Kennedy's highly public DEFCON-2 alert signal masked the president's intensive effort to hold US military might in check, even in the event of a selective initial nuclear attack by the Soviets.

Several months after the Cuban missile drama, a postmortem of the confrontation was apparently prepared by State Department policy planner Walt Rostow and Assistant Secretary of Defense Paul Nitze. I say "apparently," because I have found no reference to the Rostow/Nitze paper anywhere except in a 1967 book coauthored by journalists Charles Bartlett and Edward Weintal entitled *Facing the Brink*.[36] Citing a thirteen-page "critique of the 1962 confrontation" written by the two top Kennedy administration officials and dated February 14, 1963,[37] the two journalists noted that the memorandum "concluded that Kennedy and his advisers had erred in laying too much stress upon the danger of nuclear war," and that in fact "a Soviet nuclear initiative was a negligible prospect throughout the crisis because its consequences would have been suicidal to the Soviet Union." Hilsman would later agree: "The truth of the matter is that there were no conceivable circumstances in which the Soviet Union would have taken even the tiniest risk of war with the United States to save Castro and a Communist Cuba." Secretary McNamara had evidently drawn the same conclusion in testimony he gave before Congress a week earlier. In McNamara's view, Khrushchev "knew without any question whatsoever that he faced the full military power of the United States, including its nuclear weapons," and this was "the reason, and the only reason, why he withdrew those weapons."[38]

Four years later, the CIA updated its analysis of how to detect early warning signals of Soviet preparations for a strategic nuclear attack on the United States. An earlier analysis of this kind had been prepared in 1961,[39] but this had preceded both the Berlin tank standoff of October 1961 and the Cuban crisis of October 1962. The 1966 report, therefore, was the agency's first formal comment of this kind that took advantage of the specific strategic warning lessons learned from those two crises. It is interesting, therefore, to note the 1966 CIA report's conclusion that Khrushchev took no serious steps to ready Soviet forces for imminent conflict on either occasion. Rather, "The Soviet preparations probably fell far short of those we should expect in case they were to decide to make full-scale preparations for conflict with the US, and that there was a large element of bluff in their actions in both crises."[40]

Why was this so? During the Cuban missile crisis the Soviet premier was fully aware of the US October 24, 1962, action bringing its strategic nuclear strike forces to DEFCON-2, the highest state of attack readiness short of hot war, and that the American president had knowingly taken this action while in possession of a nuclear advantage so overwhelming that the Soviet Union would have been effectively extinguished if Kennedy had issued a first-strike order. Why didn't Khrushchev upgrade Soviet strategic readiness at least to the point of being able to mount a counterstrike threat that could have deterred his rival from launching a first-strike attack?

There can really be only one answer: Khrushchev must have been confident that the best way to avoid the feared first-strike attack was to remain cool and collected and not engage in any similarly provocative or aggressive behavior. That was certainly the view of Khrushchev's assistant, Oleg Troyanovsky. In a 1992 interview he told a journalist working with *Peter Jennings Reports* and ABC News that "from the very beginning, as far as Khrushchev was concerned, war was the last thing he had in his mind. . . . Khrushchev would have backed down because he would not, he might have gone to the very edge, but not war."[41] Thus, it would appear to be a fact that in terms of the two leaders' intentions, there was no realistic way hostilities would have broken out during the missile crisis in Cuba unless the American side had been the first to "pull the trigger."

Ray Cline, who had served as deputy director of the CIA during the Cuban crisis, later expressed his view that the chances of war breaking out over the missile confrontation in the Caribbean were small. In an op-ed piece he wrote for the *Washington Post* from the sidelines of an international conference on the crisis held in Moscow in January 1989, Cline wrote: "I think it is clear that both sides were scrupulous in avoiding any remote chance of an actual nuclear exchange for the simple reason that, as we all assured the president, the United States had at least a four-to-one advantage in ICBMs and perhaps an eight-to-one superiority in nuclear weapons capability if our powerful bomber aircraft force of that era were entered into the equation. . . . While it is exciting to speculate on how brilliantly we escaped the nuclear holocaust, none of the informed officials I talked with at the time thought the chances were more than one in a thousand."[42]

Marc Trachtenberg also concluded that the Kremlin's "strategic 'inferiority' appears to have had a profound effect on their behavior in the crisis."[43] Bundy made this same point in *Danger and Survival*, noting that in the face of the president's "plain warning" in his October 22 address to the nation "that any missile fired from Cuba would require 'a full retaliatory response' on the Soviet Union," Khrushchev made it clear in his October 26 letter "that he understood this warning. He was in control, he said, and he never had any intention whatever of attacking the United States with these defensive weapons."[44] According to Khrushchev's biographer, the chairman did not believe his Cuba venture was putting peace at risk because he anticipated that even if the Americans discovered the missiles, "surely he could negotiate himself out of the situation. It was his 'near certainty that Kennedy would not choose war,' according to Adzhubei, that made it seem 'relatively safe' to provoke the U.S. president."[45]

Finally, it is worth noting that the CIA placed Khrushchev at the top and center of Soviet decision-making regarding both the cause and the termination of the crisis. In two separate retrospective studies conducted by the agency in an effort to understand the Soviet decision-making process during the Cuban missile crisis, a consistent conclusion emerged: "Both studies correctly believed that Khrushchev was the main author of the missile venture, and the main voice in deciding on the withdrawal of the missiles."[46]

KENNEDY, TOO, WAS IN CONTROL

The Soviets had no reason to worry about the United States launching a first-strike attack either. It is true that there were individuals inside the American government and among the media who urged just such an attack while the "window of opportunity" seemed to be open. Nevertheless, while President Kennedy did participate in internal National Security Council deliberations on the consequences of such a strategy, and while the president went so far as to allow disclosure of some of this thinking to be "leaked" via press commentary in ways that would surely reach the Soviets and cause them anxiety (see chapter 3), Kennedy in fact never seriously considered seeking the dubious victory that his country's nuclear superiority might have achieved from a nuclear exchange. Although he was briefed on numerous occasions about the conditions that gave the United States a first-strike capability, there was never a time when President Kennedy came close to a decision to unleash this latent power.[47]

As with Khrushchev, the historical record leaves little doubt that Kennedy was in control of US strategic nuclear policy and the specific decision-making that produced the resolution of the Cuban crisis. We can be sure of this because the ultimate US concessions that resolved the crisis came straight from the Oval Office, and because there were directly contrary and highly provocative recommendations coming from some of his top advisers in the ExComm and subordinates in the Pentagon, which were being steadily delayed in execution or rejected outright by the president himself. As it turned out, the president settled the Cuba crisis personally based on his own secret Turkey-for-Cuba missile swap. Yet he also had at least two backup plans in the event the missile swap proposal proved to be insufficient.

The Cordier Ploy

His first fallback plan—developed with Rusk and later labeled "Cordier ploy"—used diplomacy. UN secretary-general U Thant would be asked by a Kennedy intermediary, former UN official Andrew Cordier, to make a public plea to the superpowers to reach the same missile trade compromise. As historian Sheldon Stern concluded: "U Thant was to propose, ostensibly spontaneously and of his own accord, that the UN oversee the swap of the offensive missiles in Cuba for the U.S. missiles in Turkey. Given the stakes, Kennedy reasoned, the Soviets might accept this neutral third-party, face-saving solution if all else failed. . . . Simply put, JFK was determined not to allow any reasonable chance for an accommodation to slip away if the probable alternative was war, and possibly a catastrophic nuclear one."[48]

The Cordier channel was never used, but Kennedy's willingness to have it ready if need be underscored the lengths to which the president was prepared to go to avert conflict over the Cuba crisis: "He had created his own emergency shutdown valve, which he could activate at any time. In doing so, Kennedy had bypassed the ExComm, which was unaware of the Cordier channel; Kennedy was acting with his own prerogative powers. In working out ways to end the crisis, he didn't try to forge a consensus among his advisers, most of whom were strongly against making a trade."[49]

Yet the president was contemplating a far more ambitious trading stratagem if the Turkey-for-Cuba missile swap and the Cordier ploy didn't work. His idea had been germinating since early in the ExComm deliberations, and had its origins in a more dramatic swap option that had been percolating in the press for months: West Berlin for Cuba.

Kennedy's Second Fallback Plan to Avert War: Let the Soviets "Grab" West Berlin

At 11:10 a.m. on Thursday, October 18, four days before Kennedy would give his address to the nation, he discussed with his ExComm advisers meeting in the Cabinet Room how the confrontation would unfold if the United States reached the stage of having to use military force to dislodge the Soviet missiles from Cuba. The president was conscious of his younger brother's warning to avoid the "Pearl Harbor guilt" that would attend launching an unprovoked attack on Cuba. He therefore asked the ExComm to consider what would happen if the United States were to give Khrushchev a verbal warning at this point, and in this context he again raised his favored solution of a Turkey-for-Cuba missile trade. But that was not the only available concession he was exploring: "If we said to Khrushchev that: 'We have to take action against it. But if you begin to pull them out, we'll take ours out of Turkey.'" The president then wondered aloud whether such a proposal might simply make Khrushchev more greedy: "Whether he would then send back: 'If you take these out, we're going to take Berlin' or 'We're going to do something else.' And then we'd be . . ."[50]

Llewelyn Thompson seemed to miss the president's point about the predicate of a verbal warning before taking military action, saying, "If you do this first strike . . . ," and the discussion turned to speculation about what Khrushchev would do in response to an actual American attack. But the president steered the discussion back to a further scenario that was running through his mind in which the quarantine was established but "we would not take these missiles that they now have out, or the planes they now have out." Kennedy continued by raising a provocative question: what if at that stage of a quarantine in place but no quick resolution, the United States were to give Khrushchev a verbal warning that an attack would be unleashed if the Soviets thereafter brought their missiles to operational status. Kennedy then offered his own answer: "Yeah. I would think it more likely he would just grab Berlin. That's the more likely."[51]

There followed a somewhat meandering discussion among the ExComm participants with the president largely silent. McNamara noted that "the question really is are we willing to pay some kind of a rather substantial price to eliminate these missiles?" He thought "the very least" price Khrushchev would demand would be "to remove the missiles in Italy and Turkey," to which Douglas Dillon added, "Well, I think they'll take Berlin." It was at that point that the president jumped back into the discussion by interjecting the next part-diplomatic, part-military chess move that he had in mind: "The point is, he's probably going to grab Berlin anyway." McNamara then said he "suspected" that "the price we pay to Khrushchev will be about the same, whether we give him the advance warning or don't give him the advance warning," yet McNamara added that he favored advance warning because he thought it might "*possibly* giv[e Khrushchev] an out that would reduce the requirement that we enter with military force."[52]

Neither the president nor McNamara continued this line of thought at that juncture nor pressed the point to its logical conclusion: supposing Khrushchev would likely grab West Berlin anyway, might it be possible to employ the chairman's unavoidable countermove as part of a longer strategy of achieving what the United States most wanted—withdrawal of the missiles in Cuba without triggering nuclear war between the superpowers. But the president revisited his private Berlin-for-Cuba swap game-strategizing in conversations a few days later with his closest confidants and with the ExComm. Before examining those discussions, it is useful to review briefly the public discussion of this more ambitious swap idea encompassing Berlin that had been appearing sporadically in the press.

David Coleman has traced the origin of this strategic Berlin-for-Cuba trade back to a statement Dean Rusk made during a September 30, 1962, television interview in which the secretary of state "dismissed rumors of a Berlin-for-Cuba trade because 'you cannot support freedom in one place by surrendering freedom in another.'" It was not clear at the time, however, what rumors exactly the secretary was referring to. Two weeks later, an article in the October 15 edition of the *New York Times* reported that several weeks earlier a high-level official of an unidentified Communist nation had claimed to be delivering an offer from Khrushchev "to moderate his course with Cuba if the United States relaxed its stand on West Berlin." This in turn prompted Rusk to comment at the initial meeting of the nascent ExComm group on October 16 that the Soviets "may be thinking that they can either bargain Berlin and Cuba against each other, or that they could provoke us into a kind of action in Cuba which would give an umbrella for them to take action with respect to Berlin."[53]

These comments apparently prompted the president to seek the views of his National Security Council regarding the impact on developments in Cuba of a possible Soviet move against Berlin. On October 19, David Klein, a member of the NSC staff, prepared two memoranda, one on White House letterhead ("The Defense of Berlin if Cuba Is Blockaded") and a second note for Bundy with an attached draft "Immediate Military Measures" analysis, each examining the prospect that American pressure for removal of the Soviet missiles in Cuba would stimulate Soviet countermoves against West Berlin. In his "Defense of Berlin" memorandum, Klein offered an opinion that appears to have captured the president's attention: "It is a strong probability that Khrushchev would trade Berlin for Cuba any day." Klein immediately offered his further opinion that "such a trade would be a heavy net loss for the U.S." Then Klein underscored the core problem that was uppermost in the president's mind: the fact that threatening use of American nuclear weapons "under present contingency plans" would not be a rational or credible alternative: "These plans are slow and incomplete and they depend for their execution upon a degree of allied resolution which is uncertain even now. Under prolonged blockade, with us sharing the blame, the morale of Berlin would be very likely to crack, and no one would fight a nuclear war for a dying city."[54]

Two days later, President Kennedy invited his friend British ambassador David Ormsby-Gore to a private meeting at the White House shortly before 12:30 p.m. on Sunday, October 21. No documentation of this meeting has been located in Kennedy Library or State Department files.[55] It is possible and even likely that the president shared with his friend his emerging thoughts about the eventual need for a Berlin trade. Referring to the first cable about the private October 21 meeting not sent to the British prime minister until the next day, Len Scott has noted that Ormsby-Gore "chose not to impart to Macmillan some of Kennedy's more private and highly significant views, including those concerning the Jupiter missiles."[56] The ambassador's second cable describing the October 21 meeting, sent on October 23, finally mentioned the president's consideration of a Turkey-for-Cuba missile swap, but that second cable also revealed that Berlin, too, might need to be an element in an eventual deal: Ormsby-Gore added on October 23 that the president had also expressed at their private meeting his expectation that "the crisis will be resolved through East-West discussions and he realizes that these discussions will include, as well as Cuba, Berlin, foreign bases, disarmament, etc."[57]

That this general reference to Berlin might have left unreported Kennedy's more specific thinking about an eventual Berlin-for-Cuba trade is strongly suggested by Ormsby-Gore's extraordinary remark in his October 23 cable to Macmillan: "There were other comments he made in the Berlin context which I could not possibly put on record, but I know you would be reassured by them."[58] Ormsby-Gore offered to fly back to England to report these comments in person, but that did not occur. Ultimately, the delays and hesitation that attended Ormsby-Gore's reporting of his private White House meeting with the president, coupled with the lack of time and opportunity afforded for a personal meeting with his prime minister, leave documentation of this provocative part of the two friends' conversation on October 21 incomplete. As Len Scott has observed, Kennedy's private comments to the ambassador "had potentially enormous implications for British and European diplomacy and security, and it is a matter of interest that the Ambassador did not immediately report these statements to Macmillan, reflecting the importance which Ormsby-Gore attached to their sensitivity and confidentiality."[59]

Nevertheless, just one day later, the president conveyed his thoughts about a possible Berlin-for-Cuba trade to Macmillan directly. On October, 24, 1962, as the first day of the quarantine produced early indications that at least some Soviet ships were stopping and others were turning back, but with no sign yet that the Russians were suspending work on bringing their Cuba-based missiles to operational status, Kennedy returned to the question McNamara had raised with the ExComm on October 18 about what "substantial price" Khrushchev would demand for actual removal of the missiles. This time, however, he shared his thoughts about a possible Berlin-for-Cuba trade first with the ExComm and then shortly afterward with British prime minister Macmillan. The president revealed in these back-to-back discussions that he was giving active consideration to the sequential steps he had first alluded to on October 18, tantamount to making two major accommodations for the Soviets as a means to avoid escalation to nuclear warfare: first, the United States would postpone its planned invasion of Cuba, and second, it would in effect allow the Soviets to take over ("grab") West Berlin without determined US military resistance, which would in turn give a pretext or cover for the Americans to invade Cuba as needed, yet without thereby risking a further escalation by the Soviets.

Thus, late in the afternoon of Wednesday, October 24 at a meeting with his key advisers, the president articulated "this problem" that he asked them to ponder:

> PRESIDENT KENNEDY: . . . Well, in any case we've got to think, and we can see in the next 24 hours more, but . . . what we've got to be thinking about is *this problem*, of our blockade being successful and this work going on, and being faced in November with 50 or 60 of these missiles. Well, we're faced with 30 of them now, so it's . . . but anyway faced with 60 of them. Under what conditions would the Russians fire them? *They might be more reluctant to fire them if they've already grabbed Berlin than they would be if we suddenly go in, there.* But anyway these are the . . . that's what we've got to make a judgment on.[60]

Kennedy then spoke by telephone with Prime Minister Macmillan a short time later, and their conversation was transcribed by a British notetaker. Early in the discussion the president asked Macmillan to consider the same question, which he referred to a second time as "this problem," although this time he positioned the question as a "second stage" of the unfolding crisis. Kennedy then added more explicitly his working assumption that the Soviet move on West Berlin would allow the United States to take Cuba by invasion as a kind of reciprocal exchange sparing both leaders the need to respond with nuclear force on either front.

> If they respect the quarantine, then we get the second stage of this problem, and work continues on the missiles. Do we then tell them that if they don't get the missiles out, that we're going to invade Cuba? He will then say that if we invade Cuba that there's going to be a general nuclear assault, and he will in any case grab Berlin. Or do we just let the nuclear work go on, figuring he won't ever dare fire them, and when he tries to grab Berlin, we then go into Cuba. That's what I'd like to have you think about.[61]

It appears that Macmillan never answered the critical second part of the president's question. Referring to this as "the 64 000 dollar question" in his written reply the following day, Macmillan replied opaquely: "After much reflection, I think that events have gone too far. While circumstances may arise in which such action would be right and necessary, I think that we are now all in a phase where you must try to obtain your objectives by other means." The prime minister then turned to a need for a system of inspection and the comment that the United States "will no doubt continue with your military buildup for any emergency." It is interesting that Len Scott, who meticulously tracked this exchange, failed to comment either on the audacity of the president's Berlin-for-Cuba hypothetical scenario, or the prime minister's abject refusal to respond to the "64 000 dollar question" that it posed.[62]

The president's seemingly outlandish idea of ceding West Berlin to a Soviet "grab" as a quid pro quo for a reciprocal American seizure of Cuba—and thereby hopefully relieving each of the superpowers of their most vulnerable forward positions—may have had an even longer provenance. It eerily echoed a comment the president had made to Khrushchev's son-in-law, Alexei Adzhubei, in their private meeting held in the White House on January 31, 1962, with Georgi Bolshakov, likely serving as translator, the only other person in attendance. According to the *Izvestia* editor's later report to the Kremlin recounting the president's demeanor and comments made at the meeting, Adzhubei recounted that as soon as he arrived, Kennedy, who had been "waiting and walking around the corridor" burst in:

> He immediately came into the room and in a nervous tone began the conversation. Gesticulating, he said: "Your armies are in Europe. I know the strength and potential of your military machine. Khrushchev can, of course"—and Kennedy made a gesture with his hands—"can take West Berlin. But then this would possibly provoke a rupture of relations between the Western nations and your nation and lead to tension."[63]

One can only marvel at the massive understatement embodied in Kennedy's prediction that a Soviet seizure of West Berlin would "possibly provoke a rupture" with Western nations, and "lead to tension." Even more startling, the president apparently made no mention of any NATO military response to a forceful Soviet "taking" of West Berlin, far less any need for the United States to resort to nuclear weapons as contemplated by then-current SIOP plans.[64]

This Berlin-for-Cuba scenario appears to be the clearest recorded expression of the president's actual thinking about his probable next steps at this critical stage of the Cuban drama if the standoff continued beyond the Turkey missile-trading phase. If the Soviets appeared to be standing firm in their resolve not to take down their missile installations in Cuba, then the president's working plan appears to have been to continue increasing pressure until the Soviets responded by taking West Berlin, which the United States would have acceded to much as it had a year earlier allowed the sudden erection of the Berlin Wall. The United States would then have countered by invading Cuba, but only after the Kremlin had acted first, thereby avoiding the "Pearl Harbor" problem Robert Kennedy had raised when a clear majority of ExComm members were advocating a sudden preemptive air strike against the Soviet missile installations. Kennedy apparently believed this sequence might be the best and possibly the only way to end the Cuba confrontation without resort to nuclear weapons: "It is not an exaggeration to say—because it is incontrovertibly backed up by the verbatim missile crisis recordings—that John F. Kennedy was the only person at the ExComm meetings who genuinely understood that nuclear war could never be a viable or rational choice. To the president's way of thinking, nuclear weapons had altered the very meaning of war itself, and everything—anything—had to be done to avert a nuclear apocalypse."[65]

Again and again during the ExComm discussions, the president had expressed his firm conviction—with the recent NES/NSC projections of many millions of American civilian deaths in even the best scenarios fresh in his mind—that no intelligent person, including the Soviet chairman, would consider using nuclear weapons in the circumstances then transpiring. This meant that Kennedy was ready to give considerable ground to the Soviets if that should be necessary to avoid a nuclear conflict:

PRESIDENT KENNEDY (October 16): "I would think you'd have to assume they'd be using iron bombs and not nuclear weapons. Because, obviously, why would the Soviets permit nuclear war to begin under that sort of half-assed way?"[66]

PRESIDENT KENNEDY (October 18): ". . . So there isn't any doubt that, whatever actions we take against Cuba, no matter how good our films are, are going to cause [problems] in Latin America. A lot of, a lot of people would regard this as a mad act by the United States, which is due to a loss of nerve because they will argue that, taken at its worst, the presence of these missiles really doesn't change the. . . . With all the incentives to think the other way, viewing this as you do as an American, what's everybody else going to think who isn't under the gun?"[67]

PRESIDENT KENNEDY (October 18): ". . . Now, the question really is to what action we take which lessens the chances of a nuclear exchange, which obviously is the final failure. . . . And at the same time, maintain some degree of solidarity with our allies."[68]

PRESIDENT KENNEDY (October 19): "Let me just say a little, first, about what the problem is, from my point of view. . . . On the other hand, we increase the chance greatly, as I think—there's bound to be a reprisal from the Soviet Union, there always is—[of] their just going in and taking Berlin by force. Which leaves me only one alternative, which is to fire nuclear weapons—which is a hell of an alternative—and begin a nuclear exchange, with all this happening."[69]

PRESIDENT KENNEDY (October 19): "Well, it is a fact that the number of missiles there, let's say . . . no matter what they put in there, we could live today under. If they don't have enough ICBMs today, they're going to have them in a year."[70]

The October 24 discussions with his top advisers and with Prime Minister Macmillan demonstrated the lengths President Kennedy was prepared to go to avoid an outbreak of nuclear warfare. As indicated by the "problem" to which the president invited the consideration of his key advisers and the British prime minister, Kennedy meant to foreswear military action in the face of extreme provocation and instead concede major US assets in order to induce Khrushchev to remove his missiles from Cuba and end the threat of a possible nuclear war:

First as to provocation, the president was willing to at least postpone and most likely foreswear entirely the use of American military force against Cuba despite multiple, major challenges by a hostile power: installation of nuclear-armed ballistic missiles a mere one hundred miles from the US mainland; refusal to remove the missiles in defiance of the president's red-line demand that they be removed; and the shoot-down of an American U-2, causing the death of the pilot. Each of these challenges to US power during the Cuba crisis was provocation enough, standing alone, for a concerted military response in the minds of many of the president's advisers. Each of these incidents was a casus belli. All three taken together were clearly so. Yet the president held back.

Next, what accommodation in those circumstances was the president willing to make to gain the cooperation of his belligerent adversary? Kennedy was willing to trade US forward-based missiles in Turkey and Italy for the Soviet missiles in Cuba, so long as the arrangement was masked in secrecy. In addition, he appears to have been willing to allow the Soviets to strike US bases in Turkey and Italy with nuclear weapons—allowing the Soviets to commit the dreaded act of first nuclear use, likely causing the deaths of hundreds of US military personnel and thousands of Turkish and Italian civilians—without reflexively mounting any local defense and without meting out reciprocal retaliatory punishment. At a minimum he took great pains to ensure that any decision to respond to such a Soviet attack against these particular targets in Turkey or Italy would be his alone.

And finally, the president seemed to be prepared to allow Khrushchev to "grab" West Berlin—a declared "vital interest" of the United States and an asset for which the Eisenhower administration had drawn, and Kennedy himself had endorsed,[71] a red line that the Soviets could only cross on pain of nuclear retaliation. Kennedy would have given up all these assets if it became necessary to do so in order to get the Soviet missiles withdrawn from Cuba without triggering nuclear warfare. It is for these reasons that one can confidently conclude that there was no probability that President Kennedy would have been the first to use nuclear weapons, whatever the provocation, during the Cuba crisis.

Like Khrushchev, Kennedy recognized that the US possessed an overwhelming nuclear war-fighting advantage. Yet what Khrushchev suspected, but didn't fully grasp, was the extent to which the American president recoiled in horror from the idea of actually using one of these deadly new weapons. Khrushchev may have been boasting about weapons he couldn't use due to his side's overwhelming military inferiority. But Kennedy was boasting about weapons he couldn't and wouldn't use due to his personal adherence to an overriding moral imperative.

One of the iconic moments of the Kennedy presidency occurred at the Net Evaluation Sub-Committee meeting on July 20, 1961, where the president received his first full briefing on the nation's long-standing contingency plan for scenarios in which nuclear weapons might be used. It has been reported that the president left the meeting after hearing Defense Department officials speculate about the many millions of civilian casualties that would result from various first-strike and retaliatory strike scenarios, and that he ruefully commented at that time to one of his advisers: "And we call ourselves the human race." As Dean Rusk explained in his memoirs, *As I Saw It*, published in 1990: "President Kennedy clearly understood what nuclear war meant and was appalled by it." While Rusk recalled that the president "brooded" at that meeting and on other occasions "over whether it would be his fate to push the nuclear button," the 1961 briefing "convinced us that a nuclear war must never be fought."[72]

Theodore Sorensen attended the same July 1961 briefing of the president and would later list "the harsh facts" Kennedy "already knew: (1) that neither the Soviet Union nor the United States would 'win' a nuclear war in any rational sense of the word; (2) that, except to deter an all-out Soviet attack, our threat of 'massive retaliation' to every Communist move was no longer credible, now that it invited our own destruction; and (3) that a policy of 'pre-emptive first strike' or 'preventive war' was no longer open to either side, inasmuch as even a surprise missile attack would trigger, before those missiles reached their targets, a devastating retaliation that neither country could risk or accept."[73]

Marc Trachtenberg has observed that the Kennedy administration was "revolted by the very idea of nuclear war" and "found it hard to take such notions seriously." As a result "the nuclear strategy of 'controlled response' never really cut very deep under Kennedy; and a certain ambivalence about these basic issues was very characteristic of the administration's approach to military policy."[74]

By the time the Cuban missile crisis broke out, the president had received a second projection from the NES/NSC, and this time many more millions of US civilians would die even if the United States were to unleash a preemptive attack against the USSR in an attempt to destroy its nuclear arsenal. The 1961 projection of two to fifteen million US deaths in a hypothesized 1962 war-fighting scenario had risen in the 1962 NES/NSC estimation to fifty-five million killed in a comparable war set in 1965.[75] Kennedy's negative preexisting views about any use of nuclear weapons had, if anything, hardened. There are many examples of this in the recorded ExComm discussions, including instances where the president characterized proposed courses of action that might lead to the use of nuclear weapons as a "mad" act,[76] or a "half-assed" strategy,[77] or an incomprehensible action,[78] or a "hell of an alternative."[79] At one point he referred to any use of a nuclear weapon in the missile crisis as signifying the "final failure."[80]

Sheldon Stern has called Kennedy's handling of the Cuban missile crisis the work of a peacemaker rather than a warrior: "The irrefutable evidence on the ExComm tapes proves conclusively that JFK consistently rose above his own Cold War rhetoric and policies during these decisive meetings and subtly and even audaciously steered the ship of state away from nuclear confrontation."[81] Stern identified as a critical key to understanding Kennedy's actions during the crisis his "lifelong distrust of military leaders and military solutions to political problems, and, most significantly, his horror at the prospect of total war, especially nuclear war."[82] Kennedy's political adviser, Ken O'Donnell, held a similar view, that the president had a "deeper fear of nuclear war than most of his advisers realized." According to O'Donnell, the president "could discuss the possibility of such warfare at the conference table with a calm composure, but later reflections on that possibility in private talks with one or two of us made him distressed."[83]

At bottom, President Kennedy was "deterred" from using nuclear weapons simply by the fact that the Soviets had their own nuclear weapons, even if the Soviet arsenal was significantly smaller than what the United States possessed. Kennedy told his ExComm advisers on October 19 that "the existence of these missiles [in Cuba] does not add to the danger" because the Soviets have already "got enough to keep us, between submarines and ICBMs, whatever planes they do have" so that "they pretty well got us here anyway."[84]

The president also repeated the same point shortly after the most acute phase of the Cuban missile drama had ended. In comments made on December 5, 1962, preserved on the White House taping system, Kennedy questioned why the United States needed to continue increasing its stockpile of nuclear weapons, telling McNamara: "Even what [the Soviets] had [in nuclear weapons] in Cuba alone would have been a substantial deterrent to me."[85] As Michael Dobbs noted, the president "had privately concluded that nuclear weapons were 'only good for deterring.' He thought it 'insane that two men, sitting on opposite sides of the world, should be able to decide to bring an end to civilization.'"[86]

Marc Trachtenberg has noted that the leaders of the two superpowers saw the asymmetry in the nuclear war-fighting capabilities of the two countries in dramatically different ways. For the Kennedy administration, "fears of escalation substantially cancelled out, in its own mind, whatever benefits it might have theoretically been able to derive from 'strategic superiority.'" For the Soviets, however, "their 'strategic inferiority'" appears to have "profoundly affected them": "It really does seem that 'we had a gun to their head and they didn't move a muscle'—that their failure to make any preparations for general war was linked to a fear of provoking American preemptive action." For Khrushchev, "It was more essential than it otherwise might have been to head off an invasion of Cuba through a political settlement," because the risk "of provoking an American preemptive strike tended to rule out countermeasures—or even the serious threat of countermeasures, around Berlin or elsewhere." This concern both "limit[ed] their freedom of maneuver" and "increase[d] their incentive to settle the crisis quickly."[87]

As will be seen in the final chapter, both Kennedy and Khrushchev continued to play their double game in parallel to the sudden finish of their confrontation on Sunday morning October 28, 1962. Each leader had been successively switching from "hard ball" to "soft ball" diplomacy, often in tandem with the messages he was hearing from his adversary. Both Kennedy and Khrushchev took steps during the crisis to impede the ability of their subordinate military commanders to pull the triggers of even conventional weapons. Both leaders had also resorted on occasion to ambiguity dissimulation, each one sometimes mirroring his rival's strategy, by sending double-minded signals of his intention. But the end result on the final Sunday was their mutual resort to a soft ball peace-keeping deal. A chart illustrating the two leaders' message patterns is provided in Table 2.

Table 2. Kennedy and Khruschev Play the Double Game

"It is necessary to conduct an aggressive policy, but we need to advance rationally, not to resemble a gambler, in this game, who bets whatever is left in his pocket and then grabs a pistol and shoots himself."[1]

[Instances of double-minded/dissimulation are emboldened.]

	Khrushchev	Kennedy
Hard Ball	**Boasting of ballistic missile superiority** *"It's worthwhile playing the game."*[2]	Gilpatric speech; **JFK/RFK 1st strike hints** *"And we call ourselves the human race."*[3]
Soft Ball	**Beguiling offer to help JFK** *"[NSK] did not want to make things more difficult for President—and in fact would like to help him."*[4]	Request for reciprocal stand-down of tensions during run-up to US midterm elections
Hard Ball	Pressing forward on missile shipments to Cuba	**September "red line" warnings** *"Last month I should have said that we don't care."*[5]
Soft Ball	**NSK's "defensive-only" cover story fools the president.**[6]	**JFK's "flat lie" counter-narrative fools the press and later commentators.**[7]
Hard Ball	**War threats over quarantine** *"We should increase the pressure. . . . but don't pour the last drop to make the cup overflow. . . ."*[8]	**DEFCON-2** *"Even what [the Soviets] had [in missiles] in Cuba alone would have been a substantial deterrent to me."*[9]
Soft Ball	Scali/Feklisov 10/26 meeting "no invasion" pledge is sufficient	Offer of Turkey missile trade

[1] NSK, January 8, 1962, supra p. 15.
[2] NSK, January 8, 1962, supra p. 65.
[3] JFK, July 20, 1961, supra p. 15.
[4] NSK message to JFK, July 25, 1962, supra p. 85.
[5] JFK, October 16, 1962, supra p. 139.
[6] Chapter 4.
[7] Chapter 8.
[8] NSK, January 8, 1962, supra p. 65.
[9] JFK, December 5, 1962, supra p. 235.

CHAPTER 11
Spiking the Guns

I don't think we ought to accept the Chiefs' word on that one, Paul. . . .
Well let's do it again, Paul.

—PRESIDENT KENNEDY TO PAUL NITZE, OCTOBER 21, 1962

PRESIDENT KENNEDY, like Khrushchev, took numerous steps to defuse the confrontation, including specific measures to neutralize or even disable American military capabilities that raised the risk of escalation from actions at lower levels of military command before the president would have a chance to issue countermanding instructions. As Joseph Bouchard later commented: "In effect, then, escalation was avoided by the tactical environment having been structured in such a manner as to prevent clashes from occurring in the first place." This was exemplified by Kennedy's selection of the quarantine, "But the outcome was the result of decisions made in Moscow and Havana as well as in Washington."[1]

Both Khrushchev and Kennedy had no desire to see their respective countries reach the point of discharging even conventional weapons. This prompted both leaders to repeatedly muzzle or downgrade particular military capabilities lest they inadvertently trigger an escalation leading to unwanted war. This also prompted both Khrushchev and the president to order force-denying limitations to lower the risk of conflict—limitations that were often unpopular with military leaders and domestic political opponents on both sides, and were therefore carefully hidden from public view in order to preserve the appearance of toughness and resolve.[2] The constraints placed on their military forces by both leaders were particularly tight in relation to nuclear weapons; as the NSA history of the Cuba crisis concluded in 1995: "All evidence now supports NSA's long-held contention that Soviet forces were subject to monolithic central control and that local commanders, particularly in situations involving nuclear weapons, were strictly controlled through central release authority similar to that in the U.S. armed forces."[3]

But what of the significant risks that remained—owing to accident, human frailty, and mischance, compounded by the difficulties inherent in communications in an era before the "Washington-Moscow hotline"? Even when national leaders are acting with the noblest intentions, their plans can still miscarry when the actions they authorize are poorly considered or clumsily executed, which was demonstrably the case for both sides during the Berlin and Cuba confrontations. Equally important, even the strongest leaders do not exercise absolute control over events, especially during armed confrontations when mischance frequently occurs, and combinations of hazard, miscommunication, and perverse human behavior can produce mistakes and accidental bloodshed that can rapidly escalate to wider conflict.

The tensest moments in both the Berlin tank standoff and the Cuban drama occurred when lower-level military officials acted on their own authority, contrary to command policy. During the Berlin crisis, President Kennedy had dispatched General Clay as his "special representative" to West Berlin shortly after the Soviets had erected the infamous Berlin Wall in order to demonstrate US resolve and show moral support for the beleaguered people of that divided city. In fact, the president had already accepted the wall as a fait accompli and to a degree even welcomed the structure—however odious it may have been to Berliners—as a solution to the growing refugee flight out of East Germany that had been the Soviet bloc's primary concern. Certainly Kennedy had no intention of bringing down the wall by force of arms. Nevertheless, it turned out that General Clay had a different idea, and on his own authority ordered that American tanks be equipped with bulldozer blades and their crews secretly trained to demolish simulated wall-like structures. The Soviets had observed these exercises through undercover agents, assumed they were being conducted with the knowledge of higher authorities, and had thus come to believe they would soon face an armored attack against their wall. Their response was to mass their own tanks on the opposite side of the Friedrichstrasse Plaza. Fortunately, Khrushchev and Kennedy made a timely intervention with the help of their GRU intermediary, and the tense standoff immediately subsided.

Similar lower-level miscues occurred on numerous occasions during the thirteen-day span of the Cuban crisis. Among the most notorious and dangerous episodes were the October 27, 1962, shooting down of a United States

U-2 surveillance plane by a SAM-2 missile, causing the death of the American pilot;[4] the accidental penetration of Russian airspace that same day by a second US spy plane that caused the Soviet air force to scramble to intercept, believing an attack might be underway or imminent;[5] the failure during the crisis to suspend test launches of US ballistic missiles from Vandenberg Air Force Base in California, allowing the firing of a test missile that might have been detected by the Soviets and mistaken for the initial salvo of a US first-strike missile attack;[6] the fact that, unbeknownst to US forces, Russian troops in Cuba had been equipped with tactical nuclear weapons, including short-range nuclear-capable FKR (*frontovaya krylataya raketa*) cruise missiles that were located near America's naval base at Guantánamo Bay;[7] and aggressive action by US destroyers on Cuba quarantine duty menacing submerged Soviet submarines each of which was equipped with a nuclear-armed torpedo.[8]

Of course, any one of these military incidents could conceivably have spiraled out of control despite the best efforts of more cautious civilian leaders. But none of these situations produced an escalation, and this was not due to "plain dumb luck," as Dean Acheson would later grumpily opine.[9] Michael Dobbs speculated that, if the United States had attacked Cuba, it was "conceivable that Soviet commanders on Cuba would have used tactical nuclear weapons to defend themselves, whatever their instructions from Moscow."[10] But in fact the American president had refused to order that hypothetical attack, and the Soviet chairman had withheld preapproval for use of tactical nuclear weapons by his military forces without express approval from Moscow. Thus, rather than express gratitude for the workings of dumb luck, historians should recognize the larger debt that is owed to the two superpower leaders who repeatedly took steps to stifle their subordinates' inclinations to escalate by armed response.

KENNEDY'S MILITARY-TACTIC-CONSTRAINING ORDERS AIMED AT NUCLEAR CONFLICT AVOIDANCE

The most noteworthy of these disabling measures on the US side was the president's order that Jupiter missiles in Turkey not be fired without his express approval even if they were to come under nuclear attack.[11]

After a lunch meeting with McNamara and Gilpatric on Sunday October 21, Paul Nitze, the assistant secretary of defense for international security affairs, solicited the views of the JCS about the precautions to maintain the president's control over any launch instructions for the US Jupiter missiles in Turkey and Italy. As it happened, contrary to SAC protocols, the W-49 thermonuclear warheads were attached to the Jupiters "at all times" rather than stored separately hundreds of yards away in specially designated structures called "igloos."[12]

Nitze's inquiry to the JCS appears in a transcript of the meeting of the Joint Chiefs at 1:00 p.m. on October 21: "Capt Houser brought a memo from the DepSecDef into the JCS meeting: The President wants to be sure that Jupiters in Turkey and Italy are not fired without his authorization, even in the event of a Soviet nuclear or non-nuclear attack on those units. . . . JCS reply is JCSM-800-62, opposing any further steps."[13]

As indicated by the above JCS meeting minutes, the Joint Chiefs had resisted Nitze's effort to have a more specific instruction about presidential control over the decision to launch a nuclear counterattack. This became a problem for the president when Nitze mentioned the Joint Chiefs' resistance at a White House meeting the next morning (Monday, October 22, 11:47 a.m.–12:30 p.m.). The discussion was recorded on the president's secret taping system:

> PAUL NITZE: McNamara and I wrote out a suggested instruction from him [President Kennedy] to the Chiefs and we took it up with the Chiefs. The Chiefs came back with a paper saying that those instructions were already out.
>
> PRESIDENT KENNEDY: Well why don't we reinforce them because, as I say, we may be attacking the Cubans and they may . . . a reprisal may come on these. We don't want them firing [nuclear warheads] without our knowing about it.

There followed an exchange in which Nitze noted that the Joint Chiefs had objected that any new order would "compromise[] their standing instructions," and they had additionally emphasized the significance of this point in relation to the "European Defense Plan"—using the acronym EDP, which was unfamiliar to the president:

> PRESIDENT KENNEDY: What's the EDP?
>
> PAUL NITZE: The European Defense Plan, which is nuclear war.

This alarmed the president even more as he insisted, "Now that's why we want to get on that you see." When Nitze surprisingly still objected, saying, "No. They said the orders are that nothing can go without the presidential order," the president fired back, saying, "I don't think we ought to accept the Chiefs' word on that one, Paul," and "Well let's do it again, Paul." Nitze got the message and quickly relented ("I've got your point and we'll do it again").[14]

As it turned out, the order that was redelivered to the Joint Chiefs on October 22 actually intensified the message that Nitze had tried to convey on October 21. The more specific October 22 order not only prohibited the launch of Jupiter missiles in Turkey and Italy absent "express presidential authorization" even if they came under "selective" nuclear attack by the Soviets in response to Cuba events, the order also required that the US commander in chief, Europe, be instructed that if the missiles "are in danger of being taken by our angry allies, destroy them."[15]

In a memorandum to the Joint Chiefs apparently written by Robert McNamara on or about October 22, 1962, the secretary of defense wrote: "The President has ordered me to make certain that the Jupiters [in Italy and Turkey] will not be fired without his further authorization, even in the event of a selective nuclear or non-nuclear attack on these units by the Soviet Union in response to actions we may be taking elsewhere."[16] This order—which notably embraced Thomas Schelling's notion that a nuclear attack might be launched in a "selective" way (in this instance by the Soviets)—was in turn conveyed to Lauris Norstad, the supreme allied commander, Europe (SACEUR) through the JCS even though Nitze had told the president he believed the rules of engagement were already well understood. JCS chairman Maxwell Taylor thus sent a letter to Norstad (JCS 6866) stating: "Make certain that the Jupiters in Turkey and Italy will not be fired without specific authorization from the President. In the event of an attack, either nuclear or non-nuclear . . . US custodians are to destroy or make inoperable the weapons if any attempt is made to fire them."[17]

The Jupiter missiles in Turkey were located at the US/NATO air base in Cigli, near the Turkish city of Izmir on the Aegean coast, whose 1960 population was 371,000. The Jupiters in Italy were based in the Apulia region, south of the city of Bari (1951 population: 268,000) in the surrounding area near the town of Gioia del Colle (2015 population 27,923).[18] There is no indication whether the president or his secretary of defense considered the likely loss of life in either or both of those moderately populated areas if the Soviets in fact had subjected them to a nuclear attack. Given the uncertain accuracy of Soviet strategic bombers and ballistic missiles at the time, the probable casualties both directly from the nuclear detonations and from the ensuing radiation fallout would have been substantial for at least two related reasons. First, some of the bombs and missiles would surely have missed their targets and impacted the surrounding areas' civilian populations. Second, having knowledge of the uncertain accuracy of their weapons, Soviet military planners would undoubtedly have built redundancy into their attack plans to ensure that the Jupiters would in fact be destroyed. That redundancy—meaning an increase in number of nuclear bombs and missiles dedicated to the attack in order to ensure success—would have greatly increased the number of casualties.

The fact that the president ordered that there should be no instant retaliation provides strong evidence that his aversion to the possibility of nuclear escalation was a powerful safeguard against the Cuba crisis evolving to a catastrophic war between the superpowers even supposing there had been an initial selective attack by Soviet nuclear forces or some other highly provocative circumstance that could have arisen at the time. As Philip Nash has noted, at an ExComm gathering on October 27, "Bundy remarked, 'We were going to *let* him [Khrushchev] have his strike in Turkey, as I understood it last week. At one point, at least, that was the way we talked about it.'"[19]

And what of the risks posed by tactical nuclear-capable weapons held by Soviet forces in Cuba? A low-level US surveillance aircraft had discovered the presence of short-range, tactical nuclear-capable LUNA/FROG (Free Rocket Over Ground) missiles near Remedios, Cuba, as early as October 25.[20] Subsequently, the commander in chief of the Atlantic theater (CINCLANT), Admiral Robert L. Dennison, "expressed his concern, and proposed to have tactical nuclear weapons readily available in his invasion force." The Joint Chiefs and defense secretary McNamara, however, "ultimately authorized only part of Dennison's request, allowing him to equip the invasion force with nuclear-capable delivery systems such as Honest John missiles and eight-inch howitzers. They did not authorize him to include nuclear *warheads* without explicit JCS approval."[21]

There is a revealing memorandum sent to President Kennedy on November 2, 1962, by Maxwell Taylor, the JCS chairman, responding to the president's request for JCS views on "the possible effect upon our Cuban invasion plan of the presence in Cuba of the large quantities of modern army equipment found in recent photography," including the FROG missile, "which has an atomic capability." Noting that JCS had sought Admiral Dennison's views on "whether tactical nuclear weapons, both air and ground, should be included in the arsenal of our invasion and supporting forces," Taylor reported that Dennison had concluded that "no change in plan or in the forces committed to the plan is necessary at this time." Dennison was satisfied that because "nuclear capable delivery vehicles" were a part of CINCLANT's forces, "nuclear munitions" need not be added immediately but could "be provided to these forces, when and if required."

Speaking for the JCS, Taylor observed that "we must accept the possibility that the enemy may use nuclear weapons to repel invasion," though they downplayed this possibility as a "foolhardy step" given the US ability to respond "in overwhelming nuclear force." Taylor concluded that "the more likely case [was] that atomic weapons would not be used by either side" in an invasion scenario and that therefore "our present plan of invasion is adequate and feasible."[22]

But what of Dobbs's worry that Soviet forces on the ground in Cuba could have unilaterally fired their tactical nuclear weapons at Guantánamo Bay to defend themselves in response to their fear of an attack by invading forces even if no invasion had in fact been launched?[23] Yet to do so, they would have first needed to obtain the nuclear warheads from the central nuclear storage maintained by Colonel Nikolai Beloborodov, who, as noted above, was under orders from Moscow on October 27 not to release the warheads without specific permission from Moscow.[24] Moreover, the Guantánamo naval base had not been prepared as an invasion launch point; only five thousand US Marine reinforcements had been quickly added to the base, and this relatively modest increment would have been readily visible to Cuban spies working at the facility and reported back to their contacts across the fence inside Cuba. That was a force size demonstrably more suited to defending the facility than to spearheading any serious invasion outward. Nor could the covert Cuban observers have missed the telltale absence of the kinds of massed vehicles, armor, and logistical support that would ordinarily be expected to back up a military force being assembled to invade hostile territory.[25]

By contrast, as Dobbs recognized, the attack force US planners were actually assembling in the event the president reached the ultimate decision to order an invasion amounted to 120,000 troops, and the landing beaches selected for invasion were in the north and west near Havana and the MRBM and IRBM launch sites, nowhere near Guantánamo Bay, which lay far to the south. This being so, it seems highly speculative and most unlikely that the Soviet officials in charge of the FKRs near Guantánamo Bay would have seen any activity within the naval base of a magnitude presaging an imminent invasion from that direction. Thus, Dobbs appears to have overstated the risk that the FKR units on October 27, 1962—the penultimate day of the crisis, and a matter of only a few hours before the settlement that effectively ended the confrontation—would have simultaneously experienced a "breakdown in military communications" and become disoriented to the point of believing they needed to reflexively "use[] tactical nuclear weapons to defend themselves" even though no actual US attack was in progress and an emphatic order from Moscow prohibiting use of any tactical nuclear weapon without specific, prior authorization had been specifically issued and repeated by telegram that very same day.[26]

Certainly the most consequential of the president's precautionary decisions was to impose only a naval quarantine around Cuba rather than launch an air strike on the missile sites or a full-scale invasion of Cuba. Many of the ExComm members had recommended an immediate armed response both to demonstrate US resolve and to neutralize the Soviet ballistic missiles before they could become operational. The president himself had initially believed that prompt air strikes and even an early invasion would be required ("We're certainly going to do number one; we're going to take out these missiles"),[27] but he soon changed his mind and opposed these military actions.

Kennedy's choice of a naval quarantine rather than a military strike had an immediate and profound impact on the Kremlin. When Khrushchev summoned his Presidium leadership at about seven in the evening on October 22 (Moscow time), all they knew was that President Kennedy would soon be addressing the American people on "a matter of national" importance.[28] The Soviet leaders had received no advance notice of the specific subject of the president's speech. Yet they experienced "deep uncertainty," suspecting it meant that US surveillance had "probably discovered our rockets," as Khrushchev ruefully told his son. When the Presidium gathered, Khrushchev was "red-faced and very agitated," scowling, "You blew it" to a defenseless Malinovsky, and claiming to the others that "we were not going to unleash war" and "we just wanted to intimidate them, to deter the anti-Cuban forces." Khrushchev had assured his colleagues all along that the American president was intelligent, and he had comforted himself, according to Taubman, that if the missiles were prematurely discovered, "surely he could negotiate himself out of the situation."[29] Now his reassurances were being exposed as little more than wishful thinking. As they waited fitfully in their Kremlin offices into the early morning hours of October 23 to receive news of the president's speech,[30] the Presidium had to ponder Khrushchev's new prediction: "They can attack us, and we shall respond. This may end up in a big war."[31]

It therefore came as a mixture of both disappointment and relief to Khrushchev when he absorbed the two main messages Kennedy conveyed in his speech. First, there was disappointment at the president's flat refusal to accept the missiles, a turn of events that abruptly demolished the "consensus in the Soviet government that even if the United States learned about the missiles before they became operational, Anadyr would succeed because John Kennedy would swallow whatever he found in Cuba" and "not do anything about them."[32] Yet at the same time there was "relief rather than anxiety" because the quarantine "did not look like an ultimatum or a direct threat of an attack on Cuba."[33] Nevertheless, Khrushchev recognized that he had been caught in a trap of his own making and determined at that juncture to begin the process of backing down. In Mikoyan's words describing the pivotal action set in motion that same morning: "We decided to have all of our ships carrying weapons to Cuba turn back and to have our civilian vessels stay at sea until the situation surrounding the so-called quarantine was better understood."[34]

Further, Kennedy attenuated even his modest quarantine order to provide an additional precaution against armed conflict. At the suggestion over dinner of his friend, Ambassador David Ormsby-Gore, the president ordered McNamara, against protest from the navy, to reduce the quarantine line around the Cuba coast from 800 miles to 500 miles. McNamara had earlier warned that the 800 mile radius was needed to protect US warships by keeping them outside the 740-mile range of the Soviet IL-28 bombers based in Cuba.[35] McNamara also commented, however, that he didn't believe "any IL-28s are operative today," so he also mentioned that, at a minimum, the line should be drawn outside the range of MiG-21 and MiG-19 aircraft, with the latter being 450 nautical miles.[36] It has been argued that the president chose 500 miles in order to give Khrushchev more time to consider the Soviet response and take the path of restraint, but that assertion, like much else about the missile crisis, has been disputed.[37]

As the quarantine played out, several Soviet vessels stopped, and a number of them, including ones carrying ballistic missiles and their warheads, turned around and headed back to their home ports in Russia. In the meantime, Kennedy administration officials debated the conditions under which a forced stop-and-board procedure would be carried out. During an ExComm conference on October 23, the discussion turned to what response should be made if a Soviet ship were forced to stop at the approach of an American naval vessel but refused a request to board and possibly even drew small arms in defense. The president made it clear that in these circumstances the American vessel should not attempt to board the Soviet ship but rather "stay with it, and certainly for a day or so, not board it. And drift." The president wanted no gunfire, not even of the small-bore kind, thinking it better to avoid the risk of "machine gunning with 30–40 people killed on each side."[38]

The president's policy of extreme caution in implementation of the quarantine was crisply summarized by Roger Hilsman: "Kennedy deliberately chose as the first ship to be stopped a Soviet oil tanker, the *Bucharest*, precisely because it could not possibly carry any arms. The *Bucharest* was hailed on Thursday, October 25, but not boarded. Still another twenty-four hours passed. The first boarding did not occur until Friday, October 26 at 8:00 A.M., and Kennedy had ordered that the ship to be boarded should *not* be a Soviet ship. So the ship chosen was a Lebanese freighter on Soviet charter, since it would clearly not be carrying any sensitive armaments."[39]

On October 24, once it had become evident that some Soviet ships were stopping or turning back, the president issued an order to the commander of the *Essex* aircraft carrier group that he not intercept the Soviet vessel *Kirovsk*, as previously directed, but rather continue to monitor its movements. The order from the White House, sent by cable, read as follows: "SECRET . . . From highest authority. Do not stop and board. Keep under surveillance. Make continuous reports. Further instructions to follow. Acknowledge."[40]

On the penultimate day of the crisis, Kennedy decided that there would be no immediate air strike in retaliation for the Soviet shoot-down of the American U-2 on October 27, 1962, even though only four days before he had personally approved an immediate air strike subject only to final presidential approval if these circumstances were to occur. This was the agreed, standing US response plan.[41] On October 27, however, Kennedy opted for passive acquiescence despite "the 'almost unanimous agreement' in the ExComm that an attack should be launched the next morning."[42]

KHRUSHCHEV, TOO, SEVERELY CURBED HIS COUNTRY'S MILITARY CAPABILITIES

In a speech to the Supreme Soviet on December 12, 1962, Khrushchev reported that the Soviet armed forces had been brought to a high stage of alert during the Cuban missile crisis. He said that the minister of defense was instructed

> to bring the whole army, and first of all the Soviet rocket forces of intercontinental and strategic type, the country's antiaircraft rocket defense and fighter aircraft, into a state of full battle readiness. Strategic aircraft, the navy and our submarine fleet, including atomic submarines, took up prescribed positions.[43]

The Soviet premier's postcrisis pronouncement appears to have been gross exaggeration, rather than fact. Although the Soviet Union apparently brought its armed forces to an intermediate degree of readiness during the Cuban crisis, this did not include any meaningful step-up in the actual launch readiness of their nuclear forces, and certainly nothing comparable to the White House's DEFCON-2 upgrade. As Richard Betts concluded: "Whatever their perceptions or calculations, the Soviets neither prepared for a 'fateful step' in response to the U.S. nuclear alert, nor undertook significant conventional preparations in Europe."[44]

On October 24, 1962, when the Pentagon took the unprecedented step of moving its strategic forces to DEFCON-2, the Kremlin knew immediately. The Soviets became aware of the elevated alert level by their regular monitoring of open communications channels, and it was reasonable for the Kremlin to perceive that the heightened attack mode of US nuclear striking forces was the equivalent of many loaded gun barrels being raised and pointed across all the Soviet Union's borders with enemy fingers on every trigger. Yet the Soviet Union took no similar reciprocal step toward either strategic war-fighting readiness or even force-dispersion defense. Marc Trachtenberg has called this an "extraordinary asymmetry in the area of general war preparations."[45] As Kenneth Absher has written, it may have been true that Soviet defense minister Malinovsky "placed the Soviet armed forces on a war footing," and Warsaw Treaty forces commander Andrei Grechko "increased the combat readiness" of forces under his command. "But there were no threatening moves by the Soviet army in Berlin or by the Soviet naval forces in the Mediterranean. According to Sam Halpern, the Soviets never called up their reserves, there were no conscript classes called up, and there was no assembling of aircraft, trains, or ships. In short, there was no Soviet mobilization."[46]

Although the available evidence is limited, most Cuba crisis scholars have concluded "that the nuclear forces of the Soviet Union did *not* go onto any higher state of alert in October 1962."[47] The most that can be said to the contrary, based on comments of two unnamed Soviet officials several decades later, is that there is some anecdotal indication that the Soviets moved to "a higher, intermediate condition of alert during the crisis." This is based on the two officials' recollections that "indicates only that Soviet nuclear forces were put on a higher state of alert on October 24, 1962," although that testimony "does not provide any evidence on whether there were any specific emergency alerting actions taken in response to the SAC U-2 incident on October 27."[48] Dobbs observed that, like the United States, "Khrushchev had ordered his armed forces to an advanced state of alert," but he qualified this by describing the Soviet response as cancellation of "all military leave" and indefinite deferment of "discharges from the army."[49] This was no serious match for DEFCON-2's armada of nuclear-armed B-52 bombers crossing the Mediterranean Sea with targeting orders aboard, or of Polaris submarines taking up designated battle stations in the North Sea and beyond. But then Dobbs acknowledged that Khrushchev had immediately recognized there could be no consideration of a war scenario: "As he looked down the Presidium table [10:00 a.m. Moscow time on October 25], Khrushchev understood he had to prepare his colleagues for a probable retreat. He had concluded that he had 'to dismantle the missile sites.'"[50]

In 1966 the CIA prepared an analysis of the US capability to obtain advance warning of an imminent Soviet strategic nuclear attack against the United States or its European allies. The paper, designated NIE 11-10-66, replaced a similar report issued on April 6, 1961. The 1966 CIA "Warning of Intention" noted that "the Berlin crisis of 1961 and the Cuban missile crisis of 1962 have given us concrete examples of the type and nature of some of the steps the Soviets might take in preparing to attack the United States." Most notably, the CIA concluded that "it is important to recognize, however, that in both these situations the Soviet preparations probably fell short of those we should expect in case they were to decide to make full-scale preparations for conflict with the US, and that there was a large element of bluff in their actions in both crises."[51]

The 1966 CIA "Warning of Intention" identified separate key indicators of plans for such an attack depending upon the triad of nuclear weapons likely to be deployed. For ballistic missiles, the CIA noted that the opportunity to obtain advance notice of Soviet plans for an attack was low: "If the initial Soviet strike was carried out entirely by ICBMs, our ability to derive warning from the activities of these forces would be minimal." By 1966 the Soviet ICBM force was "permanently deployed and . . . maintained at a high rate of readiness. Final readying activity would not be extensive and would not be detectable by present collection means."[52]

If the Soviets were "planning a strike in which weight of attack was paramount," which would involve long-range aviation (LRA) and missile submarines in addition to land-based missiles, however, they would then "have to take a good many steps to enhance the readiness of their forces. More LRA aircraft, including some medium bombers, would participate, and a maintenance stand down of several days would be carried out. Some of the aircraft would be staged through Arctic bases. More missile submarines would put to sea and head for launch positions off the US. Various other elements of the military forces would be brought to maximum readiness and necessary deployments carried out, including preparations for a near simultaneous attack in Europe."[53]

The CIA also identified certain telltale indications that would be detectable if the Soviets were "anticipating US retaliation" and were therefore taking "some preparatory steps in other elements of their military forces than those participating in the initial strikes." These indications would include "readying air defense forces, deploying ground forces to forward areas, putting naval elements to sea, deploying tactical aircraft to advanced bases, moving key military command elements to alternate sites, etc. In addition, we believe that the USSR would undertake some measures in the civil defense field to provide some protection to its key personnel."[54]

It is useful to consider how the CIA and the National Indications Center (NIC) assessed the execution level for each of the above indications in October 1962 and July 1963, respectively, in their separate efforts to determine whether the Soviet Union took measures during the Cuba crisis either to achieve readiness for launching an attack against the United States or to protect itself from any such attack launched by its main adversary. The answer is that the USSR did not initiate either set of preparatory measures.[55]

As noted, the Soviet long-range bomber force was based entirely within the USSR landmass and so was far more constrained by sheer distance than their United States and NATO counterparts in their respective abilities to reach their adversary's homeland. As a practical matter, even long-range Soviet bombers needed to rely on aerial refueling and prepositioning on remote and inhospitable Arctic airstrips in order to maximize their chances of reaching US targets and returning to home base.[56] Yet the movement of large numbers of strategic bombers to Arctic bases would have been detected by US intelligence surveillance, and these isolated installations in a forbidding polar climate were not places where aircraft and their crews could be suitably stationed for long periods.[57] So the question arose whether Khrushchev would meet the threat posed by America's DEFCON-2 airborne readiness by similarly sending his nation's long-range bombers to their Arctic staging areas.

The US intelligence community monitored this indication with the keenest attention due to the ominous signal any actions of this kind would send regarding the threat of an attack.[58] On October 23, for example, NSA listening posts intercepted a message from Soviet air force headquarters in Moscow inquiring about the operational status of "navigational beacons at a number of Soviet strategic bomber dispersal bases in the Arctic." On the morning of October 24, NSA surveillance noted "indications that the Russians were about to deploy a unit of strategic bombers to Arctic forward staging bases," although they also found that "Soviet strategic bomber flight activity was significantly below normal operating levels."[59]

The morning sessions of ExComm typically began with a briefing by CIA director John McCone that covered any detected Soviet moves toward strategic action readiness. No major moves were observed.[60] As late as October 27, the CIA's memorandum prepared for the Executive Committee entitled "The Crisis: USSR/Cuba" noted "no significant redeployment of Soviet ground, air or naval forces."[61] Marc Trachtenberg saw an "extraordinary asymmetry in the area of general war preparations" and found this to be "one of the most striking features of the Cuban missile crisis." While the United States "was making very serious preparations for a general nuclear conflict," most clearly exemplified by the unprecedented DEFCON-2 announcement, the Soviet Union was doing nothing of equivalent magnitude. McCone's daily reports on the state of Soviet alert and readiness were always the same: "The U.S.S.R. was not making preparations for war." Thus, the CIA, on October 24, did not believe that "measures to achieve a higher degree of action readiness for Soviet and bloc forces are being taken on a crash basis." The same point was made in the October 25 memorandum; and still on October 27, at the climax of the crisis, the CIA said it simply had not been able to detect any "significant redeployment" of Soviet forces.[62]

Although much of the NIC's analysis of Soviet long-range aviation readiness measures during the Cuba crisis period remains classified, NIC reported that a number of Soviet statements appear to have given considerably less emphasis to the readiness of long-range bombers than to that of rocket forces, and the general impression is that their readiness was of somewhat less importance to the USSR than that of the rocket troops and the Air Defense Forces."[63] A later CIA staff study commented that while "the state of readiness of Soviet forces after 22 October" still remained "in question" more than a year later, "Almost all observers agree that the USSR wished to avoid a provocative appearance at this time."[64] Marc Trachtenberg, a leading Cold War scholar, has observed that "Soviet leaders might have viewed war preparations as very dangerous—and quite possibly because of the disparity in force levels and in degree of force vulnerability, risky in a way that the corresponding American alert simply was not."[65] Trachtenberg has cited in this regard a pugnacious comment by General David Burchinal, who served as the US Air Force Staff's director of plans during the crisis. General Burchinal observed in his 1975 oral history that Khrushchev "never alerted a bomber or changed his own military posture one bit," because "We had a gun at his head and he didn't move a muscle."[66] As Ray Garthoff later concluded at a conference for historians held on an anniversary of the crisis: "We never observed any Soviet alerts, though in *Pravda* it was mentioned that the Soviet forces were put on a general alert. All they did was cancel some scheduled leaves and troop rotations. They recalled to Moscow foreign diplomats who were traveling around the Soviet Union, but they went ahead with scheduled rehearsals for the military parade on November 7. Overall, they made a very low-level response to avoid provocation." Garthoff concluded that the risk of war was lower than many had believed: "I think now, as I thought then, that the odds of a Soviet military reaction to a strike on the missiles in Cuba was extremely low. I believe they would have tried to come up with some sort of political counter-measure, but they were simply too scared to risk a military response."[67]

The historical record of Soviet decision-making regarding the readiness of their intercontinental ballistic missile systems to deal with the possible outbreak of war remains sparse even after more than a half century. Nevertheless, several facts make it clear that the Soviet military made no serious effort to match the state of maximum strategic war-fighting readiness publicly displayed by the United States.

The National Security Archive at George Washington University has posted on its website a translation of the minutes of a Kremlin meeting dated October 22, 1962, but apparently convened early the next morning after the participants had been made aware of President Kennedy's October 22 speech. The minutes reflect defense minister Malinovsky's statement, "I think that we are not in a position that requires putting our rockets on full alert," which was followed by Khrushchev's comment: "I agree with Comrade Malinovsky's conclusions."[68]

The US intelligence services were keeping a close eye on any indications that the Soviets might take steps preparatory to launching an attack against either US allies in Europe or on the continental United States itself. No evidence of serious upgrading efforts was detected. A chronology of moves by Soviet bloc armed forces was prepared by the CIA's National Indications Center (NIC) in June 1963, and a heavily redacted version of that document has subsequently been made public. The NIC chronology stated that on October 23, 1962, a day after President Kennedy's address to the nation about discovery of Soviet missile installations in Cuba, the "USSR announced deferment of release of troops in the Strategic Rocket Forces, PVO [troops of national air defense] and submarine fleet, cancellation of all leaves, and orders to 'raise the battle readiness and vigilance of all troops.'"[69] Lengthy portions of the NIC chronology remain redacted to this day, so it is impossible to tell whether more specific evidence either confirming or ruling out particular upgrades to Soviet strategic missile readiness was observed.

In February 1964 the Office of the Deputy Director Intelligence of the CIA produced a staff study providing a retrospective analysis of the Soviet Union's conduct during the Cuban crisis. The study concluded that Khrushchev took no meaningful steps to set his armed forces on a war footing: "Nevertheless, there is no persuasive set of indications from which one can conclude that the Soviet Armed Forces in general were brought to an alert status at any time before the President's speech of 22 October (nor that they were subsequently placed in a position which suggested that a state of hostilities was imminent)."[70]

The 1964 CIA report declined to offer a view on the state of readiness of the Soviet Strategic Rocket Forces based upon "virtually no available evidence" one way or the other.[71] Nevertheless, one important bit of evidence, known to the US government at the time but not mentioned in either the 1963 or 1964 CIA reports cited above, strongly suggested that Khrushchev had made no serious effort to place his ICBM forces on imminent war footing during the crisis. In mid-October 1962, the Soviet rocket forces were readying one of their few long-range missile launch pads at the Baikonur Cosmodrome in Kazakhstan (also referred to as Tyuratam) for firing a series of R-7-style *Molinya* ballistic missiles—the same rocket design as the Soviet ICBMs—for a space mission aimed at probing the planet Mars. These missile launch plans were not called off, or postponed, or deterred in any way by events in the Caribbean, and the first Mars probe, designated by the CIA as "Sputnik XXIX,"[72] took off as scheduled on October 24, 1962, two days after President Kennedy's address to the nation announcing discovery of Soviet ballistic missiles in Cuba. The *Sputnik XXIX* launch failed when the rocket's third stage malfunctioned and blew up. The residual debris was detected by the US Ballistic Missile Early Warning System (BMEWS) and was determined to be a failed space mission rather than an ICBM launch.

The events surrounding the *Sputnik XXIX* failure and a follow-on Mars I mission launched from the same facility eight days later, November 1, were later documented by Russian rocket designer Boris Chertok, who was present at the launch facility on both occasions.[73] Chertok's account provides powerful evidence that the Kremlin elected not to match the White House's decision to bring strategic nuclear forces to peak readiness. The Soviets used the same basic rocket design—the R-7, or *Molinya*, rocket—for both the nonmilitary version used for space probes (designated simply "R-7," using engine no. 8K78) as well as for the military version of their most reliable ICBM (designated "R-7A," using engine no. 8K74).[74] According to Chertok, "It was possible to move forward with the proposal for human [space] flight only with the support of the military, since one way or another, every R-7 rocket needed for the new programs depended on them."[75]

Both the military and the space probe R-7 rockets used the same Tyuratam launch pads,[76] and, according to Chertok, in late 1962 "there were just four R-7A launch pads." This squares with the US national intelligence estimate prepared just a year before that identified "massive, fully rail-served launchers" for ICBMs at "Tyuratam Areas A and B" and a "simplified pair of pads at Tyuratam Area C."[77] Thus, in failing to immediately cancel the two planned R-7 Mars missions at the outset of the Cuban missile crisis and thereby maintaining sequestration of one of the few ICBM launch pads at the USSR's principal ICBM launch site at Tyuratam, the Kremlin demonstrated that Khrushchev had elected to forgo a significant measure of ICBM launch availability and readiness.

That conclusion seems inescapable when one considers Chertok's account of what happened at the launch site on October 27 as he was readying the second Mars probe for its planned October 29 launch. When he arrived at the launch facility that day, Chertok saw "groups of soldiers in full combat gear," and upon reaching the Assembly and Testing Building he "immediately saw that the 'duty' R-7A combat missile, which had always been covered and standing up against the wall, which we had always ignored, was uncovered. . . . A couple of hours ago all the servicemen had been ordered to halt operations on the Mars launch vehicle and to immediately prepare to roll the duty combat vehicle package out to the launch site."[78]

Chertok then received news from Range Chief Anatoliy Kirillov, who he said was "in charge of all the military personnel who worked with us at the engineering facility and launch site," that the firing range "must be brought into a state of battle readiness immediately," and that they were "removing the Mars rocket from the launch site" because "we're freeing up the space."[79] This sequence of events provides further corroborating evidence that up until October 27, the penultimate day of the crisis, the four R-7A launch sites had not been commandeered and assigned exclusively for military use and readied for imminent launch orders, and therefore that Khrushchev had refrained from matching the US stage of ICBM launch readiness up until the point at which the crisis was at the latest stages of being resolved.

Michael Dobbs discussed Chertok's story in *One Minute to Midnight*, but in doing so he emphasized only the personal drama of the October 27 events without considering what had happened before—or more particularly what had *not* happened before—in the opening days of the crisis. Thus, Dobbs focused on Chertok's and Kirillov's personal reflections on October 27 as each man contemplated the possible looming act of firing the nuclear-tipped R-7A as the missile was moved onto the launch pad being vacated by the R-7 Mars probe.[80] In doing so, Dobbs overlooked the fact that by October 27 Khrushchev had already made his decision to retreat, and he also missed the more remarkable fact that the Soviet missile launch site at Tyuratam had not been brought up to full alert status until the crisis was already effectively over.

If Khrushchev had wanted to match the US DEFCON-2 alert, he would have ordered the movement of Soviet missile-carrying submarines from their home bases to launch positions within 150–350 nautical miles off the coast of the United States.[81] As Robert Norris of the Federation of American Scientists concluded in his 2012 presentation at the Woodrow Wilson Center entitled "The Cuban Missile Crisis: A Nuclear Order of Battle October/November 1962," the Soviets had "many ballistic missile (and cruise missile) submarines [but] none played a role in the Cuban crisis."[82] Chief of naval operations Admiral George Anderson advised the president at a meeting on October 22 that Soviet missile-carrying submarines "could not get to the [Caribbean] area in less than ten to fourteen days."[83]

A report issued by the NIC on July 15, 1963, entitled "The Soviet Bloc

Armed Forces and the Cuban Crisis: A Discussion of Readiness Measures," attempted to assess the extent to which Khrushchev brought Soviet military forces to a state of war-fighting readiness in October 1962. One of the readiness measures on which the NIC focused was the extent to which the Kremlin dispersed top military commanders to multiple, separated locations where the command structure would be less vulnerable to targeted attacks. The NIC 1963 report found "little apparent indication that such preparations were taken during the period preceding or during the Cuban crisis." To the contrary, "During late October, most of the High Command is known to have been in the Moscow area at least on 25 October when most of them attended a Rumanian reception, and the civilian leadership made a number of conspicuous public appearances during this period. Thus, on balance, it appears unlikely that any major components of the Ministry of Defense were relocated, although the possibility that secure or underground facilities may exist fairly close to Moscow cannot be discounted."[84]

One of the Kennedy administration's greatest concerns during the Cuban crisis was that Khrushchev might retaliate against the quarantine by mounting similarly hostile provocations against Western forces in and around West Berlin.[85] Yet, despite calls by Dobrynin and other Soviet leaders for a response involving Berlin, there was no such Soviet countermove. When Deputy Foreign Minister Vasily Kuznetsov proposed a Berlin blockade to counter Washington's Cuban quarantine, Khrushchev blew up: "We're just beginning to get ourselves out of one adventure, and you're suggesting we climb into another."[86]

The Kremlin did take modest steps to suspend leaves of Warsaw Pact troops, and Malinovsky sent a message to the pact commander asking him to call together country officers and order them to implement "measures to raise the military readiness of the military, navy, and air forces of the United Military Force."[87] But these were largely formalities. No actual, aggressive, forward deployments were made evidencing prepositioning for offensive action. To the contrary, as noted by Fred Kempe: "Khrushchev began to withdraw Soviet troops from the West German border so that it would be clear he had no intention of escalating the conflict."[88]

There were some indications of a moderately increased state of alert for Soviet forces in and around East Germany, but no major mobilization or other buildup that might have raised tensions or created further provocation.[89] In its postcrisis evaluation of the Cuban events, the CIA had this to say about Soviet restraint in the Berlin theater: "Khrushchev was apparently careful, at all stages of the venture, not to make a strong threat of retaliation in Berlin. He did not do so even during the week of the crisis in late October, when the Western press was speaking of American fear of such action. It is clear that the Russians themselves were more fearful than they believed the U.S. to be."[90]

Khrushchev stopped the ongoing arms shipments to Cuba immediately upon learning that Kennedy's October 22 speech included an embargo order. As Bouchard has noted: "The Soviets thus made a decision not to challenge the quarantine even while publicly declaring their refusal to recognize it." By Wednesday morning, October 24, "All of the Soviet ships en route to Cuba, including tankers and freighters carrying nonmilitary cargo, had already stopped or turned back."[91] As for the Russian forces already on Cuban soil, they were authorized to "resist an American invasion" but not "to use nuclear weapons of any kind." Khrushchev "was determined to maintain personal control over the warheads."[92]

When Khrushchev told the Presidium on October 28, "We must retreat," he doubtless recognized the undeniable logic of his side's extreme military inferiority in the Atlantic region as well as its strategic nuclear deficit. Bundy made this point bluntly in seeking to explain Khrushchev's ultimate acceptance of US settlement terms on October 27 and 28: "But the decisive consideration, on Friday and again on Sunday morning, was that in the Caribbean Khrushchev was in a position of such inferiority at every level of conventional strength that unlike the president he must fear not only the unpredictable consequences of accident, but the certainty of defeat at every level up to common catastrophe." Bundy concluded that if Khrushchev "had been the reckless risk taker whose possible existence we were required to consider on Saturday, he might have tried one more roll. But he was prudent; he remained in charge, and he chose to end the crisis."[93]

Thus, the first indication that the Soviets were backing down from their Cuba gamble came very shortly after the president's televised speech when US surveillance detected that some of the cargo ships en route to Cuba and still outside the line of quarantine had stopped and possibly even turned around.

On September 25, 1962, Khrushchev canceled plans to deploy a Soviet naval squadron of surface vessels to guard the cargo ships "for fear that it 'would attract the attention of the entire world.'"[94] Although Khrushchev later told the Supreme Soviet that the country's submarine fleet "took up prescribed positions," in fact he had decided not to deploy a squadron of the Soviet Union's new strategic submarines capable of carrying intermediate range nuclear missiles.[95] Brugioni noted that although the Soviets had at the time "seven types of submarines capable of firing either ballistic or cruise missiles," none of these vessels was "detected patrolling in the Atlantic during the crisis."[96]

One of the great puzzles of the Cuban missile crisis presents an extraordinary and almost comical irony that seems to have been overlooked by some scholars. First, while the Soviet Union had taken extraordinary steps to conceal the transatlantic shipment of its missiles to Cuba, almost nothing was done to conceal the missiles from US detection once they had arrived on the ground at their island bases. Indeed, once the missiles and their launcher erectors reached their installation sites in Cuba, the Soviets not only stored them in plain view (or, in the case of the six missiles and their transporters discovered first, wrapped under form-fitting canvas),[97] but they also went so far as to deny to the SAM missile sites permission to fire at the American U-2 surveillance aircraft unless there were indications an attack was imminent.[98]

Correspondingly, the American side matched its Soviet rivals in self-defeating ingenuity when Dean Rusk and McGeorge Bundy ordered the suspension of those same U-2 overflights on September 10, purportedly out of fear that one of the spy planes might be shot down by a SAM missile, causing an embarrassing international incident. Yet, surprisingly, this order was issued despite the fact that US electronic intelligence surveillance (ELINT), which, according to Brugioni, had been operating "all-out . . . against the SAMs" since at least August 30,[99] had detected no signs of the air defense system's readiness to track and fire at American spy planes. Thus, the September 5 U-2 overflight of Cuba was presumably completed without ELINT detection of SAM-2 radar tracking (referred to as "Spoon Rest") or radar targeting (referred to as "Fruit Set" or "Fan Song"). By September 6 the ELINT efforts involved "specially equipped B-47's and F3D aircraft . . . specially equipped Navy Constellations and SAC U-2's configured to collect electronic data. All of these aircraft contained automatic scanning devices to acquire SAM-2-related signals."[100] ELINT missions "were flown usually three times a day around Cuba, recording all signals being emitted by Cuban surveillance radars and radars at surface-to-air missile sites."[101] Yet the first detection of switched-on "Spoon Rest" tracking radar did not occur until September 15, and then only on a test basis for one SAM site. This finding was reported in the daily "Intelligence Checklist" for the president on September 19. The first detection of test start-ups of the more ominous "Fruit Set" targeting radar occurred sometime in "early September," but it was not until October 26, following numerous undisturbed U-2 overflights and lower-altitude surveillance missions by navy and marines aircraft, that US ELINT monitors first detected simultaneous "Spoon Rest" and "Fruit Set" radar signatures indicative of actual preparation for a SAM missile attack.[102]

This odd juxtaposition of the two sides' simultaneous, counterintuitive determination to pursue policies that neutralized military readiness raises several questions. For the Soviets, why did the Kremlin deny to its Cuba-based SAM missile sites their obvious utility as a deterrent against US efforts to discover the ballistic missiles?[103] When Major Richard S. Heyser completed his consequential October 14 overflight of the island, he said his mission had been "a piece of cake—a milk run," which was "Air Force jargon for a mission in which there were no enemy fighters seen over Cuba and no anti-aircraft or SA-2 reaction."[104] Fidel Castro later vented his frustration about this astonishing lapse when Anastas Mikoyan paid a visit at Khrushchev's request in early November 1962 to try to mend relations between the two allies: "Why didn't we use the antiaircraft guided weapons, in order not to allow overflights of our territory by the U-2 planes? We were talking with you about the most solid defense, about having bases 90 miles from the United States, while at the same time we have not undertaken the necessary measures of camouflage. And it is understandable that the enemy had discovered the missiles. We relied on the Soviet military comrades—because they have both political and military experience—but what they did with the missiles was not at all what should have been done properly."[105]

There is a converse question for the Kennedy administration: Why did fear of the SAM missiles stand as an absolute bar to U-2 overflights on September 10 when the Soviet antiaircraft guidance systems were not yet fully integrated and ready to fire, whereas that same concern somehow was no longer operative on October 14, after the passage of four additional weeks' opportunity to prepare? It is noteworthy that, within two days following the discovery of Soviet missiles on October 14, and despite the presence of Soviet SAM installations throughout Cuba, the United States instituted a massive overhead surveillance campaign that would eventually number 43 U-2 overflights and 106 low-level overflights: 54 by navy aircraft and 52 by the air force.[106]

Although definitive evidence of the Kennedy administration's thinking remains elusive, the almost self-evident reason for the monthlong surveillance inaction from September 10 to October 14 is that the president and a number of his top advisers did not want problems to arise in Cuba shortly before the US midterm elections, and they did not believe a serious *national security* problem would be posed even if the Soviet weapons deliveries *did* include ballistic missiles. General William Y. Smith, who served as assistant to General Maxwell Taylor in the White House during this period, strongly suspected as much. Noting that the president had "ordered a close, need to know hold on all information about the Soviet build-up," Smith concluded that Kennedy "hoped to avoid providing ammunition to his political opponents while keeping maximum flexibility on Cuba for himself during the fall congressional elections."[107]

The idea that the president was determined to look the other way had certainly occurred to the Soviets. During a November 1962 fence-mending trip to Cuba made at Khrushchev's request, Mikoyan told the Cuban leadership on November 4, 1962, that the Kremlin had been surprised when Kennedy persisted in referring to the Soviet personnel in Cuba as "technicians" rather than as "troops": "At first, it seems that that is what he thought. Later we learned that he knew more than he was saying, but he was not revealing it not to hinder the electoral campaign."[108]

Ultimately, when a Soviet SA-2 missile shot down Major Rudolph Anderson Jr.'s U-2 on October 27, it turns out that Soviet air defense commander Lieutenant General Stepan Grechko, who served under the top Soviet commander in Cuba, General Issa Pliyev, believed the aircraft was on a preinvasion mission rather than a pure surveillance run. Pliyev could not be reached. Thinking that an attack was imminent and that the U-2 was "discovering our positions in depth," Grechko ordered the SA-2 missile launch after receiving approval from his immediate superior, Major General Leonid Garbuz. When Khrushchev learned of the downing, he was "very upset and considered it a big mistake," according to an account by his son, Sergei. Malinovsky reprimanded the Soviet commanders in Cuba, criticizing them for "hastily" shooting down the surveillance plane at a time when "an agreement for a peaceful way to deter an invasion of Cuba was already taking shape."[109]

Khrushchev took special precautions against premature or unauthorized use of nuclear weapons in Cuba. He ordered that the nuclear warheads should be stored several miles from emplacement of the missiles.[110] Those orders remained in place throughout the crisis: "According to [Soviet General Dimitrii] Volkogonov, the warheads that had arrived in Cuba were kept 'well away' from the missiles themselves, and at no time were measures taken to mate them, even when alert levels were raised following President Kennedy's speech of October 22. Had the order to prepare the missiles come down, Volkogonov claimed, they could have been targeted in four hours, and would have required a subsequent countdown of fifteen minutes."[111]

On Thursday morning October 25, 1962, McNamara informed the president that there was "much evidence" that Khrushchev had "instructed the Cubans to act very cautiously." Cuban MiGs were "not to fire on U.S. aircraft" and "not to take off from the airfields."[112] General Gribkov confirmed this in his book on the Anadyr operation, coauthored by US general William Y. Smith, where he recounted a conversation with a frustrated MiG-21 pilot in Cuba during the crisis. The pilot had asked, "Why can't we retaliate" when "the Americans can keep flying over us so brazenly," whereas "we [are] stuck here like sitting ducks." Gribkov explained that "there was an order—'Do not open fire on individual violators'—so as not to aggravate an already tense situation."[113]

After Kennedy's October 22 speech, the Kremlin took additional steps to prevent any use of tactical or strategic nuclear weapons in Cuba without explicit orders from Khrushchev. Defense minister Malinovsky ordered his commanders in Cuba on October 22 and October 27 not to fire the ballistic missiles without express approval and added that "it is categorically reconfirmed that it is forbidden to use nuclear armaments for the missiles, the FKRs, the 'Lunas' and the aircraft without authorization from Moscow."[114]

The Soviets had shipped battlefield nuclear ground-to-ground missiles to Cuba of the FKR type as well as dual-use missiles designated "Luna" by the Soviets and "FROG" by the Americans, and the presence of the FROG missiles at least had been detected by low-level US reconnaissance flights on Wednesday, October 24, or Thursday, October 25.[115] The Kremlin had drafted an order allowing General Pliyev to use tactical nuclear weapons in the event of a US invasion in circumstances where communications with the Kremlin were cut off. But that order needed two signatures, and Khrushchev had allowed only one signature to be affixed: that of Marshal Zakharov, who signed as army chief of staff. The other required signature, that of Malinovsky, was never placed on the document.[116] Mark Kramer later concluded: "At no time during the crisis did Pliyev have authority to order the use of either medium-range or tactical nuclear missiles."[117] Sergey Radchenko has written: "Thus, we know that Khrushchev never approved the instruction prepared by the Ministry of Defence in early September 1962 which would have given Pliyev the authority to use tactical nuclear weapons in case of a US invasion and if he could not contact Moscow. Khrushchev withheld his authorization even as he approved the shipment of additional tactical nukes to Cuba on 7 September."[118]

Sergei Khrushchev came to the same conclusion based on a private meeting he had with his father on the evening of October 25: "Father felt trapped. If Soviet missiles in Cuba were attacked, he had no retaliatory actions in reserve. Such an attack must be averted at all costs. Not for a moment did he contemplate a nuclear strike on the United States. The atomic bomb was fine for newspapers. Father considered any action in Berlin to be unduly dangerous. Against his wishes, it could lead to a great war. He ruled out war as a way of resolving quarrels. There was no other answer to be found. And since it was impossible to respond in kind to the use of force, such a possibility must be averted no matter what the cost."[119]

Khrushchev issued further orders that no use of Soviet nuclear weapons—whether tactical or carried by MRBMs or IRBMs—would be allowed under any circumstances without explicit authorization from Moscow. On October 27 Khrushchev had Malinovsky send an urgent message to General Pliyev: "It is categorically confirmed that it is forbidden to use nuclear weapons from the missiles, FKRs, and Lunas, without approval from Moscow. Confirm receipt."[120]

The clearest sign that Khrushchev was not interested in any outbreak of fighting with the United States, no matter the provocation, was provided on the night of October 27 when, as already mentioned, Castro perceived an imminent, massive US invasion and pleaded with his Russian patron to avert the attack by striking first with nuclear weapons. Sheldon Stern incisively captured the Soviet chairman's alarmed response: "'It became clear to us,' Khrushchev later wrote, 'that Fidel totally failed to understand our purpose. We had installed the missiles not for the purpose of attacking the United States, but to keep the United States from attacking Cuba.'[121]

Khrushchev had assured the Soviet leadership two years earlier that there would be no war between the United States and the USSR, nuclear or otherwise. In a January 6, 1961, address to a closed meeting that followed a conference of eighty-one Communist parties held in Moscow the previous fall: "Contradicting Mao, Khrushchev insisted that nuclear war would be an 'incalculable disaster' in which 'millions would die.' Nor could 'local wars' be allowed to erupt since they could escalate into major ones. The only wars the Soviet Union supported, said Khrushchev in a bow to his own Marxist-Leninism as well as to Mao's, were 'wars of national liberation.'"[122]

On October 27, 1962, the penultimate and probably the tensest day of the missile crisis, the CIA's Office of National Estimates (ONE) provided to Director McCone a memorandum containing its expectations of whether the Soviets would respond to a US attack on the missile bases in Cuba by retaliating militarily. ONE found this unlikely; rather Kremlin leaders were "trying hard to bring about negotiations." Further, "If the action is nevertheless taken, we believe that, while the Soviets will feel the need to retaliate in some way, they will try to avoid doing so in a manner which sharply or suddenly raises the risks of escalation." ONE believed Khrushchev would more likely "allow tensions to subside and the US actions to run their course in Cuba before beginning their own retaliatory moves." And retaliation would more likely involve provocation of "severe political crisis involving Turkey or other US allies as well as neutrals bordering on the USSR" as opposed to "military measures."[123]

THE PROBLEM OF UNPREVENTABLE MISTAKES, ACCIDENTS, AND OTHER MISADVENTURE

Most crisis scholars who have addressed the question whether the world actually came close to nuclear Armageddon in October 1962 have focused on the notion that, however much each side's leaders might have been trying to avert hostilities, there remained a serious danger that matters could have spiraled out of their control due to accidental events that might have led one of them to launch a nuclear weapon first, thereby perhaps unavoidably triggering further escalation to a point of no return. Many of these scholars have noted that President Kennedy had recently read and was heavily influenced by Barbara Tuchman's acclaimed cautionary tale *The Guns of August*, which explored how World War I started as the result of an unanticipated cascade of events and missteps that seemed to propel the European nations toward a war that none of them wished for.[124]

Certainly there were untoward incidents aplenty during the Cuban crisis that might have led to exchanges of fire. Few historians have openly wondered, however, whether there might be a more probative takeaway from the occurrence of so many close calls without a breakout of fighting: namely, the lesson that the two superpowers were both so risk-averse and so heavily self-constrained against escalation that none of these risky occurrences nor even the combination of a host of them would produce even a lowly conventional firefight between the combatants far less a nuclear blow. Consider the following five situations: (1) on August 30 Cuban patrol boats fired on US surveillance aircraft, yet there was no return fire; (2) numerous American warplanes overflew Cuban soil on low-level surveillance missions after October

16, whereas no Cuban or Soviet fighter aircraft rose to confront them; (3) some overflying surveillance missions experienced ground fire from Cuban antiaircraft emplacements but mounted no suppressing fire; (4) on October 27 US destroyers dropped practice depth charges equivalent to hand grenades on top of submerged Soviet submarines in an effort to force them to the surface, and the submarine commanders all complied rather than take retaliatory action; (5) the same day an overflying American U-2 was hit and destroyed when a nervous Soviet SAM-2 site fired its missiles, but there was no US response against the offending installation. Could it be that the Cuban missile crisis proved exactly the opposite of what was widely feared: namely, just how much safer and better protected the world had become from the risk of war arising between the two superpowers given the widely appreciated horrors that nuclear weapons had introduced to modern warfighting?

In his 1993 study of nuclear risk, *The Limits of Safety*, Scott Sagan identified numerous other security mishaps, miscues, foul-ups, and other perverse events that occurred during the Cuban missile crisis beyond the ones mentioned above, and yet he observed: "The sheer number and drama of the 'close calls' that did occur in the crisis should not obscure one central fact: there may have been many safety violations, false warnings, and bizarre interactions, but nonetheless no accidental or unauthorized use of a nuclear weapon took place." Sagan also found that a "curious consensus" had emerged among hawks and doves who had been contributing to the crisis literature over three decades since the crisis: that "the likelihood of a nuclear war was actually remote during the crisis, much less likely than many participants and most of the public believed at the time." The hawks were arguing that Khrushchev was "so deterred by U.S. nuclear superiority" that the Soviets "would not have escalated the use of force elsewhere in the world" even if the United States had invaded Cuba. The doves believed that Kennedy "was so deterred by even the significantly inferior Soviet nuclear arsenal that he would not have taken any risk of nuclear war by attacking Cuba."[125] Could Sagan's "central fact" that the nuclear guns remained silent during a decidedly messy crisis be explained in significant part by a related central fact of human nature: that people tend to exercise greater caution and restraint in proportion as the potential peril they perceive from taking action appears to be increased?

Michael Dobbs encapsulated this phenomenon of the two leaders' shared aversion to war in the nuclear age as he summarized the situation on

October 25, 1962, in Khrushchev's and Kennedy's deliberations with the Presidium and ExComm, respectively: "It was now clear to Khrushchev's colleagues on the Presidium that their explosive leader had no intention of going to war over the missiles. Five thousand miles and seven time zones away in Washington, ExComm members had reached a similar conclusion about Kennedy. The president regarded a nuclear exchange as 'the final failure,' to be avoided at all costs."[126]

Roger Hilsman seemed to reach this same conclusion in his 1996 history, *The Cuban Missile Crisis: The Struggle over Policy*. Hilsman had served in 1962 as chief of the State Department's Bureau of Intelligence and Research, and he has been widely regarded as one of the Kennedy administration's most astute commentators on the meaning of the crisis. Here is how Hilsman summed up the significance of the crisis in terms of the threat of war: "It is crystal clear that both Kennedy and Khrushchev very quickly decided not only that nuclear war was unthinkable but also that it was unthinkable to run any risk at all of such a war if it could be avoided, even a very small risk. Neither was seeking a confrontation, and both were doing everything they could to avoid one."[127]

To Hilsman, proof that Kennedy was doing everything he could to avoid conflict was demonstrated by the president's careful prepositioning of the Cordier option whereby UN secretary U Thant would have been asked to publicly petition both sides to "withdraw all their missiles stationed outside their borders" if the president's private proposal to Khrushchev of a Turkey-for-Cuba missile swap had not quickly borne fruit. That demonstrated for Hilsman that even if the Cordier ploy had misfired, "Kennedy was a long way from actual fighting."

So, too, Khrushchev had demonstrated he was unwilling to be drawn into a fight in perhaps the most consequential of his crisis decisions—his determination that the Soviet Union would not match America's move to DEFCON-2 war-trigger readiness: "Although it must be assumed that Khrushchev in prudence ordered an alert for the Soviet ICBM forces, he also seems to have taken care not to permit a general military alert."[128] And while Kennedy administration officials worried that US pressure in the Caribbean would prompt Soviet countermoves against West Berlin, Hilsman noted that "it became clear as the crisis progressed that Khrushchev was studiously avoiding any move that could be interpreted as a threat to Berlin."

Hilsman certainly appreciated the risks posed by the litany of "dangerous misunderstandings, slips, missteps and unauthorized actions by subordinates" that were unavoidable and produced close calls as the crisis unfolded. For Hilsman, the major lesson was "overwhelmingly obvious": "When the consequences can be nuclear war any risk at all is simply unacceptable," and "This came to be the dominating and most urgent lesson to be learned," at least for "some of the people who participated in the crisis decisions."[129] Still, Hilsman stood back from acknowledging perhaps the most curious phenomenon his long list of dangerous mistakes and close calls exhibited: the extraordinary fact that not one of them, nor all of them together, produced a single instance of an exchange of gunfire between the superpowers anywhere in the world as the crisis unfolded. Perhaps because any comment on the remarkable *peacefulness* of the Cuban events might have diminished the worthy, sobering message that Hilsman believed the crisis was meant to deliver in the dark days of the Cold War struggle, he chose to ignore the counterintuitive clue that Sherlock Holmes famously noticed—the fact that the dog was *not* barking.[130]

First, consider these significant nonevents that are often taken for granted: the Kennedy administration did not attack Cuba by land, sea, or air, though many in the ExComm and Pentagon urged a prompt military assault; the Soviets did not deploy their airborne or seaborne nuclear striking forces to forward positions, where they might have been needed to deter a possible US first-strike attack and would have posed a real threat to the United States in the event of war; the United States did not sink or even forcibly board any Soviet vessel carrying military cargo to Cuba; the Kremlin did not threaten West Berlin by ramping up its military forces adjacent to that isolated Western outpost, far less attack the city; neither side interpreted the other's ill-timed launch of a missile from an ICBM launch site as the prelude to a nuclear attack; Khrushchev did not authorize attacks by MiG-21 fighters or SAM-2 missiles on US surveillance overflights of Cuba; no Soviet submarines fired torpedoes, nuclear-tipped or otherwise, at the American warships that were harassing them. All of these possible reactions were foreseeable and would have been entirely conventional responses to the crisis that was brewing, and each of them arguably became more likely as the crisis unfolded. Yet none occurred.

Next, what about the problem posed by the many thousands of itchy trigger fingers holding the myriad weapons at the lowest layers of each side's military force structure who might have set off the trip wires leading to escalation and war accidentally or by mischance or misfortune? Yet there was no exchange of gunfire in either the 1961 Berlin or the 1962 Cuba crisis. Any single or small number of instances of a firefight breaking out during complex events of these kinds, had any such occurred, could perhaps have been attributed to the role of misfortune or (bad) luck. But it is surely no more meaningful to say that risks are high because accident or bad luck might happen as it would be to say that risks are low because smooth sailing and good luck have attended events thus far and might continue.[131] A more compelling explanation for why "the dog didn't bark" is preferable to one based on speculating about the presence or absence of luck.[132] Eric Schlosser noted at the end of his 2013 treatise on nuclear risk that "one crucial fact must be kept in mind: none of the roughly seventy thousand nuclear weapons built by the United States since 1945 has ever detonated inadvertently or without proper authorization." He followed this remarkable fact by observing that "the technological and administrative controls on those weapons have worked, however imperfectly at times—and countless people, military and civilian, deserve credit for that remarkable achievement."[133] The best that can be said to explain the peaceful outcome of the Cuban missile crisis is that many of these "countless people, military and civilian,"—beginning with the two superpower leaders—exercised extreme caution out of a shared knowledge that the consequences of actions that could precipitate a nuclear war were so unimaginably awful that those actions should be avoided at all cost.

During the Berlin tank stand-off, no guns were fired though there were ample provocations as American vehicles, both civilian and military, repeatedly and even insolently ignored VOPO orders to stop and turn back. When the face-off escalated to the point where battle tanks aimed their cannons at one another within point blank range, motors were revved in mock displays of an imminent attack, yet the guns remained silent.

A year later, there were four instances during the Cuban drama, listed briefly above, where ground-level military units on one side or the other actually fired their weapons against the putative enemy. Human nature would suggest that surely these would be occasions presenting the highest risk that retaliation would ensue, leading inexorably to tit-for-tat counterblows risking culmination in a worldwide conflagration. Yet on each occasion there was no retaliatory shooting whatsoever; the offended party's guns were silent every time. Thus:

On August 30, 1962, Cuban patrol boats fired on overflying US surveillance aircraft. There was no US response either from the aircraft under attack or from supporting forces that could easily have been deployed from nearby air bases.[134]

On October 27 the US Navy used small practice depth charges, or PDCs, which were a standard technique for detecting and tracking submerged submarines and in practice had an explosive force similar to a simple hand grenade ("harmless explosive sound signals"). The PDCs were dropped from overflying aircraft or surface ships as a signal that the submarine should come to the surface. Notice of the planned use of PDCs as a signal for submarines reaching the Cuba quarantine to come to the surface was "broadcast to the world, including the Soviet Union, in a Notice to Mariners" issued by the United States on October 25. And because the US Navy "had been tracking Soviet submarines for years in the Atlantic . . . Soviet captains knew what PDCs sounded like."[135]

One of these PDC hand grenades may have detonated close enough to inflict some modest damage on at least one of the Soviet submarines, B-59, which would have allowed its captain under his standing orders to respond to any presumed damage-causing attack by firing torpedoes, one of which available to him in this case carried a nuclear warhead.[136] But B-59's captain ultimately chose not to fire. This incident has earned an outsized place in missile crisis lore owing to reports that a Soviet naval officer named Vasili Archipov on board B-59 allegedly stood up to his vessel's captain, Valentin Savitsky; single-handedly talked him out of his threat to arm the submarine's nuclear-capable torpedo for possible firing at US naval vessels; and thereby became known as "the man who saved the world from nuclear apocalypse." It bears noting, however, that Savitsky had received notice of the American signaling policy from Moscow on October 25, and he presumably knew the difference between clusters of sound-signaling PDCs and a determined lethal attack using real, full-strength depth charges, especially as he was aware the destroyers circling above his ship knew pretty much exactly where he was and were dropping the PDCs "in series of five at a time, which was in accordance with the warning notice."[137] Surrounded by a US antisubmarine hunter-killer group consisting of destroyers in groups of three and four, S2F Tracker aircraft, and Sea King helicopters with dipping sonars, B-59 was caught in an "iron grip." With batteries low, air conditioning inoperable, and the crew's breathable air rapidly degrading; and with American destroyers circling above in a pinwheel maneuver demonstrating by signaling PDCs that they knew exactly where to aim their real depth charges if the need arose to do so; B-59 gave up: "After nearly a day of those simulated attacks, Savitsky was finally forced to surface amid his hunters to charge batteries."[138]

B-59 was just one of three Soviet submarines that were brought to the surface using PDCs during the Cuban crisis; none of the three chose to put up a fight; no Soviet protest was filed against US antisubmarine operations during the crisis; and the colorful story of Savitsky's threat and Archipov's heroism remains controversial, as the other Soviet "submarine commanders do not believe that Savitsky would have made such a command."[139] Those inclined to further speculate about apocalyptic endings for this episode must also bear in mind the ultimate futility of an order to fire a nuclear weapon in these fraught circumstances: How could a diesel submarine thus surrounded, trapped, hounded, denied freedom of maneuver, and running out of air needed for locomotion and breathing have located and picked a target? How could its captain maneuver his vessel to take aim without courting a rain of destruction? How could the nuclear torpedo have been set to hit the enemy without also destroying the submarine and its crew?[140] These undeniable top-of-mind problems surely help to underscore the essential inevitability of the actual outcome.

Also, on October 27 a Cuban-manned antiaircraft emplacement opened fire on low-flying US Crusader surveillance planes and managed to hit one of them with a 37 mm shell. There was no US counterattack either by the stricken Crusader or by any of the scores of US fighter aircraft that had been assembled at air bases in South Florida and other regional military installations to support the planned massive invasion of Cuba.[141]

By far the most serious incident also occurred on October 27 when a Soviet SA-2 battery shot down an American U-2 aircraft over eastern Cuba, killing the pilot. Although the president had approved a response plan only a few days before that called for an automatic attack on the offending SAM site in the event of exactly this kind of incident, the president on this occasion opted not to order execution of his own plan.[142]

Then there were a number of alarming episodes in which the flight paths of US military aircraft and missiles shortly before and during the Cuba crisis could have led the Soviets to mistakenly believe they were coming under attack. Three of these incidents have received considerable attention from historians: (1) the errant flight of a US B-52 bomber on August 23, 1962, along a flight path over the Arctic Ocean headed straight for the USSR until the mistake was noted and the aircraft turned back only three hundred miles from Soviet airspace, (2) the test launch of an Atlas ICBM from Vandenberg Air Force base in California on October 26, 1962, and (3) the accidental straying of an Alaska-based U-2 spy plane off its assigned flight path and into Soviet airspace on the night of October 26–27, precipitating a near-engagement with MiG interceptors that were scrambled from Wrangel Island in an attempt to shoot it down.[143] One might even mention the Soviet launch of an interplanetary space mission on October 24, 1962, using an ICBM-variant missile that took off from the Baikonur Cosmodrome ICBM site in Kazakhstan. The US intelligence agency watchers might have mistaken that launch as a signal that a nuclear attack was underway, but they didn't.

Those who point to the Vandenberg test launch and straying Alaska U-2 as concerning incidents must reckon with the overarching fact that Khrushchev and the Presidium were facing actual oncoming attack threats throughout the Cuban crisis in the form of DEFCON-2's continuously replenishing stream of B-52 sorties menacingly approaching, armed with nuclear bombs and carrying predetermined target sets, which turned back only after coming perilously close to Soviet borders. Yet the Kremlin took no responsive measures.

Many who contemplate with alarm the risks posed by any confrontation between nuclear-armed adversaries have looked back on October 1962 as a historic moment when the world came close to experiencing total destruction. But the actual experience of that episode points in another direction, providing a more reassuring explanation for the striking degree of mutual self-restraint that the key actors displayed on that occasion: the Cold War environment of October 1962 proved to be a surprisingly safe period to be alive during the post–World War II era. For it was a time when nuclear weapons were a shared monopoly of the world's two superpowers, and the rival leaders recognized that the presence of thousands of these devastating weapons on both sides of the battlefield not only rendered the option of launching a nuclear attack essentially unthinkable, it also effectively prevented the superpowers from engaging even in low-level gunfire with conventional weapons, as that might escalate to the forbidden outcome of a nuclear exchange.

Len Scott has questioned the nearly universal assumption that any nuclear first use by either side, no matter how limited, inevitably would have triggered a reciprocal strike by the other and a follow-on escalation to catastrophic all-out nuclear war. Noting that the president had elected not to retaliate even with conventional weapons when the U-2 aircraft was shot down and its pilot killed, Scott observed that a similar reluctance to respond in kind to first use of an atomic weapon was "certainly possible" if such nuclear first use "was judged to be tactical, limited or accidental": "Although the Soviets possessed a smaller strategic force whose vulnerability might have quickly raised in Moscow minds the need to 'use them or lose them,' a limited or selective American attack might have prompted a limited Soviet response (or indeed no response at all). Assessments of the risk of nuclear war (and of cataclysmic nuclear war) require a dark empathy on the part of the historian. They also require attention to the organisational processes, military imperatives, and the radioactive fog of war that could have hastened escalation despite the best endeavors of political leaders."[144]

Scott's speculative and heavily qualified assessment of the degree of likelihood that Khrushchev might actually have refrained from escalation even in the event of a limited nuclear attack by the United States was cursory, yet it is still noteworthy for its failure to mention the critical known factors that would have counseled both sides against retaliating. For the Soviets, acceptance of a limited nuclear strike would indeed have been painful, and the notion of "using" or "losing" their own nuclear counterstrike capability might indeed have come to mind. But Scott neglected to mention the most important factor known to the Kremlin that would have overwhelmed all others: the reality that Soviet striking power against the United States was so meagre in relation to the destructive capability the United States could inflict on the USSR that any Soviet nuclear response to a limited US first nuclear use would have been suicidal, as Rostow and Nitze noted in their post-crisis appraisal.

Scott's assessment did not squarely address Kennedy's likely reaction to a limited Soviet nuclear first use. Here, however, the historical record provides two reasonably clear indications that the president would not have approved a nuclear retaliation to a limited Soviet nuclear strike against United States military forces. The first was his October 21, 1962, order to the Joint Chiefs of Staff, repeated on October 22, barring the use-it-or-lose-it firing of the Jupiter missiles in Turkey and Italy without his express permission even in a scenario in which the Soviets had launched a "selective" nuclear strike against the two installations. The second was his decision to withhold tactical nuclear weapons from the US invasion forces being assembled in Florida and throughout the Caribbean even though it was known, or at least assumed, that Soviet military units in Cuba were equipped with tactical nuclear weapons that might be used against the invaders.

One can only contemplate the prospect of American losses if the Soviet defenders had unleashed one or more of their LUNA/FROG or FKR tactical weapons armed with nuclear warheads, yet the president and defense secretary must surely have gone through that mental exercise, after they received advice from the JCS, which certainly had done so, and still decided that, even the awful prospect of sustaining an initial tactical nuclear blow would not necessarily justify specifically arming the invasion force to permit a swift retaliatory use of US tactical nuclear weapons that could have escalated to general war.

The fuller record of events that is now available leaves little room for doubt that by late in the day on October 27, 1962, and continuing into that night, as both Kennedy and Khrushchev were forced to confront the possibility that a continuing deterioration of events in and around Cuba might lead to invasion and war, they both reflexively recoiled from the nuclear edge. For Kennedy, the test came when he learned of the U-2 shoot-down. The president refused to order reprisal against the offending SAM base even though instant retaliation had been the course urged by all his advisers and had been the option he himself had specifically approved only four days before.[145] Instead, the president chose at that moment to press home his back-channel deal on Khrushchev's terms, which included the mutual withdrawal of US missiles from Turkey (with the US missiles in Italy gratuitously thrown in) in exchange for immediate withdrawal of the Soviet missiles from Cuba. He therefore postponed his decision on retaliation against the SAM base at least to the next day, and left room for a further delay to the day following.[146]

Later that fall, in a private conversation with John Kenneth Galbraith, Kennedy expressed "much feeling and some anger [at] the recklessness of the professional advice he had received during the crisis just passed, in particular the proposal to bomb the missile sites." The president then said, "I never had the slightest intention of doing so."[147]

That Khrushchev had also reached his personal turning point at about the same time was confirmed at noon on October 28, 1962, Moscow time, when he opened a meeting of the Soviet Presidium with his terse announcement: "We must retreat." As Taubman has reported: "Khrushchev began by recalling one of Lenin's greatest retreats, the March 1918 Brest-Litovsk agreement in which the Bolsheviks abandoned their western borderlands and more as the price for peace with the Germans. 'Our interests dictated that decision—we had to save Soviet power. Now we find ourselves face-to-face with the danger of war and of nuclear catastrophe. . . . In order to save the world we must retreat. I called you together to consult and debate whether you are in agreement with this kind of decision.'"[148]

Khrushchev had not yet received the report of Robert Kennedy's Cuba-for-Turkey offer. So great was his apprehension about the deteriorating situation in Cuba that he was ready to withdraw based solely on Kennedy's October 27 no-invasion pledge, which was the only firm American offer then on the table. Yet suddenly, news arrived of Robert Kennedy's meeting with Dobrynin and the American offer of a secret missile trade. Dobrynin's remarkable memorandum, which was read to the Presidium verbatim, described the attorney general's distraught demeanor; included indications from Kennedy that tensions between his brother, the president, and American military leaders had reached a dangerous point, even raising the possibility of a coup; and underscored that an American invasion of Cuba might be literally hours away. The Presidium accepted the Americans' sweetened deal without further consideration, even though the secrecy condition meant that the Kremlin would be handicapped in explaining why this resolution would not appear to the world as an embarrassing Soviet defeat.[149]

The two world leaders' simultaneous acts of unusually generous, potentially even humiliating accommodation, which promptly secured a crisis-averting deal, provide very strong evidence that the Cuban missile confrontation had not in fact brought the world to the precipice of nuclear war, as the superheated press coverage at the time (and commentators for many years afterwards) would solemnly pronounce.[150] Rather, they underscore the fact that the two leaders who were directing events from start to finish both shared an unswerving determination—at whatever cost might be required—to keep their two nations from any direct use of military force that might escalate to war.

Both leaders readily welcomed personal diplomacy, including a continuous flow of back-channel communications, as their principal means to de-escalate tensions. Their messages consistently embodied expressions of a shared overriding interest and determination to find compromise solutions in circumstances where public disclosure of these olive branches might have caused both of them political harm at the hands of domestic adversaries who would be quick to label such moves as a sign of weakness or even treachery. Thus, from start to finish of both crises, the two leaders were actively looking for ways to defuse the tension, and they consistently cooperated to de-escalate the two stand-offs and restore the status quo ante.[151]

During the Cuban drama Kennedy would have faced political risk if there had been any indication that he had caved in to Soviet pressure. For his part, Khrushchev had tried to win on a long-shot bet, but he had no intention of backing up his gamble with force (or "bet[ing] whatever is left in his pocket and then grab[bing] a pistol and shoot[ing] himself"). As Taubman has noted, based on his interview with Khrushchev's son-in-law, Alexei Adzhubei: "Not thinking things through was typical of Khrushchev, especially in his last years in power. But although he lacked a contingency plan, he did have a notion: If the Americans discovered Soviet missiles before they were fully operational, surely he could negotiate himself out of the situation. It was his 'near certainty that Kennedy would not choose war,' according to Adzhubei, that made it seem 'relatively safe' to provoke the U.S. President."[152]

Once the missiles were discovered, Khrushchev needed the Cuban drama to end quickly and peaceably because he knew that there was nothing he could do militarily to stop what he credibly believed was an imminent US invasion of Cuba. A public no-invasion pledge by the president was therefore all the Soviet chairman needed to provide acceptable cover for a hasty withdrawal from his bold but deeply ill-considered gamble. The wide asymmetries in balance of forces both at the global strategic level and in the Caribbean theater of military operations simply left Khrushchev no choice but to retreat. Roger Hilsman later observed that the "best judgment" as to why the Soviets backed down was that "Cuba was close to the sources of American strength and distant from the sources of Soviet strength." As a result the United States "could apply overwhelming conventional power at the point of contact" sustained by "an umbrella of nuclear power that foreclosed any possibility of the Soviets trying to use nuclear weapons to redress the imbalance at the contact point."[153]

Both Kennedy and Khrushchev were skilled at shaping public opinion through their speeches, as well as orchestrated expressions of view by media commentators and other proxies, and both used these channels to project forceful and even combative positions during the Cuban drama. Yet the strong predilection of both men in their private exchanges was to encourage pursuit of reasonable policies for mutual advantage. The two kept up a continuing dialogue through confidential, trusted intermediaries operating along back channels as tensions rose. Although many government officials and agencies were engaged around the clock on both sides in the massive enterprise of attempting to manage the epic Cold War crisis, in the end only two men mattered, and both wanted a peaceful outcome at almost any price. As Richard Reeves has concluded: "At least two men, the two at the center—Nikita Khrushchev and John Kennedy—realized that no politician in his right mind was going to use nuclear weapons first. The price was too high: the judgment of history would be too severe."[154]

How far would Kennedy have gone to avoid a hot nuclear confrontation with the Soviets, believing that any such incident would risk rapid escalation to Armageddon? The answer to this question obviously requires much speculation, both because it is impossible to read another person's mind with absolute confidence, and because the question itself contains a counterfactual moment of truth that never actually arose.

Historians nevertheless grapple with such unanswerable questions using the evidence, both hard and more ephemeral, that is available to them from credible sources. The vast library of reminiscences from people who knew John F. Kennedy gives us many memorable and quotable statements he made privately to close colleagues and friends, leaving a kind of canon of Kennedy pronouncements that have led historians and the public to speculate about what the president believed or how he must have felt, and to explain how he would have decided to act in the challenging circumstances he actually encountered or might have faced. Thus we have heard from close advisers and friends who witnessed such memorably tough and high-minded statements attributed to Kennedy as these: his pragmatic and measured response to Khrushchev's Berlin Wall provocation (per Kenneth O'Donnell): "A wall is a helluva lot better than a war";[155] his belief that only forceful US action would block Khrushchev's aggressive thrusts (per Arthur Schlesinger Jr.): "that son of a bitch doesn't pay attention to words, he has to see you move";[156] his low regard for military advisers who advocated muscular use of the nation's nuclear might (per Dean Rusk): "And we call ourselves the human race");[157] his combative reaction upon learning of the discovery of Soviet ballistic missiles in Cuba (per McGeorge Bundy): "He can't do that to me";[158] his outrage over the Soviet foreign minister's complicity in Khrushchev's deception (per Lovett): "[Gromyko] told more barefaced lies than I have ever heard in so short a time";[159] and his dark view during the Cuban crisis that the chance of war was "between 1 and 3 and even."[160]

It is in the context of this copious and expanding notebook of private, candid, and arresting presidential pronouncements that one must attempt to understand an equally remarkable if less admirable comment that John F. Kennedy reportedly made in the presence of his young mistress in the president's White House bedroom late on the night of October 27–28, 1962, at possibly the most consequential moment of his presidency. When he retired late that evening, Kennedy had just hours before forwarded to Khrushchev his written proposal for resolving the Cuban missile crisis and averting armed conflict, and he had simultaneously transmitted over back channels a secret addendum that promised a trade of the US Jupiter missiles in Turkey if the Soviets would accept the public terms of the deal. Lying in bed next to nineteen-year-old White House intern Mimi Alford, Kennedy could not yet be certain whether the morning would bring peace or a further descent along a slippery slope that might end in nuclear war. It was at this uncertain moment that the president shared with his young companion a private thought every bit as revealing and provocative as any of the more praiseworthy utterances he made before or since that have found their way into the Kennedy canon. As Ms. Alford said: "At one point, after leaving the room to take another urgent phone call, he came back shaking his head and said to me, 'I'd rather my children be red than dead.' It wasn't a political statement or an attempt at levity. These were the words of a father who adored his children and couldn't bear them being hurt."[161]

At that point of the Cold War, it was a staple of conservative opinion in the United States that patriotic Americans should rather "be dead than red," a phrase that called to mind the ringing sentiments of famous heroes from the birth of the Nation: Patrick Henry ("Give me liberty or give me death") and Nathan Hale ("I only regret that I have but one life to give for my country"). For Kennedy at this moment of crisis to turn a similarly heroic expression of defiance backward could tempt commentators to draw a range of arguable interpretations. But one takeaway seems clear: the president was in a frame of mind that almost any option short of military action in the Cuban crisis would be preferable to one that risked armed combat of any kind with his superpower adversary, and a fortiori that any use of nuclear weapons by the United States, no matter what the provocation, would be absolutely anathema.[162] As Robert Dallek observed, diplomatically, about Kennedy's startling confession to his young mistress: "Almost anything was better, he believed, than nuclear war."[163]

Postscript

Secrecy and Concealment Placed a Cloud over the Reputations of Some of the Kennedy Administration's Most Respected Officials

Adlai Stevenson was the first and most public victim of the secrecy campaign, and surely the one most deeply harmed by it. As the first round of more detailed analyses of the missile crisis began to be published, Stevenson was singled out as the fall guy. Ironically, the first commentary that targeted Stevenson—which called him out as the one member of ExComm who supposedly favored a missile trade as a means to appease Khrushchev—was coauthored by Charles Bartlett, one of the president's secret intermediaries who was himself responsible for midwifing this key settlement proposal. Philip Nash encapsulated the vicious irony: "The Kennedy Administration selected Adlai Stevenson as post crisis scapegoat in such a way as to suggest that it had dismissed the idea of a missile trade. Stevenson was the obvious choice for fall guy; well known as dovish on international questions, outspoken in his support of a trade in early crisis deliberations, thoroughly disliked and distrusted by Kennedy and many of his top advisers, he fit the bill nicely. All it took was approval of a single leak to JFK's friend Charles Bartlett, who with Stewart Alsop was writing a major behind-the-scenes account of the crisis for the *Saturday Evening Post*." The Bartlett/Alsop article would refer to a "nonadmiring official" who charged that "Adlai wanted a Munich," an exchange of "Turkish, Italian, and British missile bases for the Cuban bases." The article portrayed Stevenson "as the lone peacenik bucking the ExComm consensus and Kennedy listening 'politely' to his proposal and then rejecting it."[1]

That Bartlett promoted the calumny knowing it to be false was bad enough, but the journalist's complicity was even more insidious because he himself had personally set in motion the precise act of supposed infamy that he was now attributing to the US ambassador to the United Nations. In the aftermath of the Alsop/Bartlett piece, Chester Bowles wrote of the president: "His failure fully to support a distinguished American who had twice been the Democratic nominee for President strengthened my determination to leave the Administration."[2]

Dean Rusk had been among the very small group of inside advisers who were present in the Oval office on the evening of October 27 when President Kennedy instructed his brother to convey the missile trade proposal to Khrushchev through Soviet Ambassador Dobrynin.[3] Thus, the US secretary of state flatly lied when he unqualifiedly denied the existence of the Turkey-Cuba linkage in his testimony before Congress on January 25, 1963:

> SENATOR HICKENLOOPER: The removal of the missiles from Turkey . . . was in no way, shape or form, directly or indirectly, connected with the settlement, the discussions or the manipulations of the Cuban situation? . . .
>
> RUSK: That is correct, sir.[4]

Robert McNamara was also part of the inner circle who were present when the missile trade proposal was fashioned by the president in the Oval Office. His testimony before Congress on at least two occasions was affirmatively dishonest. The first was February 7, 1963, where he testified: "I can say without any qualifications whatsoever there was absolutely no deal, as it might be called, between the Soviet Union and the United States regarding the removal of Jupiter weapons from either Italy or Turkey."[5]

McNamara's February 21, 1963, testimony before a Senate committee was also a tortured and highly misleading distortion of the truth, if not an outright lie, that would only be exposed when the Kennedy tapes became public many years later:

> SENATOR STENNIS: [Withdrawal of the Jupiters] has nothing to do with the Cuban situation or anything like that. . . .
>
> MCNAMARA: Absolutely not . . . the Soviet Government did raise the issue . . . [but the] President absolutely refused even to discuss it. He wouldn't even reply other than that he would not discuss the issue at all.[6]

Theodore Sorensen was present at the October 27 Oval Office meeting, he was the editor of Robert Kennedy's posthumously published description of the role he played in the Cuban missile crisis, *Thirteen Days*, and he also wrote at least two books about the Kennedy presidency—*Kennedy* (1965) and *The Kennedy Legacy* (1970). Twenty-seven years after the event, Sorensen belatedly confessed that this was not oversight but rather his deliberate excision of a critical portion of the historical record: "I have a confession to make. . . . I was the editor of Robert Kennedy's book [*Thirteen Days*]. . . . And his diary was very explicit that this [trade] was part of the deal, but at that time it was still a secret even on the American side. . . . So I took it upon myself to edit that out of his diaries."[7]

The veracity of *Thirteen Days* was thus compromised at the hands of its editor. But the author was also to blame. As Michael Beschloss would wryly observe: "Later historians who took *Thirteen Days* as gospel neglected the fact that one reason for its writing was to bolster Robert Kennedy's credentials as a potential president."[8]

Though *Charles Bartlett* was a journalist rather than an administration official, he deserves a special status of ignominy among the president's closest confidants who were enlisted in the effort to conceal the Turkey-for-Cuba missile swap. Bartlett had been a longtime personal friend of the president, and on October 21, 1962, received directly from the president himself advance knowledge both of the presence of Soviet missiles in Cuba and of the president's inclination to consider offering to remove US missiles in Turkey in exchange for a Soviet withdrawal of their missiles from Cuba. Shortly thereafter, in what can only be described as a bizarre episode with no known sensible purpose, Bartlett was given top-secret photographs of the Soviet missile sites and asked by Robert Kennedy to invite Bolshakov to his office in order to show these photos to the GRU officer. Bolshakov later described this strange meeting, which occurred before Adlai Stevenson's October 25, 1962, presentation of these same photographs to the United Nations Security Council, and a day before the photographs first appeared in the American press: "When I entered [Bartlett's] office, I immediately noticed some large map-boards covered with paper standing in the corner. On the boards were aerial photographs. The captions indicated that these were pictures of sites where Soviet missile bases were being built at San Cristobal in Cuba. . . . in the right hand corner of each map-board, whether by accident or not—I personally think that it was deliberate—the classified stamp had not been removed, and the highest classification for the Americans is 'For the President's Eyes Only.'"[9]

Bartlett was also enlisted by Kennedy on October 23, 1962, to float the president's missile swap idea by the Russians via Georgi Bolshakov.[10] Thus, Bartlett was personally aware that the source of that proposal was the White House, that is, the president himself. Nevertheless, when questions began to be raised after the crisis was resolved about whether the deal had included any Kennedy promises about the US missiles in Turkey, Bartlett collaborated with the president and another favored journalist, Stewart Alsop, on a false story that would conceal the president's role by laying blame for that proposal on Adlai Stevenson, the US ambassador to the United Nations. The Bartlett/Alsop story would even go the further step of gratuitously smearing Stevenson as a Chamberlain-like "Munich" appeaser. Bartlett dutifully incorporated the false story ("Adlai wanted a Munich")—passed to him by the president himself—into a postcrisis article he cowrote with fellow journalist and Kennedy friend Stewart Alsop for the *Saturday Evening Post.* Fittingly enough, the president was a silent editorial collaborator on the story. Evan Thomas captured part of the back story in his 2000 biography of Robert Kennedy: "Bartlett, as he later acknowledged, was used. . . . President Kennedy insisted on seeing the article before publication. He requested only one change: that the authors cut out a passage describing the role of Ted Sorensen on the ExComm (the article as published mentioned Sorensen only in passing). Sorensen had been a pacifist in World War II; it would not do to give him too prominent a role in the president's councils of war."[11]

The 2000 Thomas biography had linked the White House to the Bartlett/Alsop smear aimed at Stevenson but still left unclear the extent of the president's actual involvement. After all, the fact that Kennedy had apparently requested only one edit might have reflected nothing more than his hasty or too-casual review of the draft piece, or an entirely understandable desire not to interfere unduly with the independence of the Fourth Estate. The full extent of Kennedy's and Bartlett's collaboration in this calumny against Stevenson would not be revealed until the publication in 2014 of Gregg Herken's history of the Alsop brothers' careers in journalism and their intimate connections with the Kennedy family. Based on his review of surviving drafts of the *Saturday Evening Post* article and Stewart Alsop's personal correspondence, Herken was able to demonstrate that "in fact, the 'nonadmiring official' was Kennedy himself. The president had penciled in the 'Munich' line when he annotated a typescript of the draft article submitted by Bartlett and Alsop. Although Clay Blair, editor of *The Saturday Evening Post,* urged Stew to respond to the article's critics by identifying the president as the source of the inflammatory quotation, Alsop held firm in a letter to Blair: 'Alas, my lips are sealed. The whole business was on a sealed-lips basis, as you know, and if I so much as hinted that JFK was in any way involved, I'd be run out of town. For good reason too—there are certain rules of the game that you just can't break if you want to go on earning a living here.'"[12]

McGeorge Bundy confirmed in his oral history that the president had seen a draft of the Alsop/Bartlett article before it was published: "You know and I know that that article of Stewart Alsop's and Charlie Bartlett's wouldn't have happened if the President hadn't, at one point and for a period, been very irritated with Adlai. But it was a case where he let himself go, or let others go—whichever way you want to put it—and I will say for myself that I never saw that damned thing before it appeared—but Jack Kennedy did (and we may have to rub this part out when we redo the tape)."[13]

Notes

Introduction

1. A missile is termed "ballistic" if it is guided in the ascent of a high-arc trajectory and then falls to its target by the action of gravity. An ICBM has a range of greater than 3,400 miles. MRBM and IRBM missiles have ranges of 500–1,500 miles and 1,500–3,400 miles, respectively.

2. See James G. Blight, Bruce J. Allyn, and David A. Welch, *Cuba on the Brink: Castro, the Missile Crisis and the Soviet Collapse* (New York: Pantheon, 1993); Dino A. Brugioni, *Eyeball to Eyeball: The Inside Story of the Cuban Missile Crisis* (New York: Random House, 1991); Frederick Kempe, *Berlin 1961: Kennedy, Khrushchev and the Most Dangerous Place on Earth* (New York: G.P. Putnam, 2011); Michael Dobbs, *One Minute to Midnight: Kennedy, Khrushchev and Castro on the Brink of Nuclear War* (New York: Knopf, 2008).

3. President Kennedy contributed his own scatological twist to the victory narrative in conversations with friendly reporters and other intimates: "But presidential conversations on background with Bartlett, Lippmann, Sulzberger, and Bradley and the usual skillful leaks by the White House staff ensured that Americans would know who had won the Missile Crisis. Discussing his confrontation with Khrushchev among intimate friends, the President modestly said, 'I cut his balls off.'" Michael R. Beschloss, *The Crisis Years: Kennedy and Khrushchev, 1960–1963* (New York: HarperCollins, 1991), pp. 548–49.

4. The *New York Times* on October 29, 1961, carried an article by Sydney Gruson dated the day before under the title "U.S. and Russians Pull Back Tanks from Berlin Line," and with a subtitle: "Soviet Units Go First." On October, 29, 1962, Joseph Alsop's column in the *Washington Post* bore the title "Victory." See Gregg Herken, *The Georgetown Set* (New York: Knopf, 2014), p. 276. After the Cuban crisis settlement there were similar glowing press reports of a US victory. See James W. Hilty, *Robert Kennedy: Brother Protector* (Philadelphia: Temple University Press, 1997), p. 451 ("*Time* declared Kennedy had 'won in his courageous confrontation,' and *Newsweek* marked it as his 'greatest political triumph'"). A special CBS News evening broadcast by Charles Collingwood reported that the world had come out "from under the most terrible threat of nuclear holocaust since the sec-

ond world war," with a "humiliating defeat for Soviet policy." See http://www.theguardian.com/commentisfree/2012/oct/15/cuban-missile-crisis-russian-roulette

5. Michael Dobbs called this the "mythologization of the Cuban missile crisis" in which "Kennedy loyalists" writing instant histories of the event "accentuated the positive and played down the negative, emphasizing the president's resolve and skill in managing the test of wills with Nikita Khrushchev." See http://litresp.ru/chitat/en/D/dobbs-michael/one-minute-to-midnight-kennedy-khrushchev-and-castro-on-the-brink-of-nuclear-war

6. At the conclusion of the Cuban crisis President Kennedy told congressional leaders at a White House meeting, "We've won a great victory." Beschloss, *Crisis Years*, p. 545.

7. Many of the descriptions of Kennedy published during his short presidency or in the years following his assassination were reverential, bordering on adulatory. See, e.g., Arthur M. Schlesinger Jr., *A Thousand Days: John F. Kennedy in the White House* (New York: Houghton Mifflin, 1965), p. 716 (Kennedy's leadership during the missile crisis was a "combination of toughness and restraint, of will, nerve and wisdom, so brilliantly controlled, so matchlessly calibrated" that it "dazzled the world"); William Manchester, *Portrait of a President* (Boston: Little, Brown, 1962), p. 7 ("The figure tapers like a boxer's; the glossy hair is chestnut, with only a suggestion of gray at the temples. The face, however, is deeply lined, especially around the mouth, and the eyes give an even stronger impression of maturity. They are opaque, gray, and often hooded by long lashes. . . . It is impossible to read John Fitzgerald Francis Kennedy's mind, but obviously there is much on it"); Robert Dallek, *An Unfinished Life: John F. Kennedy 1917–1963* (New York: Back Bay Books, 2003), p. 404 (describing the first meeting of Kennedy and Khrushchev at their Vienna summit: "The youthful Kennedy towered over the short, squat sixty-seven-year-old Khrushchev"). In his 1965 biography of Kennedy, Theodore Sorensen did not profess objectivity; recalling a quip by the president that the two of them would one day write a book together, Sorensen said of his biography: "This is my substitute for the book he was going to write. It reflects to the extent possible, his views during his last eleven years. It employs, to the extent possible, his words and his thoughts." Sorensen, *Kennedy* (New York: Harper & Row, 1965), p. 3. The heroic images of President Kennedy and his brother Robert persist. See Evan Thomas, *Robert Kennedy: His Life* (New York: Simon & Schuster, 2000), p. 233 ("On the tape recordings of the ExComm deliberations, one can almost hear the blending of their complementary talents, JFK steady and reasonable, RFK urgent and probing. Given the stakes and the pressure, their performance was remarkable. Some myths *are* true: this was their finest hour").

8. William Taubman opened his highly acclaimed biography of Khrushchev with this blunt description of the Soviet leader's public standing: "Ask many Westerners, and not a few Russians, and they're likely to recall Nikita Khrushchev as a crude, ill-educated clown who banged his shoe at the United Nations." William Taubman, *Khrushchev: The Man and His Era* (New York: Norton, 2003), p. xi.

9. Ernest R. May and Philip D. Zelikow, eds., *The Kennedy Tapes: Inside the White House during the Cuban Missile Crisis* (Cambridge: Belknap Press, 1997). The Miller Center of Public Affairs at the University of Virginia subsequently produced a three-volume revised version of the tape transcriptions edited by Timothy Naftali (vol. 1), Naftali and Philip Zelikow (vol. 2), and Zelikow and Ernest May (vol. 3). See Ernest R. May and Philip Zelikow, gen. eds., *The Presidential Recordings: John F. Kennedy*, vols. 1–3, *The Great Crises* (New York: Norton, 2001).

10. See ,e.g., Aleksandr Fursenko and Timothy Naftali, *Khrushchev's Cold War* (New York: Norton, 2006), and *One Hell of a Gamble: Khrushchev, Castro & Kennedy, 1958–1964* (New York: Norton, 1997); and Timothy Naftali, "The Malin Notes: Glimpses inside the Kremlin during the Cuban Missile Crisis," *Cold War International History Project*, Wilson Center, Issue 17/18, Fall 2012, https://www.wilsoncenter.org/sites/default/files/CWIHP_Cuban_Missile_Crisis_Bulletin_17-18.pdf

11. See Jonathan Haslam, *Russia's Cold War* (New Haven: Yale University Press, 2011).

12. See Taubman, *Khrushchev*.

13. Sergei N. Khrushchev, *Nikita Khrushchev and the Creation of a Superpower* (University Park: Pennsylvania State University Press, 2000).

14. Anatoly Dobrynin, *In Confidence: Moscow's Ambassador to America's Six Cold War Presidents* (New York: Random House, 1995).

15. See Philip Nash, *The Other Missiles of October* (Chapel Hill: University of North Carolina Press, 1997).

16. See Beschloss, *Crisis Years*.

17. Dobbs, *One Minute to Midnight*; Sheldon M. Stern, *The Cuban Missile Crisis in American Memory: Myths versus Reality* (Stanford, CA: Stanford University Press, 2012).

18. As the Kennedy administration was taking its post-missile crisis "victory lap," many commentators were fond of quoting a pithy remark attributed to Secretary of State Dean Rusk as the quarantine began to take effect: "We're eyeball-to-eyeball and I think the other fellow just blinked." As our understanding of the Cuban events has become clearer in ensuing years, however, Rusk's vivid and triumphalist image has lost much of its power to inform.

19. See Robert Jervis, "The Cuban Missile Crisis: What Can We Know, Why Did It Start, and How Did It End?," in Len Scott and R. Gerald Hughes, eds., *The Cuban Missile Crisis: A Critical Reappraisal* (New York: Routledge, 2015), p. 7 ("Although the fact that it took two meetings before the Presidium agreed may show some resistance [the records are too sparse to reveal this], there is no doubt that Khrushchev was in charge").

20. See Stern, *Cuban Missile Crisis*, p. 16 ("It is not an exaggeration to say—because it is incontrovertibly backed up by the verbatim missile crisis recordings—that John F. Kennedy was the only person at the ExComm meetings who genuinely understood that nuclear war could *never* be a viable or rational choice. Nuclear weapons had altered the very meaning of war itself, and everything—

anything—had to be done to avert a nuclear apocalypse"); Taubman, *Khrushchev*, p. 347 ("[Khrushchev's] core axiom was that nuclear weapons were so destructive they would never be employed; when he first learned 'all the facts about nuclear power,' he remarked, 'I couldn't sleep for several days. Then I became convinced we could never possibly use these weapons, and . . . I was able to sleep again'").

21. See Don Munton, "The Fourth Question: Why Did John F. Kennedy Offer Up the Jupiter Missiles in Turkey," in David Gioe, Len Scott, and Christopher Andrew, eds., *An International History of the Cuban Missile Crisis* (New York: Routledge, 2013), p. 268 ("As Graham Allison suggested decades ago, both Kennedy and Khrushchev sought a peaceful negotiated solution because they feared the likely consequence of not pulling back—an uncontrolled escalation of a local conflict into a super-power nuclear war. They recognized the need to avoid, in John Kennedy's words, 'the final failure'").

22. Cf. John Mueller, *Atomic Obsession* (New York: Oxford University Press, 2010), p. 39 ("Interestingly, it seems that even in the great 'nuclear' crisis over Cuba in 1962, the central figures would have been about equally anxious to keep the conflict under control even if they could have been guaranteed that any ensuing armed conflict would remain conventional"). The shoot-down of the American U-2 aircraft by a Soviet SAM-2 was an unauthorized act that angered Khrushchev when he learned that the Soviet commander of the SAM-2 battery had decided to follow Cuban rather than Soviet rules of engagement. Taubman, *Khrushchev*, pp. 571–72.

23. Kempe, *Berlin 1961*, pp. 468, 475. Kennedy had appointed Clay as his special representative in Berlin, with the rank of ambassador, on August 30, stating at the time that "the situation in Berlin is a serious one, and I wish to have the advantage of having on the scene a person of General Clay's outstanding capacity and experience." See Curtis Cate, *The Ides of August: The Berlin Wall Crisis 1961* (New York: M. Evans, 1978), p. 458. The trouble was that Clay also had the "capacity" for recommending highly aggressive action in response to perceived Soviet pressure. In the closing days of 1961, Clay would write the president urging that the United States was "facing the ultimate challenge now," and that "if we do not have the courage, or if we are deterred by Allied weakness in the short remaining period in which military odds are in our favor, what will we do when this is no longer true?" Clay's answer to his own rhetorical question was that "we should seek the confrontation sooner rather than later." Marc Trachtenberg, *History and Strategy* (Princeton, NJ: Princeton University Press, 1991), p. 230.

24. Frederick Taylor, *The Berlin Wall: A World Divided, 1961–1989* (New York: HarperCollins, 2007), p. 283.

25. Naftali and Zelikow, *Presidential Recordings*, vol. 2, p. 583. Perhaps influenced by Robert Kennedy's panicked warnings to two different Soviet intermediaries about the president's "enemies" who "might go to any length" (to GRU officer Georgi Bolshakov on August 31, 1962), and about the "many unreasonable heads among the generals . . . itching for a fight" (to Soviet ambassador Dobrynin two months later on October 27), some commentators have portrayed LeMay as a

dangerous militarist who could have posed a threat to the president's authority. Yet these critics have failed to give LeMay credit for his striking demonstration of self-control and loyalty to the president when the October 19 meeting ended and the president and his White House advisers left the room. LeMay and his two fellow chiefs of staff, Marine Corps commandant David Shoup and army general Earle Wheeler, remained alone together in the room, none of them knowing that the president's secret taping machine was soundlessly recording their every word. Shoup launched into a tirade against the president, beginning with obsequious praise of the air force chief of staff: "You pulled the rug right out from under him." Had LeMay truly been disloyal to the president, this surely would have been his opportunity to utter a rude rejoinder unobserved. Instead, the general's response was, "Jesus Christ! What the hell do you mean?" Doubtless taken aback, Shoup rambled incoherently about the president's fear of a military escalation: "If somebody could keep 'em from doing the goddamn thing piecemeal, that's our problem. You go in there and friggin around with the missiles. You're screwed." LeMay, however, kept whatever concerns he may have had about the president and the country's leadership to himself, offering instead only a single, mildly affirming comment: "That's right." Stern, *Cuban Missile Crisis*, p. 165.

26. See Beschloss, *Crisis Years*, p. 571.

27. See Scott D. Sagan, *The Limits of Safety: Organizations, Accidents, and Nuclear Weapons* (Princeton, NJ: Princeton University Press, 1993).

28. GRU (Glavnoye Razvedyvatel'noye Upravleniye) was the military intelligence service of the Soviet Union's armed forces. Bolshakov's given name "Georgi" is sometimes found spelled "Georgy."

29. *Foreign Relations of the United States* (hereafter *FRUS*), 1961–1963, vol. 23, *Southeast Asia*, Doc. 455, Memorandum from Robert Kennedy to McGeorge Bundy, July 11, 1962 (reporting on conversation between Kennedy and Bolshakov regarding a potential pullout of US troops in Thailand).

30. Khrushchev, *Nikita Khrushchev*, p. 461.

31. James G. Hershberg, introduction to "A Trigger for Khrushchev's Deployment: Alexei Adzhubei's Report on His Conversation with John F. Kennedy, 30 January 1962," *Cold War International History Project Bulletin* 17–18 (Fall 2012), pp. 319, 321, Woodrow Wilson International Center for Scholars, www.wilson-center.org/publication/bulletin-no-17-18.

32. See Aleksandr Fursenko and Timothy Naftali, "Soviet Intelligence and the Cuban Missile Crisis," in James G. Blight and David A. Welch, eds., *Intelligence and the Cuban Missile Crisis* (London: Frank Cass, 1998), p. 79. See also Sagan, *Limits of Safety*, p. 65; Taubman, *Khrushchev*, p. 565.

Chapter 1

1. https://www.nytimes.com/1989/11/09/opinion/essay-how-many-divisions.html. See also S. M. Plokhy, *Yalta: The Price of Peace* (New York: Viking, 2010), p. 372 (attributing same comment to Stalin at Yalta conference). The au-

thenticity of this comment as attributed to Stalin at Potsdam has been questioned in a note to the US State Department Office of the Historian's *FRUS: Diplomatic Papers, The Conference of Berlin (Potsdam Conference)*, 1945, vol. 2. See https://history.state.gov/historicaldocuments/frus1945Berlinv02/d710a-65, n. 26.

2. https://www.telegraph.co.uk/news/worldnews/europe/russia/11547247/Europe-faces-a-real-threat-from-Russia-warns-US-army-commander.html

3. Naftali and Zelikow, *Presidential Recordings*, vol. 2, p. 581.

4. Naftali and Zelikow, *Presidential Recordings*, vol. 2, p. 541. The original version of the *Kennedy Tapes* transcribed this much-cited JFK term as "prime failure." May and Zelikow, *Kennedy Tapes*, p. 145.

5. See Dobbs, *One Minute to Midnight*, p. 190 ("The 'missile gap' against which Kennedy had campaigned during the 1960 presidential election did indeed exist. But it was in America's favor, not Russia's—and it was even wider than American experts believed").

6. Robert S. Norris, "The Cuban Missile Crisis: A Nuclear Order of Battle," presented at Woodrow Wilson Center, October 24, 2012, p. 10. See https://www.wilsoncenter.org/sites/default/files/2012_10_24_Norris_Cuban_Missile_Crisis_Nuclear_Order_of_Battle.pdf

7. See National Intelligence Estimate (hereafter "NIE") 11-8-61, "Soviet Capabilities for Long Range Attack," June 7, 1961, p. 22 (noting that the facilities available at the Soviet Union's arctic airfields, "together with the adverse operational conditions in the Arctic, impose limitations on the number of aircraft which can be launched for simultaneous attack"); Gareth Porter, *Perils of Dominance: Imbalance of Power and the Road to War in Vietnam* (Berkeley: University of California Press, 2005), p. 7 ("By September 1961, U.S. intelligence had very accurate data on the location of Soviet missile bases. And although the USSR now had about 100 bombers capable of reaching the United States by re-fueling on two-way missions from Arctic bases, the entire land-based Soviet strategic force was highly vulnerable to a U.S. first-strike attack").

8. See Fursenko and Naftali, *Khrushchev's Cold War*, p. 39 ("The Myasishchev-4 [M-4], designated the Bison bomber by NATO, went into serial production in 1954 but was a huge disappointment. It lacked the range to hit American targets because Myasishchev could not devise a reliable method to refuel the plane").

9. See NIE 11-4-60, "Main Trends in Soviet Capabilities and Policies, 1960–1965," December 1, 1960, Central Intelligence Agency Electronic Reading Room, p. 57 (Soviet long-range aviation "continues to consist largely of medium bombers, best suited for operations in Eurasia and capable of attacking continental US targets only through extensive use of one-way missions").

10. Haslam, *Russia's Cold War*, p. 180; Roger Hilsman, *From Nuclear Military Strategy to a World without War* (Westport, CT: Praeger, 1999), p. 60.

11. May and Zelikow, *Kennedy Tapes*, p. 32 (in the summer of 1961, although Corona "showed the Soviets hard at work on new versions of an ICBM, it provided convincing evidence that their existing ICBM arsenal numbered at most six").

12. NIE 11-8-59, "Soviet Capabilities for Strategic Attack through Mid-1964," February 9, 1960, p. 3.

13. NIE 11-8-61, "Soviet Capabilities for Long Range Attack," June 7, 1961, p. 1.

14. Leonard F. Parkinson and Logan H. Potter, "Closing the Missile Gap," Central Intelligence Agency, undated document declassified and approved for release on July 12, 2011, included in John F. Kennedy Presidential Library Symposium, *Penetrating the Iron Curtain: Resolving the Missile Gap with Technology*, https://www.cia.gov/library/publications/cold-war/resolving-the-missile-gap-with-technology/missile-gap.pdf, pp. 37–38.

15. See http://www.foia.cia.gov/sites/default/files/document_conversions/89801/DOC_0000278409.pdf

16. Id. p. 3.

17. NIE 11-8-62, "Soviet Capabilities for Strategic Attack," July 6, 1962, p. 1.

18. Fred Kaplan, *The Wizards of Armageddon* (New York: Simon & Schuster, 1983), p. 289.

19. See Taubman, *Khrushchev*, p. 379 and n. 96. See also Richard M. Pious, "The Cuban Missile Crisis and the Limits of Crisis Management," *Political Science Quarterly* 116, no. 1 (Spring 2001), p. 84 ("Even with the Soviet [Cuba] deployment, by the end of October 1962 the United States had 172 ICBMs operational and on alert and 144 Polaris missiles at sea on station. . . . The Soviets may have had 24 ICBMs operational, and the 24 SS-4s in Cuba doubled the total of missiles capable of hitting U.S. targets").

20. See Boris Chertok, *Rockets and People*, vol. 3: *Hot Days of the Cold War* (Washington, DC: NASA History Division, Office of External Relations, May 2009), p. 87.

21. Strategic Air Command, History & Research Division, *Strategic Air Command Operations in the Cuban Missile Crisis of 1962*, Historical Study No. 90, vol. 1, 1963, p. 66, http://nsarchive.gwu.edu/nsa/cuba_mis_cri/dobbs/SAC_history.pdf (hereafter "SAC Historical Study No. 90").

22. See Beschloss, *Crisis Years*, p. 328 ("Now that satellites had shown the Pentagon the location of virtually every Soviet ICBM, the system had only limited value for a first strike and almost none for a second. As the State Department intelligence chief Roger Hilsman recalled, 'The whole Soviet ICBM system was suddenly obsolescent'").

23. Kaplan, *Wizards of Armageddon*, p. 295 (the Soviet air defense system was "riddled with gaps," air-defense forces "had little value," and "the Soviets lacked the ability to coordinate an air-defense campaign and shoot down many bombers, especially if flight tactics were carefully planned").

24. NIE 11-8-62, "Soviet Capabilities for Strategic Attack," July 6, 1962, p. 4 (noting limitation of Soviet first-generation SS-6 ICBM due to its "nonstorable liquid propellants").

25. See Beschloss, *Crisis Years*, p. 328 ("Briefing Kennedy one week later [circa mid-September 1961], General Lemnitzer put the figure at ten to twenty-five (Soviet ICBMs). Unlike America's, none were in hardened silos; all were cumbersome to launch").

26. Roger Hilsman, *To Move a Nation: The Politics of Foreign Policy in the Administration of John F. Kennedy* (New York: Doubleday, 1967), pp. 162–63.

27. See May and Zelikow, *Kennedy Tapes*, p. 674 (referring to the Soviet ICBMs of the time as "monstrous weapons of doubtful reliability").

28. Haslam, *Russia's Cold War*, p. 196.

29. Nash, *Other Missiles of October*, p. 68, map 2.

30. See Niall Ferguson, *Kissinger, 1923–1968: The Idealist* (New York: Penguin, 2015), p. 382n ("The R7 that had placed *Sputnik* in orbit was the first intercontinental ballistic missile, and it had been designed specifically to deliver hydrogen bombs to U.S. targets").

31. NIE 11-8-61, "Soviet Capabilities for Long Range Attack," June 7, 1961, p. 22.

32. NIE 11-8-61, "Soviet Capabilities for Long Range Attack," June 7, 1961, p. 22.

33. NIE 11-4-61, Main Trends in Soviet Capabilities and Policies, 1961–1966, August 24, 1961, Annex A: Soviet Military Forces and Capabilities, p. 6.

34. NIE 11-4-61, Main Trends in Soviet Capabilities and Policies, 1961–1966, August 24, 1961, Annex A: Soviet Military Forces and Capabilities, p. 6. Although Annex A provided no figure for the number of one-way bombers the Soviets could deploy, an approximation of this number can be deduced from a dissenting comment on the comparable January 1962 NIE numbers provided by the assistant chief of staff, intelligence, US Air Force, who estimated that three hundred Soviet bombers would be able to carry out two-way missions and five hundred bombers able to carry out one-way missions. See http://www.foia.cia.gov/sites/default/files/document_conversions/89801/DOC_0000205719.pdf, p. 5. Using the assistant chief of staff's ratio of five to three, the "official" Annex A number of one-way bombers would most likely be approximately 333.

35. Norris, "Cuban Missile Crisis," p. 27.

36. Each assigned target was referred to as a "Designated Ground Zero" or DGZ, of which 1,060 were assigned under SIOP-62. Hilsman, *Nuclear Military Strategy*, p. 52. During the period of the Cuban missile crisis, an EWO-ready B-52 bomber "typically [carried] four H-bombs." A "typical combat mission folder carried by an SAC bomber crew" included "target identification aids" and the following additional guidance: "a high-altitude navigation chart, low-altitude operational navigation chart, the air target chart, a map of radar significant power lines and locations, the basic target graphics, the seasonal target graphics, the hard target graphics, delivery tactics, Soviet air-defense installations, and other threats on the penetration route, and the timeline of the attack (time-over-targets, bomb-release lines, etc." L. Douglas Keeney, *15 Minutes: General Curtis LeMay and the Countdown to Nuclear Annihilation* (New York: St. Martin's Press, 2011), pp. 233, 253.

37. SAC Historical Study No. 90, pp. 48, 52, 56.

38. Ken Young, *The American Bomb in Britain: US Air Forces' Strategic Presence, 1946–1964*. (Manchester: Manchester University Press, 2016), p. 134 ("All post-strike SAC aircraft were scheduled to land at 20 designated SAC overseas bases." Subsequently, concern about the vulnerability of the "recovery" bases to destruc-

tion by "enemy action," SAC identified some 156 alternative landing fields "under a scheme dubbed 'Jack Pot' . . . all within one hour's flight of the designated recovery base"). See also Keeney, *15 Minutes*, p. 100.

39. Young, *American Bomb*, p. 94.

40. Keeney, *15 Minutes*, p. 182; William E. Pinter, "Concentrating on Dispersed Operations: Answering the Emerging Antiaccess Challenge in the Pacific Rim," Air University Press, Maxwell Airforce Base, Alabama, April 2007, pp. 35–48, https://apps.dtic.mil/dtic/tr/fulltext/u2/a488573.pdf; Young, *American Bomb*, p. 94.

41. SAC Historical Study No. 90, p. 57.

42. Young, *American Bomb*, pp. 134, 266. See also Jim Wilson, *Launch Pad UK: Britain and the Cuban Missile Crisis* (Barnsley: Pen & Sword Books, 2008), p. 129.

43. Young, *American Bomb*, pp. 209, 253.

44. Young, *American Bomb*, pp. 263, 267; Wilson, *Launch Pad UK*, pp. 138–39. Wilson noted that in 1962 the combined Thor and V-bomber forces stationed in England "were capable of delivering a nuclear holocaust of 230 megatons on 230 targets" (p. 114, citing Stewart Menaul, *Countdown: Britain's Strategic Nuclear Forces* [London: Robert Hale, 2000]). During the missile crisis American General Lauris Norstad served as SACEUR.

45. Norris, "Cuban Missile Crisis," pp. 23–24, 31; Wilson, *Launch Pad UK*, pp. 114, 128. The combat radius of each of these aircraft was as follows: Canberra (950 miles); F-100 Super Sabre (600 miles); F-84 Thunderstreak (705–1,000 miles). The flight distance from Frankfurt to Moscow is approximately 1,260 miles.

46. Young, *American Bomb*, p. 266.

47. Dobbs, *One Minute to Midnight*, p. 250.

48. "Memorandum to Holders of Annexes A and B, NIE 11-4-61: 'Main Trends in Soviet Capabilities and Policies, 1961–1966,' Dated 24 August 1961," http://www.foia.cia.gov/sites/default/files/document_conversions/89801/DOC_0000205719.pdf, pp. 5–6. This meant that any Soviet effort to launch missiles from submarines required, first, that the submarine be brought close in to striking distance and, second, that the vessel surface. Both conditions carried very significant vulnerability to destruction by US antisubmarine defenses. Four Soviet attack submarines of the F-class—each equipped with a single nuclear-armed torpedo but no missiles—had been sent into the Atlantic to protect the Soviet cargo ships bound for Cuba. See *The Submarines of October: U.S. and Soviet Naval Encounters During the Cuban Missile Crisis*, National Security Archive Electronic Briefing Book No. 75, William Burr and Thomas S. Blanton, editors, http://nsarchive.gwu.edu/NSAEBB/NSAEBB75/

49. Porter, *Perils of Dominance*, p. 7; Minutes of the 506th Meeting of the National Security Council, October 21, 1962, in *FRUS*, 1961–1963, vol. 11, *Cuban Missile Crisis and Aftermath*, pp. 141–49, cited in May and Zelikow, *Kennedy Tapes*, p. 211 (Soviet missile-carrying submarines remained in their home bases during the crisis and "could not get to the [Caribbean] area in less than ten to fourteen days"). See also Haslam, *Russia's Cold War*, p. 198 (according to Soviet general Makhmut Gareev, even by March 1963, when Soviet subsurface-launched mis-

siles first came into service, "SLBMs only had an accuracy for use against economic potential and industrial infrastructure and therefore were very poor weapons for anything but retaliatory strikes").

50. Andreas Wenger, *Living with Peril: Eisenhower, Kennedy and Nuclear Weapons* (Lanham, MD: Rowman & Littlefield, 1997), p. 243.

51. Wilson, *Launch Pad UK*, p. 129.

52. Steven J. Cimbala, *Coercive Military Strategy* (self-published, 1998), pp. 50–51, table 9.

53. Beschloss, *Crisis Years*, p. 65.

54. See Blight, Allyn, and Welch, *Cuba on the Brink*, p. 23.

55. Robert J. McMahon, *The Cold War: A Very Short Introduction* (New York: Oxford University Press, 2003), p. 92.

56. Haslam, *Russia's Cold War*, p. 200.

57. Chertok, *Rockets and People*, vol. 3, p. 88.

58. Evan Thomas, *Ike's Bluff: President Eisenhower's Secret Battle to Save the World* (New York: Little, Brown, 2012), pp. 267–68.

59. David L. Snead, *The Gaither Committee, Eisenhower, and the Cold War* (Columbus: Ohio State University Press, 1999), p. 122.

60. Snead, *Gaither Committee*, p. 161; Herken, *Georgetown Set*, p. 234; Gaither Report pp. 6–7, http://nsarchive.gwu.edu/NSAEBB/NSAEBB139/nitze02.pdf. See Ferguson, *Kissinger*, p. 393 (Gaither Committee believed that "the United States could soon become vulnerable to a Soviet surprise nuclear attack if it did not accelerate the production of intercontinental and submarine-launched ballistic missiles").

61. Nash, *Other Missiles of October*, pp. 27, 36.

62. Snead, *Gaither Committee*, p. 161.

63. Norris, "Cuban Missile Crisis," p. 14.

64. Dobbs, *One Minute to Midnight*, p. 92.

65. Haslam, *Russia's Cold War*, p. 179.

66. Fursenko and Naftali, *Khrushchev's Cold War*, pp. 245–46.

67. Kaplan, *Wizards of Armageddon*, p. 295.

68. Taubman, *Khrushchev*, p. 537. Taubman incorrectly referred to the first-generation Soviet missile as the "R-16," whereas in fact it was the R-7A, referred to by the US military as the SS-6. The R-16 was a later-generation rocket that would use solid fuel and be launched from an underground silo. See Fursenko and Naftali, *Khrushchev's Cold War*, p. 246.

69. Parkinson and Potter, "Closing the Missile Gap," pp. 32–34; James Lloyd, "Death on the Steppes: The Nedelin Rocket Disaster," NASA, November 7, 2005, https://sma.nasa.gov/docs/default-source/safety-messages/safetymessage-2005-11-01-nedelinrocketdisaster-vits.pdf?sfvrsn=4

70. Fursenko and Naftali, *Khrushchev's Cold War*, p. 246.

71. Fursenko and Naftali, *Khrushchev's Cold War*, pp. 247–48. See Fursenko and Naftali, *Gamble*, p. 138 ("production of the first generation of Soviet interconti-

nental ballistic missiles [ICBMs] had been stopped, after the delivery of fewer than thirty-five of them, because of design flaws").

72. Barry Leonard, ed., *History of Strategic and Ballistic Missile Defense*, vol. 2: *1956–1972*, pp. 118–19, https://archive.org/stream/bub_gb_HoxycYhoKZkC/bub_gb_HoxycYhoKZkC_djvu.txt

Chapter 2

1. When Khrushchev set in place the plan for erecting the Berlin Wall, he made sure the process moved in a deliberate sequence that would have allowed a pause or even abandonment of the project if the West had reacted militarily. As Taubman determined in his biography of the Soviet leader: "As an extra precaution, Khrushchev decreed that the wall go up in stages; first, barbed wire, with concrete to follow only if the West acquiesced. Even so, the Soviets held their breaths on August 13, waiting to see how the Americans would react. There was a crisis atmosphere in the Foreign Ministry. When it became clear that the wire wouldn't be torn down, Sergei Khrushchev later wrote, 'Father sighed with relief. Things had turned out all right.'" Taubman, *Khrushchev*, p. 506.

2. Kempe, *Berlin 1961*, p. 281.

3. Kempe, *Berlin 1961*, p. 298.

4. An excellent discussion of Kissinger's role as a consultant to the Kennedy White House strategic nuclear policy planning is contained in Niall Ferguson's biography of Kissinger, covering his career through 1986. Ferguson, *Kissinger*, pp. 461–513. In considering why Kissinger's role remained that of a consultant, though the then-young Harvard professor longed to become a full-time member of Kennedy's administration, Ferguson offers the view that Kissinger's way in was blocked by the president's national security adviser, McGeorge Bundy, most likely based on a combination of professional jealousy and wariness that Kissinger retained ties to his first major political patron, Nelson Rockefeller, who remained a credible aspirant to the Republican Party's hopes for the presidency in 1964. In offering this explanation, the biographer was surely echoing the views of his subject that it was all a matter of "personal competitiveness." See p. 509. Yet in fairness, it would seem that a further and perhaps more plausible explanation for Kissinger's inability to penetrate the inner circle of Kennedy's national security advisers was the professor's reputation as the country's leading proponent for the proactive use of tactical nuclear weapons, a viewpoint that was anathema to the president's determination never to pull the nuclear trigger under any circumstances.

5. See http://prospect.org/article/did-us-military-plan-nuclear-first-strike-1963; Trachtenberg, *History and Strategy*, p. 224 n. 203.

6. Thomas Schelling, "Nuclear Strategy in the Berlin Crisis," July 5, 1961, *FRUS*, 1961–1963, vol. 14, *Berlin Crisis, 1961–1962* (emphasis added), Doc. 56, John F. Kennedy Library, Boston, MA (hereafter "JFKL"), National Security Files, Ger-

many, Berlin, General, https://history.state.gov/historicaldocuments/frus1961-63v14/d56

7. Kempe, *Berlin 1961*, p. 307.

8. NSAM 109, October 23, 1961, National Security Files, Meetings & Memoranda, Papers of President Kennedy, JFKL, NSC Box 332.

9. Letter from President Kennedy to General Norstad, October 20, 1961, Eisenhower Library, Norstad Papers, Subject File, Kennedy, John F., Top Secret, https://2001-2009.state.gov/r/pa/ho/frus/kennedyjf/xiv/15865.htm. See Trachtenberg, *History and Strategy*, pp. 225–26 (noting that instructions delivered to General Norstad at this time "stated that 'before any transition from non-nuclear to nuclear,' he would 'receive specific directives,' and that 'such transition would probably occur when Soviet forces sufficient to defeat non-nuclear efforts are brought into play'").

10. http://belfercenter.ksg.harvard.edu/files/CMC50/ScottSaganSIOP62TheNuclearWarPlanBriefingtoPresidentKennedyInternationalSecurity.pdf

11. Scott D. Sagan, *Moving Targets: Nuclear Strategy and National Security* (Princeton, NJ: Princeton University Press, 1989), p. 29.

12. Sagan, *Moving Targets*, p. 29.

13. Sagan, *Moving Targets*, p. 30.

14. See Ferguson, *Kissinger*, p. 493.

15. Trachtenberg, *History and Strategy*, p. 219 (citing *New York Times*, August 8, 1961, p. 8).

16. Trachtenberg, *History and Strategy*, p. 233.

17. Michael Beschloss noted that, apart from Kennedy's visit to Berlin in June 1963, the president mentioned the Berlin Wall in only three speeches, and each time only in passing. The first such mention would not occur until December 1961, during a speech in Bogotá, Columbia. See Beschloss, *Crisis Years*, p. 282.

18. Kempe, *Berlin 1961*, p. 379; Beschloss, *Crisis Years*, p. 278.

19. Kempe, *Berlin 1961*, pp. 378, 385.

20. Kempe, *Berlin 1961*, p. 388.

21. Jean Edwards Smith, *Lucius D. Clay: An American Life* (New York: Henry Holt, 1990), p. 660.

22. Fursenko and Naftali, *Khrushchev's Cold War*, p. 402.

23. *FRUS*, 1961–1963, vol. 14, *Berlin Crisis, 1961–1962*, Doc. 181, Letter from the President's Special Representative in Berlin (Clay) to President Kennedy, October 18, 1961.

24. Walter Isaacson and Evan Thomas, *The Wise Men: Six Friends and the World They Made* (New York: Simon & Schuster, 1986), pp. 456, 615.

25. As reported by Campbell Craig, General Clay spoke with the president by telephone on October 24, 1961, to discuss the mounting Berlin tensions directly. Campbell Craig, *Destroying the Village: Eisenhower and Thermonuclear War* (New York: Columbia University Press, 1998), p. 149.

26. Kempe, *Berlin 1961*, p. 454.

27. Fursenko and Naftali, *Khrushchev's Cold War*, p. 402.

28. Kempe, *Berlin 1961*, p. 418. Kempe cited later personal correspondence by General Bruce C. Clarke, the US Army's commander in Europe, indicating that the moment he had learned of the Clay plan in late September he "stopped it and got rid of what had been done" (p. 418). But, as will be seen, that was not, in fact, the last that would be seen of Clay's tank bulldozer brainchild.

29. Kempe, *Berlin 1961*, pp. 475–76.

30. Raymond L. Garthoff, "Berlin 1961: The Record Corrected," *Foreign Policy* 84 (Fall 1991), pp. 147–48; Kempe, *Berlin 1961*, p. 418.

31. Nikita S. Khrushchev, *Khrushchev Remembers: The Glasnost Tapes*, trans. and ed. Jerrold L. Schechter with Vyacheslav Luchkov (Boston: Little, Brown, 1990), p. 459.

32. *FRUS*, 1961–1963, vol. 14, *Berlin Crisis, 1961–1962*, Doc. 193. Rusk's October 26 telegram was in response to Clay's telegram nos. 834 (October 25, 1961) and 835 (October 26, 1961), both of which sought instructions regarding the proposed "raid in force." Clay's two telegrams can be found in the JFKL, Papers of President Kennedy, National Security Files, Countries, Germany, Berlin, General Lucius Clay 8/28/61–10/31/61, Box 86.

33. Kempe, *Berlin 1961*, p. 474. Rusk's telegram to Clay was sent on October 26, 1961: see *FRUS*, 1961–1963, vol. 14, *Berlin Crisis, 1961–1962*, Doc. 193, Telegram from the Department of State to the Mission at Berlin, Washington, October 26, 1961, 8:11 p.m.

34. Kempe, *Berlin 1961*, p. 477.

35. On October 23, 1961, the day after the initial border-crossing incident involving Allan Lightner and his wife had been resolved when a senior Soviet official arrived on the scene, Clay had told the press that "the 'fiction is now destroyed' that it was the East Germans who were responsible for preventing Allied access to East Berlin." Kempe, *Berlin 1961*, p. 454. As Clay would later explain to his biographer, "But these were Russian tanks, not East German tanks. It was obvious that the Russians did not trust the East Germans in this situation. As soon as they did that, I was no longer concerned. The Russians had come out of hiding, and I was sure they were not going to do anything." Smith, *Lucius D. Clay*, p. 660.

36. The Kennedy-Clay open-line telephone conversation, which was being monitored and recorded by the Soviets, included a jovial exchange that has gone down in history as a kind of signature display of American doughtiness in the face of crisis. In response to the president's question whether Clay was keeping his nerve, the general responded: "Mr. President, we're not worried about our nerves. We're worrying about those of you people in Washington." Craig, *Destroying the Village*, p. 150.

37. Garthoff, "Berlin 1961," p. 152.

38. Fursenko and Naftali, *Khrushchev's Cold War*, p. 403. See also Kempe, *Berlin 1961*, p. 478.

39. National Defense University, General Lyman L. Lemnitzer Papers. My explanatory comments are added in brackets:

Top Secret [scratched out]

27 Oct

White House Meeting on Friedrichstrasse [title]

P, Sec State, Sec Def, Kohler, Nitze, Atty General, Bundy, Hillebrant, L.

1. Berlin is low level Autobahn

2. I reported latest events—Norstad cable

3. Clay -

Probes are considered to have accomplished purpose

Norstad—Temporarily defer probes with military force or escort [accompanied by checkmark]

pending or until US govt goes back to Moscow [accompanied by checkmark]

Refer to Gro[myko] & Thom[pson] meetings as unsatisfactory

Mil[itary] pers[onnel] will be in uniform

State will try to get uniform OK & Fr[iedrichstrasse] agreement re: mil[itary] personnel

Importance to US interests not a setback—will not

Will not send in US civilians who show passes to VOPOS

Will send in two [drivers?]

40. David E. Murphy, Sergei A. Kondrashev, and George Bailey, *Battle Ground Berlin: CIA vs KGB in the Cold War* (New Haven: Yale University Press, 1997), p. 392.

41. The curious episode of the president making an "open air" call to General Clay on October 27, 1961, would be duplicated a year later when on October 24, 1962, General Thomas Power, the SAC commander, would use the telephone to issue verbal instructions to his command regarding his momentous upgrade of the air force's strategic readiness to DEFCON-2. Power's telephone message would also be transmitted on open air (*en clair*) channels, guaranteeing that the Soviets would be able to intercept the message simultaneously. Some commentators have questioned General Power's action, attributing it to personal bravado. See Raymond L. Garthoff, *Reflections on the Cuban Missile Crisis—Revised to Include New Revelations from Soviet and Cuban Sources* (Washington, DC: Brookings, 1989), p. 62. It is evident, however, that the underlying decision moving force readiness to DEFCON-2 was made by the president (see Dobbs, *One Minute to Midnight*, p. 96) and that the Soviets learned of this action even before Power's message when they intercepted the preceding directive from the Joint Chiefs of Staff authorizing General Power to upgrade SAC readiness to DEFCON-2. The JCS order was also transmitted *en clair*, immediately intercepted by GRU officials in Washington, and promptly reported to Moscow by cable from Dobrynin. See Fursenko and Naftali, "Soviet Intelligence," p. 79 (citing Dobrynin to MFA, October 25, 1962, Folio 3, List 65, File 905, pp. 69–70, Archive of the President of the Russian Federation.

42. *FRUS*, 1961–1963, vol. 14, *Berlin Crisis, 1961–1962*, Doc. 197, https://history.state.gov/historicaldocuments/frus1961-63v14/d197. See also Kempe, *Berlin 1961*, pp. 478–79.

43. Robert F. Kennedy, Oral History, JFKL, vol. 1, March 1, 1964, p. 69 ("They were in their tanks, and I asked, got in touch with Bolshakov and said the president would like them to take their tanks out of there . . . in twenty-four hours. He said he'd speak to Khrushchev, and they took their tanks out in twenty-four hours"). See Beschloss, *Crisis Years*, p. 334n ("One pattern in Robert Kennedy's discussion of the meetings with Bolshakov and other Russians in 1964 and 1965 oral histories is his inclination to suggest that the Soviets caved in at crucial moments to unilateral demands by himself and the President without mentioning American concessions that were actually the key to solutions. The most prominent example of this is his treatment of the bargaining that ended the Cuban Missile Crisis, distorted to suggest that he and his brother were tougher bargainers than they actually were").

44. Fursenko and Naftali, *Khrushchev's Cold War*, p. 404.

45. See Frederick Kempe, "Kennedy's Showdown at Checkpoint Charlie," http://blogs.reuters.com/berlin1961/2011/06/14/kennedys-showdown-at-checkpoint-charlie/. See also Kempe, *Berlin 1961*, p. 479 ("What no one recorded were the details of the [RFK-Bolshakov] agreement. However, from that point forward, the U.S. stopped its military escorts of civilians, and Clay no longer challenged East German authority at the border points. Whatever contingencies Clay had scripted to knock through portions of the Wall were shelved, and the shovels mounted to tanks to knock portions of the Wall were removed and put in storage").

46. Fursenko and Naftali, *Khrushchev's Cold War*, pp. 404–7.

47. Cate, *Ides of August*, p. 491.

48. Craig, *Destroying the Village*, p. 150.

49. Central Intelligence Agency, "A Handbook on the Berlin Problem, December 27, 1961, p. 67, https://archive.org/details/CentralIntelligenceAgencyBerlinHandbook

50. Hershberg, introduction to "Trigger for Khrushchev's Deployment," p. 321.

51. Richard D. Williamson, *First Steps toward Détente: American Diplomacy in the Berlin Crisis, 1958–1963* (Lanham MD: Lexington Books, 2012), p. 174 (citing Rusk memo for Kennedy, "Contingency Planning for Soviet-GDR Peace Treaty," August 2, 1962, JFKL, National Security Files, Box 84A, Folder 8/62).

52. Naftali, *Presidential Recordings*, vol. 1, p. 269.

53. Naftali, *Presidential Recordings*, vol. 1, p. 636. The editors of *Presidential Recordings* explained in a note that the president's comment that "we won't go over" referred to refraining from going over to East Berlin (p. 636).

54. Cate, *Ides of August*, p. 491 ("By one of those ironies that so frequently mark the course of human affairs, the Friedrichstrasse confrontation, although tactically a victory, undermined rather than enhanced Clay's overall prestige").

55. Craig, *Destroying the Village*, pp. 150–51.

56. Taylor, *Berlin Wall*, p. 287.

57. Taylor, *Berlin Wall*, p. 281 (Khrushchev had told Konev "to match the Americans exactly. But no shooting").

58. Taylor, *Berlin Wall*, p. 286.

59. Khrushchev would later write in his memoirs: "This was how we gained de facto recognition of the establishment of borders and the transfer of functions for guarding them to the German Democratic Republic. It ceased being a cause of aggravation in our relations." Khrushchev, *Nikita Khrushchev*, p. 466.

60. Here is how Khrushchev's son, Sergei, would describe his father's approach to the Berlin settlement process: "Father proposed a solution. We had to make the first step, to blink, and the tension would be relieved. The Soviet tanks and accompanying infantry were ordered to pull back into the side streets and, after turning off their engines, remain concealed there." Khrushchev, *Nikita Khrushchev*, p. 466.

Chapter 3

1. Fursenko and Naftali, *Khrushchev's Cold War*, p. 7.
2. Fursenko and Naftali, *Khrushchev's Cold War*, p. 232.
3. *Bulletin of the Atomic Scientists*, April 1988, pp. 41–42; Fursenko and Naftali, *Khrushchev's Cold War*, p. 255.
4. Fursenko and Naftali, *Khrushchev's Cold War*, p. 248.
5. Telegram, Salinger to the President, August 8, 1961, cited in Wenger, *Living with Peril*, p. 219.
6. Fred I. Greenstein, *The Presidential Difference: Leadership Style from FDR to Barack Obama*, 3rd ed. (Princeton, NJ: Princeton University Press, 2009), p. 65.
7. See Herken, *Georgetown Set*, p. 199 ("Nitze's NSC 68 had identified 1954 as the so-called year of maximum danger, when the Soviet Union's nuclear capability would be such that 'the Kremlin might be tempted to strike swiftly and with stealth'"). See also Norman Freedman, *The Fifty-Year War: Conflict and Strategy in the Cold War* (Annapolis, MD: Naval Institute Press, 2000), p. 254; Beschloss, *Crisis Years*, p. 63n.
8. Kaplan, *Wizards of Armageddon*, p. 287; Beschloss, *Crisis Years*, p. 65.
9. Fursenko and Naftali, *Khrushchev's Cold War*, p. 400.
10. Stephen Dowling, "The Monster Atomic Bomb That Was Too Big to Use," *BBC Future*, August 16, 2017, http://www.bbc.com/future/story/20170816-the-monster-atomic-bomb-that-was-too-big-to-use
11. See http://www2.gwu.edu/~nsarchiv/NSAEBB/NSAEBB56/BerlinC6.pdf
12. Beschloss, *Crisis Years*, p. 331.
13. Beschloss, *Crisis Years*, pp. 351, 701.
14. Wenger, *Living with Peril*, p. 244.
15. Thomas, *Ike's Bluff*, p. 15.
16. Thomas, *Ike's Bluff*, p. 15.
17. Kennedy himself had joined the chorus of "missile gap" critics during the presidential campaign. In a speech to the American Legion Convention on October 18, 1960, Kennedy urged that "we must step up crash programs on the ultimate weapon. The Polaris submarine, the Minuteman missile, which will eventually close the missile gap." See http://www.presidency.ucsb.edu/ws/?pid=74096

18. 1961 Report of the Net Evaluation Subcommittee, National Security Council, pp. x, xvii, National Security Archive's Nuclear Documentation Project, George Washington University, https://nsarchive2.gwu.edu/nukevault/ebb480/

19. Notes on National Security Council Meeting, July 20, 1961, http://nsarchive.gwu.edu/nukevault/ebb480/. Despite the president's order to maintain secrecy, news of the July 20, 1961, meeting of the Net Evaluation Subcommittee somehow eventually leaked and found its way into a column written by journalist Fletcher Knebel in the November 21, 1961, issue of *Look* magazine. The president was evidently dismayed, and McGeorge Bundy subsequently provided him with a memorandum pointing out numerous errors in the article. See Bundy's November 21, 1961, Memorandum for the President, http://nsarchive.gwu.edu/nukevault/ebb480/

20. See http://belfercenter.ksg.harvard.edu/files/CMC50/ScottSaganSIOP-62TheNuclearWarPlanBriefingtoPresidentKennedyInternationalSecurity.pdf; Lemnitzer Daily Journal, September 13, 1961 ("4:30 President—SIOP"), General Lemnitzer Private Collection, National Defense University, Box 56.

21. Scott Ritter, *Dangerous Ground: America's Failed Arms Control Policy, from FDR to Obama* (New York: Nation Books, 2010), p. 99.

22. Beschloss, *Crisis Years*, pp. 308–9.

23. Richard K. Betts, *Nuclear Blackmail and Nuclear Balance* (Washington, DC: Brookings Institution, 1987), p. 103.

24. President Kennedy had stated at a press conference on February 8, 1961, "We have the realization that the United States will not strike first, and therefore we have to consider what will be available to the United States if an attack took place on us, not only in missiles, but also in the other arms of the arsenal, SAC, the Navy, Polaris and all the rest." *Public Papers of the Presidents of the United States—John F. Kennedy, 1961*, p. 67.

25. Deputy defense secretary Roswell Gilpatric gave a speech on January 21, 1962, in which he stated: "The reason we have to be ahead, the reason that we have to have an edge in our military power is because we have foreclosed ourselves from the initiative in the sense that we will never strike first in a preemptive attack." Tristram Coffin Reports, *Bulletin of the Atomic Scientists*, April 1962, p. 32.

26. http://www.oldtimeradiodownloads.com/historical/meet-the-press/meet-the-press-61-09-24-robert-f-kennedy. See Lawrence Freedman, *Kennedy's Wars: Berlin, Cuba, Laos and Vietnam* (New York: Oxford University Press, 2000), p. 433 and n. 38. The next day, an article by Joseph Alsop appeared in the *Washington Post* (September 25, 1961, p. A13) that summarized the great advantage in nuclear firepower possessed by the United States and ended with a similar warning: "For the present, what is chiefly important is to make Khrushchev understand that if he pushes the Berlin crisis to the ultimate crunch, the great power which the United States still possesses will not remain unused."

27. *FRUS*, 1961–1963, vol. 5, *Soviet Union*, p. 298, Memorandum of Conversation, September 25, 1961.

28. See https://news.google.com/newspapers?nid=888&dat=19620202&id=mQVZAAAAIBAJ&sjid=e1IDAAAAIBAJ&pg=7133,614950&hl=en

29. Fursenko and Naftali, *Khrushchev's Cold War*, p. 424 and n. 32; Fursenko and Naftali, *Gamble*, p. 155. See also Christopher Andrew and Vasili Mitrokhin, *The Mitrokhin Archive* (London: Penguin, 2000), pp. 237–38 (characterizing the GRU intelligence assessment as "woefully inaccurate").

30. See Nash, *Other Missiles of October*, pp. 1, 103; see also James M. Grimwood and Frances Strowd, "History of the Jupiter Missile System," US Army Ordnance Missile Command, July 27, 1962, p. 104 (gives April 1962 as the operational date).

31. Albert Wohlstetter, "The Delicate Balance of Terror," *Foreign Affairs* 37 (January 1959), p. 229. See also Yoshikazo Sakamoto, "Unilateral Initiative as an Alternative Strategy," in Yoshikazo Sakamoto, ed., *Strategic Doctrines and Their Alternatives* (New York: Gordon and Breach Science Publishers, 1987), p. 120.

32. Nash, *Other Missiles of October*, p. 96 (emphasis added).

33. Nash, *Other Missiles of October*, p. 174.

34. Stewart Alsop, "Kennedy's Grand Strategy," *Saturday Evening Post*, March 31, 1962; Herken, *Georgetown Set*, p. 262; Taubman, *Khrushchev*, p. 536 and n. 22; James W. Douglass, *JFK and the Unspeakable: Why He Died and Why It Matters* (New York: Simon & Schuster, 2010), p. 237. It was probably to this magazine article that McGeorge Bundy was referring when he noted that the president "watched constantly to prevent the appearance of belligerence" and "made his dissatisfaction plain" when in "one magazine account" a "single phrase out of context was seized upon by Soviet propaganda." McGeorge Bundy, "The Presidency and the Peace," *Foreign Affairs* 42 (April 1964), p. 356.

35. Fursenko and Naftali, *Gamble*, pp. 178, 195–96.

36. Fursenko and Naftali, *Gamble*, p. 185 (citing Dobrynin to MFA, June 4, 1962, Folio 3, List 66, File 313, pp. 96–97, APRF). See also Evans, *Robert Kennedy* p. 206 (calling Kennedy's comments to Bolshakov "remarkably indiscreet").

37. Naftali, *Presidential Recordings*, vol. 1, p. 187. The president was furious when he learned of the leak and immediately ordered his brother to launch an FBI investigation, which included wiretapping Baldwin's private telephone line (p. 187). The Kremlin might well have believed this was an authorized leak, however, representing an official effort to intimidate them.

38. http://www2.gwu.edu/~nsarchiv/bayofpigs/chron.html. See James G. Hershberg, "Before 'The Missiles of October': Did Kennedy Plan a Military Strike on Cuba?," in James A. Nathan, ed., *The Cuban Missile Crisis Revisited* (New York: St. Martin's Press, 1992), p. 243.

39. Thomas, *Robert Kennedy*, p. 149.

40. Fursenko and Naftali, *Gamble*, p. 152. Immediately following this meeting attended by an official State Department translator, there ensued at Kennedy's initiative a two-way private meeting between Adzhubei and the president at which Bolshakov served as the sole translator. Hershberg, introduction to "Trigger for Khrushchev's Deployment," p. 319.

41. Hershberg, introduction to "Trigger for Khrushchev's Deployment," p. 319.

It is interesting to compare Adzhubei's description of Kennedy's comments on Cuba/Hungary with the considerably more succinct description provided in the "Memorandum of Conversation" prepared by the State Department's official interpreter, Alexander Akalovsky: "The President pointed out that the USSR would have the same reaction if a hostile group arose in the vicinity of its borders. In this connection, the President referred to the Soviet reaction to the Hungarian uprising." *FRUS*, 1961–1963, vol. 5, *Soviet Union*, Doc. 150, https://1997-2001.state.gov/about_state/history/vol_v/150_159.html

42. Fursenko and Naftali, "Soviet Intelligence," p. 71. See also Fursenko and Naftali, *Khrushchev's Cold War*, pp. 420–21 (Kennedy's comments "suggested to the Soviet leader that Kennedy felt strong enough to challenge Soviet interests in Europe and the Caribbean and was not about to budge in negotiations"); Hershberg, introduction to "Trigger for Khrushchev's Deployment," pp. 316–23.

43. Brugioni, *Eyeball to Eyeball*, pp. 80–81.

44. See Fursenko and Naftali, "Soviet Intelligence," p. 74 and n. 79. See also Mark J. White, *The Cuban Missile Crisis* (London: Macmillan, 1996), p. 59 ("And to Khrushchev, [the Lantphibex-62 exercise] may have spurred him or at least strengthened his resolve to make a decision, the potential consequences of which made it the most grave in the history of the Cold War"); Garthoff, *Reflections*, p. 6.

45. Hershberg, "Before the Missiles," p. 250.

46. Brugioni, *Eyeball to Eyeball*, p. 221. An Editorial Note of the Avalon Project—Cuban Missile Crisis at Yale University stated that Operation PHIBRIGLEX was scheduled to last from October 15 to October 30. http://avalon.law.yale.edu/20th_century/msc_cuba017.asp. See also Norman Polmar and John D. Gresham, *DEFCON-2: Standing on the Brink of Nuclear War during the Cuban Missile Crisis* (Hoboken, NJ: John Wiley & Sons, 2006), pp. 133 ("As part of these preparations for an actual assault against Cuba, in addition to Atlantic Fleet marines, a ten thousand-man marine brigade from the West Coast had embarked in amphibious ships and was steaming toward the Panama Canal and the Caribbean. The West Coast marines had been training specifically for a landing in Cuba").

47. See Hershberg, "Before the Missiles," p. 255; Garthoff, *Reflections*, p. 60.

48. Brugioni, *Eyeball to Eyeball*, p. 221. See Polmar and Gresham, *DEFCON-2*, p. 133.

49. Dobbs, *One Minute to Midnight*, pp. 17, 104. See also http://www.smithsonianmag.com/smart-news/never-before-seen-photos-taken-50-years-ago-during-preparations-for-cuba-invasion-77664326/?no-ist

50. See NSAM 181, Box 338, Cuba (B) 9/62, JFKL, http://fas.org/irp/offdocs/nsam-jfk/nsam181.htm

51. Even the "Plan B Plus" nomenclature seemed to be fluid. An August 16, 1962, file memorandum prepared by CIA director McCone summarized a meeting of the Special Action Group (Augmented) held that day in which General Lansdale discussed "his Plan B Augmented," and in which the word "sabotage" appeared several times. *FRUS*, 1961–1963, vol. 10, *Cuba, January 1961–September 1962*, Doc. 378.

52. *FRUS*, 1961–1963, vol. 10, *Cuba, January 1961–September 1962*, Doc. 399.

53. Minutes of Meetings of Special Action Group (Augmented) on Mongoose, September 6 and 14, 1962, released under the John F. Kennedy Assassination Records Collection Act of 1992, October 26, 2017.

54. Thomas, *Robert Kennedy*, p. 203.

55. Memorandum from William K. Harvey to Brigadier General E.G. Lansdale, Subject: Operation MONGOOSE—Sabotage Operations, October 11, 1962, released under the John F. Kennedy Assassination Records Collection Act of 1992, October 26, 2017.

56. Thomas, *Robert Kennedy*, pp. 211–12.

57. Beschloss, *Crisis Years*, pp. 331, 351. See also Richard Ned Lebow and Janice Gross Stein, *We All Lost the Cold War* (Princeton, NJ: Princeton University Press, 1994), p. 49 (the president's actions "had the unanticipated consequence of convincing Khrushchev of the need to protect the Soviet Union and Cuba from American military and political challenges"); Brugioni, *Eyeball to Eyeball*, p. 81 (quoting Malinovsky: "These declarations correspond to the conception of preventive war using nuclear and other weapons of mass destruction, contained in the military doctrine of the United States, and clearly show the aggressive trend in American military plans"); Herken, *Georgetown Set*, p. 262 ("Immediately after Stewart's *Post* article appeared, the Russian leader ordered Soviet military forces to heightened alert, in a tacit signal of his displeasure").

58. Taubman, *Khrushchev*, p. 536.

59. Fursenko and Naftali, *Gamble*, p. 177.

60. Beschloss, *Crisis Years*, pp. 393, 437.

61. Seymour Topping, "Soviet Denounces U.S. on War Aims," *New York Times*, April 1, 1962; see Hufstader at http://patch.com/connecticut/avon/bp--the-cold-wars-deadly-pitfall-misunderstanding-the95eaac2803

62. Herken, *Georgetown Set*, p. 262 and n. 35.

63. Dobbs, *One Minute to Midnight*, p. 37.

64. Fursenko and Naftali, *Khrushchev's Cold War*, p. 246.

65. Fursenko and Naftali, *Khrushchev's Cold War*, pp. 413–14.

66. Fursenko and Naftali, *Khrushchev's Cold War*, p. 414.

67. Fursenko and Naftali, *Khrushchev's Cold War*, p. 414.

68. Fursenko and Naftali, *Khrushchev's Cold War*, p. 415. See also Haslam, *Russia's Cold War*, p. 200.

Chapter 4

1. Khrushchev, *Khrushchev Remembers*, cited in Taubman, *Khrushchev*, p. 573.

2. This method of reinforcing the disinformation campaign by repetition on numerous occasions and in identical formulations across multiple communication channels was known during the Cold War as *kombinatsiya*, "combination."

3. Hilsman, *To Move a Nation*, p. 165; Roger Hilsman, *The Cuban Missile Crisis: The Struggle over Policy* (London: Praeger, 1996), p. 20.

4. Dobrynin, *In Confidence*, pp. 68–69. Kennedy would later claim that Dobrynin assured him specifically at the September 4 meeting that the Soviets had not sent any ground-to-ground missiles to Cuba.

5. Theodore C. Sorensen, Special Counsel to the President, September 6, 1962, Memorandum for the Files, *FRUS*, 1961–1963, vol. 10, *Cuba, January 1961–September 1962*, Doc. 415 (emphasis added); Sorensen, *Kennedy*, p. 668. A later CIA analysis of the "flat lie" theory would describe Dobrynin's comments to Sorensen as "seriously misleading" but "still short of a flat lie." See Central Intelligence Agency, "The Soviet Missile Base Venture in Cuba," CIA/RSS, DD/I Staff Working Paper, February 17, 1964, p. 80, https://www.cia.gov/library/readingroom/docs/1964-02-27.pdf (hereafter "CIA/DDI Venture").

6. Garthoff, *Reflections*, p. 29.

7. Garthoff, *Reflections*, p. 30; Hilsman, *Cuban Missile Crisis*, p. 20.

8. Barton J. Bernstein, "Reconsidering the Missile Crisis: Dealing with the Problems of the American Jupiters in Turkey," in Nathan, *Cuban Missile Crisis Revisited*, p. 66.

9. For a further discussion of the exact date of this meeting, see chapter 8.

10. Georgy Bolshakov, "The Hot Line: The Secret Communication Channel between John Kennedy and Nikita Khrushchev," *New Times* 5 (1989), p. 42. Robert Kennedy would later state that Bolshakov had told him at this meeting that Khrushchev's message was different and more specific: that no "surface-to-surface missiles" would be sent to Cuba. For an assessment of the conflicting accounts of Georgi Bolshakov and Robert Kennedy, see chapter 8.

11. Chester Bowles, *Promises to Keep: My Years in Public Life, 1941–1969* (New York: Harper & Row, 1971), p. 418; Memorandum from the Ambassador at Large (Bowles) to President Kennedy, October 13, 1962, *FRUS*, 1961–1963, vol. 11, *Cuban Missile Crisis and Aftermath*; see also Taubman, *Khrushchev*, p. 556 (incorrectly placing the meeting on October 15). Note that Brugioni (*Eyeball to Eyeball*, p. 176) incorrectly suggests Dobrynin denied the presence of "offensive missiles" in response to Bowles's question using that term, whereas Bowles's file memorandum makes no reference to missiles and cites only Dobrynin's party line assurance that there were no "offensive weapons." See also Hilsman, *To Move a Nation*, p. 166, accurately referring to "offensive weapons."

12. Kohler cable 133, *FRUS*, 1961–1963, vol. 15, *Berlin Crisis, 1961–1962*, https://history.state.gov/historicaldocuments/frus1961-63v15/d133; Hilsman, *To Move a Nation*, p. 166.

13. Hilsman, *To Move a Nation*, p. 199; http://microsites.jfklibrary.org/cmc/oct18/doc1/html

14. President Eisenhower had sought the recommendations of an expert Technological Capabilities Panel of the White House's Science Advisory Committee on the question whether to develop and deploy IRBM missiles. The Killian Committee, named for the panel's chairman, James R. Killian, supported development and deployment of these weapons in large part on the basis of defensive

purposes exemplified by the title of the committee's report: "Meeting the Threat of Surprise Attack." See Nash, *Other Missiles of October*, p. 7 and n. 5.

15. Text of Declaration and Communique, December 19, *Department of State Bulletin* 38 (January 6, 1958), pp. 13 et seq.

16. Nash, *Other Missiles of October*, p. 11 ("Eisenhower still supported the deployment of IRBMs for political reasons—first, to develop a ballistic missile to facilitate the deterrence of Soviet *threats* as soon as possible, and second, to help repair the Anglo-American relationship [after the Suez crisis]").

17. Nash, *Other Missiles of October*, p. 23 (quoting from Secretary of State John Foster Dulles's announcement of the IRBM base offers to NATO allies at the organization's December 1957 meeting in Paris: "If this council so desires, and in order to strengthen NATO's deterrent power, the United States is prepared to make available to other NATO countries intermediate-range ballistic missiles, for deployment in accordance with the plans of SACEUR [Supreme Allied Commander Europe]").

18. Robert A. Divine, *The Sputnik Challenge* (New York: Oxford University Press, 1993), p. 193.

19. Divine, *Sputnik Challenge*, p. 193.

20. Beschloss, *Crisis Years*, p. 382.

21. Nash, *Other Missiles of October*, p. 185 n. 14.

22. North Atlantic Treaty Organization, "NATO's Nuclear Deterrence Policy and Forces," May 17, 2018, https://www.nato.int/cps/em/natohq/topics_50068.htm; Bojan Pancevski, "'Nuclear Sharing' Stirs Debate in Berlin," *Wall Street Journal*, February 13, 2019, p. A8.

23. Nash, *Other Missiles of October*, p. 101.

24. Zelikow and May, *Presidential Recordings*, vol. 3, p. 47.

25. Nash, *Other Missiles of October*, p. 99 (citing Khrushchev's reference to the US missiles deployed in Turkey and Iran followed by his comment: "The USSR is stronger than Turkey and Iran, just as the U.S. is stronger than Cuba. This situation may cause miscalculation").

26. Taubman, *Khrushchev*, p. 541.

27. Taubman, *Khrushchev*, p. 546. Not surprisingly, the Kennedy administration took exactly the opposite position. By the time the Cuban missile crisis had become a public event, administration officials were working from talking points that proclaimed the US Jupiters in Turkey were a defensive response to Soviet threats, whereas the Soviet missiles in Cuba could "only be assumed to be aggressive." Nash, *Other Missiles of October*, p. 122 (citing Tobin, "Attempts to Equate Soviet Missile Bases," 1; official replies to reporters' questions, Christian Science Monitor, October 25, 1962, 1; Thomas Sorensen, "Information Policy Guidance on Cuba," 3; MemCon, October 22, 1962, 5:00 p.m., (drafted October 24), McAuliffe, *CIA Documents*, p. 277.) See also Bernstein, "Reconsidering the Missile Crisis," p. 64.

28. Nash, *Other Missiles of October*, p. 63.

29. Nash, *Other Missiles of October*, p. 103, table 2.

30. Taubman, *Khrushchev*, p. 541. See also Nash, *Other Missiles of October*, p. 106 (Khrushchev vowed to "get even" with the United States for its "intolerable provocation"); Khrushchev, *Khrushchev Remembers*, p. 174 ("[We] were not inventing anything new. We were just copying the methods used against us by our adversaries when they encircled us with bases").

31. Fursenko and Naftali, *Gamble*, p. 182.

32. Taubman, *Khrushchev*, p. 545.

33. Fursenko and Naftali, *Gamble*, p. 196.

34. Fursenko and Naftali, *Gamble*, p. 196.

35. Naftali and Zelikow, *Presidential Recordings*, vol. 2, p. 451.

36. Naftali and Zelikow, *Presidential Recordings*, vol. 2, p. 410.

37. Naftali and Zelikow, *Presidential Recordings*, vol. 2, p. 451; Nash, *Other Missiles of October*, p. 118.

38. See Bernstein, "Reconsidering the Missile Crisis," p. 59 (the Jupiter missiles in Turkey were "liquid-fuel IRBMs, taking hours to fire, quite inaccurate, very vulnerable, and hence only useful militarily for a first strike and thus provocative"); Young, *American Bomb*, p. 95 (citing SAC commander in chief Thomas Power's objection to both Thor and Jupiter missiles for being "fragile, vulnerable, difficult to fuel and too slow in alert reaction"). Tellingly, Roger Hilsman, the chief of the State Department's Bureau of Intelligence and Research, would later make the same point about the Soviet missiles installed in Cuba: "Both the MRBMs and the IRBMs were above ground and 'soft'—very vulnerable to attack—and therefore useful mainly in a first strike." Hilsman, *Cuban Missile Crisis*, p. 77.

39. Nash, *Other Missiles of October*, p. 174.

40. The McGhee memorandum is held in the Papers of President Kennedy, National Security File, Regional Security, NATO Weapons, Cables, Turkey, Box 226A, JFKL.

41. Jack S. Levy, "The Offensive/Defensive Balance of Military Technology: A Theoretical and Historical Analysis," *International Studies Quarterly* 28 (1984), p. 226. See also, e.g., Keir A. Lieber, "Grasping the Technological Peace: The Offense-Defense Balance and International Security," *International Security* 25, no. 1 (Summer 2000), reprinted in Michael E. Brown, Owen R. Cote Jr., Sean M. Lynne-Jones, and Steven E. Miller, eds., *Offense, Defense and War: An International Security Reader* (Cambridge: MIT Press, 2004), p. 373 ("Proponents have struggled to provide objective and consistent criteria for distinguishing between offensive and defensive technologies. The few explicit discussions of differentiation criteria have often been supported by ambiguous arguments or contradictory examples").

42. Julian E. Zelizer, *Arsenal of Democracy: The Politics of National Security from World War II to the War on Terrorism* (New York: Basic Books, 2010), p. 157.

43. McGeorge Bundy, *Danger and Survival: Choices about the Bomb in the First Fifty Years* (New York: Random House, 1988), p. 392.

44. Sorensen, *Kennedy*, p. 671.

45. SNIE 85-3-62, "The Military Buildup in Cuba," September 19, 1962, Conclu-

sions para. C (emphasis added). See Mary S. McAuliffe, ed., *CIA Documents on the Cuban Missile Crisis* (Washington, DC: History Staff, Central Intelligence Agency, 1992), Doc. 33, p. 91.

46. See Khrushchev to Kennedy, October 26, 1962, in *FRUS*, 1961–1963, vol. 11, *Cuban Missile Crisis and Aftermath*, pp. 235–36.

47. Dobrynin, *In Confidence*, p. 71n.

48. David G. Coleman, "The Missiles of November, December, January, February . . . : The Problem of Acceptable Risk in the Cuban Missile Crisis Settlement," *Journal of Cold War Studies* 9, no. 3 (Summer 2007), p. 20, citing Lawrence Freedman, *The Evaluation of Nuclear Strategy*, 3rd ed. (Houndmills, UK: Palgrave Macmillan, 2003), pp. 105–6.

49. Nash, *Other Missiles of October*, p. 124.

50. Beschloss, *Crisis Years*, p. 496.

51. Elie Abel, *The Missile Crisis* (Philadelphia: J.B. Lippincott, 1966), pp. 13–14 (emphasis added).

52. Naftali and Zelikow, *Presidential Recordings*, vol. 2, p. 534.

53. Dean Rusk, Oral History, recorded interview by Dennis J. O'Brien, February 19, 1970, pp. 118–19, JFKL.

54. Brugioni, *Eyeball to Eyeball*, pp. 126.

55. Taubman, *Khrushchev*, p. 545.

56. Andrei Kokoshin, "Reflections on the Cuban Missile Crisis in the Context of Strategic Stability," Harvard Kennedy School, Belfer Center for Science and International Affairs, September 2012, https://www.ciaonet.org/attach ments/21711/uploads

57. Professors Allison and Zelikow posed three "central questions" about the Cuban missile crisis that had "eluded satisfactory answers" even after three decades of close study, of which the first question was, "Why did the Soviet Union place offensive missiles in Cuba?" Graham Allison and Philip Zelikow, *Essence of Decision: Explaining the Cuban Missile Crisis*, 2nd ed. (New York: Longman, 1999), p. 1.

58. Beschloss, *Crisis Years*, p. 447.

59. Raymond Garthoff, "US Intelligence in the Cuban Missile Crisis," in Blight and Welch, *Intelligence*, p. 24.

60. Allison and Zelikow, *Essence of Decision*, pp. 1, 107.

61. Beth A. Fischer, "Perception, Intelligence Errors and the Cuban Missile Crisis," in Blight and Welch, *Intelligence*, p. 158.

62. Aleksandr Fursenko, ed., *Prezidium TsK KPSS*, p. 617 (cited in Sergey Radchenko, "On Hedgehogs and Passions," in Scott and Hughes, *Cuban Missile Crisis*, p. 186). See also Ferguson, *Kissinger*, p. 549 ("What the Soviets did not know for sure but strongly suspected was that the Americans were already contemplating an attack on Cuba, even before the scale of the Soviet operation was clear. Both air strikes and a naval blockade were already under discussion in September"). The full-scale invasion was indeed being practiced by two US marine and two airborne divisions that were being transported by forty warships for a full-scale invasion exercise to be launched against the Caribbean island of Vieques on Oc-

tober 17, 1962. The exercise was initially delayed by stormy weather and ultimately transformed into a stand-by Cuba invasion force after the U-2 photographed the Soviet missile bases. Dobbs, *One Minute to Midnight*, pp. 17, 104. See also http://www.smithsonianmag.com/smart-news/never-before-seen-photos-taken-50-years-ago-during-preparations-for-cuba-invasion-77664326/?no-ist

63. Quoted in Blight, Allyn, and Welch, *Cuba on the Brink*, p. 335 n. 13.

64. Laurence Chang and Peter Kornbluh eds., *The Cuban Missile Crisis, 1962*, National Security Archive Documents Reader (New York: New Press, 1992), Doc. 4, "Minutes of First Operation Mongoose Meeting with Attorney General Robert Kennedy, December 1, 1961"; Doc. 7, "Brig. Gen. Edward Lansdale, Review of Operation Mongoose, Phase 1, July 25, 1962."

65. See generally, Thomas G. Patterson, "The Defense-of-Cuba Theme and the Missile Crisis," *Diplomatic History* 14, no. 2 (Spring 1990), pp. 249–56.

66. Chang and Kornbluh, *Cuban Missile Crisis, 1962*, Doc. 9.

67. Naftali and Zelikow, *Presidential Recordings*, vol. 2, p. 594.

68. George Washington University, National Security Archive, http://nsarchive.gwu.edu/NSAEBB/NSAEBB400/docs/Interview%20with%20Oleg%20Troyanovsky.pdf. See also Taubman, *Khrushchev*, p. 535; Stern, *Cuban Missile Crisis*, p. 2 ("In addition, evidence from the Soviet archives suggested that Khrushchev's original explanation for his dangerous gamble in Cuba had been fundamentally true: despite the firm convictions of JFK and his advisers, tensions over Berlin were not a decisive factor in the chairman's decision to ship nuclear missiles and warheads to Cuba. Nor did he intend these missiles as an aggressive threat to the security of the United States. From the perspective in Moscow, the missiles were meant to provide a beleaguered Cuban ally with deterrence against covert or overt U.S. attacks and to give the Americans 'a little of their own medicine' after JFK's decision to activate the Jupiter missiles in Turkey").

69. Andrew and Mitrokhin, *Mitrokhin Archive*, p. 238.

70. Fursenko and Naftali, *Gamble*, pp. 149–50.

71. Naftali and Zelikow, *Presidential Recordings*, vol. 2, p. 409.

72. Fursenko and Naftali, *Gamble*, pp. 188–89.

73. Patterson, "Defense-of-Cuba Theme," p. 256.

74. Sheldon M. Stern, "The Cuban Missile Crisis 45 Years Later: A Personal and Professional Remembrance," http://www.washingtondecoded.com/site/2007/10/cmc-45th.html

Chapter 5

1. See Thomas G. Paterson and William J. Brophy, "October Missiles and November Elections: The Cuban Missile Crisis and American Politics, 1962," *Journal of American History* 73, No. 1 (June 1996), p. 90 ("Only once in the twentieth century, in 1934, had the party of an incumbent president improved at midterm its position in the House of Representatives; and not since that year had the party in power in the White House enhanced its strength in the Senate").

2. Richard Reeves, *President Kennedy: Profile of Power* (New York: Simon & Schuster, 1993), p. 325.

3. Naftali, *Presidential Recordings*, vol. 1, pp. xli–xlii (introduction by Naftali).

4. David G. Coleman, *The Fourteenth Day: JFK and the Aftermath of the Cuban Missile Crisis* (New York: Norton, 2012), p. 10.

5. Coleman, *Fourteenth Day*, pp. 94, 97.

6. White, *Cuban Missile Crisis*, p. 106.

7. Department of State, Central Files, 762.00/7-2562, Top Secret, Priority, https://2001-2009.state.gov/r/pa/ho/frus/kennedyjf/xv/45990.htm. See Fursenko and Naftali, *Khrushchev's Cold War*, p. 447.

8. Haslam, *Russia's Cold War*, p. 203. See Taubman, *Khrushchev*, p. 448 ("It was the largest Soviet sealift to Cuba, and the timing seemed unusual").

9. Matthew M. Aid, *The Secret Sentry: The Untold Story of the National Security Agency* (New York: Bloomsbury Press, 2009), p. 65.

10. Telegram 230 from Moscow, July 26; Department of State, Central Files, 761.5411/7-2662; see https://history.state.gov/historicaldocuments/frus1961-63v05/d215. At a meeting of the Soviet Presidium a few weeks earlier, on July 1, 1962, comments in the discussion "Concerning Cuba" included, "Regarding the flights buzzing our ships—say that this impedes shipping," according to the official meeting notes prepared by Vladimir Malin, the chief of the General Department of the Central Committee. See Naftali, "The Malin Notes," pp. 299, 304.

11. Naftali, *Presidential Recordings*, vol. 1, p. 3.

12. Fursenko and Naftali, *Gamble*, p. 194 n. 48; Fursenko and Naftali, *Khrushchev's Cold War*, pp. 448–49; Appointment Books of President John F. Kennedy, Tuesday July 31, 1962, JFKL ("6:43–7:00 [Georgi Bolshakov] [Editor, USSR] [Hon. Robert Kennedy] OFF THE RECORD"); Robert Kennedy Desk Diaries, 1962, JFKL, for Tuesday July 31, 1962 ("6:00 Georgi Bolshakov, 6:30 Mtg with President"). Thompson met with the president in the Oval Office on August 8, 1962, from 10:36 to 11:12 a.m., and their conversation was recorded by the president's secret taping system. Neither Thompson nor the president mentioned the air surveillance issue, however. See Naftali, *Presidential Recordings*, vol. 1, pp. 261–71.

13. Fursenko and Naftali, *Gamble*, p. 194 and n. 48 (citing "Instructions to Soviet ambassador (Dobrynin)" [n.d., but in response to RFK-Bolshakov meeting of July 31, 1962], Folio 3, List 66, File 316, pp. 194–95, APRF); Fursenko and Naftali, *Khrushchev's Cold War*, pp. 448–49; Barbara Leaming, *Jack Kennedy: The Education of a Statesman* (New York: Norton, 2006), pp. 390–91; Naftali, *Presidential Recordings*, vol. 1, p. 131.

14. Fursenko and Naftali, *Gamble*, p. 193 and n. 46. The authors were unable to determine the precise date of Khrushchev's instructions to Bolshakov, nor of Bolshakov's initial contact with the Kennedys on this subject.

15. In late 1943 Franklin Delano Roosevelt was engaged in protracted and ultimately futile efforts to persuade Joseph Stalin to respect the postwar independence and self-determination of Poland and other Eastern European countries that at the time were being overrun by a counterattacking Red Army. Roosevelt

appealed to Stalin "on the grounds of high morality" and the tenets of the Atlantic Charter, which included "no territorial changes that do not accord with the freely expressed wishes of the peoples concerned," and "the right of all peoples to choose the form of government under which they will live." See John Lewis Gaddis, *The United States and the Origins of the Cold War, 1941–1947* (New York: Columbia University Press, 2005), pp. 15, 136. During the Tehran conference in December 1943 Roosevelt also cited American public opinion favoring Poland's right to independence. Stalin turned a cold, deaf ear to these comments and spoke rather about his plan to move the borders of Poland westward, meaning that parts of eastern Poland would be absorbed by the USSR and parts of eastern Germany would become part of Poland. The president felt he had no choice but to accept Stalin's wishes given the Red Army's uncontestable predominance of power on the ground. Yet Roosevelt asked for a personal accommodation closely similar to what Kennedy would seek from Khrushchev almost two decades later. According to the official US notes of a private meeting between the two leaders held at the Tehran conference on December 1, 1943, Roosevelt told Stalin he wanted to speak "briefly and frankly" on a matter involving "internal American politics." The president said he "might have to" run again in the upcoming 1944 presidential election, and "added that there were in the United States from six to seven million Americans of Polish extraction, and as a practical man, he did not wish to lose their vote." Referring to Stalin's boundary-shifting proposal for Poland, Roosevelt said that "personally he agreed with the views of Marshal Stalin as to the necessity of the restoration of a Polish state," but he hoped "that the Marshal would understand that for political reasons outlined above, he could not participate in any decision here in Tehran or even next winter on this subject and that he could not publicly take part in any such arrangement at the present time." That was good enough for Stalin, who replied that "now [that] the President [had] explained, he had understood." But Roosevelt wanted something more. Recognizing that "the big issue in the United States insofar as public opinion went, would be the question of referendum and the right of self-determination," the president said he "thought that world opinion would want some expression of the will of the people, perhaps not immediately after their re-occupation by Soviet forces, but some day." The president then made plain what he needed from Stalin: "It would be helpful for him [Roosevelt] personally if some public declaration in regard to the future elections to which the Marshal had referred, could be made." Stalin responded only with a vague comment that "there would be plenty of opportunities for such an expression of the will of the people," and the leaders' conversation then turned to other subjects. See *FRUS*: Diplomatic Papers, *The Conferences at Cairo and Tehran, 1943*, December 1, 1943, 3:20 p.m., Doc. 378, https://history.state.gov/historicaldocuments/frus1943CairoTehran/d378. Gaddis would later observe: "It is impossible to know precisely what Stalin made of this peculiar conversation . . . but it seems likely that Stalin emerged from this talk convinced that the President's main concern would be to present Russian policy to the American people in the most favorable light, not to secure literal compliance with the principles of the Atlantic Charter." Gaddis, *Origins*, p. 139.

16. Thomas, *Robert Kennedy*, pp. 207–8; Taubman, *Khrushchev*, p. 555.

17. David M. Barrett and Max Holland, *Blind over Cuba: The Photo Gap and the Missile Crisis* (College Station: Texas A&M University Press, 2012), p. 14.

18. Fursenko and Naftali, *Gamble*, p. 194.

19. Fursenko and Naftali, *Gamble*, p. 194; Fursenko and Naftali, *Khrushchev's Cold War*, p. 449 and n. 35.

20. Robert Kennedy Desk Diaries, 1962, JFKL.

21. See Naftali, *Presidential Recordings*, vol. 1, p. 131 ("Nothing came of President Kennedy's Berlin condition and so the President's own promise to suspend overhead surveillance was not kept").

22. Thomas, *Robert Kennedy*, pp. 208, 209.

23. Khrushchev would subsequently tell US ambassador Kohler in a meeting on October 16, 1962, that "he regretted that things had not worked in accordance with his discussion with Ambassador Thompson." Kohler cable 133, *FRUS*, 1961–1963, vol. 15, *Berlin Crisis, 1962–1963*, https://history.state.gov/historicaldocuments/frus1961-63v15/d133

24. Aid, *Secret Sentry*, pp. 65–66. Compare this entry in the President's "Intelligence Checklist" for August 29, 1962: "We note that deliveries of industrial equipment, foodstuffs and other nonmilitary items are being made largely on chartered Western ships, probably because so many Soviet ships are involved in hauling military gear." http://www.foia.cia.gov/sites/default/files/document_conversions/1827265/DOC_0005995903.pdf

25. Department of State, Presidential Correspondence, Lot 77D163, www.loyola.edu, Kennedy-Khrushchev Exchanges. Parenthetically, if this was the Soviet chairman's attitude entering the critical month of October 1962, it is easy to discern a mindset that treated the US president as a novice warranting condescension who could be expected to accept the Soviet missile installations in Cuba if only they could be concealed until completed and presented as a fait accompli after the US midterm elections.

26. National Security Council, 1962 Report of the Net Evaluation Subcommittee, p. 109, National Security Archive's Nuclear Documentation Project, George Washington University, https://nsarchive2.gwu.edu/nukevault/ebb480/. The president would receive a further SIOP-63 briefing on nuclear war fighting from General Lemnitzer three weeks later, on September 14, 1962, but documentation of that meeting has not yet been declassified. Lemnitzer Memorandum for the President, Subject: SIOP 63 Briefing, September 22, 1962.

27. Fursenko and Naftali, *Gamble*, p. 202 ("The concern shared by most of Kennedy's advisers was that Khrushchev would choose this moment to act on his four-year-old threat to sign a peace treaty with the East Germans, ending all Soviet rights in East Berlin and calling on NATO to do the same in West Berlin").

28. Bundy to Sorensen, August 23, 1962, *FRUS*, 1961–1963, vol. 15, *Berlin Crisis, 1962–1963*, pp. 284–85.

29. Jeremy Pressman, "September Statements, October Missiles, November Elections: Domestic Politics, Foreign Policy Making, and the Cuban Missile Crisis," *Security Studies* 10, no. 3 (Spring 2001), pp. 94–95; see https://history.state.gov/historicaldocuments/frus1961-63v10/d415; *FRUS*, 1961–1963, vol. 15, *Berlin Crisis, 1962–1963*, Doc. 103, n. 3 (citing Sorensen file memorandum), https://2001-2009.state.gov/r/pa/ho/frus/kennedyjf/xv/45993.htm

30. See "August 28, 1962—Conversation of Cde N.S. Khrushchev and acting United Nations Secretary General U Thant, 28 August 1962," Wilson Center Digital Archive, http://digitalarchive.wilsoncenter.org/document/113342.pdf?v=9a800e0b87da59638953e2b51ea18718

31. Khrushchev, *Nikita Khrushchev*, p. 528.

32. See Pressman, "September Statements," pp. 87, 90.

33. Gregory W. Pedlow and Donald E. Welzenbach, *The Central Intelligence Agency and Overhead Reconnaissance: The U-2 and OXCART Programs, 1954–1974*, HR70-14, History Staff, Central Intelligence Agency, 1992, pp. 200–201, https://www.cia.gov/library/readingroom/docs/2002-07-16.pdf

34. Brugioni, *Eyeball to Eyeball*, pp. 104, 105.

35. Hilsman, *To Move a Nation*, p. 171; Hilsman, *Nuclear Military Strategy*, p. 62; Raymond L. Garthoff, "Soviet Actions and Reactions in the Cuban Missile Crisis," presented to the colloquium "A New Look at the Cuban Missile Crisis," June 18, 1992, Naval History and Heritage Command, p. 10 ("The coastal defense forces included 4 fixed 'Sopka' S-2 [Samlet] coast defense cruise missile sites, each with a battery of two launchers, and in all 32 missiles with an 80km range"), https://www.history.navy.mil/research/library/online-reading-room/title-list-alphabetically/n/new-look-cuban-missile-crisis.html; Andrei Kokoshin, "Reflections on the Cuban Missile Crisis in the Context of Strategic Stability," Belfer Center ("Cuba, the 'Island of Freedom,' also planned to host IL-28 bombers [NATO designation Beagle] that were capable of carrying nuclear weapons, Luna tactical missiles with nuclear warheads [NATO designation FROG-7], and Sopka coastal-defense missile systems that were also nuclear armed"), https://www.belfercenter.org/sites/default/files/legacy/files/09.25.12.%20kokoshin%20paper%20final%20combined.pdf; Graham Allison, "The Cuban Missile Crisis," in Steve Smith, Amelia Hadfield, and Tim Dunne, eds., *Foreign Policy: Theories, Actors, Cases* (New York: Oxford University Press 2016), p. 264 ("The first nuclear warheads for the MRBMs arrived on 4 October, along with dozens of nuclear warheads for the Sopka coastal defense cruise missiles"). Dobbs states (*One Minute to Midnight*, p. 388n) that the Sopkas "did not carry a nuclear warhead."

36. See Thomas, *Robert Kennedy*, p. 219 (Kennedy's handwritten memorandum of October 22, 1962, was discovered by Thomas in the "Robert F. Kennedy 'Confidential File,'" JFKL).

37. Report to the President's Foreign Intelligence Advisory Board on Intelligence Community Activities Relating to the Cuban Arms Build-up (April 14 through October 14, 1962), by the Director of Central Intelligence, p. 24. A later transmittal memorandum by DD/CI Marshall Carter confirms that the DCI Re-

port to PFIAB was approved as final on January 3, 1963. See https://www.cia.gov/library/readingroom/docs/CIA-RDP80B01676R001800050001-9.pdf.

38. Brugioni, *Eyeball to Eyeball*, pp. 107–8; see also Fursenko and Naftali, *Gamble*, p. 205.

39. *Washington Post*, August 31, 1962, p. A4.

40. http://nsarchive.gwu.edu/nsa/cuba_mis_cri/620829_620909%20Chronology%202.pdf, p. 18.

41. Bundy served as the president's top national security adviser; Kaysen was deputy national security adviser; Clifton was military representative to the president; and Shepard was naval aide to the president.

42. *FRUS*, 1961–1963, vol. 10, *Cuba, January 1961–September 1962*. The Bundy memorandum may also be found at JFKL, NSAM 181, Box 338.

43. Brugioni, *Eyeball to Eyeball*, pp. 111–12 (citing August 31, 1962, article in *New York Herald Tribune*).

44. Sorensen, *Kennedy*, p. 670; Allison and Zelikow, *Essence of Decision*, p. 330.

45. Lyman B. Kirkpatrick, memo for the director, "Action Generated by DCI Cables Concerning Cuban Low-Level Photography and Offensive Weapons," n.d., McAuliffe, *CIA Documents*, Doc. 12.

46. Fursenko and Naftali, *Gamble*, p. 204.

47. Fursenko and Naftali, *Gamble*, pp. 106, 107.

48. See August 31, 1962, *Congressional Record—Senate*, p. 18359.

49. August 31, 1962, *Congressional Record—Senate*, p. 18360; see also Brugioni, *Eyeball to Eyeball*, pp. 112–13.

50. August 31, 1962, *Congressional Record—Senate*, p. 18361; see also Pressman, "September Statements," p. 87.

51. Reeves, *President Kennedy*, p. 345.

52. JFKL, Box 338, Cuba (B) 9/62 (Kaysen's transmittal note); *FRUS*, 1961–1963, vol. 10, *Cuba, January 1961–September 1962*, Doc. 405 (Kaysen's memorandum to the president).

53. *FRUS*, 1961–1963, vol. 10, *Cuba, January 1961–September 1962*, Doc. 405.

54. The *FRUS* editors noted that "CINCLANTFLT had issued instructions to conform with the new rules of engagement." Ibid.

55. Robert M. Beer, "The U.S. Navy and the Cuban Missile Crisis," submitted to the US Naval Academy and accepted by its Trident Scholar Committee in May 1990, pp. 37–38, https://vdocuments.net/ar-mil-a-trident-scholar-project-mil-a-trident-scholar-project-report-lc.html. McCabe was interviewed on November 4, 1989. Reports of revelations by Oleg Penkovsky, a GRU colonel working in Russia as a spy for the CIA and Britain's MI-6, were coded IRONBARK and CHICKADEE and were among the most important and highly classified materials within the US intelligence community. They included "key technical details of the R-12 medium-range missiles that the Soviet Union sent to Cuba in the fall of 1962, especially the range of the missiles and the time required to make them operational." David E. Hoffman, *The Billion Dollar Spy: A True Story of Cold War Espionage and Betrayal* (New York: Knopf Doubleday, 2015), p. 15. Penkovsky was exposed to the Soviets by a double agent working in the United States, arrested on October 22, 1962, at the height of the Cuban missile crisis, and eventually executed.

Although no definitive conclusion can be reached on the basis of the scant evidence noted above, it seems unlikely that the president would have issued his "red line" warning to the Soviets on September 4, 1962, that no offensive ground-to-ground missiles should be placed in Cuba if he had known at the time that such missiles were on the way or already there.

56. Bolshakov, "The Hot Line," p. 40.

57. Dean Rusk's presence was shown by a printed notation in the Appointment Books of President John F. Kennedy for Friday, August 31, 1962. Robert Kennedy's presence at the meeting is documented in Evelyn Lincoln's "Day at a Glance" for that date, which bears the entry "Bobby" at 4:45. Both documents are maintained at the JFKL. RFK's Desk Diary for that date bears the entry "4:45 Signing of Satellite Bill in President's Office," but the President's Appointment Book states that that ceremony occurred earlier, at 9:45–10:00 a.m. on August 31.

58. See Hershberg, introduction to "Trigger for Khrushchev's Deployment," p. 320. Adzhubei's report of the private meeting on January 31 also included the following comment about Kennedy's use of Bolshakov: "Then Kennedy said that he personally welcomes the contact which existed between Bolshakov and Robert Kennedy, insofar as it gives him the possibility to manage without the services of a translator from the State Department" (p. 321). Adzhubei would have needed a translator for this private meeting with the president, and Bolshakov would have served that role, just as he done the day before at the president's request.

59. Bolshakov, "The Hot Line," p. 40. Bolshakov provided the same exact account, almost word for word, in a lunch conversation with Pierre Salinger on January 31, 1989, just after Salinger had attended a conference on the Cuban missile crisis that had been hosted in Moscow. See Pierre Salinger, *PS: A Memoir* (New York: St. Martin's Press, 1995), pp. 253–54. See also Talbot, *Hidden History*, p. 32.

60. Beschloss, *Crisis Years*, p. 409.

61. Department of State, Presidential Correspondence, Lot 77D163, FRUS, 1961-1963, Volume VI, Kennedy-Khrushchev Exchanges, Doc. 56, pp. 152–61.

62. Fursenko and Naftali, *Gamble*, p. 194.

63. Bolshakov, "The Hot Line," p. 41. There is one possible, though speculative, basis for tying Robert Kennedy's outburst to the White House meeting on July 31: involving worrisome events on the other side of the world, in Laos. The attorney general had for several months been using the Bolshakov/Khrushchev back-channel in conjunction with his brother's efforts to defuse military conflict in Laos. The president had made successive conciliatory gestures in reliance on Khrushchev's return assurances that aggression by Pathet Lao and North Vietnamese forces would be reduced. On May 12, after an important Laotian base was overrun by communist forces, Robert Kennedy told Bolshakov to inform Khrushchev that the president "felt he had been double-crossed." In mid-May President Kennedy ordered between 5,000–6,000 Marines and other troops deployed into Thailand. On July 23 the "International Agreement on the Neutrality of Laos" was signed in Geneva by the United States, USSR, and others requiring all foreign troops to leave that country. Also on July 23 Bolshakov told Robert Kennedy that Khrushchev wanted the president to remove the US troops that had recently been deployed to Thailand, the president immediately agreed to do so, and the

US troops were gone by July 31. Those Laos developments would surely have been discussed during the ensuing July 31 White House meeting between Bolshakov and the two Kennedys. It is therefore quite possible that Robert Kennedy was worried that his brother's conciliatory moves in Thailand would cause problems with the Pentagon and CIA, and also that Khrushchev might once again renege on his reciprocal commitments, in particular his obligation under the July 23 Laos Neutrality Agreement to ensure that North Vietnamese forces would leave that country. If so, the attorney general's anxiety on both fronts could have triggered his July 31 parting outburst. See History of the Joint Chiefs of Staff, The Joint Chiefs of Staff and National Policy, Volume VIII 1961–1964, Walter S. Poole (2011) pp. 134–35, 137, https://www.jcs.mil/Portals/36/Documents/History/Policy/Policy_V008.pdf; and *The Joint Chiefs of Staff and the War in Vietnam 1960–1968 Part 1*, Jack Schulimson (2011) pp. 227–28, 231, https://www.jcs.mil/Portals/36/Documents/History/Vietnam/Vietnam_1960-1968_P001.pdf.

64. Bolshakov, "The Hot Line," p. 41. Note that Khrushchev also met with Secretary of the Interior Udall on September 6 during his vacation in Pitsunda and then with Bolshakov in the same place "several days later." See Taubman, *Khrushchev*, pp. 555–56.

65. Memorandum from SAC, WFO to Director, FBI, 7/12/62, Subject: Georgi N. Bolshakov ("The subject is scheduled to return to the Soviet Union on 8/3/62. He plans to stay there for one month . . ."); Report of Edward J. Kaier, Bureau File No. 105-18268, 7/19/62 Title: Georgi Nikitovich Bolshakov ("The subject will be returning to the United States (US) in approximately one month"); Memorandum from SAC, WFO to Director, FBI, 11/19/62 Subject: Georgi Nikitovich Bolshakov ("Subject returned to the Soviet Union on 8/3/62, reportedly for a vacation, and reported back to the U.S. on 10/2/62") National Archives.

66. Beer, "U.S. Navy," p. 69.

67. NSAM 181.

68. Naftali and Zelikow, *Presidential Recordings*, vol. 2, pp. xxiii–xxiv, 21–22, 29.

69. Leaming, *Jack Kennedy*, p. 399. Kennedy's close friendship with Ormsby-Gore extended far back to the president's days as son of the US ambassador to the Court of St. James when he lived in London in the late 1930s. As will be seen hereafter, the president would soon be sharing with his British friend some of the most salient and confidential aspects of his thinking as he struggled with the challenge of finding a peaceful resolution to the Cuban missile crisis.

70. Naftali and Zelikow, *Presidential Recordings*, vol. 2, p. 80.

71. Dobrynin described an "oral message" in his memoirs as a customary diplomatic practice that is "used in order to make a communication sound less official and informal." The message might be dictated so that the recipient could take notes or even faithfully recreate an exact duplicate of the message on his own paper, or it might be conveyed by the messenger handing over "a strictly unofficial but complete text" he had prepared himself that, although certainly a "written document," was a document "which officially did not exist." Dobrynin, *In Confidence*, pp. 69–70.

72. Theodore Sorensen, Memorandum for the Files, September 6, 1962, *FRUS*, 1961–1963, vol. 10, *Cuba, January 1961–September 1962*, Doc. 415.

73. Theodore Sorensen, Memorandum for the Files, September 6, 1962, *FRUS, 1961–1963*, vol. 10, *Cuba, January 1961–September 1962*, Doc. 415. Notably, Sorensen neglected to give details about his September 6 conversation with Dobrynin in his 2008 memoirs other than to say that Khrushchev's assurances conveyed by the ambassador to the effect that the Soviets were doing nothing "new or extraordinary" in Cuba "were false." Theodore Sorensen, *Counselor: A Life at the Edge of History* (New York: HarperCollins, 2008), p. 286.

74. White, *Cuban Missile Crisis*, p. 107.

75. Beschloss, *Crisis Years*, p. 421. Khrushchev's son-in-law, Aleksei Adzhubei, provided further evidence supporting this conclusion when he told William Taubman in an interview that the Soviet chairman told him that if the Americans discovered the missiles before they were operational, he believed to a "near certainty that Kennedy would not choose war" and that the confrontation could be resolved by negotiation. Taubman, *Khrushchev*, p. 552.

76. Memorandum, Assistant Director, Research and Reports, to Deputy Director (Intelligence), *Further Analysis of Bloc and Western Shipping Calling at Cuban Ports*, September 11, 1962, CIA Electronic FOIA Reading Room, Doc. 0000307720, https://www.foia.cia.gov/library/readingroom/docs/doc_0000307720.pdf

77. Aid, *Secret Sentry*, p. 67.

78. Dobrynin, *In Confidence*, p. 69. Robert Kennedy's desk diary (at JFKL) confirms that he met with Dobrynin at 11:15 a.m. on September 18, 1962.

79. No mention of Dobrynin's delivery of Khrushchev's fifteen-page "oral message" can be found in Michael Beschloss's encyclopedic *Crisis Years*, despite the author presumably having been granted full access to the John F. Kennedy Presidential Library. Notably, Beschloss's comprehensive treatment of the missile crisis was published four years before the arrival of Dobrynin's memoirs in 1995. But why was Dobrynin's 1995 recounting of his momentous September 18, 1962, meeting with Robert Kennedy not mentioned by Fursenko and Naftali in their 1997 *Gamble*, or by Taubman in his 2003 biography of Khrushchev, or by Dobbs in his 2008 *One Minute to Midnight*?

80. Dobrynin, *In Confidence*, p. 70.

81. Dobrynin, *In Confidence*, pp. 69–70 (emphasis added).

82. Taubman, *Khrushchev*, p. 564.

83. https://history.state.gov/historicaldocuments/frus1961-63v06/d59. The "September 28" Khrushchev letter actually bears no date. State Department archivists have assigned September 28 as its date based upon the letter President Kennedy sent back on October 8, which responded to Khrushchev's comments on the nuclear test ban issue but then said, "I shall want to comment separately on other aspects of your letter." No such separate comments by the president to the chairman have yet emerged from the historical record.

84. Dobrynin's memoir discussion of the "September 18" letter and the actual text of the "September 28" letter have the following parallels, which appear in the two renderings of the letter in the same order:

Dobrynin memoirs
"unnatural situation" in Berlin
"freeze matters until after the election"
"nice conversation" with Udall
Soviets "doing nothing to provoke tensions"
US making "piratical demands" regarding Soviet ships headed for Cuba
September 28 letter
"abnormal situation in West Berlin"
"German problem, so to say, on ice until the end of the elections"
Udall "made a good impression on me" . . . "friendly"
Soviets "haven't done anything that could give a pretext"
Soviet ships won't "yield to any pirate demands"

85. September 28, 1962, letter from Khrushchev to Kennedy, https://history.state.gov/historicaldocuments/frus1961-63v06/d56

86. Garthoff, "US Intelligence," pp. 47–48.

87. Naftali and Zelikow, *Presidential Recordings*, vol. 2, p. 189.

88. Bolshakov, "The Hot Line," p. 40.

89. Georgi Bolshakov, "Bolshakov on Cuban Missile Crisis—Conclusion, the Kennedy-Khrushchev 'Secret Channel,'" 90UMO283A. *Moscow KOMMUNIST VOORUZHENNYKH SIL*, in Russian, No. 21, November 1989, republished in JPRS Report, *Soviet Union Military Affairs*, March 23, 1990, p. 113. A nearly identical rendition of this message was published in Bolshakov's *New Times* article, "The Hot Line," p. 42.

90. Zelikow and May, *Presidential Recordings*, vol. 3, p. 100; see also http://avalon.law.yale.edu/20th_century/msc_cuba045.asp

91. "Meeting of the Secretariat of the CRI with Mikoyan at the National Palace, Sunday, 4 November 1962," contained in James G. Hershberg, "New Evidence on the Cuban Missile Crisis: More Documents from the Russian Archives," *Cold War International History Project Bulletin* 8–9 (Winter 1996–97), p. 340, Woodrow Wilson International Center for Scholars.

92. See Beschloss, *Crisis Years*, p. 382, quoting Sergo Mikoyan on Khrushchev's objective of defending Cuba: ("Khrushchev's solution: send nuclear missiles to Cuba! Sergo recalled, 'The idea was that their very existence would deter an American invasion. It would not be necessary to launch them . . . the intention was to do it very speedily, in September and October, but not to reveal it before the American elections on November'").

93. Beschloss, *Crisis Years*, pp. 398, 399.

94. Haslam, *Russia's Cold War*, p. 204.

95. SNIE 85-3-62, "The Military Buildup in Cuba," September 19, 1962, p. 4, para. 8 (emphasis added).

96. Fursenko and Naftali, *Gamble*, p. 194.

97. Robert Kennedy's Attorney General's Office Desk Diaries are located at JFKL.

98. Naftali, *Presidential Recordings*, vol. 1, p. 131 ("Nothing came of President Kennedy's Berlin condition and so the President's own promise to suspend overhead surveillance was not kept").

99. See CIA, Office of the Deputy Director (Intelligence), Office of Research and Reports, "Cuba 1962: Khrushchev's Miscalculated Risk," February 13, 1964, SC 03387/64, p. 50, LBJ Library and at http://historyinpieces.com/documents/documents/cia-cuban-missile-crisis-khrushchevs-miscalculated-risk ("The missiles and other unit equipment then at the sites had been delivered to Cuba aboard five or six large-hatch ships that arrived between approximately mid-September and mid-October"). See also Garthoff, "US Intelligence," p. 23 (first missile-carrying ship, the *Omsk*, was unloaded in Cuba on September 9, 1962).

100. Dobrynin, *In Confidence*, pp. 67–68. No Sorensen file memo on this conversation has been located.

101. Theodore C. Sorensen, Memorandum for the Files, September 6, 1962, *FRUS*, 1961–1963, vol. 10, *Cuba, January 1961–September 1962*, Doc. 415. See also Sorensen, *Kennedy*, pp. 667–68.

102. Telegram from the Embassy in the Soviet Union to the Department of State, July 25, 1962, Moscow 225, *FRUS*, 1961–1963, vol. 15, *Berlin Crisis, 1962–1963* ("Khrushchev suggested that when I got home I personally ask President—not through State Department—whether it would be better for him if Berlin question brought to a head before or after our Congressional elections. He did not want to make things more difficult for President—and in fact would like to help him").

103. Kennedy, *Thirteen Days*, p. 4; Reeves, *President Kennedy*, p. 346; Sorensen, Memorandum for the Files, September 6, 1962, JFKL, cited in Fursenko and Naftali, *Gamble*, p. 197, n. 64; Beschloss, *Crisis Years*, p. 420; Abel, *Missile Crisis*, p. 19.

104. Taubman, *Khrushchev*, pp. 554–55. Taubman opined that Khrushchev was most likely "encouraging" Kennedy "to do what he assumed the president wanted to do anyway—namely, look the other way so as to avoid a pre-election crisis and pave the way for a postelection summit" (p. 555).

105. Beschloss, *Crisis Years*, p. 438.

106. Beschloss, *Crisis Years*, p. 209.

107. Taubman, *Khrushchev*, p. 555; Beschloss, *Crisis Years*, p. 421; Fursenko and Naftali, *Gamble*, pp. 197, 252–53; Blight, Allyn, and Welch, *Cuba on the Brink*, p. 375 (citing Sorensen memorandum on the conversation); see also Dobrynin, *In Confidence*, p. 68.

108. Anatoli I. Gribkov and William Y. Smith, *Operation Anadyr: U.S. and Soviet Generals Recount the Cuban Missile Crisis*, ed. Alfred Friendly Jr. (Chicago: Edition q, 1994), p. 109.

109. Dobrynin, *In Confidence*, p. 70.

110. Beschloss, *Crisis Years*, p. 426n. Bartlett would later report to President Kennedy on a subsequent conversation he had with Zinchuk on October 29, 1962, in which the Soviet embassy official said that "he knew nothing about the missiles and does not know why Khrushchev allowed the impression to develop that they were only short-range." Bartlett to "Mr. President," October 29, 1962, NARA Digital Archives.

111. See Thomas, *Robert Kennedy*, pp. 205–6 (citing an entry in Robert Kennedy's desk diary reflecting meeting with Bolshakov on that date).

112. Bolshakov, "Secret Channel," pp. 113–18.

113. Fursenko and Naftali, *Khrushchev's Cold War*, pp. 462–63 (citing Dobrynin to NSK, October 9, 1962, Volkogonov Collection, Library of Congress).

114. Kohler cable to US Department of State, Moscow 970, October 16, 1962, https://history.state.gov/historicaldocuments/frus1961-63v05/d248, cited in May and Zelikow, *Kennedy Tapes*, p. 88 n. 5; see also Kohler cable no. 133, *FRUS*, 1961–1963, vol. 15, *Berlin Crisis 1962–1963*; Beschloss, *Crisis Years*, pp. 438–39; Taubman, *Khrushchev*, p. 556. Khrushchev's reference to an announcement about a Cuban fishing village evidently referred to charges that the Soviets were using a fishing village in Cuba as cover for construction of a Soviet naval base at that location. See Kennedy, *Thirteen Days*, pp. 20–21.

115. Beschloss, *Crisis Years*, p. 438. A typewritten document found in journalist Edward Weintal's personal papers at the Georgetown University Library entitled "Summary of Deceptions," maintained in Weintal's backup files for a book he and Charles Bartlett were writing on the Cuban missile crisis, includes the following comment about US ambassador Kohler's October 16 meeting with Khrushchev: "[Khrushchev] said he did not want to embarrass the President in the midst of the elections and gave his most profound assurances that this was in fact nothing but a fishing village." Weintal Personal Papers, Box 7, Folder 15. See also Edward Weintal and Charles Bartlett, *Facing the Brink* (New York: Charles Scribner's Sons, 1967).

116. Memorandum of Conversation, October 18, 1962, Office of the Historian, *FRUS*, 1961–1963, vol. 15, *Berlin Crisis, 1962–1963*, https://history.state.gov/historicaldocuments/frus1961-63v15/d135; Haslam, *Russia's Cold War*, p. 205.

117. Beschloss, *Crisis Years*, p. 426n.

118. Naftali and Zelikow, *Presidential Recordings*, vol. 2, p. 555.

Chapter 6

1. Bolshakov, "The Hot Line," p. 42.
2. White, *Cuban Missile Crisis*, p. 109.
3. *FRUS*, 1961–1963, vol. 10, *Cuba, January 1961–September 1962*, Doc. 405.
4. Brugioni, *Eyeball to Eyeball*, p. 123.
5. Brugioni, *Eyeball to Eyeball*, pp. 124–26.
6. Brugioni, *Eyeball to Eyeball*, p. 127.
7. Brugioni, *Eyeball to Eyeball*, p. 127. See also Hilsman, *Cuban Missile Crisis*, p. 36 ("Very early in the crisis [Kennedy] recognized that if the Soviets did put missiles in Cuba, he would need time to work out a response. Therefore he instituted the special Psalm security clearance restricting information about 'offensive weapons' in Cuba to those who would need to know to do their jobs in both the intelligence and policy-making communities").
8. May and Zelikow, *Kennedy Tapes*, p. 53 n. 10. Brugioni was aware of the pres-

ident's restriction on evidence dissemination, but he described it in a notably subdued way. Referring to the "startling discovery" of a Soviet tactical missile site near Banes, Cuba, Brugioni stated: "Because the president and his brother had shown such interest in new developments in Cuba, [Ray] Cline asked that the information not be disseminated until the president had seen it and pressed Lundahl to complete his analysis as soon as possible." Brugioni, *Eyeball to Eyeball*, p. 121.

9. Report to the President's Foreign Intelligence Advisory Board on Intelligence Community Activities Relating to the Cuban Arms Build-up (April 14 through October 14, 1962), by the Director of Central Intelligence, pp. 50–52.

10. Barrett and Holland, *Blind over Cuba*, p. 6 (citing Bundy, *Danger and Survival*, pp. 393, 413), https://www.cia.gov/library/center-for-the-study-of-intelligence/csi-publications/csi-studies/studies/vol49no4/Photo_Gap_2.htm; Telephone Conversation between Marshall Carter and Carl Kaysen, September 1, 1962, CREST, NARA, *FRUS*, 1961–1963, vol. 10, *Cuba, January 1961–September 1962*, pp. 1023–24.

11. McAuliffe, *CIA Documents*, Doc. 10, p. 33.

12. Pedlow and Welzenbach, *Overhead Reconaissance*, p. 205 n. 10 (citing Memorandum for DDCI Carter from James Q. Reber, Chairman, COMOR, "Historical Analysis of U-2 Overflights of Cuba," October 24, 1962, IC Staff, COMIREX records).

13. Brugioni, *Eyeball to Eyeball*, p. 133.

14. The Special Group, created in 1955 by NSC Intelligence Document 5412/2 and sometimes referred to as the "5412 Committee," consisted of the director of central intelligence, the deputy secretary of defense, the undersecretary of state, and the military adviser to the president. Pedlow and Welzenbach, *Overhead Reconaissance*, p. 188.

15. Barrett and Holland, *Blind over Cuba*, p. 7.

16. *FRUS*, 1961–1963, vol. 10, *Cuba, January 1961–September 1962*, Doc. 421, Memorandum prepared in the Central Intelligence Agency, written on February 28, 1963, by Ernest deM. Berkaw Jr. for the Executive Director based on information provided by Reber and Cunningham "and to some extent the Lehman report." The Lehman Report was a postmortem prepared in the aftermath of the U-2 "photo gap" controversy. See Memorandum for DCI from Richard Lehman, "CIA Handling of the Soviet Build-up in Cuba, 1 July–16 October 1962," November 14, 1962, CREST, NARA, 12. See also Barrett and Holland, *Blind over Cuba*, p. 150 n. 50.

17. Barrett and Holland, *Blind over Cuba*, p. 8.

18. Polmar and Gresham, *DEFCON-2*, p. 80. See Brugioni, *Eyeball to Eyeball*, pp. 138–39.

19. Brugioni, *Eyeball to Eyeball*, pp. 135–39. Brugioni, citing an unnamed source, reported that Robert Kennedy stated at one point, "Let's sustain the overflights and the hell with the international issues" (p. 137).

20. *FRUS*, 1961–1963, vol. 10, *Cuba, January 1961–September 1962*, Doc. 421, Memorandum prepared in the Central Intelligence Agency by Ernest deM.

Berkaw Jr. for the Executive Director. The memo quoted Carter as stating: "I want to put you people on notice that it remains our intention to fly right p over those SAMs to see what is there." Then the memo noted, "To this, there was no response—positive or negative."

21. Pedlow and Welzenbach, *Overhead Reconaissance*, p. 205.

22. Barrett and Holland, *Blind over Cuba*, p. 9.

23. Brugioni, *Eyeball to Eyeball*, p. 139.

24. Dobbs, *One Minute to Midnight*, pp. 184–87 (SIGINT from the USS *Oxford* at sea); Brugioni, *Eyeball to Eyeball*, p. 107 (ELINT operating "all-out . . . against the SAMs" since August), p. 116 (U-2 mission on September 5), p. 118 (listing multiple "specially equipped" US intelligence-gathering aircraft that had been "thrown into the gap," all of which "contained automatic scanning devices to acquire SA-2-related signals"); There may have been some exaggeration in Brugioni's comment that "all-out" ELINT surveillance had begun as early as August. Self-published research by Colonel Wayne W. Whitten (Ret.) has demonstrated that the first RB47 ELINT flight did not occur until September 14, and that these ELINT flights were conducted only once per day for a few hours until October 22. Correspondence between Whitten and the author on file. Richelson noted that in September "attempts to use RB-47s and specially modified B-52s" to collect electronic intelligence (ELINT) "proved unsuccessful," and he described the impressive US intelligence-gathering capabilities that were deployed when NSA "launched a massive SIGINT effort" on October 16. Jeffery T. Richelson, *A Century of Spies: Intelligence in the Twentieth Century* (New York: Oxford University Press, 1995), pp. 315–16 (RB-47H and RC-121 Super Constellation ELINT aircraft overhead). The question remains: why weren't these "massive" intelligence-gathering assets deployed much earlier, when the growing presence of SAM-2 sites under development in Cuba signaled the presence of a looming threat to the United States?

25. Chronology of JCS Decisions Concerning the Cuban Crisis, January 4, 1963, Maxwell Taylor Special Collection, Box 16, Folder G#1, National Defense University Library.

26. Minutes of the Special Group Meeting, October 4, 1962, in Memorandum for DCI McCone from J. S. Earman, Inspector General, "Handling of Raw Intelligence Information during the Cuban Arms Buildup," November 20, 1962, DCI Records, Job 80-B-1676R, Box 17 (TS Codeword), in Pedlow and Welzenbach, *Overhead Reconaissance*, p. 206, https://issuu.com/tonycronin/docs/u2__history_complete.pdf.crdownload

27. McAuliffe, *CIA Documents*, Doc. 42, "Memorandum of Discussion with Mr. McGeorge Bundy, Friday, October 5, 1962, 5:15 p.m.," p. 115.

28. Robert F. Kennedy, Oral History, JFKL, vol. 8, February 27, 1965, p. 611. Kennedy went so far as to accuse McCone of disseminating a misleading story to protect his own reputation. See p. 612 ("And then we all knew John McCone was sort of moving around among senators and congressmen, peddling this idea because it got him off the hook. Who was primarily responsible for not knowing there were missiles in Cuba earlier? CIA. He wasn't going to have that on his back. So he got it off his back in this way").

29. See Kenneth M. Absher, "Mind Sets and Missiles: A First Hand Account of the Cuban Missile Crisis," Strategic Studies Institute, September 2009, pp. 29–30 ("From August 10–23, 1962, DCI McCone warned President Kennedy a total of four times that he thought the Soviets intended to place offensive missiles in Cuba"); CIA, Chronology of Specific Events Relating to the Military Buildup in Cuba, compiled for the President's Foreign Intelligence Advisory Board, pp. 9–11, https://nsarchive2.gwu.edu//nsa/cuba_mis_cri/590102_620827%20Chronology%202.pdf

30. Blight and Welch, *Intelligence*, p. 5; Dobbs, *One Minute to Midnight*, pp. 123–24.

31. SNIE 85-3-62, "The Military Buildup in Cuba," September 19, 1962, p. 8, para. 31.

32. Jerrold L. Schecter and Peter S. Deriabin, *The Spy Who Saved the World: How a Soviet Colonel Changed the Course of the Cold War* (New York: Charles S. Scribner's Sons, 1992), pp. 68, 79. See Matthias Uhl and Vladimir I. Ivkin, "'Operation Atom'—the Soviet Union's Stationing of Nuclear Missiles in the German Democratic Republic, 1959," in *Cold War International History Project Bulletin* 12–13 (Fall–Winter 2001), n. 33, Woodrow Wilson International Center for Scholars, citing "Intelligence Note: Deployment of Soviet Medium Range Missiles in East Germany," Memorandum from Hugh S. Cumming Jr. (INR) to the Secretary of State, January 4, 1961, National Archives, Record Group 59, Lot 65DR478: Records of the Special Assistant to the Secretary of State for Atomic Energy/Country and Subject Files Relating to Atomic Energy Matters, 1950–1962, Box 5, 1961/USSR/Intelligence Reports; "Current Support Brief—Possible Shyster Missile Base in East Germany," August 11, 1960, Office of Research and Reports, Central Intelligence Agency CIA/RR CB-60-41. See Matthias Uhl, *Krieg um Berlin? Die Sowjetische Militär- und Sicherheitspolitik in der zweiten Berlin-Krise 1958–1962* [War over Berlin? Soviet Military and Security Policy in the Second Berlin Crisis, 1958–1962] (Munich: Oldenbourg, 2008).

33. For a further discussion of the exact date of the Bolshakov-Kennedy meeting see chapter 8.

34. Bolshakov, "The Hot Line," p. 42.

35. Pedlow and Welzenbach, *Overhead Reconaissance*, pp. 206–7; Max Holland, "The 'Photo Gap' That Delayed Discovery of Missiles," *CIA Studies in Intelligence* 49, no. 4 (2005), p. 9, https://www.cia.gov/library/center-for-the-study-of-intelligence/csi-publications/csi-studies/index.html

36. Jeffrey T. Richelson, *The Wizards of Langley: Inside the CIA's Directorate of Science and Technology* (Boulder, CO: Westview, 2001), p. 53.

37. Holland, "Photo Gap," p. 9 (citing CIA, Office of the Deputy Director (Intelligence), Office of Research and Reports, "Cuba 1962: Khrushchev's Miscalculated Risk," p. 28, which Holland had found in 1964, National Security File, Country File: Cuba, Box 35, LBJ Presidential Library, pp. 2–3).

38. Notes on a meeting with the President by Roswell L. Gilpatric; Washington National Records Center, RG 330, OASD (C) A Files: FRC 71 A 2896, RLG's Notes re Cuba, Editorial Note, Avalon Project—Cuban Missile Crisis, Yale University,

http://avalon.law.yale.edu/20th_century/msc_cuba017.asp. Volume 8 of the subsequent *History of the Joint Chiefs of Staff* would report that as of October 19 "a DIA briefer" advised the JCS that twenty-two SAM sites had been located, "nine of which were believed to be operational." The DIA representative also predicted that "in just a few weeks . . . a couple of air defense nets would have real capability." Walter S. Poole, *History of the Joint Chiefs of Staff*, vol. 8, *The Joint Chiefs of Staff and National Policy, 1961–1964* (Washington, DC: Office of Joint History, Office of the Chairman of the Joint Chiefs of Staff, 2011), p. 169, https://www.noexperiencenecessarybook.com/JKOJj/the-joint-chiefs-of-staff-and-national-policy-1961-1964.html

39. Typed version of General Taylor's handwritten notes, p. 24, maintained in Box 16, Folder 4, T644A-71, Maxwell Taylor Special Collection, National Defense University Library.

40. Gribkov and Smith, *Operation Anadyr*, pp. 51–52.

41. Brugioni, *Eyeball to Eyeball*, pp. 135–36. According to Colonel Whitten, on September 14, 1962, the director of the JCS Joint Reconnaissance Committee, Colonel Steakley, would brief the Mongoose Group on the capabilities of two tactical reconnaissance aircraft: the RF-8A and the RF-101, but no decision was made because "the group wanted to wait for specific targets to come from U-2 missions." Colonel H. Wayne Whitten, USMC (Ret). *Countdown to 13 Days and Beyond*, 2nd ed. (Self-published, September 2012), p. 32.

42. See Holland, "Photo Gap."

43. Hilsman, *Nuclear Military Strategy*, p. 63.

44. CIA/DDI Venture, p. 73.

45. Taubman, *Khrushchev*, p. 555. The CIA ultimately dismissed the above hypothesis of willful blindness as "over-stated," positing that "Khrushchev could not have concluded, even if he had available a complete tracking of the [U-2] flights, that the new pattern would persist." CIA/DDI Venture, p. 74.

46. Gioe, Scott, and Andrew, *International History*, p. 121; Michael B. Petersen, *Legacy of Ashes, Trial by Fire: The Origins of the Defense Intelligence Agency and the Cuban Missile Crisis Crucible*, Defense Intelligence Historical Perspectives No. 1 (Washington, DC: Defense Intelligence Agency, Historical Research Division. 2011), pp. 15–17 (citing Wright Diary; *FRUS*, 1961–1963, vol. 10, *Cuba, January 1961–September 1962*, pp. 1054–55). See Wright briefing of SECDEF and JCS at https://history.state.gov/historicaldocuments/frus1961-63v11/pg_1

47. Typed version of General Taylor's handwritten notes, pp. 4, 10, maintained in Box 16, Folder 4, T644A-71, Maxwell Taylor Special Collection, National Defense University Library. See Holland, "Photo Gap," p. 9. See Beschloss, *Crisis Years*, p. 425 ("Photointerpreters studying the pictures of the SAM installations noticed the same trapezoidal pattern that U-2 cameras had found around missile bases in the Soviet Union").

48. See Brugioni, *Eyeball to Eyeball*, p. 165n (obliquely mentioning Wright's key role), p. 199 (noting that MRBM site recognition was aided by "information pro-

vided by the Soviet Penkovsky"), and p. 541 (noting that "Penkovsky had provided information and documents on field deployment of Soviet weapons"); Christopher Andrew, *For the President's Eyes Only* (New York: HarperCollins, 1995), pp. 270 (Penkovsky provided "information on missile site construction"), p. 290 ("Without Penkovsky's material 'on Soviet missile procedures and site construction' US analysts "would have been unable to interpret a significant part of what the [U-2] photographs revealed"); Absher, "Mind Sets and Missiles," p. 7 ("By comparing the U-2 photography with information in the manuals provided by Penkovsky, analysts were able to identify positively the specific missiles being placed in Cuba"); Blight and Welch, *Intelligence*, p. 57 n. 26 ("Of particular value was detailed information on the readiness and operating procedures of the SS-4 missile system earlier provided by U.S. (and U.K.) agent GRU Col. Oleg Penkovsky, including the SS-4 operating manual. . . . this information . . . complemented earlier U-2 and satellite photography that had made US analysts familiar with the pattern of SS-4 and SS-5 site preparation and construction in the Soviet Union").

49. Naftali and Zelikow, *Presidential Recordings*, vol. 2, p. 432 n. 34; Parkinson and Potter, "Closing the Missile Gap," p. 34. See Supplement 3 to Joint Evaluation of Soviet Missile Threat in Cuba, October 22, 1962, in McAuliffe, *CIA Documents*, Doc. 81, stamped "IRONBARK," pp. 281–82 ("These sites presently contain unrevetted, field-type launchers which rely on mobile erection, checkout and support equipment. These missiles are probably those reported moving into this area in September").

50. Barrett and Holland, *Blind over Cuba*, p. 15. Halpern was executive officer of Task Force W (TFW), which was "the Mongoose component at CIA headquarters" (p. 15)

51. Peter A. Huchthausen, *October Fury* (Hoboken, NJ: John Wiley & Sons, 2002), p. 26.

52. McCone file memorandum entitled "Memorandum on Donovan Project," McAuliffe, *CIA Documents*, Doc. 44 pp. 123–34. See http://avalon.law.yale.edu/20th_century/msc_cuba012.asp

53. "Notes taken from transcripts of meetings of the Joint Chiefs of Staff, October–November 1962, dealing with the Cuban Missile Crisis (handwritten notes were made in 1976 and typed in 1993)," released under the Freedom of Information Act, copy made available by National Security Archive. See *Cold War International History Project Bulletin* 8–9 (Winter 1996–97), pp. 272 and nn. 9 and 10, Woodrow Wilson International Center for Scholars, https://www.wilsoncenter.org/sites/default/files/CWIHP_Bulletin_8-9.pdf

Chapter 7

1. See Beer, "U.S. Navy," p. 59 (at a mid-August 1962 meeting of the JCS, two flag officers who were members of the Joint Strategic Survey Committee [JSSC] presented their case that "the Soviets were basing ballistic missiles in Cuba" and

"the service chiefs all agreed with the JSSC assessment, but the new JCS chairman, General Taylor, did not, and he was unwilling to sound the alarm without further evidence and refused to convey their argument to McNamara or the president").

2. Sorensen, *Kennedy*, p. 332. Sorensen would say much the same thing when speaking of the president, and the presidency, in his memoirs written more than four decades later: "All of us on the president's staff knew that we were in part the president's political advisors and that the White House is inherently a political institution." Does the president "play politics"? "Of course he is playing politics—the president in a democracy is required to play politics with every issue, if this country is to be governed with the consent of the governed." "I soon learned that foreign policy, domestic policy, budgetary policy, congressional relations, and the president's own political fortunes all intersect and overlap." Sorensen, *Counselor*, pp. 209, 312.

3. Kenneth P. O'Donnell and David F. Powers, *Johnny We Hardly Knew Ye: Memories of John Fitzgerald Kennedy* (Boston: Little, Brown, 1970), p. 307. Bundy noted that "most of the more intense [ExComm] arguments of the first week took place in his absence." Bundy, *Danger and Survival*, p. 397.

4. Naftali and Zelikow, *Presidential Recordings*, vol. 2, pp. 440–41.

5. Naftali and Zelikow, *Presidential Recordings*, vol. 2, p. 443.

6. Naftali and Zelikow, *Presidential Recordings*, vol. 2, p. 528. See also Trachtenberg, *History and Strategy*, pp. 245–46 (citing October 17, 1962, Sorensen memorandum stating that it was "generally agreed that these missiles, even when fully operational, do not significantly alter the balance of power"). Trachtenberg called Sorensen "simply wrong on this point," citing the contrary views of the Pentagon and the CIA, yet it would seem Sorensen's term "generally" referred to the White House and its earliest ExComm advisers.

7. Thomas, *Robert Kennedy*, pp. 219–20.

8. O'Donnell and Powers, *Johnny*, p. 314.

9. See Thomas, *Robert Kennedy*, p. 225. See also Kennedy, *Thirteen Days*, p. 54; Dobbs, *One Minute to Midnight*, p. 86; Howard Jones, *Crucible of Power: A History of American Foreign Relations from 1945* (Lanham, MD: Rowman & Littlefield, 2009), p. 121.

10. O'Donnell and Powers, *Johnny*, pp. 306–7.

11. Paterson and Brophy, "October Missiles," p. 94.

12. Sorensen, *Kennedy*, p. 670; see also Allison and Zelikow, *Essence of Decision*, p. 330.

13. Paterson, *November Elections*, p. 90.

14. Denise M. Bostdorff, *The Presidency and the Rhetoric of Foreign Crisis* (Columbia: University of South Carolina Press, 1999), p. 38.

15. O'Donnell and Powers, *Johnny*, p. 310; see also Zelizer, *Arsenal of Democracy*, p. 163; Reeves, *President Kennedy*, p. 371. In fact, Capehart would lose his seat in the 1962 midterm election, though for reasons "not directly related to the Cuban issue," according to Paterson and Brophy. Democrats lost four seats in the House

and Republicans gained two. In the Senate five incumbent senators lost their seats: three Republicans and two Democrats. Paterson and Brophy, "October Missiles," pp. 112, 115. Kenneth Keating did not have to face election until 1964, when he lost his Senate seat to Robert F. Kennedy.

16. Beschloss, *Crisis Years*, p. 420; see also Pressman, "September Statements"; Taubman, *Khrushchev*, p. 554.

17. Lebow and Stein, *We All Lost*, p. 92.

18. Naftali and Zelikow, *Presidential Recordings*, vol. 2, pp. 442–43.

19. Taubman, *Khrushchev*, p. 554.

20. White, *Cuban Missile Crisis*, p. 111. Keating would go on to make another twenty-four public statements on Cuba through October 25, 1962 (White, p. 103). There was much speculation in August 1962 and continuing for many years thereafter about who Senator Keating's source may have been. No firm answers have been found. See, e.g., Thomas G. Paterson, "The Historian as Detective: Senator Kenneth Keating, the Missiles in Cuba, and His Mysterious Sources," *Diplomatic History* 11, no. 1 (Winter 1987), pp. 67–71; Max Holland, "A Luce Connection: Senator Keating, William Pawley, and the Cuban Missile Crisis," *Journal of Cold War Studies* 1, no. 3 (1999), pp. 139–67, Project MUSE, muse.jhu.edu/article/9114

21. Julian E. Zelizer, *Arsenal of Democracy: The Politics of National Security—From World War II to the War on Terrorism.* New York: Basic Books, 2010, p. 157.

22. Brugioni, *Eyeball to Eyeball*, p. 158.

23. See Paterson, *November Elections*, p. 96.

24. Paterson, *November Elections*, p. 96.

25. O'Donnell and Powers, *Johnny*, p. 309.

26. Beschloss, *Crisis Years*, p. 438 ("In his haste to remedy his domestic political worries" the president issued a statement that "locked him into a specific course of action").

27. Beschloss, *Crisis Years*, p. 448.

28. Dobbs, *One Minute to Midnight*, pp. 5–6. An "excited utterance" made after a shocking incident is an exception to the hearsay rule. It has been deemed sufficiently credible to be admissible into evidence, despite its hearsay character, based on the commonsense notion that a speaker in an excited or stressful state after a shocking event would not likely be able to intentionally lie. See Federal Rule of Evidence 803 (2). Arthur Best, *Evidence: Practice, Problems and Rules* (n.p.: Wolters Kluwer Law & Business, 2017), p. 264.

29. Barrett and Holland, *Blind over Cuba*, p. 6.

30. O'Donnell and Powers, *Johnny*, p. 309.

31. Naftali and Zelikow, *Presidential Recordings*, vol. 2, pp. 441, 443.

32. Naftali and Zelikow, *Presidential Recordings*, vol. 2, p. 464.

33. Naftali and Zelikow, *Presidential Recordings*, vol. 2, p. 22.

34. Richard Ned Lebow, "The Traditional and Revisionist Interpretations Revisited: Why Was Cuba a Crisis?," in Nathan, *Cuban Missile Crisis Revisited*, p. 183 n. 34.

35. Naftali and Zelikow, *Presidential Recordings*, vol. 2, pp. 576–77; May and Zelikow, *Kennedy Tapes*, p. 172.

36. The draft of the president's October 22, 1962, speech together with General Taylor's comments is maintained in the Maxwell Taylor Special Collection, Box 15, T-194–69, Folder A, at the National Defense University Library.

37. See, e.g., Dobbs, *One Minute to Midnight*, p. 68; Thomas, *Robert Kennedy*, pp. 222, 224 (mentioning Robert Kennedy's reference to "Holeman" and the president's observation, "It looks really mean, doesn't it?" but ignoring the two brothers' expressions of concern about the risk of impeachment).

38. It is evident that the two Kennedys had forgotten that the taping system was capturing their conversation because they left the room without switching off the recorder, which continued to tape silence until the recording reel ended.

39. Robert Caro mentioned this unusual, almost coded method of fraternal communication in the third volume of his biography of Lyndon Johnson, where Caro noted that President Kennedy "was not just a brother, but a brother with whom Robert Kennedy had been so close that they finished each other's sentences, or communicated without any words at all, in a 'perfect,' 'almost telepathic' understanding." Robert Caro, *Lyndon Johnson: The Passage of Power* (New York: Knopf, 2012), p. 573. Evan Thomas's biography of Robert Kennedy provides a similar insight, picking up on a comment Isaiah Berlin made about the apparently "telepathic" way that the two brothers communicated: "Though the brothers sat far apart at the table, they picked up on each other's jokes, asides and glances. 'They hardly had to speak with each other. They understood each other from a half word,' Berlin recalled. 'There was a kind of constant, almost telepathic, contact between them.'" Thomas, *Robert Kennedy*, p. 233.

40. Regarding the president's speaking style, see Naftali, *Presidential Recordings*, vol. 1, pp. lii–liii (introduction by Naftali). For the attorney general's often tangled comments in meetings, see Thomas, *Robert Kennedy*, p. 134 ("His inarticulateness was an impediment: the Soviets were sometimes baffled by his colloquial utterances"), p. 210 (at ExComm meeting RFK "asked awkward questions [sometimes awkwardly; stress did not improve his syntax]").

41. The longtime historian of the John F. Kennedy Presidential Library, Sheldon Stern, has produced his own transcription of the Kennedy tapes that corrects numerous passages provided in the May and Zelikow *Presidential Recordings* transcriptions. In this instance, Stern's transcription corrected "It's just a question of where they go about it next" to read, "Jesus Christ! What are they gonna fuck up next?" Sheldon Stern, *Averting "The Final Failure": John F. Kennedy and the Secret Cuban Missile Meetings* (Stanford, CA: Stanford University Press, 2003), p. 204. In another passage, Stern (Author's Translation, "AT") corrected an important and substantive error in the transcription of Llewelyn Thompson's view of Walter Lippmann's October 25 article:

> [May and Zelikow, *Presidential Recordings*], [vol.] 3, [p.] 470: Thompson: "I think they've been put **up** by the Lippmann piece. **It occurs to me** that we

really **aren't** prepared to talk Turkey for Cuba."

AT: Thompson: "I think they've been put **off** by the Lippmann piece—**encouraged to think** that we *really* **are** prepared to **swap** Turkey for Cuba."

Stern, p. 438. See a representative sample of the Stern transcription corrections at pp. 427–40.

42. Again, Sheldon Stern provided this slightly different transcription of the same comment by the president: "Anyway, it's a sickening thing that we were told, is that he's [Khrushchev] very mad about being revealed about this. *How* is that embarrassing in the election." Stern, *Averting the Final Failure*, p. 205.

43. Zelikow and May, *Presidential Recordings*, vol. 3, pp. 177–79.

44. Further confirmation of the notion that the president was considering the option of doing nothing comes in the question he asked at the October 18 Ex-Comm meeting at 11:00 a.m. to which no one in the room provided an audible response: "Well, let me ask you this. Is there anyone here who doesn't think that we ought to do something about them?" Naftali and Zelikow, *Presidential Recordings*, vol. 2, p. 557.

45. Len V. Scott, *Macmillan, Kennedy and the Cuban Missile Crisis* (London: Macmillan, 1999), pp. 41, 43.

46. Scott, *Macmillan, Kennedy*, p. 96 (emphasis added).

47. Fursenko and Naftali, *Gamble*, p. 196.

48. Sorensen, *Kennedy*, pp. 682, 683; see also Sorensen, *Counselor*, p. 288 ("From the beginning, the president made certain that all his options were reviewed, including the option of doing nothing at all").

49. Sorensen, *Kennedy*, p. 683.

50. Naftali and Zelikow, *Presidential Recordings*, vol. 2, p. 422. See White, *Cuban Missile Crisis*, pp. 133–34 ("Kennedy's performance on 16 October made clear that his own instincts coupled with a desire to keep his September public promises to take resolute action if missiles were placed in Cuba led him down the path towards military action").

51. Sorensen, *Counselor*, pp. 292, 308.

52. Naftali and Zelikow, *Presidential Recordings*, vol. 2, pp. 442–43.

53. Naftali and Zelikow, *Presidential Recordings*, vol. 2, pp. 528–29.

54. Naftali and Zelikow, *Presidential Recordings*, vol. 2, p. 541.

55. Naftali and Zelikow, *Presidential Recordings*, vol. 2, p. 541.

56. Naftali and Zelikow, *Presidential Recordings*, vol. 2, p. 557.

57. Naftali and Zelikow, *Presidential Recordings*, vol. 2, pp. 587–88.

58. Naftali and Zelikow, *Presidential Recordings*, vol. 2, p. 590.

59. Thomas, *Robert Kennedy*, p. 219.

60. See Stern, *Averting the Final Failure*, p. 204 (the impeachment risk would arise "after the mid-term elections, on the grounds of failure to live up to his public pledge to prevent an offensive military buildup in Cuba").

61. Lebow and Stein, *We All Lost*, p. 97.

62. Bernstein, "Reconsidering the Missile Crisis," p. 104.

63. Lebow, "Traditional and Revisionist Interpretations," p. 167.

64. Sorensen, *Kennedy*, pp. 688, 775; Reeves, *President Kennedy*, p. 381; Morton H. Halperin and Priscilla Clapp, *Bureaucratic Politics and Foreign Policy*, 2nd ed. (Washington, DC: Brookings Institution Press, 2006), p. 64.

65. See chapter 9.

66. Evan Thomas speculated about what the president meant by his question whether Holeman was "with us," and guessed the attorney general might have been "holding back . . . from his brother" by not saying more about the Holeman and Bartlett initiatives, perhaps in order to preserve "plausible deniability." Thomas, *Robert Kennedy*, pp. 222–23. It seems more likely, however, that the president knew what was going on and had authorized the attorney general to launch the missile swap feelers through at least one and probably both of the journalists, given the president's active personal perseverance regarding his missile swap idea, the urgent need to resolve the crisis, the specific mention of both journalists' names during the Kennedy brothers' private October 23 exchange, the president's having spoken to Bartlett about his missile trade idea only two days before, and the two prompt follow-on meetings between Bartlett and the president on the evenings of October 23 and 24.

67. Thomas, *Robert Kennedy*, p. 222; Kempe, *Berlin 1961*, p. 191 ("Bolshakov had worked Holeman as an unpaid informant from the time they had met at a 1951 Soviet embassy lunch in the American correspondent's honor"). Thomas wrote that Holeman had become "temporarily unemployed" due to the New York newspaper strike, and as of October 23 was working for Ed Guthman, Robert Kennedy's spokesman at the Department of Justice. This chronology seems inaccurate, as the New York newspaper strike would not commence until several weeks later, on December 8, 1962, and Holeman wrote an October 28, 1962, article for the *Daily News* reporting on the Kennedy-Khrushchev agreement that day which appeared to end the crisis. http://www.nydailynews.com/news/world/cuban-missiles-crisis-1962-article-1.2414732

68. NYT obituary, February 19, 2017, citing Bartlett comments reported in Sallie Bedell Smith, *Grace and Power: The Private World of the Kennedy White House* (New York: Random House, 2004).

69. Memorandum of A. I. Mikoyan's Conversation with Comrades F. Castro, O. Dorticós, E. Guevara, E. Aragonés, and C. R. Rodriguez, November 22, 1962 (emphasis added), http://nsarchive.gwu.edu/NSAEBB/NSAEBB393/.

70. As previously noted, Sheldon Stern, the longtime historian of the John F. Kennedy Presidential Library, produced his own transcription of the Kennedy tapes that yielded numerous differences from the Zelikow/May transcription. For the immediately preceding sentence as an example, Stern's transcription reads: "Anyway, it's a sickening thing that we were told, is that he's [Khrushchev] very mad about being revealed about this. *How* is that embarrassing in the election." Stern, *Averting the Final Failure*, p. 205.

71. Zelikow and May, *Presidential Recordings*, vol. 3, p. 100; see also http://avalon.law.yale.edu/20th_century/msc_cuba045.asp

72. Charles Bartlett letter addressed to "Mr. President," November 5, 1962, Georgetown University Library, Edward Weintal Personal Papers, Box 2, Folder 5. The Bartlett letter may also be found in the John F. Kennedy Presidential Library in President's Office Files, Series 1, Special Correspondence, Bartlett, Charles L. 9/62-12-62, Box 28.

73. Naftali and Zelikow, *Presidential Recordings*, vol. 2, p. 555.

Chapter 8

1. There was, however, one strange dissenting voice: that of Secretary of Defense McNamara. At a meeting with congressional leaders on October 24, 1962, McNamara made a "most unusual statement," memorialized in CIA director McCone's meeting memorandum, which noted the ambiguities attending characterization of the Soviet missiles as offensive or defensive: "He said: 'One might question whether the missiles are or are not offensive. However, there is no question about the IL-28s.'" McCone added a parenthetical note in his meeting memorandum that "this was the first time anyone has raised doubt as to whether the MRBMs and the IRBMs are offensive missiles." McCone, Memorandum for the File, October 24, 1962, in McAuliffe, *CIA Documents*, p. 277.

2. See, e.g., Hamid Karimianpour, *Nation Building: Or Democracy by Other Means* (New York: Algora Publishing, 2011), p. 198 (referring to widespread accusations in the aftermath of the Iraq war that "the British Government had 'sexed up' the dossier to build a case for war").

3. Lebow and Stein, *We All Lost*, p. 78 (citing comments by Bundy and Sorensen at later conferences convened to analyze the Cuban missile crisis confirming that "the president would have found it extraordinarily difficult to have opposed an open deployment" of the Soviet missiles because "world opinion would be receptive to the Soviet claim that the missiles in Cuba were a legitimate response to the Jupiters in Turkey").

4. Naftali and Zelikow, *Presidential Recordings*, vol. 2, pp. 455–57. See also Beschloss, *Crisis Years*, p. 455 ("Rusk and Thompson advised the President not to show Gromyko the U-2 pictures" because this would "give Khrushchev the initiative").

5. Beschloss, *Crisis Years*, p. 458.

6. CIA/DDI Venture, p. 80. Dean Rusk expressed the same view in his oral history, recorded in 1970: "But Gromyko simply repeated the formulation which their ambassador had earlier given us that there were only defensive weapons in Cuba." Oral History, JFKL, p. 118.

7. http://microsites.jfklibrary.org/cmc/oct18/doc1/html

8. October 24, 1962, Telegram from Soviet Ambassador to the USA Dobrynin to the USSR MFA, http://digitalarchive.wilsoncenter.org/document/111625

9. Sorensen, *Kennedy*, pp. 689–90.

10. http://www.historywiz.com/primarysources/kennedyspeechcuba.html

11. Stewart Alsop and Charles Bartlett, "In Times of Crisis," *Saturday Evening Post*, December 8, 1962, http://www.saturdayeveningpost.com/wp-content/uploads/satevepost/1962-12-08-missile-crisis.pdf. See Herken, *Georgetown Set*, pp. 277–79.

12. In his memoirs, Bowles said of his October 13 meeting with Dobrynin only that the Soviet ambassador was "genuinely surprised" upon hearing from Bowles that the Americans had obtained photographic evidence of Soviet "heavy IL-28 bombers" in Cuba, and "insisted that the report must be untrue." Bowles, *Promises to Keep*, p. 418.

13. Alsop and Bartlett, "In Times of Crisis."

14. Kennedy, *Thirteen Days*, pp. 3, 5.

15. See Hilsman, *To Move a Nation*, p. 166 ("only antiaircraft missiles . . . which could not reach American targets").

16. Beschloss, *Crisis Years*, p. 426.

17. See, e.g., Khrushchev's statement in May 1962 that "we are in fact stronger than imperialism, because our forces include not only the socialist states but also progressive and peace-loving peoples on earth, all people who hold peace dear." John Gooch and Amos Perlmutter, eds., *Military Deception and Strategic Surprise* (New York: Routledge, 2012), pp. 48–49.

18. CIA/DDI Venture, p. 72.

19. The report considered, for example, whether Khrushchev might have concluded that he had been wrong in thinking that the United States would acquiesce in the buildup, and that "his situation was now serious enough to justify the use of the most extreme form of deception." CIA/DDI Venture, p. 72.

20. CIA/DDI Venture, p. 77.

21. Robert Kennedy told the president on the morning of September 4 that Dobrynin had asked for the meeting but hadn't provided the reason: "He wants to see me at 2:15. He said anytime and anyplace. He wants to talk just . . . I don't know what it's about." Naftali and Zelikow, *Presidential Recordings*, vol. 2, p. 12.

22. Kennedy, *Thirteen Days*, p. 3.

23. See Beschloss, *Crisis Years*, p. 420; Brugioni, *Eyeball to Eyeball*, p. 115 (citing Kennedy, *Thirteen Days*). Beschloss also picked up on Kennedy's observation that he was "skeptical about Dobrynin's assurances" and therefore "persuaded the president to issue a public warning to the Soviets." *Crisis Years*, p. 420. See the same purported attribution to Dobrynin in James Hansen, "Soviet Deception in the Cuban Missile Crisis," CIA report, posted April 14, 2007—but Hansen cites as support Brugioni, *Eyeball to Eyeball*, p. 115, which in turn cited Robert Kennedy's *Thirteen Days* as its source, https://www.cia.gov/library/center-for-the-study-of-intelligence/csi-publications/csi-studies/studies/vol46no1/article06.html

24. Kennedy, *Thirteen Days*, p. 4.

25. Abel, *Missile Crisis*, p. 19.

26. Naftali and Zelikow, *Presidential Recordings*, vol. 2, p. 34.

27. Brugioni, *Eyeball to Eyeball*, p. 115.

28. Hilsman, *To Move a Nation*, p. 165; Hilsman, *Cuban Missile Crisis*, p. 20.

29. See Lebow and Stein, *We All Lost*, p. 86 ("Anatoly Dobrynin, the man on the spot in Washington, was neither consulted nor informed about the missiles").

30. Dobrynin, *In Confidence*, pp. 68–69. Fursenko and Naftali found the same summary of the Dobrynin/Kennedy conversation of September 4, 1962, in the portion of the ambassador's diary written on September 13, 1962. See *Khrushchev's Cold War*, p. 453 and n. 48.

31. Dobrynin, *In Confidence*, p. 69. Dobrynin provided the same response in answer to a question posed to him in 1992 by a journalist working with *Peter Jennings Reporting*, ABC News:

> SHERRY JONES: And about the deployment?
>
> DOBRYNIN: . . . I was simply told that in case somebody asked you about missiles, you just simply you should answer there is no offensive weaponry in Cuba. Solely defensive weaponry, period. No other details you shouldn't provide and you will not explain why, so on all the questions about missiles, we always answer, there is no offensive missiles, no offensive weapons in Cuba. This is our standard answer for all Soviet diplomats, including myself.

George Washington University National Security Archives, http://nsarchive.gwu.edu/NSAEBB/NSAEBB400/docs/Interview%20with%20Anatoly%20Dobrynin.pdf

32. McGeorge Bundy acknowledged that it was a mystery to him how Dobrynin could have flatly lied when the Soviet ambassador lacked any underlying knowledge of the true facts. Bundy, *Danger and Survival*, p. 414.

33. Theodore C. Sorensen, Special Counsel to the President, September 6, 1962, Memorandum for the Files, *FRUS*, 1961–1963, vol. 10, *Cuba, January 1961–September 1962*, Doc. 415.

34. Sorensen, *Kennedy*, p. 668. In a 1964 CIA DD/I staff working paper on the Cuban missile crisis, reflecting information available through December 1963, the agency called Dobrynin's comments to Sorensen "seriously misleading," though not a "flat lie," and the agency found no flat lie in statements by Soviet Foreign Minister Gromyko. CIA/DDI Venture, pp. x, 61, 80.

35. CIA/DDI Venture, pp. 75–76.

36. CIA/DDI Venture, p. 77.

37. CIA/DDI Venture, p. 77; Beschloss, *Crisis Years*, p. 770.

38. See Bolshakov, "The Hot Line," pp. 41–42; Thomas, *Robert Kennedy*, pp. 205–6, 206n. Fursenko and Naftali also concluded, based on the Kennedy diary entry, that October 5 was the most likely date of the meeting. Fursenko and Naftali, *Gamble*, p. 219 and n. 10.

39. See Fursenko and Naftali, *Khrushchev's Cold War*, p. 462 and n. 72 (citing Dobrynin to NSK, October 9, 1962, Volkogonov Collection, Library of Congress).

40. The authors of the CIA postcrisis report were "uncertain" as to the date of

actual transmission of this message to American officials. They saw "no reason to doubt, however, that Khrushchev *meant* to have this message transmitted in the first week of October." CIA/DDI Venture, pp. 77n, 82. As to the various other dates that have been ascribed to the RFK/Bolshakov meeting: Brugioni wrote at a subsequent meeting two days later that Robert Kennedy mistakenly placed the meeting on September 11 (*Eyeball to Eyeball*, pp. 177–78); Richard Reeves concluded that October 4 and 6 were the correct dates (*President Kennedy*, p. 366); James Hansen, a former CIA official, providing no source, placed the meeting on October 17 ("Soviet Deception," p. 47); and Raymond Garthoff placed the meeting on October 24 (*Reflections*, p. 47 and n. 76), citing an incorrect page in Sorensen's *Kennedy* (p. 753 rather than p. 668). Sorensen's report of the Kennedy/Bolshakov meeting, which was also cited by Graham Allison (*Essence of Decision: Explaining the Cuban Missile Crisis* [Boston: Little Brown, 1971], p. 41), provided no date for the meeting and no source for the information. Sorensen also noted that Bolshakov's message was not conveyed to the president until "after he knew of the missiles' existence"—i.e., after October 16. *Kennedy*, p. 668. Schlesinger placed the date of the Bolshakov/Kennedy meeting on October 24. *A Thousand Days*, p. 820. Roger Hilsman gave no specific date for the Kennedy/Bolshakov meeting. *To Move a Nation*, p. 166.

41. Bolshakov, "The Hot Line," p. 41.

42. Evan Thomas has established that this RFK-Bolshakov meeting most likely occurred on October 5, 1962, based on an entry in Kennedy's daily diary maintained in the RFK Papers at JFKL. See Thomas, *Robert Kennedy*, pp. 205–6, 206n.

43. Bolshakov, "Secret Channel," p. 115.

44. *Thirteen Days*, p. 5.

45. Robert F. Kennedy, Oral History, JFKL, vol. 1, March 1, 1964, p. 70. See Kempe, *Berlin 1961*, p. 478; Thomas, *Robert Kennedy*, pp. 134–35.

46. See also Thomas, *Robert Kennedy*, p. 231 (referring to Robert Kennedy's draft memo to the Secretary of State purporting to summarize his October 27 meeting with Dobrynin, Thomas wrote, "In what one scholar has described as a 'blatant falsification of history,' Kennedy apparently also tried to cleanse the record in the files of the United States government"); Beschloss, *Crisis Years*, p. 334n ("One pattern in Robert Kennedy's discussion of the meetings with Bolshakov and other Russians in his 1964 and 1965 oral histories is his inclination to suggest that the Soviets caved in at crucial moments to unilateral demands by himself and the President without mentioning American concessions that were actually the key to solutions").

47. Bolshakov, "The Hot Line," p. 42. See also Bolshakov, "Secret Channel," p. 113 (nearly identical version of Bolshakov's recounting of Khrushchev's remarks published in the Soviet Union in November 1989).

48. It remains unclear how many pieces of confidential correspondence that passed by secret courier between Kennedy and Khrushchev remain protected from disclosure to historians and the public. In his 2008 memoirs, Sorensen mentioned Bolshakov by name only twice: once for having delivered Khrushchev's "first" private letter to the president, and a second time for having on a Saturday morning

passed to Sorensen on a Washington, DC, street corner a daily newspaper that concealed in its folds a "sealed envelope from the Soviet chairman." Sorensen, *Counselor*, pp. 5–6. No further details were provided by the president's loyal aide.

49. Bolshakov, "The Hot Line," p. 42.

50. See Blight and Welch, *Intelligence*, p. 175 (Bolshakov was unaware of the Soviet missile deployment until he learned about it on October 22, when it was announced by the president of the United States).

51. CIA/DDI Venture, pp. 72–77. In a contemporaneous FBI memorandum referencing the Joseph Alsop article of November 5, 1962, agency officials referenced a source, whose identity has been redacted from the memorandum, who reported that Bolshakov was overheard "discussing this article" on November 5, 1962 "with another Soviet and referred to it 'as propaganda.'" Memorandum from SAC, WFO to Director, FBI [date partially obscured but date-stamped in November 1962], Subject: Georgi Nikitovich Bolshakov, National Archives.

52. CIA/DDI Venture, p. 75.

53. Brugioni, *Eyeball to Eyeball*, pp. 177–78.

54. See Bolshakov, "The Hot Line," p. 41 (placing his meeting with Khrushchev and Mikoyan as occurring some time "between September 10 and 15"); see also Taubman, *Khrushchev*, pp. 555–56 (Khrushchev met with Secretary Udall in Pitsunda on September 6 and then with Bolshakov "several days later").

55. Brugioni's comment that Bolshakov used a "blue notebook" at the "early October" meeting is curious. Brugioni's only source citation—to *Thirteen Days*—does not mention a blue notebook. A postcrisis magazine article published by journalists Charles Bartlett and Stewart Alsop on December 8, 1962, mentioned that Bolshakov took down Mikoyan's comments in a "little blue notebook," but they also reported that these comments did not reach the president until after he had already become aware of the Soviet missiles in Cuba. See http://www.saturdayeveningpost.com/wp-content/uploads/satevepost/1962-12-08-missile-crisis.pdf. And while Charles Bartlett had written two earlier letters memorializing his meeting with Bolshakov, neither of them mentioned a blue notebook. See also Beschloss, *Crisis Years*, p. 426 (referring to Bolshakov writing down the Khrushchev/Mikoyan message in his "blue notebook," presumably so he would be able to convey it exactly, citing a Bartlett interview and Bartlett's memo to Robert Kennedy dated October 26, 1962, as his sources.)

56. Brugioni, *Eyeball to Eyeball*, p. 177.

57. Brugioni, *Eyeball to Eyeball*, p. 177.

58. Thomas, *Robert Kennedy*, pp. 205–6.

59. It is evident that Bartlett's October 23 approach to Bolshakov to buttress the "flat lie" story was instigated by Robert Kennedy without involvement by the president. This conclusion finds support in the following exchange between the two brothers that was captured on the White House taping system on the evening of October 23. The president posed the following odd question, indicating his ignorance of the nature of his brother's discussions with Soviet intermediaries about the capabilities of Soviet weapons in Cuba, and leaving Robert Kennedy in the embarrassing position of having to clarify the record as to what he had been told:

JFK: But did any of them tell you that they were going to put missiles there?
RFK: No. Remember, when I told you that.

60. In Beschloss's rendition of the Bartlett/Bolshakov meeting, no comment by Mikoyan is mentioned, but only a statement attributed to Bolshakov that he "could not believe" there were ground-to-ground missiles in Cuba. Beschloss, *Crisis Years*, p. 500.

61. Memo to the Attorney General, October 26, 1962, Georgetown University Library, Edward Weintal Personal Papers, Box 2, Folder 5.

62. Letter to Mr. President, November 5, 1962, Georgetown University Library, Edward Weintal Personal Papers, Box 2, Folder 5. The Bartlett letter may also be found in the John F. Kennedy Presidential Library in President's Office Files, Series 1, Special Correspondence, Bartlett, Charles L. 9/62-12-62, Box 28.

63. See, e.g., Herken, *Georgetown Set*, p. 277 (finding that Robert Kennedy "lost faith" in Bolshakov, Joe Alsop wrote a November 5, 1962, column "outing the Russian" as a measure of "the Kennedys' revenge," whereupon the GRU agent was "promptly recalled to Moscow").

64. Fursenko and Naftali, *Gamble*, pp. 249–50 (October 23 messages); Bolshakov, "Secret Channel," p. 113 (Bartlett demonstration of the U-2 photos); A. A. Fursenko, "Georgy Bolshakov, Khrushchev's Orderly to Kennedy," *Znamya* (ISSN 0321-1878) 7 (1997), pp. 161–83 (Glenn Bryant translation in author's files) (Robert Kennedy's approaches to Bolshakov to resolve inclusion of the IL-28 bombers). An FBI memorandum dated November 20, 1962 captured the still-friendly relationship between Bolshakov and the attorney general. When Bolshakov called on that date to wish Kennedy "Happy Birthday." Based on a source whose identity was redacted in the memorandum, the following conversation transpired: "Bolshakov asked 'You got what you wanted?' The Attorney General replied 'Yes, that was very good. I think it helped.' He continued and asked Bolshakov if he was going to come in (apparently to see the Attorney General) and Bolshakov replied in the affirmative and the time was set for 4:45 p.m." FBI Memorandum from Mr. Branigan to Mr. Sullivan, 11/20/62, Subject: Georgi N. Bolshakov, National Archives.

65. Bolshakov, "The Hot Line," p. 39; see also Fursenko, "Georgy Bolshakov, Khrushchev's Orderly."

66. Bartlett to "Mr. President," October 29, 1962, JFKL, NARA Digital Archives.

67. October 24, 1962, Telegram from Soviet Ambassador to the USA Dobrynin to the USSR MFA, http://digitalarchive.wilsoncenter.org/document/111625; see also Taubman, *Khrushchev*, p. 564.

68. Memorandum for the President from the Attorney General, October 24, 1962, JFKL, Attorney General Confidential File, Box 218.

69. Kennedy, *Thirteen Days*, p. 3.

70. October 24, 1962, Telegram from Soviet Ambassador to the USA Dobrynin to the USSR MFA, http://digitalarchive.wilsoncenter.org/document/111625. See also Dobrynin, *In Confidence*, pp. 81–82. In response to Robert Kennedy's statement that "even the ambassador himself had no reliable information at the time of our earlier meeting," Dobrynin noted, "He was right, and I had not much to

say to him in reply except to confirm that I had no real information from my government."

71. See CIA/DDI Venture, pp. 63–64 ("This [TASS] specification of defensive *purpose* rather than capability was the model for most subsequent descriptions of the weapons sent to Cuba").

72. Hilsman, *Cuban Missile Crisis*, p. 105.

Chapter 9

1. Beschloss, *Crisis Years*, p. 281n. (noting that Kennedy ended the Berlin Wall and Cuban missile crises in "exactly" the same manner "by proposing a solution in talks of the highest secrecy with a private Khrushchev emissary, taking extraordinary pains to assure that the concession remained secret out of fear of deep political harm should the Americans discover what he had done").

2. Max Frankel, *High Noon in the Cold War: Kennedy, Khrushchev and the Cuban Missile Crisis* (New York: Ballantine Books, 2004), p. 80.

3. Barrett and Holland, *Blind over Cuba*, p. 4; see also Fursenko and Naftali, *Gamble*, p. 204 (McCone "suggested that the United States pull its Jupiter missiles out of Turkey so that they would not pose such an inviting target for Soviet vengeance").

4. Nash, *Other Missiles of October*, p. 109; see also May and Zelikow, *Kennedy Tapes*, p. 36 (citing to the same effect McCone's personal notes of the August 23 meeting: "McCone questioned value of Jupiter missiles in Turkey and Italy. McNamara agreed they were useless but difficult politically to remove them").

5. Holland, "Photo Gap"; Absher, "Mind Sets and Missiles," p. 31.

6. NSAM 181.

7. *FRUS*, 1961–1963, vol. 10, *Cuba, January 1961–September 1962*, Doc. 402, Att. 2.

8. Naftali and Zelikow, *Presidential Recordings*, vol. 2, pp. 532, 538. See Nash, *Other Missiles of October*, pp. 128–29.

9. Naftali and Zelikow, *Presidential Recordings*, vol. 2, p. 613.

10. Zelikow and May, *Presidential Recordings*, vol. 3, pp. 18, 19, 47.

11. Zelikow and May, *Presidential Recordings*, vol. 3, p. 312.

12. Zelikow and May, *Presidential Recordings*, vol. 3, pp. 363, 364, 366, 380, 381, 443, 481.

13. Trachtenberg, *History and Strategy*, p. 243.

14. Scott, *Macmillan, Kennedy*, pp. 41–44.

15. Quoted in Scott, *Macmillan, Kennedy*, p. 48.

16. Fursenko and Naftali, *Gamble*, p. 237. Shortly afterward the president initiated another highly unorthodox dissemination of top-secret information through his friend Bartlett. At the president's or his brother's request, the original story board displays of the U-2 photographs showing Soviet missile installations in Cuba that had been marked "For the President's Eyes Only" were given to Bartlett so that he could show them to Georgi Bolshakov over lunch on October 24 at the National Press Club. Andrew, *President's Eyes Only*, p. 297.

17. Polmar and Gresham, *DEFCON-2*, pp. 211–12.

18. See Frankel, *High Noon*, p. 123: "Bobby still kept him [Bolshakov] at arm's length, but he sent two friends in the Washington press corps to tell Bolshakov that a withdrawal of the missiles might, in calmer days, be reciprocated with an American withdrawal of the Jupiters from Turkey. The president's hand has never been detected in this suggestion, but Bobby well knew that his voice carried presidential weight in Moscow."

19. Fursenko and Naftali, *Gamble*, p. 249, based on GRU *Spravka*, Archives of the Main Department of the General Staff of the Russian Federation. According to Evan Thomas's biography of Robert Kennedy, Holeman was at the time "temporarily unemployed" due to a newspaper strike and "had taken a job with Ed Guthman, Kennedy's spokesman at the Justice Department." Thomas, *Robert Kennedy*, p. 222. Thomas's explanation of Holeman's availability is unsatisfactory, however, since the New York newspaper strike did not begin until December 8, 1962. See https://en.wikipedia.org/wiki/1962%E2%80%9363_New_York_City_newspaper_strike

20. Robert Kennedy Desk Diaries, 1962, JFKL.

21. Beschloss, *Crisis Years*, p. 500.

22. Fursenko and Naftali, *Gamble*, p. 250, based on GRU *Spravka*, Archives of the Main Department of the General Staff of the Russian Federation.

23. Thomas, *Robert Kennedy*, p. 222.

24. See chapter 7.

25. The Kennedys and Ormsby-Gores were very close personal friends. Kennedy's younger sister had married Ormsby-Gore's first cousin. During the Cuban crisis, the president apparently offered the ambassador and his family places in "the Presidential nuclear shelter deep beneath the Appalachian Mountains." Wilson, *Launch Pad UK*, p. 128. In 1968, after both the president and the British ambassador's wife had died, Ormsby-Gore proposed marriage to the president's widow. She turned him down in favor of the Greek shipping magnate Aristotle Onassis. See Steven Erlanger, "Letters from Jacqueline Kennedy to the Man She Wouldn't Marry," *New York Times*, February 9, 2017, p. A1.

26. Zelikow and May, *Presidential Recordings*, vol. 3, pp. 177–79.

27. Evan Thomas aptly expressed the matter of Robert Kennedy's apparent authority in this passage from *Robert Kennedy*, which considered Khrushchev's likely thinking when he received the Kennedy feeler through Bolshakov: "Khrushchev knew that the GRU agent had a direct line to the Kennedys. By sending Khrushchev a back-channel peace feeler, did RFK unwittingly exacerbate the crisis, inadvertently emboldening the Kremlin leader to make new demands?" (p. 226).

28. JFKL, Evelyn Lincoln "Day at a Glance." Bartlett also dined with the attorney general and the president at the White House on the evening of October 24. Dobbs, *One Minute to Midnight*, p. 107.

29. Fursenko and Naftali, *Gamble*, p. 236.

30. It is also interesting in this regard to note that the first public viewing of the U-2 surveillance photographs of the Soviet missile sites did not occur in the United States but rather in the United Kingdom, after the White House gave the

BBC permission to broadcast to the British public "the most highly classified U.S. imagery intelligence ever to be released." Andrew, *President's Eyes Only*, p. 296.

31. Michael Graham Fry, ed., *History, the White House and the Kremlin: Statesmen as Historians* (New York: Bloomsbury, 1991), pp. 74–75.

32. Bruce J. Allyn, James G. Blight, and David A. Welch, "Essence of Revision," *International Security* 14, no. 3 (Winter 1989–90), p. 158.

33. Lebow, "Traditional and Revisionist Interpretations," p. 168. Lebow placed the date of the meeting on October 24 (p. 168), Raymond Garthoff on October 25 (*Reflections*, p. 52), and Laurence Chang on October 26 ("The View from Washington and the View from Nowhere: Cuban Missile Crisis Historiography and the Epistemology of Decision Making," in Nathan, *Cuban Missile Crisis Revisited*, p. 150). Dobrynin's recollection at the 1989 conference was that the meeting occurred on October 26.

34. Khrushchev, *Nikita Khrushchev*, p. 595. Stern has observed that no contemporaneous written records were made regarding this conversation, and he concludes that "the historical jury is still out" on whether the meeting ever took place. Stern, *Avoiding the Final Failure*, pp. 289–90.

35. Fursenko and Naftali, *Gamble*, p. 275.

36. Herken, *Georgetown Set*, pp. 256–57 ("Kennedy instructed his press secretary, Pierre Salinger, that only four newsmen—Joe Alsop, Phil Graham, Scotty Reston and Walter Lippmann—were to be put through to him immediately when they telephoned the White House"); Barrett and Holland, *Blind over Cuba*, p. 33 (Lippmann included among "list of journalists who were to be 'contacted privately'—in other words, who would receive selective leaks from ExComm members").

37. Barrett and Holland, *Blind over Cuba*, pp. 33–34 and nn. 49 and 50.

38. Barrett and Holland, *Blind over Cuba*, p. 13 and n. 75.

39. Zelikow and May, *Presidential Recordings*, vol. 3, p. 29.

40. Zelikow and May, *Presidential Recordings*, vol. 3, p. 107.

41. Yale University Library, Walter Lippmann Papers, Engagement Book 1962 (2), Group No. 326, Series VII, Box 239, Box 243, Folder 68; Diaries, Series VII, Box 239, microfilm.

42. *FRUS*, 1961–1963, vol. 11, *Cuban Missile Crisis and Aftermath*, Telegram No. 56 (with notation that the telegram had been drafted by Ball). Ball himself had apparently come to the conclusion that reaching a "political arrangement" with the Soviet's was the only way to end the crisis. Gregg Herken discovered a shorthand note written by Paul Nitze at an ExComm meeting on October 25 quoting the following "ominous prediction" uttered by George Ball: "Unless we return to political arrangement we will all fry." Herken, *Georgetown Set*, p. 274.

43. Lippmann, Today & Tomorrow, "Blockade Proclaimed," *Washington Post*, October 25, 1962, p. A25; Scott, *Macmillan, Kennedy*, p. 48; Nash, *Other Missiles of October*, p. 131 and n. 31 (referring to "Ormsby-Gore to Macmillan 23 October 1962"). Interestingly, Lippmann's Engagement Book and Diary also note that the columnist dined with the Ormsby-Gores at a large British embassy luncheon on October 23, but these documents contain no indication whether there was any opportunity for private discussion of the missile crisis with the ambassador at that time.

44. See Dobrynin November 1, 1962 Cable to Foreign Office contained in *Cold War International History Project Bulletin* 8–9 (Winter 1996–97), p. 308, Woodrow Wilson International Center for Scholars. Http://cwihp.si.edu/default/htm

45. Cf. Herken, *Georgetown Set*, p. 277 n. 29 ("In an ExComm meeting on November 2, Kennedy observed of press coverage of the crisis, 'But I think if we can hold it as tight as possible, then we can put it out in our own way'").

46. See Dobrynin cable to Foreign Ministry, November 1, 1962 (forwarding memorandum reflecting meeting G. A. Zhukov attended on October 31 with Llewelyn Thompson, Pierre Salinger, Averill Harriman, and Lippmann in which the American attendees were emphasizing the administration's need to have credible monitoring mechanisms working before the midterm elections in order to demonstrate to the American public that the Soviet bases in Cuba were actually being dismantled), contained in *Cold War International History Project Bulletin* 8–9 (Winter 1996–97), pp. 307–8, Woodrow Wilson International Center for Scholars. Http://cwihp.si.edu/default/htm

47. Dobbs, *One Minute to Midnight*, p. 199. See also Richard Ned Lebow, *Coercion, Cooperation and Ethics in International Relations* (New York: Routledge, 2007), p. 228 (the Soviet embassy thought Lippmann column was "a trial balloon sent aloft by the White House"); Freedman, *Kennedy's Wars*, p. 210 (noting that Khrushchev "found it telling that the Jupiter trade had been intruded into the discussion by the well-connected—indeed semi-official—Lippmann"). An article by Max Frankel in the *New York Times* on October 24 had also mentioned the possibility of a Turkey-for-Cuba missile trade, although he noted that Kennedy administration officials were denying any parallels between the missile bases in the two countries. Nash, *Other Missiles of October*, p. 133.

48. Evan Thomas has concluded with considerable reason that the Bolshakov message must have been the "more influential" of the two because it reportedly originated at the White House and had further weight given that "Khrushchev knew that the GRU agent had a direct line to the Kennedys." Thomas, *Robert Kennedy*, p. 226.

49. See Wisniewski, *Lippmann*, pp. 209–10 (citing Mikoyan's comment to Castro on November 4, 1962: "Speaking frankly, we were not thinking about bases in Turkey at all . . . but during discussion of the dangerous situation we received information from the United States of America, including an article by Lippmann, where it was said that the Russians could raise the question of liquidating the USA bases in Turkey").

50. Khrushchev, *Nikita Khrushchev*, p. 591. Austrian Foreign Minister Bruno Kreisky was reported to have made a statement at this same time similar to Lippmann's proposal of a possible missile trade solution.

51. Zelikow and May, *Presidential Recordings*, vol. 3, p. 421. See also Nash, *Other Missiles of October*, p. 135.

52. Zelikow and May, *Presidential Recordings*, vol. 3, p. 427.

53. Letters from Khrushchev to Kennedy, October 23 and 24, 1962, Thomas, *Robert Kennedy*, p. 223.

54. Letter to Mr. President, November 5, 1962, Georgetown University Library, Edward Weintal Personal Papers, Box 2, Folder 5. The Bartlett letter may also be found in the John F. Kennedy Presidential Library in President's Office Files, Series 1, Special Correspondence, Bartlett, Charles L. 9/62-12-62, Box 28.

55. Hilsman, *Cuban Missile Crisis*, p. 121; Hilsman, *Nuclear Military Strategy*, p. 65.

56. Hilsman, *Cuban Missile Crisis*, p. 122. Fomin, whose real name was Aleksandr Semyonovich Feklisov, was the KGB station chief (resident) in Washington, DC. Andrew, *President's Eyes Only*, p. 299.

57. Aid, *Secret Sentry*, pp. 73–74. This information was not relayed to Secretary of Defense McNamara until noon on October 24, due to the navy's belief that it first needed to be "confirmed by visual sightings." McNamara was not happy about the delay, and subjected the chief of naval operations "to an abusive tirade" (Aid, pp. 75, 76).

58. Dobbs, *One Minute to Midnight*, p. 113.

59. Taubman, *Khrushchev*, p. 567. See also Fursenko and Naftali, *Gamble*, p. 259 ("Khrushchev was now convinced that the Soviet Union could not keep ballistic missiles in Cuba without going to war, and he wanted the rest of the Presidium to understand that Moscow would have to find another way to protect Fidel Castro").

60. Khrushchev, *Nikita Khrushchev*, p. 582.

61. Khrushchev, *Nikita Khrushchev*, p. 581.

62. Khrushchev, *Nikita Khrushchev*, p. 584.

63. Khrushchev, *Nikita Khrushchev*, p. 589.

64. Beschloss, *Crisis Years*, p. 522.

65. Fursenko and Naftali, *Gamble*, p. 276; Polmar and Gresham, *DEFCON-2*, p. 216.

66. Fursenko and Naftali, *Gamble*, p. 274.

67. Zelikow and May, *Presidential Recordings*, vol. 3, pp. 362, 365.

68. Zelikow and May, *Presidential Recordings*, vol. 3, p. 378. The attorney general's use of the expression "double-crossed" is revealing, for it signifies "betray[al] by acting in contradiction to *an agreed course of action*." *Webster's New College Dictionary* (1999) (emphasis added).

69. Zelikow and May, *Presidential Recordings*, vol. 3, pp. 363–64; Stern, *Averting the Final Failure*, pp. 294–97.

70. See Fursenko and Naftali, *Gamble*, p. 259 ("Trying not to display a sense of urgency, he suggested that before dismantling the R-12s, the Kremlin should 'look around' and be sure that Kennedy would not yield"); Taubman, *Khrushchev*, p. 567.

71. Taubman, *Khrushchev*, pp. 572–73.

72. Taubman, *Khrushchev*, p. 573.

73. Taubman, *Khrushchev*, p. 573.

74. Allison and Zelikow, *Essence of Decision*, p. 363.

75. Naftali and Zelikow, *Presidential Recordings*, vol. 2, pp. 413–14.

76. Bernstein, "Reconsidering the Missile Crisis," p. 105.

77. Thomas, *Robert Kennedy*, p. 231.

78. Bernstein, "Reconsidering the Missile Crisis," p. 105.

79. Fursenko and Naftali, *Gamble*, p. 249.

80. Polmar and Gresham, *DEFCON-2*, p. 211; see also Thomas, *Robert Kennedy*, p. 222.

81. Beschloss, *Crisis Years*, p. 525.

82. See http://nsarchive.gwu.edu/nsa/cuba_mis_cri/moment.htm

83. See http://nsarchive.gwu.edu/nsa/cuba_mis_cri/moment.htm

84. See Beschloss, *Crisis Years*, pp. 546–47; Nash, *Other Missiles of October*, pp. 151–52.

85. Beschloss, *Crisis Years*, p. 536n; Nash, *Other Missiles of October*, p. 142 and n. 59.

86. See Jervis, "Cuban Missile Crisis," p. 20 ("In this regard, it is telling that the US removed the missiles from Italy as well as from Turkey even though Khrushchev never called for this").

87. Nash, *Other Missiles of October*, pp. 161–62.

88. Nash, *Other Missiles of October*, pp. 161–62.

89. See http://www.historywiz.com/primarysources/kennedyspeechcuba.html (emphasis added).

90. Fursenko and Naftali, *Gamble*, p. 263.

91. See https://history.state.gov/historicaldocuments/frus1961-63v06/d68

92. Ferguson, *Kissinger*, p. 555. As Michael Dobbs has reported, the IL-28s in Cuba that the Soviets had assembled were not capable of carrying nuclear weapons. Additional nuclear-capable IL-28s had been transported to the island, but they were not removed from their crates, and their Tatyana 12-kiloton bombs were kept in separate storage locations. Nevertheless, US military planners worked under the assumption that the IL-28s on the island were nuclear-capable. Dobbs, *One Minute to Midnight*, pp. 246–48.

93. See, e.g., Beschloss, *Crisis Years*, pp. 557–61; Coleman, *Fourteenth Day*, pp. 146–48.

94. Fursenko, "Georgy Bolshakov, Khrushchev's Orderly."

95. Khrushchev letter quoted in Beschloss, *Crisis Years*, p. 560.

Chapter 10

1. See Zelikow and May, *Presidential Recordings*, vol. 3, p. 235 (McCone: "We still see no signs of any crash procedure in measures to increase the readiness of the Soviet armed forces. The Watch Committee concludes in their report this morning as follows: 'We conclude that Soviet bloc armed forces are continuing to increase their status of readiness and some units are on alert. We have, however, noted no significant redeployments'").

2. Thomas R. Johnson, *American Cryptology during the Cold War, 1946–1989*, "Book II: Centralization Wins, 1960–1972" ([Fort George G. Meade, MD]: Center for Cryptological History, National Security Agency, 1995), Top Secret Umbra, Excised copy, p. 331, https://nsarchive2.gwu.edu/NSAEBB/NSAEBB260/nsa-3.pdf.

Curiously, NSA had detected that Soviet defensive forces were put on a similar state of heightened alert on October 11, 1962, but this alert level was ended ten days later, on October 21. The NSA historians speculated that the alert "may have been called because Moscow suspected that Kennedy had found out about the missiles." Johnson, pp. 330–31. A potentially relevant contemporaneous predicate for this theory was the decision by the National Security Council Special Action Group (Augmented) on October 9, 1962, to accept the COMOR recommendation to resume U-2 overflights of Cuba by sending a special mission over the western part of the island. Might the Kremlin have somehow learned of that momentous action, which produced the October 14 U-2 overflight that discovered the Soviet MRBM missiles at the San Cristóbal site, and which also created severe interdepartmental turbulence by transferring the U-2 piloting duty from the CIA to the air force? See Richelson, *Wizards of Langley*, pp. 52–53.

3. See Absher, "Mind Sets and Missiles," p. 68.

4. Johnson, *American Cryptology*, p. 331.

5. See Blight and Welch, *Intelligence*, p. 79 ("The U.S. military routinely transmitted changes to the Defense Condition (DefCon) status of Americans [*sic*] forces *en clair* in an unclassified form"). See Norris, "Cuban Missile Crisis," p. 20 (B-52 daily launches on preplanned attack missions targeted at the Soviet Union increased from twelve per day to sixty-six per day with a peak rate of seventy-five per day on November 5, 1962). The one-eighth figure meant that at least one out of every eight B-52 war planes "was always in the air, armed with nuclear weapons and ready to strike upon order." Garthoff, *Reflections*, p. 61 n. 100.

6. SAC Historical Study No. 90, pp. 34, 36, 38; Poole, *Joint Chiefs of Staff*, pp. 173–74.

7. See Dobbs, *One Minute to Midnight*, p. 52 ("Even as Kennedy finished speaking [on October 22], nearly two hundred planes began crisscrossing America with live nuclear weapons on board, headed in many cases for civilian airports"); Eric Schlosser, *Command and Control: Nuclear Weapons, The Damascus Accident, and the Illusion of Safety* (New York: Penguin, 2013), p. 292 (listing the civilian airports to which nearly two hundred B-47 bombers were dispersed as including Portland, Spokane, Minneapolis, Chicago, Detroit, Birmingham, Philadelphia, and Tulsa); http://historyinpieces.com/video/footage/sac-b47s-memphis-airport-cuban-missile-crisis (Memphis airport); http://www.mitchellgallery.org/flightlines/art/b-47 cuban-missile-crisis-milwaukee.pdf (Milwaukee airport); http://www.businessinsider.com/that-time-when-nuclear-weapons-were-at-your-local-airport-2015-7 (Logan and Memphis airports).

8. Although not necessarily a core feature of President Kennedy's personal crisis management style, this tactic of delivering a highly sensitive national security message *en clair*, knowing that it would thereby come immediately to the attention of an adversary, is reminiscent of the president's telephone call to General Clay over a nonsecure line at the height of the Berlin tank standoff, which ensured that history would preserve that private discussion care of a KGB intercept. See chapter 2.

9. Lebow and Stein, *We All Lost*, p. 341.

10. Sagan, *Limits of Safety*, pp. 66. Sagan observed that "U.S. leaders in 1962 believed that the alert was critical in signaling U.S. resolve and contributing to deterrence" (p. 67).

11. Marc Trachtenberg, "The Influence of Nuclear Weapons in the Cuban Missile Crisis," *International Security* 10, no. 1 (Summer 1985), p. 157.

12. See Poole, *Joint Chiefs of Staff*, p. 174; SAC Historical Study No. 90, pp. 34–35; May and Zelikow, *Kennedy Tapes*, p. 347 n. 2 (referencing McNamara's approval under JCS 6917 to CINCSAC, October 23, 1962); Brugioni, *Eyeball to Eyeball*, p. 398 ("Joint Chiefs of Staff issued Defcon 2"); Dobbs, *One Minute to Midnight*, p. 96. Cf. Poole, *Joint Chiefs of Staff*, p. ix ("During 1961–1962, relations between the JCS and their civilian superiors were often awkward and even confrontational. . . . The appointment of General Maxwell D. Taylor as Chairman, in October 1962, ameliorated the situation. Taylor expressed deep regard for McNamara, which the Secretary reciprocated").

13. Brugioni, *Eyeball to Eyeball*, p. 401.

14. Len Scott and Stephen Twigge, *Planning Armageddon: Britain, the United States, and Command of Western Nuclear Forces, 1945–1964* (New York: Routledge, 2013), p. 128.

15. Haslam, *Russia's Cold War*, pp 208–9.

16. Keeney, *15 Minutes*, p. 252; SAC Historical Study No. 90, p. 38; see also Norris, "Cuban Missile Crisis," p. 20 (reversing the northern and southern route figures).

17. Richard K. Smith, "Seventy-Five Years of Inflight Refueling: Highlights, 1923–1998, Air Force History and Museums Program, 1998, p. 47, https://media.defense.gov/2010/Sep/29/2001309638/-1/-1/0/AFD-100929-015.pdf.

18. Keeney, *15 Minutes*, p. 282.

19. Naftali and Zelikow, *Presidential Recordings*, vol. 2, pp. 437–38 (October 16, 6:30 p.m. meeting), vol. 3, p. 74 (October 22, 5:30 p.m. meeting with congressional leadership).

20. Allison and Zelikow, *Essence of Decision*, p. 218.

21. Sagan, *Limits of Safety*, p. 65 (citing Cuba Fact Sheet, Cuba General Folder, October 26–27, 1962, National Security Files, box 36A, JFKL).

22. The SAC's 1963 historical study of its DEFCON-2 performance during the missile crisis noted that the extreme requirements of one-eighth airborne alert required "a slight relaxation of the stringent operating criteria applied to airborne alert at the indoctrination level," deployment of B-52 aircraft "with one engine shut down," and use of certain classes of B-52 bombers and KC-135 in-air refueling aircraft "with low oil pressure on one or more engines." SAC Historical Study No. 90, p. 40.

23. Betts, *Nuclear Blackmail*, p. 118.

24. See Dave Philipps, "In Sick Airmen, Echo of '66 Nuclear Crash," *New York Times*, June 20, 2016, p. A1.

25. Keeney, *15 Minutes*, p. 284.

26. SAC Historical Study No. 90, p. 96 (citing *Washington Post*, December 8, 1962).

27. See, e.g., Robert Dallek, "JFK vs. the Military," *The Atlantic*, Fall 2013 ("Even Curtis LeMay, Power's superior, described him as 'not stable' and a 'sadist'"), https://www.theatlantic.com/magazine/archive/2013/08/jfk-vs-the-military/309496/

28. Kaplan, *Wizards of Armageddon*, pp. 245–46.

29. May and Zelikow, *Kennedy Tapes*, October 22, 1962, 5:00 p.m., Cabinet Room, pp. 281–82.

30. Kaplan, *Wizards of Armageddon*, pp. 301–2.

31. See, e.g., Dobbs, *One Minute to Midnight*; Blight, Allyn, and Welch, *Cuba on the Brink*.

32. Hilsman, *Nuclear Military Strategy*, p. 74.

33. Scott and Hughes, *Cuban Missile Crisis*, p. 7.

34. Taubman, *Khrushchev*, p. 513.

35. Fursenko and Naftali, *Gamble*, p. 273. See also Haslam, *Russia's Cold War*, at 176 (quoting Soviet general Dmitrii Yazov, a regimental commander closely involved in the Cuba operation, as saying: "After the decision was taken, only then were Malinovsky and Zakharov asked for advice about the planning; that you must do this, that, and the other. This is not advice, it is the implementation of instructions. That is how it was").

36. Weintal and Bartlett, *Facing the Brink*.

37. The specific date of the Rostow/Nitze memorandum appears in a summary of the memorandum prepared by the two journalist-authors that is held in the Weintal Papers at the Georgetown University Library, Box 7, Folder 2. The summary indicates the title of the memorandum was "Lessons from Cuba."

38. Weintal and Bartlett, *Facing the Brink*, pp. 54–55; Hilsman, *Nuclear Military Strategy*, p. 61; US Congress, House of Representatives, Committee on Appropriations, Subcommittee on Department of Defense Appropriations, "Department of Defense Appropriations for 1964," February 6, 1963, p. 31 (cited in Trachtenberg, "Influence of Nuclear Weapons," p. 141).

39. NIE 11-61, "Probable Intelligence Warning of Soviet Attack on the US," April 6, 1961.

40. NIE 11-10-66, "Warning of Soviet Intention to Attack," August 18, 1966.

41. George Washington University National Security Archives, http://nsarchive.gwu.edu/NSAEBB/NSAEBB400/docs/Interview%20with%20Oleg%20Troyanovsky.pdf

42. Ray S. Cline, "Nuclear War Seemed Remote . . . ," *Washington Post*, February 6, 1989.

43. Trachtenberg, *History and Strategy*, p. 258.

44. Bundy, *Danger and Survival*, p. 425; see also Blight, Allyn, and Welch, *Cuba on the Brink*, p. 70 ("Bundy: We never thought there was any chance anyone was going to push that button deliberately").

45. Taubman, *Khrushchev*, p. 552.

46. Garthoff, "US Intelligence," pp. 37, 39. See also Dean Rusk, Oral History, JFKL, p. 125: "Khrushchev's leadership was more personal in character. While he was in office he had full control."

47. See Garthoff, *Reflections*, p. 160 ("In the Cuban missile crisis the American strategic nuclear superiority was overwhelming. . . . That the United States could launch 3,000 strategic weapons against the Soviet Union and possibly be hit by only 30 (or at most a few dozen more than that) was no consolation. The mere possibility of nuclear war was the deterrent").

48. Stern, "Cuban Missile Crisis 45 Years Later."

49. Richard M. Pious, "Why Do Presidents Fail," *Presidential Studies Quarterly* 32, no. 4 (December 2002), p. 729.

50. Naftali and Zelikow, *Presidential Recordings*, vol. 2, p. 532.

51. Naftali and Zelikow, *Presidential Recordings*, vol. 2, pp. 532–33. Kennedy had made the same point, and used the same expression "grab," at an earlier White House meeting with advisers Chip Bohlen and Llewellyn Thompson on September 29, before the crisis began. Naftali and Zelikow, *Presidential Recordings*, vol. 2, p. 200.

52. Naftali and Zelikow, *Presidential Recordings*, vol. 2, p. 539. Campbell Craig has cited this exchange as clear evidence that McNamara was so firmly set against any nuclear use during the missile crisis "that he was ready to abandon Berlin to prevent it." There should be no thought given to "the Schelling strategy" of "a demonstrative nuclear attack to force the Soviets to think about all-out war," an idea Craig believed "must have struck McNamara as obscene." Craig, *Destroying the Village*, pp. 160–61.

53. Coleman, *Fourteenth Day*, pp. 178–80.

54. JFKL, National Security File, Box 85, https://www.jfklibrary.org/Asset-Viewer/Archives/JFKNSF-085-002.aspx

55. See *FRUS*, 1961–1963, vol. 11, *Cuban Missile Crisis and Aftermath*, 37, Editorial Note.

56. Scott, *Macmillan, Kennedy*, p. 47.

57. Scott, *Macmillan, Kennedy*, p. 48.

58. Scott, *Macmillan, Kennedy*, p. 96.

59. Scott, *Macmillan, Kennedy*, p. 48.

60. Zelikow and May, *Presidential Recordings*, vol. 3, p. 224 (emphasis added).

61. Zelikow and May, *Presidential Recordings*, vol. 3, p. 227; see also Scott, *Macmillan, Kennedy*, p. 98.

62. Scott, *Macmillan, Kennedy*, pp. 98–99.

63. Hershberg, introduction to "Trigger for Khrushchev's Deployment," p. 320.

64. See chapter 3; see also http://belfercenter.ksg.harvard.edu/files/CMC50/ScottSaganSIOP62TheNuclearWarPlanBriefingtoPresidentKennedyInternationalSecurity.pdf and discussion.

65. Stern, *Cuban Missile Crisis*, p. 16. See Munton, "The Fourth Question," p. 268 ("As Graham Allison suggested decades ago, both Kennedy and Khrushchev

sought a peaceful negotiated solution because they feared the likely consequence of not pulling back—an uncontrolled escalation of a local conflict into a superpower nuclear war. They recognized the need to avoid, in John Kennedy's words, 'the final failure'").

66. Naftali and Zelikow, *Presidential Recordings*, vol. 2, p. 420.

67. Naftali and Zelikow, *Presidential Recordings*, vol. 2, p. 529.

68. Naftali and Zelikow, *Presidential Recordings*, vol. 2, p. 541.

69. Naftali and Zelikow, *Presidential Recordings*, vol. 2, p. 581, Friday, October 19, 1962, 9:45 a.m., Cabinet Room.

70. Naftali and Zelikow, *Presidential Recordings*, vol. 2, pp. 587–88.

71. Kennedy had told Soviet ambassador Dobrynin as recently as July 17, 1962, that West Berlin was "a vital interest of the United States." Naftali, *Presidential Recordings*, vol. 1, p. xlvii (introduction by Naftali, citing *FRUS*, vol. 15, *Berlin Crisis, 1962–1963*, pp. 223–24).

72. Dean Rusk, *As I Saw It* (New York: Norton, 1990), pp. 246–47; Dobbs, *One Minute to Midnight*, p. 228. See also George Washington National Security Archive: "This was President Kennedy's first exposure to a NESC report, but the secret studies of nuclear war scenarios had been initiated by his predecessor, Dwight D. Eisenhower. It may have been after this briefing, described by Secretary of State Dean Rusk as 'an awesome experience,' that a dismayed Kennedy turned to Rusk, and said: 'And we call ourselves the human race.'" http://nsarchive.gwu.edu/nukevault/ebb480/

73. Sorensen, *Kennedy*, p. 513.

74. Trachtenberg, "Influence of Nuclear Weapons," pp. 151–52.

75. National Security Council, 1962 Report of the Net Evaluation Subcommittee, p. 109, National Security Archive's Nuclear Documentation Project, George Washington University, https://nsarchive2.gwu.edu/nukevault/ebb480/.

76. Naftali and Zelikow, *Presidential Recordings*, vol. 2, p. 529.

77. Naftali and Zelikow, *Presidential Recordings*, vol. 2, p. 420:

> PRESIDENT KENNEDY: I would think you'd have to assume they'd be using iron bombs and not nuclear weapons. Because, obviously, why would the Soviets permit nuclear war to begin under that sort of half-assed way?

78. Naftali and Zelikow, *Presidential Recordings*, vol. 2, pp. 440, 528:

> DILLON: What if [Soviet or Cuban aircraft attacking the United States from Cuba] carry a nuclear weapon?
>
> PRESIDENT KENNEDY: Well, if they carry a nuclear weapon. . . . You assume they wouldn't do that. . . .
>
> PRESIDENT KENNEDY: But at least as far as their . . . except with nuclear. I would think you would have to go on the assumption that they are not going to permit nuclear weapons to be used against the United States from Cuba unless they're going to be using them from everyplace.

79. Naftali and Zelikow, *Presidential Recordings*, vol. 2, p. 581:

> PRESIDENT KENNEDY: . . . On the other hand, we increase the chance greatly, as I think they—there's bound to be a reprisal from the Soviet Union, there always is—of their just going in and taking Berlin by force at some point. Which leaves me only one alternative, which is to fire nuclear weapons—which is a hell of an alternative—and begin a nuclear exchange, with all this happening.

80. Naftali and Zelikow, *Presidential Recordings*, vol. 2, p. 541.
81. Stern, *Averting the Final Failure*, pp. 32–33.
82. Stern, *Averting the Final Failure*, p. 34.
83. O'Donnell and Powers, *Johnny*, p. 285. See also Wenger, *Living with Peril*, p. 296 ("As in the Berlin crisis, the Kennedy administration at no point concluded that a war in which nuclear weapons were employed would end with anything less than common disaster").
84. Naftali and Zelikow, *Presidential Recordings*, vol. 2, p. 590.
85. Barton J. Bernstein, "Examining the Fourteenth Day," in Scott and Hughes, *Cuban Missile Crisis*, p. 61; Dobbs, *One Minute to Midnight*, p. 229.
86. Dobbs, *One Minute to Midnight*, p. 229 (citing Goodwin, *Remembering America* (Boston: Little Brown, 1988), p. 218.)
87. Trachtenberg, *History and Strategy*, p. 259.

Chapter 11

1. Joseph F. Bouchard, *Command in Crisis: Four Case Studies* (New York: Columbia University Press, 1991), pp. 130–31.
2. John F. Kennedy seemed to perceive that he and Khrushchev faced similar challenges in dealing with their respective military establishments. At a meeting with *Saturday Review* editor Norman Cousins on April 22, 1963, Kennedy said: "One of the ironic things about this entire situation is that Mr. Khrushchev and I occupy approximately the same political positions inside our governments. He would like to prevent a nuclear war but is under severe pressure from his hard-line crowd. . . . I've got similar problems. . . . The hard-liners in the Soviet Union and the United States feed on one another, each using the actions of the other to justify his own position." Quoted in Beschloss, *Crisis Years*, p. 588.
3. Johnson, *American Cryptology*, p. 330.
4. Dobbs, *One Minute to Midnight*, p. 242.
5. Dobbs, *One Minute to Midnight*, pp. 268–72.
6. See http://www.archives.gov/publications/prologue/2012/fall/cuban-missiles.html
7. Dobbs, *One Minute to Midnight*, pp. 124–27, 178–81, 205–6.
8. Dobbs, *One Minute to Midnight*, p. 317.
9. Dobbs, *One Minute to Midnight*, p. 353.

10. Dobbs, *One Minute to Midnight*, p. 351.

11. See May and Zelikow, *Kennedy Tapes*, Saturday October 20, 1962, Oval Room of the Executive Mansion, p. 200.

12. Nash, *Other Missiles of October*, pp. 87 and 125 n. 19.

13. Notes Taken from Transcripts of Meetings of the Joint Chiefs of Staff, October–November 1962, Dealing with the Cuban Missile Crisis (handwritten notes were made in 1976 and typed in 1993), p. 14 (hereafter "JCS Transcripts"), http://nsarchive.gwu.edu/nsa/cuba_mis_cri/621000%20Notes%20Taken%20from%20Transcripts.pdf

14. Zelikow and May, *Presidential Recordings*, vol. 3, pp. 33–35.

15. JCS Transcripts, p. 15.

16. Nash, *Other Missiles of October*, pp. 126–27 (emphasis added), citing untitled document, n.d. [October 22], NATO-Weapons, Cables-Turkey, Box 226, Regional Security File, National Security File, Presidential Papers, 1961–1963, John F. Kennedy Papers, JFKL; see Zelikow and May, *Presidential Recordings*, vol. 3, p. 459:

> BUNDY: We were going to *let* him have his strike in Turkey, as I understood it last week.

17. Herken, *Georgetown Set*, p. 272; May and Zelikow, *Kennedy Tapes*, October 22, 1962, 11:30 A.M., the Cabinet Room, p. 223 n. 16; Nash, *Other Missiles of October*, pp. 87, 125–27; Sagan, *Limits of Safety*, pp. 109–10.

18. Nash, *Other Missiles*, pp. 78, 80.

19. Nash, *Other Missiles of October*, pp. 126–27 (emphasis added), citing untitled document, n.d. [October 22], NATO-Weapons, Cables-Turkey, box 226, Regional Security File, National Security File, Presidential Papers, 1961–1963, JFKL, Boston, Massachusetts; for Bundy remark, see Zelikow and May, *Presidential Recordings*, vol. 3, p. 459.

20. May and Zelikow, *Kennedy Tapes*, p. 475 n. 4 (citing McAuliffe, *CIA Documents*, p. 325); Whitten, *Countdown*, pp. 51–52. See also Hilsman, *Nuclear Military Strategy*, p. 64 (US Navy low-level reconnaissance flights authorized on October 24 "revealed the presence of battlefield nuclear weapons. A total of fourteen such weapons were eventually identified").

21. Coleman, "Missiles of November," p. 22. See McNamara, *In Retrospect*, p. 341; Chang and Kornbluh, *Cuban Missile Crisis, 1962*, Doc. 41, "CINCLANT's request to have tactical nuclear weapons available for U.S. invasion force, December 29, 1962."

22. Maxwell D. Taylor, Memorandum for the President, "Evaluation of the Effect on US Operational Plans of Soviet Army Equipment Introduced into Cuba," November 2, 1962, CM-85-62, declassified by Joint Staff September 29, 2000.

23. Dobbs, *One Minute to Midnight*, p. 351.

24. Beloborodov, whose later report of the crisis was described by Dobbs as "the most authoritative account available about the handling of Soviet nuclear weapons on Cuba" (*One Minute to Midnight*, p. 372n) would later state categorically, "At no point did I receive any signals to issue warheads for either the medium-range missiles or the tactical weapons." Kramer, "Lessons of the Crisis," p. 353 n. 17.

25. Dobbs, *One Minute to Midnight*, pp. 48, 128–29.

26. Dobbs, *One Minute to Midnight*, pp. 104, 351–52. See telegram from Trostnick (Soviet Defense Minister Rodion Malinovsky) to Pavlov (General Issa Pliyev), October 27, 1962, http://digitalarchive.wilsoncenter.org/document/117326.

27. White, *Cuban Missile Crisis*, p. 119.

28. Fursenko and Naftali, *Khrushchev's Cold War*, p. 467; Sergo Mikoyan, *The Soviet Cuban Missile Crisis* (Stanford, CA: Stanford University Press, 2012), p. 156 (quoting Anastas Mikoyan's notes of October 22 events dictated in January 1963: "We decided to await Kennedy's speech there at the meeting so that . . . without needlessly wasting time, we would be able to take responsive measures since anything could be expected").

29. Taubman, *Khrushchev*, pp. 545, 552.

30. Dobbs, *One Minute to Midnight*, p. 55 ("Forbidden by Khrushchev to leave the Kremlin, Soviet leaders spent an uncomfortable night in their offices on couches and chairs").

31. Taubman, *Khrushchev*, pp. 560–61.

32. Fursenko and Naftali, *Gamble*, p. 196.

33. Taubman, *Khrushchev*, p. 562 (citing Troyanovsky's recollection of these events).

34. Mikoyan, *Soviet Cuban Missile Crisis*, p. 157.

35. Wilson, *Launch Pad UK*, p. 131.

36. Zelikow and May, *Presidential Recordings*, vol. 3, pp. 157–58.

37. See, e.g., Bouchard, *Command in Crisis*, p. 112 ("President Kennedy did *not* order the quarantine line moved in, but directed McNamara to delay the initial boarding of Soviet ships and suggested that moving the quarantine line closer to Cuba would be a means of achieving that objective. McNamara consulted with the CNO, who recommended that the quarantine line be left at five hundred nautical miles until the extent of the threat from Cuban aircraft could be determined").

38. Zelikow and May, *Presidential Recordings*, vol. 3, p. 167.

39. Hilsman, *Nuclear Military Strategy*, p. 64.

40. Copy of cable accessible at http://nsarchive.gwu.edu/nsa/cuba_mis_cri/dobbs/

41. Zelikow and May, *Presidential Recordings*, vol. 3, p. 115:

> PRESIDENT KENNEDY: Then I would think what we would do is, if the first one [is shot down], we have to take it out [the offending SAM site], and then announce what's happened.

See Beschloss, *Crisis Years*, p. 490 (at the ExComm meeting on October 23, 1962, "All agreed that if one of the U-2s now repeatedly photographing Cuba were downed, American bombers and fighters should destroy a SAM site, but only after the President's specific order"). See also Chang, "View from Washington," p. 146.

42. Lebow and Stein, *We All Lost*, p. 128.

43. CIA, National Indications Center, "Soviet Bloc Armed Forces and the Cuban Crisis: A Chronology," June 18, 1963, p. 121, https://www.cia.gov/library/readingroom/docs/DOC_0001161985.pdf

44. Betts, *Nuclear Blackmail*, p. 120.

45. Trachtenberg, "Influence of Nuclear Weapons," p. 157.

46. Absher, "Mind Sets and Missiles," p. 68.

47. Sagan, *Limits of Safety*, p. 143.

48. Sagan, *Limits of Safety*, p. 144.

49. Dobbs, *One Minute to Midnight*, p. 113.

50. Dobbs, *One Minute to Midnight*, p. 113.

51. NIE 11-10-66, "Warning of Soviet Intention to Attack," August 18, 1966, pp. 9–10. Writing in 1998, Raymond Garthoff would conclude: "At least on the basis of US intelligence materials declassified to date, there is no indication that the United States was aware of any special alert measures taken by the Soviet strategic missile forces during the crisis." Garthoff, "US Intelligence," p. 59 n. 38.

52. NIE 11-10-66, "Warning of Soviet Intention to Attack," August 18, 1966, p. 11.

53. NIE 11-10-66, "Warning of Soviet Intention to Attack," August 18, 1966, p. 12.

54. NIE 11-10-66, "Warning of Soviet Intention to Attack," August 18, 1966, p. 12.

55. See Raymond Garthoff, "The Cuban Missile Crisis: An Overview," in Nathan, *Cuban Missile Crisis Revisited*, pp. 46–47 ("Even the Soviet response to the unparalleled American alert of its strategic forces and most forces worldwide was an announced, but actually hollow, Soviet and Warsaw pact alert").

56. See NIE 11-8-62, "Soviet Capabilities for Strategic Attack," July 6, 1962, p. 7 ("In attempting to overcome the range limitations of Long Range Aviation for intercontinental attack, the Soviets have given considerable emphasis to aerial refueling and Arctic training in BADGER and BISON units").

57. Addressing a congressional subcommittee in 1963 on the ability of the Soviet Air Force to mount an attack against the United States, defense Secretary McNamara testified, "To mount such an attack, the Soviets would either first have to deploy their bomber force to Arctic bases or stage them through these bases in successive waves. Such action would greatly jeopardize their chance of surprising us and, equally important, their bombers would become vulnerable to our missile attack during their staging operation." Statement of Secretary of Defense Robert S. McNamara before the House Subcommittee on Department of Defense Appropriations, The Fiscal Year 1964–1968 Defense Program and the 1964 Defense Budget, February 6, 1963, p. 50, National Security Archives, Washington, DC. See Sagan, *Moving Targets*, p. 31.

58. See NIE 11-10-66, "Warning of Soviet Intention to Attack," August 18, 1966, p. 12 ("In planning a strike in which weight of attack was paramount, the Soviets would have to take a good many steps to enhance the readiness of their forces. . . . Some of the aircraft probably would be staged through Arctic bases").

59. Aid, *Secret Sentry*, pp. 72, 75. Berezovka Air Base, located near Murmansk,

was one such forward arctic staging installation capable of handling Soviet Badger bombers. Even in 2014 Berezovka was equipped with "only a radio beacon, control tower, and a small shelter." https://www.urbanghostsmedia.com/2014/12/12-abandoned-cold-war-airfields-soviet-union-russia/. See also Hilsman, *Nuclear Military Strategy*, p. 52 ("If intelligence showed that the Soviets were preparing to attack by . . . moving bombers to advance bases in the Arctic, . . . SIOP-62 provided the president with the option of ordering the United States to strike first—to 'launch on warning'").

60. The single exception was a comment about some evidence of *preparations* for deployment that Director McCone made at the ExComm meeting on the morning of October 24, where he said, "There are indications of preparations for the deployment of some long-range aircraft to Arctic bases. We have so far noted no major re-deployment of other Soviet-Bloc forces." Zelikow and May, *Presidential Recordings*, vol. 3, p. 185. There were no further updates indicating this had led to an actual, meaningful forward air deployment, however.

61. McAuliffe, *CIA Documents*, p. 328.

62. Stern, *Averting the Final Failure*, pp. 208–9. See also Richard N. Lebow, *Nuclear Crisis Management: A Dangerous Illusion* (Ithaca, NY: Cornell University Press, 1987), p. 67 ("Western analysts have speculated that Moscow failed to put any strategic forces on alert in either the Cuban or the Middle East crisis because the Soviets wanted to avoid the kind of provocative action which might have significantly increased the risk of war with the United States").

63. CIA, National Indications Center, "The Soviet Bloc Armed Forces and the Cuban Crisis: A Discussion of Readiness Measures," July 15, 1963, p. 22.

64. CIA/DDI Venture, p. 102n.

65. Trachtenberg, *History and Strategy*, pp. 256–57.

66. Transcript of oral history interview of General David Burchinal, April 11, 1975, p. 116, Office of Air Force History, Bolling Air Force Base, Washington, DC, cited in Trachtenberg, "Influence of Nuclear Weapons," p. 161.

67. Blight, Allyn, and Welch, *Cuba on the Brink*, p. 91.

68. National Security Archive, http://nsarchive.gwu.edu/nsa/cuba_mis_cri/dobbs/, providing a link to the minutes, which were apparently archived at and translated by the Miller Center of Public Affairs at the University of Virginia.

69. CIA, National Indications Center, "Soviet Bloc Armed Forces and the Cuban Crisis: A Chronology," p. 52.

70. CIA, Office of the Deputy Director (Intelligence), Office of Research and Reports, "Cuba 1962: Khrushchev's Miscalculated Risk," p. 88.

71. CIA, National Indications Center, "The Soviet Bloc Armed Forces and the Cuban Crisis: A Discussion of Readiness Measures," p. 21.

72. NIE 11-1-62, "The Soviet Space Program," December 5, 1962, p. 25.

73. Chertok, *Rockets and People*, vol. 3, pp. 96, 102; see also https://nssdc.gsfc.nasa.gov/nmc/spacecraftDisplay.do?id=1962-057A; https://en.wikipedia.org/wiki/Mars_2MV-4_No.1

74. Chertok, *Rockets and People*, vol. 3, pp. 18, 23, 74, 94, 96.

75. Chertok, *Rockets and People*, vol. 3, p. 18. See NIE 11-1-62, "The Soviet Space Program," December 5, 1962, p. 9 ("Since its inception, the USSR's space program has been closely linked to its military missile program. The two programs have used the same boosters and launching facilities, and are mutually supporting in other respects as well. We believe that many of the scientists, engineers and technicians who are working on space projects are also involved in the Soviet missile program").

76. NIE 11-1-62, "The Soviet Space Program," December 5, 1962, p. 9.

77. Chertok, *Rockets and People*, vol. 3, p. 87. See also Boris Chertok, *Rockets and People*, vol. 2: *Creating a Rocket Industry* (Washington, DC: NASA History Division, Office of External Relations, June 2006), p. 601 (two of the R-7 launch pads were located at Plesetsk in Arkangelsk Oblast 800 km north of Moscow and two were located at Tyuratam); Taubman, *Khrushchev*, p. 379 ("It wasn't until the 1960s that the first Soviet ICBMs, a grand total of four of them, actually became operational"). NIE 11-8/1-61, "Strength and Deployment of Soviet Long Range Ballistic Missile Forces," September 21, 1961, p. 8. NIE 11-8/1-61 also identified (p. 9) three additional ICBM complexes under construction: two near Yur'ya and Yoshkar-Ola "in a region several hundred miles northeast of Moscow," and the third "near Yerkhnya Salda in the Urals." It also mentioned "a fourth complex similar to the others" in Plesetsk, "farther to the northwest," about which information "was too limited either to confirm or rule out this location as an ICBM deployment complex."

78. Chertok, *Rockets and People*, vol. 3, pp. 96–97.

79. Chertok, *Rockets and People*, vol. 3, pp. 94, 98.

80. Dobbs, *One Minute to Midnight*, p. 189.

81. See Norris, "Cuban Missile Crisis," p. 25; NIE 11-10-66, "Warning of Soviet Intention to Attack"August 18, 1966, p. 12 ("In planning a strike in which weight of attack was paramount, the Soviets would have to take a good many steps to enhance the readiness of their forces. . . . More missile submarines would probably put to sea and head for launch positions off the US").

82. Norris, "Cuban Missile Crisis," p. 25.

83. Minutes of the 506th Meeting of the National Security Council, October 21, 1962, in *FRUS*, 1961–1963, vol. 11, *Cuban Missile Crisis and Aftermath*, pp. 141–49, cited in May and Zelikow, *Kennedy Tapes*, p. 211.

84. NIC 1964 Report, pp. 32–33.

85. See, e.g., Naftali and Zelikow, *Presidential Recordings*, vol. 2, p. 533 (President Kennedy's comment at an ExComm meeting on October 18, 1962: "Yeah. I would think it more likely he [Khrushchev] would just grab Berlin").

86. Taubman, *Khrushchev*, p. 538; Dobbs, *One Minute to Midnight*, p. 218; May and Zelikow, *Kennedy Tapes*, p. 430–31 (citing Dobrynin's expressed view and quoting Khrushchev's comment in response to Kuznetsov differently: "[I can] do without such advice . . . [W]e had no intention to add fuel to the conflict").

87. Fursenko and Naftali, *Gamble*, p. 248.

88. Kempe, *Berlin 1961*, p. 497; see also Dobbs, *One Minute to Midnight*, p. 217

("the Soviets did not increase the pressure on Berlin in response to the U.S. blockade of Cuba").

89. Aid, *Secret Sentry*, p. 76 (noting October 26, 1962, NSA confirmation that "some Soviet army units had suddenly left their barracks in East Germany and moved to concentration points closer to the border with West Germany").

90. CIA/DDI Venture, p. 70n. See also Brugioni, *Eyeball to Eyeball*, p. 383 ("It was significant . . . that there were no threatening moves by the Soviet Army in Berlin or by the Soviet naval forces in the Mediterranean").

91. Bouchard, *Command in Crisis*, p. 114.

92. Dobbs, *One Minute to Midnight*, pp. 43–44. See Gioe, Scott, and Andrew, *International History*, p. 3 ("Indeed it is now clear that Khrushchev had made up his mind—and secured the unanimous agreement of the Presidium—to retreat by Thursday 25 October"); May and Zelikow, *Kennedy Tapes*, October 25–26, 1962, p. 439.

93. Bundy, *Danger and Survival*, p. 440.

94. Haslam, *Russia's Cold War*, p. 208 (quoting from a September 25, 1962, "Memorandum for the Presidium" authored by Zakharov and Fokin); Garthoff, "US Intelligence," p. 52.

95. Fursenko and Naftali, *Gamble*, p. 213 and nn. 51 and 53; Fursenko and Naftali, *Khrushchev's Cold War*, pp. 481–82.

96. Brugioni, *Eyeball to Eyeball*, p. 543.

97. The October 14 U-2 photographs revealed at one site "six long canvas-covered objects . . . more than sixty feet long" that were quickly determined to be "missile transporters" for SS-4 MRBM missiles, and at a second site eight missile transporters and four "large objects" that looked at first like boats but turned out on closer inspection to be "launcher erectors." Brugioni, *Eyeball to Eyeball*, pp. 197, 201, 213.

98. Gribkov and Smith, *Operation Anadyr*, p. 52 ("Moscow had sent them [the SA-2s] to Cuba to defend against air attack, not aerial surveillance"); Mikoyan, *Soviet Cuban Missile Crisis*, p. 107 ("It was odd that the Americans were 'given' an opportunity to detect the launchers and perform aerial photography from the U-2 aircraft").

99. Brugioni, *Eyeball to Eyeball*, p. 107.

100. Brugioni, *Eyeball to Eyeball*, p. 118.

101. Brugioni, *Eyeball to Eyeball*, p. 179.

102. Dobbs, *One Minute to Midnight*, p. 187. I am indebted to Colonel H. Wayne Whitten (USMC, Ret.) for his privately published research and scholarship on the timing of these two ELINT discoveries in his book (*Countdown*, pp. 30, 54, 58), pamphlet (*Without a Warning: The Shootdown of a U-2 Spyplane during the Cuban Missile Crisis*, pp. 10, 12), and correspondence with the author.

103. Barrett and Holland, *Blind over Cuba*, p. 134, Appendix ("Castro confirmed, however, that there had been a very strict order not to fire on the U-2s, meaning that the Kennedy administration's earlier caution had been unwarranted, though

the White House had no reasonable way to know that"); May and Zelikow, *Kennedy Tapes*, p. 681, citing Gribkov, "The View from Havana and Moscow," p. 52 ("Soviet troops in Cuba had tracked the U-2 overflights of October 14, 15, and 17, but, strangely, they had orders not to fire at U.S. planes unless attacked").

104. Brugioni, *Eyeball to Eyeball*, p. 186.

105. Memorandum of A. I. Mikoyan's Conversation with Comrades F. Castro, O. Dorticos, E. Guevara, E. Aragones, and R. Rodriguez, November 22, 1962, https://stationhypo.com/2016/08/05/without-a-warning-the-story-of-the-shoot-down-of-a-u-2-spy-plane-during-the-cuban-missile-crisis-guest-post-part-ii/. Fidel Castro would later comment at a conference on the Cuban missile crisis held on January 9–12, 1992, that Khrushchev's "very strict orders" that the SAM missiles were "not to shoot, not to fire on the U-2s" was "a clear political mistake." Blight, Allyn, and Welch, *Cuba on the Brink*, p. 86.

106. Keeney, *15 Minutes*, p. 283.

107. Gribkov and Smith, *Operation Anadyr*, p. 99.

108. Hershberg, "New Evidence," p. 340. See also Taubman, *Khrushchev*, p. 777 n. 89 ("According to what Mikoyan later told Castro, by mid-September Moscow had good reason to believe the Americans knew of Soviet missile deployment").

109. Keeney, *15 Minutes*, p. 283; Beschloss, *Crisis Years*, p. 532; Fursenko and Naftali, *Gamble*, pp. 277–78; Taubman, *Khrushchev*, p. 571.

110. Stern, *Cuban Missile Crisis*, p. 2.

111. Allyn, Blight and Welch, "Essence of Revision," p. 154. See also Beschloss, *Crisis Years*, p. 495.

112. Zelikow and May, *Presidential Recordings*, vol. 3, p. 239.

113. Gribkov and Smith, *Operation Anadyr*, p. 57.

114. Gribkov and Smith, *Operation Anadyr*, pp. 62–63. See Dobbs, *One Minute to Midnight*, 330 ("Malinovsky had prepared a decree authorizing Soviet troops on Cuba to use 'all available means' to defend the island. The formula alarmed Khrushchev. 'If they were to use all means without exception, that would include the [medium range] missiles,' he objected. 'It would be the start of a thermonuclear war. How can we imagine such a thing?'").

115. Hilsman placed the discovery on October 24 (*Cuban Missile Crisis*, p. 116), but later researchers cited October 25 as the correct date. See Coleman, "Missiles of November," p. 21 and n. 61.

116. Fursenko and Naftali, *Gamble*, p. 212. See also id. p. 243 ("Persuaded by Malinovsky, the Kremlin decided to send the first set of conservative instructions immediately, barring the use of any nuclear weapons").

117. Kramer, "Lessons of the Crisis," p. 349. Kramer summarized a controversy that had arisen based upon the later testimony of General Gribkov that Pliyev had issued orders for the release of tactical nuclear warheads for attachment to the FKR missiles. Gribkov had no documentation or other supporting evidence, however, and his statement was contradicted by Colonel Nikolai Beloborodov, the Soviet officer who was in charge of the "central nuclear base" where all nuclear warheads were stored. Beloborodov stated unequivocally that he had never

received any orders or other authorization to release the warheads for attachment to any tactical weapons, and that his approval and use of special authorizing codes would have been needed before any such release could have occurred. See Kramer, p. 349 and n. 17.

118. Radchenko, "History, Hearsay and Hotchpotch," in Scott and Hughes, *Cuban Missile Crisis*, p. 193. See also Absher, "Mind Sets and Missiles," p. 34 ("The next day, September 8, 1962, the Ministry of Defense drafted an order delegating the Soviet commander in Cuba, General Issa Pliyev, the authority to use these tactical battlefield nuclear weapons should communications with Moscow be cut and a US-led invasion be underway. However, Khrushchev had already given Pliyev this authority orally during a meeting in July. Malinovsky decided not to sign or send the instructions to Pliyev in writing. According to Gribkov, even this oral authority was later withdrawn by Moscow in a cable sent to Pliyev hours before Kennedy's October 22, 1962, crisis speech, which ordered Pliyev to use "all the power of the Soviet forces" to repel an invasion, except nuclear weapons").

119. Khrushchev, *Nikita Khrushchev*, p. 582.

120. Dobbs, *One Minute to Midnight*, pp. 200–201. It is equally clear that US decision-makers doubted the Soviets would be the first to resort to nuclear weapons. In their early consideration on October 16, 1962, of the option of a US attack on the Soviet installations in Cuba, which in turn led to a discussion of the strong likelihood that this would trigger a responsive air attack on Miami or elsewhere in southern Florida, the president, Bundy, Rusk and Taylor were agreed that there was little likelihood any such strike would include a nuclear weapon. Naftali and Zelikow, *Presidential Recordings*, vol. 2, p. 440.

121. Stern, *Cuban Missile Crisis*, p. 142.

122. Taubman, *Khrushchev*, p. 487.

123. Central Intelligence Agency, Board of National Estimates, October 27, 1962, Memorandum for the Director, Reactions to US Air Strike against Soviet Missile Bases, MiG-21s and IL-28s, TS No. 185480, pp. 1–2, http://nsarchive.gwu.edu/NSAEBB/NSAEBB397/docs/doc%2015%2010-27-62%20ONE%20paper%20on%20reactions%20to%20air%20strike.pdf

124. See, e.g., Evans, *Robert Kennedy*, p. 211; Beschloss, *Crisis Years*, p. 491; Dobbs, *One Minute to Midnight*, pp. 226–27.

125. Sagan, *Limits of Safety*, pp. 53–54, 153–54.

126. Dobbs, *One Minute to Midnight*, p. 114.

127. Hilsman, *Cuban Missile Crisis*, p. 143.

128. Hilsman, *Cuban Missile Crisis*, pp. 143–44.

129. Hilsman, *Cuban Missile Crisis*, p. 147.

130. See Arthur Conan Doyle, *The Memoirs of Sherlock Holmes*, 1892, "Silver Blaze."

131. See Sagan, *Limits of Safety*, p. 155 ("I do not want to push the point about good fortune to an extreme. There was also plenty of bad luck—garbled messages, the bear climbing the fence, the bright aura borealis coming out—at the heart of these incidents").

132. Cf. Elise Rowan, "A Perfect Record: Assessing Risk and the Human Factor in Avoiding Nuclear Catastrophe," in Sarah Minot, ed., *Nuclear Scholars Initiative: A Collection of Papers from the 2014 Nuclear Scholars Initiative* (Washington, DC: Center for Strategic and International Studies, August 2015), pp. 161, 166 (after noting comments by Robert McNamara and William Perry speculating that "luck" may have been a factor in avoiding accidental detonation of nuclear weapons, Rowan observes that "human judgment adds a fascinating layer. Scrutiny of past close calls has focused largely on human error and technical failures and less on the judgment of individuals who, in all cases of near nuclear use so far, have resisted launching nuclear weapons, sometimes against protocol. For instance, in the dozens of examples in the literature of false warnings—caused by faulty computer chips, training tapes mistaken for actual events, and failures in communication—caution and critical thinking led to what was later determined to be the 'appropriate' outcome" [citation omitted]), https://www.nti.org/media/pdfs/A_Perfect_Record_Rowan.pdf?_=1441212952?_=1441212952

133. Schlosser, *Command and Control*, p. 480.

134. Brugioni, *Eyeball to Eyeball*, pp. 107–8.

135. Bouchard, *Command in Crisis*, pp. 120–23.

136. Bouchard, *Command in Crisis*, p. 126; Huchthausen, *October Fury*, p. 18.

137. Huchthausen, *October Fury*, p. 169. Bouchard noted that "navy patrol planes and HUK groups had been tracking Soviet submarines for years in the Atlantic . . . so Soviet captains knew what PDCs sounded like." *Command in Crisis*, p. 123. See also Gary E. Weir and Walter J. Boyne, *Rising Tide: The Untold Story of the Russian Submarines That Fought the Cold War* (New York: Basic Books, 2003), pp. 94, 102 (Soviet submarines at the area of quarantine were subjected to sequences of "three grenades used as a signal" also described as "the customary three-grenade explosion signal ordering them to surface").

138. Huchthausen, *October Fury*, p. 169; https://www.ussbealedd-dde471.org/about1-c1yri

139. See Bouchard, *Command in Crisis*, p. 125; William Burr and Thomas S. Blanton, eds., "The Submarines of October: US and Soviet Naval Encounters During the Cuban Missile Crisis," National Security Archive Electronic Briefing Book No. 75, October 31, 2002, https://nsarchive2.gwu.edu/NSAEBB/NSAEBB75/ (concluding that "fortunately, the U.S. and Soviet leadership, from heads of state to naval commanders wanted to avoid open conflict; cool heads, professionalism, and some amount of luck, kept the crisis under control"). See also Dobbs, *One Minute to Midnight*, p. 303.

140. The Soviets had conducted a total of only two live-fire tests of their nuclear torpedoes, and both had been hair-raisingly dangerous for those involved. See Weir and Boyne, *Rising Tide*, pp. 79–80. The admiral who had been selected to lead the squadron of Foxtrot class diesel submarines deployed to Operation Anadyr, Leonid F. Rybalko, had balked when informed of the nuclear-armed torpedoes these vessels would be carrying, saying to his commanding officer: "Sir, you're aware that few of our submarines have ever test-fired atomic weapons at

sea," and "Sir, we still don't know the effects on the launch platforms of such weapons, or at what range the blast will be lethal to the firing unit. We might destroy one of our own subs if we fire one of these at an American target." Huchthausen, *October Fury*, pp. 18–19.

141. Dobbs, *One Minute to Midnight*, pp. 286–87; Allison and Zelikow, *Essence of Decision*, p. 241.

142. Hilsman, *Cuban Missile Crisis*, p. 145.

143. See, e.g., Sagan, *Limits of Safety*, pp. 74, 79, 135–36.

144. Len Scott, "The Only Thing to Look Forward To's the Past," in Scott and Hughes, *Cuban Missile Crisis*, p. 241. Michael Beschloss found a related comment by Secretary of Defense McNamara during a 1980s interview by WGBH Boston in which he was discussing a speech he had given in February 1962 explaining a possible US counterforce strategy aimed at limiting damage "to ourselves and our allies" by destroying "the enemy's bases before he has had time to launch his second salvos." McNamara's later comment was, "I don't know anybody who thinks that a nuclear war, once started today, can be limited. But that was our hope then." Beschloss, *Crisis Years*, p. 406n.

145. See Zelikow and May, *Presidential Recordings*, vol. 3, p. 115; Fursenko and Naftali, *Gamble*, pp. 280–81 ("The president faced a terrible decision. It was established U.S. policy to retaliate against any Cuban SA-2 site that fired on a U-2. For days, sixteen U.S. planes had been standing by on thirty-minute alert to destroy any SA-2 site . . . Kennedy decided to wait until morning to decide whether to retaliate").

146. Zelikow and May, *Presidential Recordings*, vol. 3, p. 492 ("Let me say, I think we ought to wait till tomorrow afternoon"; "if we don't get some satisfaction . . . tomorrow night, figure that Monday we're going to do something about the SAM sites").

147. John Kenneth Galbraith, *A Life in Our Times* (New York: Houghton Mifflin, 1981), p. 388. The president's comment came well after crisis tensions had abated, and it overlooked the fact, confirmed by transcripts from his own secret White House taping system, that the president himself had initially favored bombing the missile sites. Yet this early reaction seems to have reflected a transient moment of desperation or even panic, and the fuller record of the president's recorded comments throughout the crisis strongly corroborate his later pacific remark.

148. Taubman, *Khrushchev*, p. 574.

149. Taubman, *Khrushchev*, p. 574. In his memoir of the Cuban missile Crisis, *Thirteen Days*, Robert Kennedy stated that he had told Dobrynin that "there could be no quid pro quo or any arrangement" about the US missiles in Turkey "made under this kind of threat or pressure." Nevertheless, Kennedy recalled telling the Soviet ambassador that the president "had been anxious to remove those missiles from Turkey and Italy for a long period of time," and "had ordered their removal some time ago," so that "within a short time after this crisis was over, those missiles would be gone." *Thirteen Days*, p. 83.

150. In his response to Castro's inflammatory plea for a Soviet first-strike attack, Khrushchev told his ally that Castro's cable, with its "proposal that we be the first to launch a nuclear strike against the enemy," had prompted him to yield. For "we are not struggling against imperialism in order to die," but rather to "achieve the victory of communism," and "now, as a result of the measures we have taken, we have reached the goal sought when we agreed with you to send missiles to Cuba." Taubman, *Khrushchev*, p. 580 and n. 10.

151. "Despite all their differences, both personal and ideological, the two men had reached similar conclusions about the nature of nuclear war. Nikita Khrushchev and John Kennedy both understood that such a war would be far more terrible than anything mankind had known before. . . . They believed that the risks of war had become unacceptably high, and it was necessary to act decisively to cut what Khrushchev had called 'the knot of war.'" Dobbs, *One Minute to Midnight*, p. 324.

152. Taubman, *Khrushchev*, p. 552.

153. Hilsman, *Nuclear Military Strategy*, p. 72.

154. Reeves, *President Kennedy*, p. 425.

155. O'Donnell and Powers, *Johnny*, p. 350.

156. Schlesinger, *A Thousand Days*, p. 363.

157. Douglass, *JFK and the Unspeakable*, p. 237.

158. Stern, *Final Failure*, p. 31.

159. Beschloss, *Crisis Years*, p. 458.

160. Graham Allison, "The Cuban Missile Crisis at 50: Lessons for U.S. Foreign Policy Today," *Foreign Affairs* 91, no. (2012), p. 11; Allison, *New York Times*, op-ed, June 15, 2012.

161. Mimi Alford, *Once upon a Secret: My Affair with President John F. Kennedy and Its Aftermath* (New York: Random House, 2012), pp. 93–94. See Dallek, "JFK vs the Military; Robert Dallek, *Camelot's Court: Inside the Kennedy White House* (New York: HarperCollins, 2013), p. 330.

162. Kennedy would later refer to one of his children in a remarkably similar context in late May 1963. In the course of discussing with then-undersecretary of State Chester Bowles the prospects for a treaty with the Russians limiting atmospheric testing of nuclear weapons, the president said, "It may sound corny, but I am thinking not so much of our world but the world that Caroline will live in," and that even if he could "muster only ten votes in the Senate," he was determined to present the treaty with his recommendation for approval." Bowles, *Promises to Keep*, p. 452.

163. Dallek, "JFK vs the Military."

Postscript

1. Nash, *Other Missiles of October*, p. 158.
2. Bowles, *Promises to Keep*, p. 431.
3. McGeorge Bundy, who was also present at the Oval Office meeting, later

identified the participants as "the president, Dean Rusk, Robert McNamara, Robert Kennedy, George Ball, Roswell Gilpatric, Llewellyn Thompson, Theodore Sorensen, and I." Bundy, *Danger and Survival*, pp. 432–33.

4. Nash, *Other Missiles of October*, p. 157.

5. Cited in Barrett and Holland, *Blind over Cuba*, p. 66, US House Appropriations Committee, Department of Defense Appropriations for 1964, 88th Cong., 1st Sess., Part I, p. 57, cited in Bernstein, "Examining the Fourteenth Day," p. 56 ("On 7 February 1963, for example, in testimony before a U.S. House of Representatives Appropriations subcommittee, McNamara, loyal to the President and possibly untroubled by deceiving Congressional committee members, denied that there had been such an arrangement. McNamara was actually one of only a few high-level administration members, besides the Kennedy brothers, Rusk, and Bundy, who knew about this secret deal").

6. See Bernstein, "Examining the Fourteenth Day," p. 56.

7. Stern, *Cuban Missile Crisis*, p. 39.

8. Beschloss, *Crisis Years*, p. 536n.

9. Bolshakov, "Secret Channel," p. 113.

10. See Fursenko and Naftali, *Gamble*, p. 250.

11. Thomas, *Robert Kennedy*, p. 232. In a subsequent interview with authors Fursenko and Naftali, Bartlett denied having ever mentioned Turkey to Bolshakov. See Fursenko and Naftali, *Gamble*, p. 389 n. 20.

12. Herken, *Georgetown Set*, p. 279.

13. McGeorge Bundy, recorded interview by Richard Neustadt, March 1964, p. 18, John F. Kennedy Library Oral History Program.

Selected Sources

US and USSR Government Documents, Books, and Papers

Carter, Donald A. The U.S. Military Response to the 1960–1962 Berlin Crisis, The US Army Center of Military History, accessed https://www.archives.gov/files/research/foreign-policy/cold-war/1961-berlin-crisis/overview/us-military-response.pdf

Central Intelligence Agency, Board of National Estimates. October 27, 1962. Memorandum for the Director, Reactions to US Air Strike against Soviet Missile Bases, MiG-21s and IL-28s, TS No. 185480.

Central Intelligence Agency. "The Soviet Missile Base Venture in Cuba." CIA/RSS, DD/I Staff Study. February 17, 1964. Located at https://www.cia.gov/library/readingroom/docs/1964-02-27.pdf

Central Intelligence Agency, Office of the Deputy Director (Intelligence), Office of Research and Reports. "Cuba 1962: Khrushchev's Miscalculated Risk," February 13, 1964. SC 03387/64.

Killian Report. "Meeting the Threat of Surprise Attack." Report to the President by the Technological Capabilities Panel of the Science Advisory Committee, 1955.

McAuliffe, Mary S. *Cuban Missile Crisis: The CIA Documents.* Washington, DC: History Staff, Central Intelligence Agency, October 1992.

Meeting of Soviet Presidium. Minutes # 60 of October 22, 1962, National Security Archive. http://nsarchive.gwu.edu/nsa/cuba_mis_cri/dobbs/

Minutes of the 506th Meeting of the National Security Council, October 21, 1962. In *Foreign Relations of the United States*, 1961–63, vol. 11, *Cuban Missile Crisis and Its Aftermath.*

National Indications Center. "The Soviet Bloc Armed Forces and the Cuban Crisis: A Discussion of Readiness Measures." July 15, 1963.

National Intelligence Estimate 11-1-62. "The Soviet Space Program." December 5, 1962.

National Intelligence Estimate 11-10-66. "Warning of Soviet Intention to Attack." August 18, 1966, https://www.cia.gov/library/readingroom/docs/DOC_0000283838.pdf

National Security Council. 1961 Report of the Net Evaluation Subcommittee, National Security Archive's Nuclear Documentation Project, George Washington University, https://nsarchive2.gwu.edu/nukevault/ebb480/

National Security Council. 1962 Report of the Net Evaluation Subcommittee, National Security Archive's Nuclear Documentation Project, George Washington University, https://nsarchive2.gwu.edu/nukevault/ebb480/

Notes taken from transcripts of meetings of the Joint Chiefs of Staff, October-November 1962, dealing with the Cuban missile crisis. Handwritten notes were made in 1976 and typed in 1993. http://nsarchive.gwu.edu/nsa/cuba_mis_cri/621000%20Notes%20Taken%20from%20Transcripts.pdf

Parkinson, Leonard F., and Logan H. Potter. "Closing the Missile Gap." Central Intelligence Agency. Undated document declassified and approved for release on July 12, 2011, included in John F. Kennedy Presidential Library Symposium, *Penetrating the Iron Curtain: Resolving the Missile Gap with Technology*. https://www.cia.gov/library/publications/cold-war/resolving-the-missile-gap-with-technology/missile-gap.pdf

Pedlow, Gregory W., and Donald E. Welzenbach. *The Central Intelligence Agency and Overhead Reconnaissance: The U-2 and OXCART Programs, 1954–1974*. HR70-14. History Staff, Central Intelligence Agency, 1992. https://issuu.com/tonycronin/docs/u2__history_complete.pdf.crdownload

Poole, Walter S. *History of the Joint Chiefs of Staff*. Vol. 8, *The Joint Chiefs of Staff and National Policy, 1961–1964*. Washington, DC: Office of Joint History, Office of the Chairman of the Joint Chiefs of Staff, 2011.

Schelling, Thomas. "Nuclear Strategy in the Berlin Crisis." July 5, 1961, *FRUS* 1961–1963, vol. 14, *Berlin Crisis, 1961–1962*. Doc. 56, JFK Library, National Security Files, Germany, Berlin, General, https://history.state.gov/historicaldocuments/frus1961-63v14/d56

Smith, Richard K. "Seventy-Five Years of Inflight Refueling: Highlights, 1923–1998." Air Force History and Museums Program, 1998. https://media.defense.gov/2010/Sep/29/2001309638/-1/-1/0/AFD-100929-015.pdf

Strategic Air Command Operations in the Cuban Missile Crisis of 1962. Historical Study No. 90, History and Research Division, Strategic Air Command, vol. 1, 1963.

US Air Force, Strategic Air Command, History and Research Division. "History of the Joint Strategic Target Planning Staff: Preparation of SIOP-63." January 1964. http://www2.gwu.edu/~nsarchiv/nukevault/ebb236/SIOP-63.pdf

Various additional national intelligence estimates and special national intelligence estimates located at www.foia.cia.gov and found there under Historical/Missile Gap.

Articles

Allison, Graham. "The Cuban Missile Crisis at 50." *Foreign Affairs* 91, no. 4 (July 2012), pp. 11–16.

Allyn, Bruce J., James G. Blight, and David A. Welch. "Essence of Revision." *International Security* 14, no. 3 (Winter 1989–90).

Bainbridge, John. "Die Mauer: The Early Days of the Berlin Wall." *New Yorker*, October 27, 1962.

Bolshakov, Georgi. "Bolshakov on Cuban Missile Crisis—Conclusion, 'The Kennedy-Khrushchev 'Secret Channel.'" 90UMO283A *Moscow KOMMUNIST VOORUZHENNYKH SIL*. In Russian. No. 21, November 1989, republished in JPRS Report, *Soviet Union Military Affairs*, March 23, 1990.

Bolshakov, Georgy. "The Hot Line: The Secret Communication Channel between John Kennedy and Nikita Khrushchev." *New Times, nos. 4-6* 5 (1989), pp. 38–40 (no. 4), 40–42 (no. 5), 38–41 (no. 6).

Bundy, McGeorge. "The Presidency and the Peace." *Foreign Affairs* 42 (April 1964), pp. 353–65.

Coleman, David G. "The Missiles of November, December, January, February . . : The Problem of Acceptable Risk in the Cuban Missile Crisis Settlement." *Journal of Cold War Studies* 9, no. 3 (Summer 2007), pp. 5–48.

Fursenko, Alexandr, and Timothy Naftali. "Soviet Intelligence and the Cuban Missile Crisis (1998)." In James G. Blight and David A. Welch, eds., *Intelligence and the Cuban Missile Crisis*. London: Frank Cass, 1998. pp. 64–87.

Fursenko, Andrei A. "Georgii Bolshakov—svyaznoi Khrushchev s prezidentom Kennedy" [Georgi Bolshakov—Khrushchev's liaison to President Kennedy]. Znamya 7 (1997), pp. 161–83.

Galbraith, James K., and Heather A. Purcell. "Did the U.S. Military Plan a Nuclear First Strike for 1963?" http://www.maryferrell.org/wiki/index.php/Essay_-_Did_the_US_Military_Plan_a_Nuclear_First_Strike_for_1963

Garthoff, Raymond L. "Berlin 1961: The Record Corrected." *Foreign Policy* 84 (Fall 1991), pp. 142–56.

Hansen, James. "Soviet Deception in the Cuban Missile Crisis: Learning from the Past." Central Intelligence Agency report. https://www.cia.gov/library/center-for-the-study-of-intelligence/csi-publications/csi-studies/studies/vol46no1/article06.html

Hershberg, James G. "Before 'The Missiles of October': Did Kennedy Plan a Military Strike on Cuba?" *Diplomatic History* 14, no. 2 (Spring 1990), pp. 163–98.

Hershberg, James G. *The Cold War International History Project Bulletin* 5 (Spring 1995) ("Anatomy of a Controversy").

Hershberg, James G. Introduction to "A Trigger for Khrushchev's Deployment: Alexei Adzhubei's Report on His Conversation with John F. Kennedy, 30 January 1962." *Cold War International History Project Bulletin* 17–18 (2012), https://www.wilsoncenter.org/publication/bulletin-no-1718-fall-2012, Woodrow Wilson International Center for Scholars, pp. 316–23.

Hershberg, James G. "New Evidence on the Cuban Missile Crisis: More Documents from the Russian Archives." *Cold War International History Project Bulletin* 8–9, (Winter 1996–97), Woodrow Wilson International Center for Scholars, pp. 270–354.

Hoffmann, Stanley. "Restraints and Choices in American Foreign Policy." *Daedalus* 91, no. 4 (Fall 1962), pp. 668–704.

Holland, Max. *The "Photo Gap" That Delayed Discovery of Missiles: Politics and Intelligence.* https://www.cia.gov/library/center-for-the-study-of-intelligence/csi-publications/csi-studies/studies/vol49no4/Photo_Gap_2.htm

Kaplan, Fred. "JFK's First Strike Plan." *The Atlantic*, October 1, 2001.

Kokoshin, Andrei. "Reflections on the Cuban Missile Crisis in the Context of Strategic Stability." Harvard Kennedy School, Belfer Center for Science and International Affairs, September 2012. https://www.ciaonet.org/attachments/21711/uploads

Levy, Jack S. "The Offensive/Defensive Balance of Military Technology: A Theoretical and Historical Analysis." *International Studies Quarterly* 28 (June 1984), pp. 219–38.

McAuliffe, Mary S. "Return to the Brink: Intelligence Perspectives on the Cuban Missile Crisis." *Society for Historians of American Foreign Relations Newsletter* 24, no. 2 (June 1993), pp. 4–18.

Naftali, Timothy. "The Malin Notes: Glimpses inside the Kremlin during the Cuban Missile Crisis." *Cold War International History Project Bulletin* 17–18 (2012), https://www.wilsoncenter.org/publication/bulletin-no-1718-fall-2012, Woodrow Wilson International Center for Scholars, pp. 299–315.

Nitze, Paul. "Atoms, Strategy and Policy." *Foreign Affairs* 34 No. 2 (1956), pp. 187–98.

Norris, Robert S. "The Cuban Missile Crisis: A Nuclear Order of Battle." Presented at Woodrow Wilson Center, October 24, 2012. https://www.wilsoncenter.org/sites/default/files/2012_10_24_Norris_Cuban_Missile_Crisis_Nuclear_Order_of_Battle.pdf

Patterson, Thomas G. "Commentary: The Defense-of-Cuba Theme and the Missile Crisis." *Diplomatic History* 14, no. 2 (1990), pp. 249–56.

Patterson, Thomas G. "The Defense-of-Cuba Theme and the Missile Crisis." *Diplomatic History* 14, no. 2 (Spring 1990), pp. 249–56.

Patterson, Thomas G. "The Historian as Detective: Senator Kenneth Keating, the Missiles in Cuba, and His Mysterious Sources." *Diplomatic History* 11, no. 1 (Winter 1987), pp. 67–71.

Patterson, Thomas G., and William J. Brophy. "October Missiles and November Elections." *Journal of American History* 73, no. 1 (June 1986), pp. 87–119.

Pious, Richard M. "The Cuban Missile Crisis and the Limits of Crisis Management." *Political Science Quarterly* 116, no. 1 (Spring 2001), pp. 81–108.

Preble, Christopher. "The Uses of Threat Assessment in Historical Perspective: Perception, Misperception and Political Will." Cato Institute.

Pressman, Jeremy. "September statements, October Missiles, November Elections: Domestic Politics, Foreign Policy Making, and the Cuban Missile Crisis." *Security Studies* 10, no. 3 (Spring 2001), pp. 80–114.

Sagan, Scott. "SIOP-62: The Nuclear War Plan Briefing to President Kennedy." *International Security* 12, no. 1 (Summer 1987). http://belfercenter.ksg.harvard.

edu/files/CMC50/ScottSaganSIOP62TheNuclearWarPlanBriefingtoPresidentKennedyInternationalSecurity.pdf
Schwartz, Benjamin. "The Real Cuban Missile Crisis." *The Atlantic*, January–February 2013. http://www.theatlantic.com/magazine/archive/2013/01/the-real-cuban-missile-crisis/309190/
Smirnoff, Yuri, and Vladislav Zubok. "Nuclear Weapons after Stalin's Death: Moscow Enters the H-Bomb Age." *Bulletin, Cold War International History Project* 4 (Fall 1994), pp. 1, 14–18.
Steininger, Rolf. "Kennedy and the Berlin Wall." http://www.rolfsteininger.at/kennedy_berlin_wall.html
Stern, Sheldon M. "The Cuban Missile Crisis 45 Years Later: A Personal and Professional Remembrance." http://www.washingtondecoded.com/site/2007/10/cmc-45th.html
Trachtenberg, Marc. "American Policy and the Shifting Nuclear Balance." In Melvyn P. Leffler and David S. Painter, eds., *Origins of the Cold War*. New York: Routledge, 1994.
Trachtenberg, Marc. "The Influence of Nuclear Weapons in the Cuban Missile Crisis." *International Security* 10, no. 1 (Summer 1985), pp. 137–63.
Trauschweizer, Ingo Wolfgang. "Tanks at Checkpoint Charlie: Lucius Clay and the Berlin Crisis—1961–62." *Cold War History* 6, no. 2 (May 2006), pp. 205–28.
Wohlstetter, Albert. "The Delicate Balance of Terror." *Foreign Affairs* 37 (January 1959), pp. 211–34.

Books

Abel, Elie. *The Missile Crisis*. Philadelphia: J.B. Lippincott, 1966.
Aid, Matthew M. *The Secret Sentry: The Untold Story of the National Security Agency*. New York: Bloomsbury Press, 2009.
Alford, Mimi. *Once upon a Secret: My Affair with John F. Kennedy and Its Aftermath*. New York: Random House, 2012.
Allison, Graham, T. *Essence of Decision: Explaining the Cuban Missile Crisis*. Boston: Little, Brown, 1971.
Allison, Graham T., and Philip Zelikow. *Essence of Decision: Explaining the Cuban Missile Crisis*. New York: Longman, 1999.
Andrew, Christopher. *For the President's Eyes Only*. New York: HarperCollins, 1995.
Andrew, Christopher, and Vasili Mitrokhin. *The Mitrokhin Archive*. London: Penguin, 2000.
Barrett, David M., and Max Holland. *Blind over Cuba: The Photo Gap and the Missile Crisis*. Texas A& M University Press, 2012.
Beschloss, Michael R. *The Crisis Years: Kennedy and Khrushchev, 1960–1963*. New York: HarperCollins, 1991.
Beschloss, Michael R. *May Day: Eisenhower, Khrushchev and the U-2 Affair*. New York: Open Road, 1986.

Betts, Richard K. *Nuclear Blackmail and Nuclear Balance*. Washington, DC: Brookings Institution, 1987.

Blight, James, Bruce Allyn, and David Welch. *Cuba on the Brink: Castro, the Missile Crisis and the Soviet Collapse*. New York: Pantheon, 1993.

Blight, James G., and David A. Welch, eds. *Intelligence and the Cuban Missile Crisis*. London: Frank Cass, 1998.

Bobbitt, Philip. *Democracy and Deterrence*. New York: St. Martin's Press, 1988.

Bobbitt, Philip, Lawrence Freedman, and Gregory Treverton. *U.S. Nuclear Strategy*. New York: New York University Press, 1989.

Bouchard, Joseph F. *Command in Crisis: Four Case Studies*. New York: Columbia University Press, 1991.

Bowles, Chester. *Promises to Keep: My Years in Public Life, 1941–1969*. New York: Harper & Row, 1971.

Brugioni, Dino A. *Eyeball to Eyeball: The Inside Story of the Cuban Missile Crisis*. New York: Random House, 1991.

Brugioni, Dino A. *Eyes in the Sky: Eisenhower, the CIA, and Cold War Aerial Espionage*. Annapolis, MD: Naval Institute Press, 2010.

Bundy, McGeorge. *Danger and Survival: Choices about the Bomb in the First Fifty Years*. New York: Random House, 1988.

Cate, Curtis. *The Ides of August: The Berlin Wall Crisis, 1961*. New York: M. Evans, 1978.

Chertok, Boris. *Rockets and People*. Vol. 3: *Hot Days of the Cold War*. Washington, DC: NASA History Division, Office of External Relations, May 2009.

Coleman, David G. *The Fourteenth Day: JFK and the Aftermath of the Cuban Missile Crisis*. New York: Norton, 2012.

Craig, Campbell. *Destroying the Village: Eisenhower and Thermonuclear War*. New York: Columbia University Press, 1998.

Dallek, Robert. *JFK: An Unfinished Life*. New York: Back Bay Books, 2003.

Divine, Robert A. *The Sputnik Challenge*. New York: Oxford University Press, 1993.

Dobbs, Michael. *One Minute to Midnight: Kennedy, Khrushchev and Castro on the Brink of Nuclear War*. New York: Alfred A. Knopf, 2008.

Dobrynin, Anatoly. *In Confidence: Moscow's Ambassador to America's Six Cold War Presidents*. New York: Random House, 1995.

Douglass, James W. *JFK and the Unspeakable: Why He Died and Why It Matters*. New York: Simon & Schuster, 2010.

Ferguson, Niall. *Kissinger, 1923–1968: The Idealist*. New York: Penguin , 2015.

Freedman, Lawrence. *Kennedy's Wars: Berlin, Cuba, Laos and Vietnam*. New York: Oxford University Press, 2000.

Freedman, Norman. *The Fifty-Year War: Conflict and Strategy in the Cold War*. Annapolis, MD: Naval Institute Press, 2000.

Fursenko, Alexandr, and Timothy Naftali. *Khrushchev's Cold War: The Inside Story of an American Adversary*. New York: Norton, 2006.

Fursenko, Alexandr, and Timothy Naftali. *"One Hell of a Gamble": Khrushchev, Castro and Kennedy, 1958–1964*. New York: Norton, 1997.

Gaddis, John Lewis. *The United States and the Origins of the Cold War, 1941–1947*. New York: Columbia University Press. 2005.

Garthoff, Raymond L. *Reflections on the Cuban Missile Crisis—Revised to Include New Revelations from Soviet and Cuban Sources*. Washington, DC: Brookings, 1989.

Gioe, David, Len Scott, and Christopher Andrew, eds. *An International History of the Cuban Missile Crisis: A 50-Year Retrospective*. New York: Routledge, 2014.

Gribkov, Anatoli I., and William Y. Smith. *Operation Anadyr: U.S. and Soviet Generals Recount the Cuban Missile Crisis*. Chicago: Edition q, 1994.

Haslam, Jonathan. *Russia's Cold War*. New Haven: Yale University Press, 2011.

Herken, Gregg. *The Georgetown Set*. New York: Alfred A. Knopf, 2014.

Hilsman, Roger. *The Cuban Missile Crisis: The Struggle over Policy*. London: Praeger, 1996.

Hilsman, Roger. *From Nuclear Military Strategy to a World without War*. Westport, CT: Praeger, 1999.

Hilsman, Roger. *To Move a Nation: The Politics of Foreign Policy in the Administration of John F. Kennedy*. New York: Doubleday, 1967.

Hilty, James W. *Robert Kennedy: Brother Protector*. Philadelphia: Temple University Press, 1997.

Huchthausen, Peter A., *October Fury*. Hoboken, NJ: John Wiley & Sons, 2002.

Kaplan, Fred, *The Wizards of Armageddon*. New York: Simon & Schuster, 1983.

Keeney, L. Douglas. *15 Minutes: General Curtis LeMay and the Countdown to Nuclear Annihilation*. New York: St. Martin's Press, 2011.

Kempe, Frederick. *Berlin 1961: Kennedy, Khrushchev and the Most Dangerous Place on Earth*. New York: G.P. Putnam, 2011.

Kennedy, Robert F. *Thirteen Days: A Memoir of the Cuban Missile Crisis*. New York: Norton, 1971.

Khrushchev, Nikita. *Khrushchev Remembers: The Glasnost Tapes*. Trans. and ed. Jerrold I. Schecter with Vyacheslav V. Luchkov. Boston: Little, Brown, 1990.

Khrushchev, Sergei N. *Nikita Khrushchev and the Creation of a Superpower*. University Park: Pennsylvania State University Press, 2000.

Leaming, Barbara. *Jack Kennedy: The Education of a Statesman*. New York: Norton, 2006.

Lebow, Richard Ned. *Coercion, Cooperation and Ethics in International Relations*. New York: Routledge, 2007.

Lebow, Richard Ned. *Nuclear Crisis Management: A Dangerous Illusion*. Ithaca, NY: Cornell University Press, 1987.

Lebow, Richard Ned, and Janice Stein. *We All Lost the Cold War*. Princeton, NJ: Princeton University Press, 1994.

May, Ernest R., and Philip D. Zelikow, eds. *The Kennedy Tapes: Inside the White House during the Cuban Missile Crisis*. Cambridge: Belknap Press, 1997.

Naftali, Timothy, and Philip Zelikow, gen. eds. *The Presidential Recordings: John F. Kennedy*. Vols. 1–3: *The Great Crises*. New York: Norton, 2001.

McMahon, Robert J. *The Cold War: A Very Short Introduction*. New York: Oxford University Press, 2003.

McNamara, Robert S. *In Retrospect: The Tragedy and Lessons of Vietnam*. New York: Random House, 1995.

Mikoyan, Sergo. *The Soviet Cuban Missile Crisis*. Stanford, CA: Stanford University Press, 2012.

Mueller, John. *Atomic Obsession*. New York: Oxford University Press, 2010

Murphy, David E., Sergei A. Kondrashev, and George Bailey. *Battle Ground Berlin: CIA vs KGB in the Cold War*. New Haven: Yale University Press, 1997.

Nash, Philip. *The Other Missiles of October: Eisenhower, Kennedy, and the Jupiters, 1957–1963*. Chapel Hill: University of North Carolina Press, 1997.

Nathan, James A., ed. *The Cuban Missile Crisis Revisited*. New York: St. Martin's Press, 1992.

O'Donnell, Kenneth P., and David F. Powers. *Johnny We Hardly Knew Ye: Memories of John Fitzgerald Kennedy*. Boston: Little, Brown, 1970.

Polmar, Norman, and John B. Gresham. *DEFCON-2: Standing on the Brink of Nuclear War during the Cuban Missile Crisis*. Hoboken, NJ: John Wiley & Sons, 2006.

Porter, Gareth. *Perils of Dominance: Imbalance of Power and the Road to Vietnam*. Berkeley: University of California Press, 2005.

RAND Corporation. "Striking First: Preemptive and Preventive Attack in US National Security Policy." 2006.

Reeves, Richard. *President Kennedy: Profile of Power*. New York: Simon & Schuster, 1993.

Richelson, Jeffery T. *A Century of Spies: Intelligence in the Twentieth Century*. New York: Oxford University Press, 1995.

Richelson, Jeffrey T. *The Wizards of Langley: Inside the CIA's Directorate of Science and Technology*. Boulder, CO: Westview, 2001.

Ritter, Scott. *Dangerous Ground: America's Failed Arms Control Policy, from FDR to Obama*. New York: Nation Books, 2010.

Rosenberg, David. "The Origins of Overkill: Nuclear Weapons and American Strategy, 1945–1960." In Steven Miller, ed., *Strategy and Nuclear Deterrence*. Princeton, NJ: Princeton University Press, 1984.

Sagan, Scott D. *The Limits of Safety: Organizations, Accidents, and Nuclear Weapons*. Princeton, NJ: Princeton University Press, 1993.

Sagan, Scott D. *Moving Targets: Nuclear Strategy and National Security*. Princeton, NJ: Princeton University Press, 1989.

Scott, Len V. *Macmillan, Kennedy and the Cuban Missile Crisis*. London: Macmillan, 1999.

Scott, Len, and R. Gerald Hughes, eds. *The Cuban Missile Crisis: A Critical Reappraisal*. New York: Routledge, 2015.

Smith, Jean Edwards. *Lucius D. Clay: An American Life*. New York: Henry Holt, 1990.

Snead, David L. *The Gaither Committee, Eisenhower, and the Cold War*. Columbus: Ohio State University Press, 1999.

Sorensen, Theodore C. *Counselor: A Life at the Edge of History*. New York: Harper Collins, 2008.
Sorensen, Theodore C. *Kennedy*. New York: Harper & Row, 1965.
Stern, Sheldon. *Averting "The Final Failure": John F. Kennedy and the Secret Cuban Missile Meetings*. Stanford, CA: Stanford University Press, 2003.
Stern, Sheldon. *The Cuban Missile Crisis in American Memory: Myths versus Reality*. Stanford, CA: Stanford University Press, 2012.
Talbot, David. *Brothers: The Hidden History of the Kennedy Years*. New York: Free Press, 2007.
Taubman, William. *Khrushchev: The Man and His Era*. New York: Norton, 2003.
Taylor, Frederick. *The Berlin Wall: A World Divided, 1961—1989*. New York: Harper-Collins, 2007.
Thomas, Evan. *Ike's Bluff: President Eisenhower's Secret Battle to Save the World*. New York: Little, Brown, 2012.
Thomas, Evan. *Robert Kennedy: His Life*. New York: Simon & Schuster, 2000.
Trachtenberg, Marc. *History and Strategy*. Princeton, NJ: Princeton University Press, 1991.
Walker, Martin. *The Cold War: A History*. New York: Holt, 1995.
Weintal, Edward, and Charles Bartlett. *Facing the Brink*. New York: Charles Scribner's Sons, 1967.
Wenger, Andreas. *Living with Peril: Eisenhower, Kennedy and Nuclear Weapons*. Lanham, MD: Rowman & Littlefield, 1997.
White, Mark J. *The Cuban Missile Crisis*. London: Macmillan, 1996.
Whitten, H. Wayne. *Countdown to 13 Days and Beyond*. Self-published, 2012.
Wilson, Jim. *Launch Pad UK: Britain and the Cuban Missile Crisis*. Barnsley: Pen & Sword Books, 2008.
Young, Ken. *The American Bomb in Britain: US Air Forces' Strategic Presence, 1946–1964*. Manchester: Manchester University Press, 2016.

Index